Understanding and Managing Customers

We work with leading authors to develop the
strongest educational materials in business,
finance and marketing, bringing cutting-edge
thinking and best learning practice to a
global market.

Under a range of well-known imprints, including
Financial Times Prentice Hall, we craft high quality
print and electronic publications which help readers
to understand and apply their content, whether
studying or at work.

To find out more about the complete range of our
publishing please visit us on the World Wide Web at:
www.pearsoned.co.uk

Understanding and Managing Customers

Edited by

Isobel Doole
Peter Lancaster
Robin Lowe

 Prentice Hall

FINANCIAL TIMES

An imprint of **Pearson Education**

Harlow, England • London • New York • Boston • San Francisco • Toronto • Sydney • Singapore • Hong Kong
Tokyo • Seoul • Taipei • New Delhi • Cape Town • Madrid • Mexico City • Amsterdam • Munich • Paris • Milan

Pearson Education Limited
Edinburgh Gate
Harlow
Essex CM20 2JE
United Kingdom

and Associated Companies throughout the world

Visit us on the World Wide Web at:
www.pearsoned.co.uk

———————————————

First published 2005

ISBN 0 273 68562 7

British Library Cataloguing-in-Publication Data
A catalogue record for this book is available from the British Library

Library of Congress Cataloging-in-Publication Data
Understanding and managing customers / edited by Isobel Doole, Peter Lancaster, Robin Lowe.
      p. cm.
   Includes bibliographical references and index.
   ISBN 0-273-68562-7 (alk. paper)
    1. Customer services. I. Doole, Isobel. II. Lancaster, Peter, 1952- III. Lowe, Robin,
1945-

   HF5415.5.U46 2004
   658.8'12--dc22

                                                                                      2004056329

10 9 8 7 6 5 4 3 2 1
09 08 07 06 05

Typeset in 10/12.5 pt Palatino by 30
Printed and bound by Asford Colour Press, Gosport

The publisher's policy is to use paper manufactured from sustainable forests.

Contents

Case studies   xi

Figures   xii

Tables   xiv

The contributors   xv

Preface   xvii

Acknowledgements   xx

Structure of the book   xxii

Part One Identifying the customer

1 Customers, quality and exchange   3
Robin Lowe

Learning outcomes   3
Key words   3
Introduction   4
1.1 The challenge of providing customer satisfaction   4
1.2 Organisations and customer satisfaction   5
1.3 The concept of exchange   9
1.4 The concept of quality and value   13
1.5 Quality   16
1.6 The different customer situations   17
1.7 Influencing the customer   19
Summary   21
Discussion questions   21
Case study 1.1: Customer–supplier exchange at university 22
Further reading   23
Website   23

2   Who is the customer?   24
Isobel Doole

Learning outcomes   24
Key words   24
Introduction   25
2.1   Are customers different from consumers?   25
2.2   Are customers buying goods different from those
         buying services?   26
2.3   Are customers different from clients?   26
2.4   Different types of customer   27
2.5   The individual/family customer   28
2.6   How do customers make their purchasing decisions?   31
2.7   Are there different types of purchasing decision?   36
2.8   Typologies of individual customers   37
2.9   Buying roles   38
2.10   The organisational customer   39
2.11   The business-to-business customer   40
2.12   The government as a customer   43
2.13   Not-for-profit customers   45
2.14   Internal customers   45
Summary   46
Discussion questions   46
Case study 2.1: Stadium Ltd   47
Further reading   48
References   48

3   The marketing environment   49
Jeanette Baker

Learning outcomes   49
Key words   49
Introduction   50
3.1   The marketing environment   51
3.2   Environmental scanning   52
3.3   Analysing the environment   53
Summary   70
Discussion questions   71
Case study 3.1: The Day Chocolate Company   72
Further reading   75
References   75

4   Building information on the customer   76
Debbie Hill

Learning outcomes   76
Key words   76
Introduction   77

4.1 Why do organisations need information?   77
4.2 Information sources   86
4.3 The process of information collection   93
Summary   103
Discussion questions   104
Case study 4.1: Males boost use of cosmetics in Europe   104
Further reading   106
References   106

Part Two Understanding the customer

5 Why organisations need to understand customer behaviour   109

Peter Lancaster

Learning outcomes   109
Key words   109
Introduction   110
5.1 The scope and importance of customer behaviour
      to business organisations   110
5.2 How customers make buying decisions   112
5.3 Motivation   117
5.4 Learning   120
5.5 Attitudes   126
Summary   131
Discussion questions   132
Case study 5.1: Tokai Guitars   132
Further reading   136
References   136

6 How customers are segmented and organised   137

Chris Dawson

Learning outcomes   137
Key words   137
Introduction   138
6.1 Principles and process of market segmentation   138
6.2 What is market segmentation?   139
6.3 Advantages and disadvantages of market segmentation   140
6.4 The necessary requirements for viable segmentation   142
6.5 Recognising the criteria used to identify consumer and
      industrial market segments   145
6.6 Profile segmentation   145
6.7 Psychographic segmentation   148

6.8   Behavioural segmentation   150
6.9   Critical events segmentation   153
6.10   Hybrid segmentation   153
6.11   Segmenting industrial markets   155
6.12   Customer segmentation in the business-to-business area   158
Summary   159
Discussion questions   159
Case study 6.1: Levi's leaps into the mass market   160
Further reading   161
References   161

7 What the customer is looking for   163
Mark Godson

Learning outcomes   163
Key words   163
Introduction   164
7.1   Meeting customer demands   164
7.2   Products and services for industrial customers   167
7.3   The difference between products and services   169
7.4   The different levels of a product   172
7.5   Branding   175
7.6   New product development and innovation   180
Summary   185
Discussion questions   185
Case study 7.1: Driving the past   186
Further reading   187

8 Customers' perceptions of quality   188
Robin Lowe

Learning outcomes   188
Key words   188
Introduction   189
8.1   What quality means to customers   189
8.2   Service quality and the total customer experience   197
8.3   Quality issues for customers in business-to-business sectors 205
8.4   Customers expect quality companies to behave ethically   207
Summary   209
Discussion questions   210
Case study 8.1: New-style quality is just a fiddle   210
Further reading   211
Website   211
References   211

Part Three Influencing the customer

9 Organising internally to serve external customers   215
Andy Cropper

Learning outcomes   215
Key words   215
Introduction   216
9.1 So what do we mean by the 'customer'?   218
9.2 Customer and supplier interaction   220
9.3 Adopting a service culture   226
9.4 Building and managing the service culture   232
9.5 Managing the external customer relationship   237
Summary   241
Discussion questions   241
Case study 9.1: Who lost the sale?   241
Case study 9.2: Outside, looking in – a customer experience   243
Further reading   244

10 Customer-led communications   245
Rod Radford

Learning outcomes   245
Key words   245
Introduction   246
10.1 Customer communication   246
10.2 Influencing external and internal customers   253
10.3 How communications influence customers   261
Summary   269
Discussion questions   269
Case study 10.1: Metro   270
Further reading   271
References   272

11 Developing and managing customer relationships   273
Simon Kelly

Learning outcomes   273
Key words   273
Introduction   274
11.1 Why are customer relationships important?   274
11.2 What is value?   275
11.3 The case for customer relationships   276
11.4 What is relationship marketing?   279
11.5 What is customer relationship management?   280

11.6 Principles of relationship marketing   281
11.7 Types of customer relationship   286
11.8 Properties of effective relationships   291
11.9 Planning effective relationships   297
Summary   301
Discussion questions   301
Case study 11.1: Text R for relationships?   302
Further reading   303
References   303

12 The emergence of the 'new consumer': coming to terms with the future   305
Colin Gilligan

Learning outcomes   305
Key words   305
Introduction   306
12.1 The changing marketing environment
       (or the emergence of a new marketing reality)   306
12.2 The rise of the new consumer   308
12.3 The changing social, cultural and demographic environments   310
12.4 The rise of the new consumer and the implications for
       marketing planning   318
12.5 The new consumer and the growth of relationship marketing   322
Summary   325
Discussion questions   326
*Case study 12.1: The new consumer and the rise of the Internet – new
rules for the new world*   326
Further reading   329
References   329

Index   331

Companion Website resources

Visit the Companion Website at www.booksites.net/doole

For lecturers
- Complete, downloadable Instructor's Manual
- PowerPoint slides that can be downloaded and used as OHTs

Case studies

Chapters	Case study outline
	Part One Identifying the customer
1	**Customer–supplier exchange at university** Criteria for satisfaction
2	**Stadium Ltd** Customer client relationships
3	**The Day Chocolate Company** Environmental and competition analysis
4	**Males boost use of cosmetics in Europe** Improving popularity of skin care products in the EU
	Part Two Understanding the customer
5	**Tokai Guitars** Explores how a Japanese guitar manufacturer can obtain customer belief and favourable attitudes
6	**Levi's leaps into the mass market** Segmentation by outlet and price
7	**Driving the past** Product relevancy to customers
8	**New-style quality is just a fiddle** Techniques to achieve customer satisfaction
	Part Three Influencing the customer
9	**Who lost the sale?** **Outside, looking in – a customer experience** Problems with suppliers
10	**Metro** Has a tired medium still got legs?
11	**Text R for relationships?** Relationship marketing in the mobile phone industry
12	**The new consumer and the rise of the Internet – new rules for the new world** Satisfying the new customer with new technology

Figures

Figure 1.1	The exchange process	9
Figure 1.2	Customer expectation and satisfaction	11
Figure 1.3	The exchange process and the environment	12
Figure 2.1	The decision-making process	31
Figure 3.1	Chapter overview	50
Figure 3.2	The changing environmental dynamics	51
Figure 3.3	The marketing environment	53
Figure 4.1	Customer information system	83
Figure 4.2	CIS revisted	92
Figure 4.3	Information collection process	93
Figure 4.4	Primary information	96
Figure 4.5	Market share of cosmetics and toiletries (%), 1998	105
Figure 5.1	A simplified model of customer decision making	111
Figure 5.2	The customer decision-making process	113
Figure 5.3	Types of customer decision-making process	115
Figure 5.4	The motivation process	117
Figure 5.5	A hierarchy of needs	119
Figure 5.6	Schools of learning	122
Figure 5.7	Pavlov's experiment	123
Figure 5.8	Skinner's experiment	123
Figure 5.9	The traditional tricomponent model of attitudes	127
Figure 5.10	The contemporary view of attitude components	128
Figure 5.11	The interaction of attitudes and behaviour	130
Figure 6.1	Selected methods for segmenting business markets	155
Figure 7.1	The different levels of a product	173
Figure 7.2	The four stages of product adoption	184
Figure 7.3	The demand curve of a product	184
Figure 9.1	Elements of the business chains	217
Figure 9.2	Stylised company structure	219
Figure 9.3	Company functional relationships	219
Figure 9.4	The many levels of contact	221
Figure 9.5	The organisation as a process and functions	227
Figure 9.6	The elements of customer relationship	230

Figure 10.1   Extended mix communications   247
Figure 10.2   Communications model   248
Figure 10.3   Levels of communication   249
Figure 10.4   Commercial communications process   250
Figure 10.5   Communications ladder   257
Figure 10.6   Brand repositioning map   258
Figure 10.7   Map of internal stakeholder awareness   260
Figure 10.8   Consumer decision-making model   263
Figure 11.1   The shift from mass marketing to one-to-one marketing   275
Figure 11.2   The transition to relationship marketing   277
Figure 11.3   The consequences of a 5% reduction in customer
               losses in different fields   277
Figure 11.4   The development of value categories in the course of a
               customer relationship   278
Figure 11.5   Relationship marketing and CRM – a hierarchy   280
Figure 11.6   Loyalty snakes and ladders   281
Figure 11.7   The five steps of permission marketing   284
Figure 11.8   B2B decision making   287
Figure 11.9   Planning for effective relationships – the five
               building blocks   297
Figure 12.1   The shift from the old to the new consumer   319

Tables

Table 1.1	Some examples of what can be exchanged	9
Table 2.1	Customers versus clients	27
Table 2.2	The UK consumer	29
Table 2.3	How UK consumers spend their money	29
Table 4.1	Sources of secondary data	88
Table 5.1	Consumer decision processes for high- and low-involvement purchase decisions	116
Table 6.1	Market segmentation type and selected variables for consumer markets	145
Table 6.2	Lifestyle dimensions	148
Table 6.3	ACORN User Guide	154
Table 7.1	The world's biggest brands, 2002	176
Table 8.1	B2B purchasing responsibilities	206
Table 10.1	Properties of commercial communication tools	254
Table 10.2	Commercial medium attributes	266
Table 12.1	The changing marketing environment and the emergence of a new marketing reality	307
Table 12.2	The emergence of the new consumer	308
Table 12.3	European consumers: the changing PEST environment	316
Table 12.4	The three nations society	317

The contributors

Dr Isobel Doole is subject leader for the Marketing Group at Sheffield Hallam University. Isobel's teaching specialism is international marketing and she has co-authored the textbook *International Marketing Strategy* (Thomson Learning), the fourth edition of which was published in 2004. She has also co-authored a marketing research book specifically written for the smaller firm. Isobel is a senior examiner for Diploma stage of the Chartered Institute of Marketing.

Peter Lancaster has spent several years in industry both in the marketing of services and consumer durables. He has also spent over 20 years teaching marketing in the university sector, specialising in consumer behaviour and marketing planning. He is currently a senior lecturer in marketing at Sheffield Hallam University.

Robin Lowe had 25 years experience in industry before joining Sheffield Hallam University so he probably must share responsibility for some occasional poor quality of textile fibres, paper and healthcare products! He is a principal lecturer in international marketing and is still surprised by the mistakes companies make, upsetting their customers in the process. Robin also works in the university's Enterprise Centre, encouraging students and staff to commercially exploit their ideas, always hoping that their own businesses will not make the same mistakes.

Jeanette Baker is senior lecturer in marketing at Sheffield Hallam University with a special interest in market analysis, information use and market understanding. Whatever area of marketing you are in, this understanding is valuable in allowing companies to compete successfully.

Andy Cropper has never managed to make a permanent move to academia and has always combined his lecturing with a range of activities within the business arena. Starting his career with a major multinational, he has latterly chosen to work mainly with SMEs and now spends a significant proportion of his time with companies based in the emerging Central and Eastern European economies. The highs and lows of his career include saving a Siberian company from the brink of extinction and taking eight attempts before passing an exam for one of his professional qualifications. Curiously he doesn't talk too much about the latter.

Chris Dawson is an associate lecturer at Sheffield Hallam University. Having spent more time than he would like to admit in the pharmaceutical industry, acted as a direct marketing consultant, and more recently in the IT industry helping to bring innovative products to market, he has worked with major retailing chains in the UK with their website development.

Colin Gilligan is Professor of Marketing at Sheffield Hallam University and a Visiting Professor at the University of Northumbria. He is the author of twelve books on marketing and has acted as a consultant to a variety of organisations in both the private and the public sectors.

Mark Godson has practical experience of managing products and services in both business-to-business and business-to-consumer markets and many of the examples used in his chapter reflect this. These include working in new product development for five years in the building products industry and later as UK Marketing Manager for an international retail chain. He is currently employed as a senior lecturer in marketing at Sheffield Hallam University.

Debbie Hill is a senior lecturer in marketing at Sheffield Hallam University. Given that Debbie has a background in strategic marketing management, it is not surprising that her aim is to provide academically well-qualified practitioners of marketing. With interests in strategic marketing management, customer orientation and new product development, Debbie remains committed to this cause.

Simon Kelly is an associate lecturer in marketing at Sheffield Hallam University. He now runs his own marketing and sales practice which focuses on the B2B arena. He has 21 years experience in marketing to business customers in the telecommunications industry.

Rod Radford is currently a senior lecturer in marketing communications at Sheffield Hallam University and an examiner in marketing communications for the Chartered Institute of Marketing. With a background in public relations, merchandising and sales management both here and abroad, he is sadly aware of 'still making almost every mistake in the communications lexicon on a daily basis'.

Preface

As business becomes ever more complex and managers come under even greater pressure, it is only too easy for them to fall into the trap of paying insufficient attention to customers. However, the simple fact is that without customers there is no business. Moreover, customers are changing at an ever increasing pace and becoming much more demanding. Therefore businesses ignore customers and their changing needs at their peril. To achieve continued success it is essential that organisations grasp the necessity to both understand and manage their customers and for managers in organisations to develop the skills, knowledge and aptitudes that are necessary to achieve this.

Understanding and Managing Customers aims to provide readers with a comprehensive understanding of customers. An introductory business text, the book provides an easy introduction to the subject of customers and ensures that the needs of business students will be met in an up-to-date and innovative manner. As students are under constant time pressure, we have been particularly conscious in maintaining readability and clarity as well as providing a straightforward and logical structure that will enable students to apply their learning to the tasks ahead.

THE MARKET

This text is clearly intended for students coming to business studies and marketing courses for the first time. The book is aimed at first year undergraduate students on both business studies and marketing degrees and also HND students. The book is also extremely useful to students of the Chartered Institute of Marketing studying for the certificate stage of the Institute's examinations. However, since it is intended to provide a thorough understanding of the process and pitfalls of understanding and managing customers, it has a wider application and is also suitable for students of social sciences, engineering and sciences who will have an involvement with customers. Practitioners in the early stages of their careers should find it useful as a reference text and source of information on both method and practice.

ORGANISATION

Part One Identifying the customer

Part One focuses on identifying customers and the importance of customer orientation. It provides an introduction to customer orientation and explores how customers can be defined and identified. A framework for analysing the customers' environment and an outline for analysing competitors are developed. The final chapter in the section provides an outline to researching customers and building information systems.

Part Two Understanding the customer

Part Two explains why it is important for businesses to understand their customers not only in terms of their behaviour but also how they can be segmented, and provides an insight into what customers want from the company and also how organisations can identify how customers view quality and value. These are key decisions for many organisations as they are the doorway to creating a competitive advantage.

Part Three Influencing the customer

This section addresses the ways in which organisations organise themselves to influence their customers. It deals with how companies can organise themselves to serve external customers, how they communicate with customers via various media, how they manage the customer in the long term, and how customers evolve and change over time.

PEDAGOGY

To help reinforce key learning points, each chapter includes the following:

- Learning Outcomes, which allow the readers to test their knowledge against the outcomes.
- Introduction, which summarises what has gone before and also explains the topics to be covered in the body of the chapter.
- Sections and sub-sections break up the main text to help students digest and retain the information.
- Tables, figures and other illustrative material help the reader grasp the essential facts.
- Spotlights and dilemmas throughout the text cover extended examples, mini-cases, interesting research results or more technical issues.

- Case studies provide a basis for class discussion or assessment on an in-depth set of issues.
- Discussion questions provide a basis for self-assessment by the students or revision topics at the end of the programme.
- Selected further readings offer the opportunity to refer to other more specialised or specific sources of information on many subjects.
- Case studies at the end of each chapter demonstrate the importance of how success in business is achieved through the ability to integrate the many facets of the organisation in a way that can deliver value to the customers in the market- place. They also provide a basis for class discussion or assessment on an in-depth set of questions.

DISTINCTIVE CHARACTERISTICS

- **Not a simple marketing or consumer behaviour text.** Although marketing is referred to, the book is primarily designed to give a comprehensive grasp of the importance of both understanding and managing customers. This is a crucial aspect of successful business.
- **Consistent European flavour.** All aspects and the focus of the application and discussion of the concepts are based within the European sector.
- **Accessible and readable.** Easy to read and with a clear structure, this book is an ideal offering for a 12 week teaching semester. It can also be used on shorter modules. Its broad view of organisations and their customers with examples of both good and bad practice from many parts of Europe make it suitable for use with courses combining multi-cultural students.

Acknowledgements

There are many individuals to thank for their contributions.

We'd like to thank our colleagues, Mark Godson, Rod Radford, Jeanette Baker, Colin Gilligan, Debbie Hill, Andy Cropper, Chris Dawson, Simon Kelly for their chapters and their forbearance for all our chasing and chivvying during the writing of the book.

We are also grateful to the following reviewers who provided comments during the writing process:

Rita Carmouche, The University of Huddersfield
Charles Dennis, Brunel University
Jillian Farquhar, Oxford Brookes University
Mari-Ann Karlson, Orebro University
Ashok Ranchhod, Southampton Institute
Cleopatra Veloutsou, University of Glasgow

At Pearson Education, we'd like to thank Senior Acquisitions Editor, Thomas Sigel, Editorial Assistant, Peter Hooper, and Desk Editor, Nicola Chilvers.

We believe that faculty will find this book a useful tool in structuring courses and delivering content and that students will find it a valuable resource in developing an appreciation for understanding and managing the customer.

Isobel Doole
Peter Lancaster
Robin Lowe
Sheffield Hallam University
Summer 2004

This book is dedicated to our students past, present and yet to come.
(adapted from *A Christmas Carol*, Charles Dickens, London 1843)

PUBLISHER'S ACKNOWLEDGEMENTS

We are grateful to the following for permission to reproduce copyright material:

Table 2.1 adapted from *The Lifebelt: The Definitive Guide to Managing Customer Retention*, Murphy, J.A. 2000. © John Wiley & Sons Limited. Reproduced with permission; Table 4.1 adapted from *Principles of Marketing, 3rd Edition*, Brassington, F. and Pettitt, S., © Pearson Education Limited 2003; Figure 4.5 from *The European Cosmetic, Toiletry and Perfumery Market 1998*, Colipa, June 1999 reprinted with permission from Colipa. Table 6.2 reprinted with permission from 'The concept and application of lifestyle segmentation', *Journal of Marketing*, published by the American Marketing Association, Plummer, J.T., 1974, volume 34 (January); Table 6.3 from Caci Ltd. (www.caci.co.uk); Table 7.1 from Interbrand; Figure 10.2 from Kotler, *Marketing Management: Millenium Edition*, 10th Edition, © 2002. Adapted by permission of Pearson Education, Inc., Upper Saddle River, NJ. Figure 11.1 reprinted from *Strategic Marketing Planning*, Gilligan, C.T. and Wilson, R.M.S. Copyright 2003, with permission from Elsevier; Figures 11.2 and 11.5 reprinted from *Relationship Marketing*, Christopher, M., Payne, A. and Ballantyne, D. Copyright 2002 with permission from Elsevier; Figure 11.3 reprinted by permission of Harvard Business School Publishing from 'The Loyalty Effect' by Frederick F. Reichheld. Boston, MA 1996, pp 36. Copyright © 1996 by Bain & Company, Inc. All rights reserved. Figure 11.4 reprinted by permission of *Harvard Business Review*. From 'Zero defections: quality comes for services', by Reichheld, F.F. and Sasser, W., August-September 1990. Copyright © 1990 by the Harvard Business School Publishing Corporation; all rights reserved.

We are grateful to the Financial Times Limited for permission to reprint the following material:

Males boost use of cosmetics in Europe, © *Financial Times*, 25 June 1999; Finding new niches in a saturated market, FT.com, © *Financial Times*, 30 April 2003; Chocolate fingered, © *Financial Times*, 2 May 2003; Front Page Companies & Markets: Doubt on Hutchison target for 3G units, © *Financial Times*, 5 May 2003; Features Marketing: Levi's leaps into mass market, © *Financial Times*, 1 May 2003.

We are grateful to the following for permission to use copyright material:

Let us spray from *Wecherd FT*, Issue 44, The Financial Times Limited, November 1999, © Lucia van der Post; Haymarket Reprints for permission to reproduce an extract from 'T-mobile vs. O2: The First Year' by J. Curtis published in *Marketing* 10th April 2003; Dilemma 2.3 reprinted with kind permission of Anthony Grimes, University of Hull; Chapter 5 case study reprinted with kind permission of Bob Murdoch and Shohei Adachi, Tokai Gakki Japan.

In some instances we have been unable to trace the owners of copyright material, and we would appreciate any information that would enable us to do so.

Structure of the book

Parts	Chapters	Key ideas
Part One Identifying the customer	1, 2, 3, 4	Importance of customer orientation, identifying different types of customer and their environment, and building information systems on customers.
Part Two Understanding the customer	5, 6, 7, 8	Understanding customer behaviour, how to segment customers and identify what they require from the organisation, and understanding how they perceive quality and value.
Part Three Influencing the customer	9, 10, 11, 12	Understanding how organisations organise to serve external customers, how to communicate with customers and manage them in the long term, and how customers change and evolve.

Identifying the customer

Part One of this book, *Identifying the customer*, is the foundation on which Part Two, *Understanding the customer*, and Part Three, *Influencing the customer*, are built. In this part we examine who customers are and why they are important to companies; we explore the environment in which they operate as customers; and we examine how companies can build information in order to understand and influence their existing and potential customers.

In Chapter 1 we examine why it is important for organisations to be customer oriented. This chapter discusses why the success of any commercial enterprise is dependent on the exchanges that take place and the relationships that are developed between the organisation and its customers. It argues that without customers, businesses cannot operate. Companies have to know who their customers are and why they buy so they can ensure they offer customers superior value over and above that of their competitors. The chapter explains the rationale behind the book and briefly introduces the reader to a number of concepts that will be examined in some depth as the reader moves through the remaining chapters of the book.

In Chapter 2 we seek to develop our understanding of who customers actually are and gain some insights into the process they undergo in a buying situation. We explore in some depth what customers actually buy. We look at the different types of customer, both external and internal, and their characteristics and discuss the differences between the varying types of customer in business-to-business marketing and business-to-consumer marketing. We then go on to explore the decision-making process in a buying situation and examine the components of the purchasing decision-making units in organisational as well as individual/family buying situations.

In Chapter 3 we explore the marketing environment in which customers and competitors are located. If companies are to understand customers, they need to understand the environment in which those customers exist. The chapter uses the PEST (Political, Economic, Social and Technological) framework to explore the different facets and changing trends within the environment and the implications these trends have on the way customers behave.

Finally, Chapter 4 examines how companies can build information on the markets and their customers. It looks at what constitutes information and the importance of collecting relevant data which can help companies understand who their customers are and how they operate in the market. The chapter distinguishes between secondary data and primary data. The sources of the different types of data are examined and data is used to understand customer dynamics. The chapter also takes the reader through the steps of the marketing research process in collecting primary data on customers and consumers.

After reading Part One of this book readers should understand the dynamics of different types of customer, appreciate the challenges of the environment in which companies compete for customers, and be able to carry out the necessary investigations to access relevant information on the customer.

1 Customers, quality and exchange

Robin Lowe

LEARNING OUTCOMES

After reading this chapter you should be able to:

- Discuss the complexity of customer satisfaction, and the importance of delivering value and quality in a fast-changing, competitive market

- Explain to colleagues the concepts and significance of customers, exchanges and quality as they apply in the market

- Compare the types of input and output from suppliers and customers that contribute to the exchange and customer satisfaction

- Appreciate the organisational basis for understanding and managing customers and thus understand the rationale for the book

KEY WORDS

Barter
Competition
Competitive environment
Customer
Customer-focused
Customer satisfaction
Customer segments
Dissatisfiers
Exchanges
Expectations
For-profit businesses

Marketing
Markets
Not-for-profit organisations
Perceived value
Products
Quality
Satisfiers
Services
Suppliers
Tangible and intangible benefits
Total customer value

INTRODUCTION

At some stage of every day just about all of us become a **customer**. Customers are at the heart of our society because the economy revolves around **exchanges**, in which customers receive from **suppliers** the physical goods, services and ideas that satisfy them and give something in return. In this chapter we begin by discussing some instances of **customer satisfaction** and dissatisfaction with the products and services they receive from organisations. The purpose of all **for-profit businesses**, such as Marks & Spencer, British Airways and McDonald's, is to find, satisfy and keep customers, because customers provide the revenue for businesses that will enable them to survive and grow. The majority of **not-for-profit organisations**, such as the RSPCA, Greenpeace and the Labour Party, and organisations that do not take customers' money directly, such as hospitals and schools, exist by satisfying the **expectations** of the individuals that have an interest in their activities.

We then go on to explain the role of customers and the nature of the exchanges that take place between the supplier and the customer. We discuss the idea that the success of these exchanges and customer satisfaction is dependent upon the customers' perception of the value of the products, services, ideas and money that are exchanged and the kinds of judgement that customers make about the quality of every aspect of the interaction that takes place between the customer and the supplier.

What must also be remembered is that organisations only exist because customers are prepared to engage with them. The majority of us will survive and prosper throughout our lives by serving customers, either personally or as part of an organisation, both within and outside the company. To be successful, however, it is necessary for organisations to go much further than simply designing **quality products** and **services**. Everything they do must be **customer-focused** and so contribute positively to the whole customer experience. In this way organisations influence their customers by communicating effectively and building up relationships with them over a long period of time. Ultimately the most admired organisations consistently delight their customers by anticipating their new needs and expectations and so provide **total customer value**.

1.1 THE CHALLENGE OF PROVIDING CUSTOMER SATISFACTION

As customers, our expectations are deceptively simple. We want customer satisfaction. By this we mean we expect all the products, services and ideas that are offered to us to be of high quality and we expect to be treated as well as we would treat others.

Total customer value

Some organisations have grown steadily over many years by routinely providing total customer value to their customers. Tesco has become the leading UK supermarket chain by being customer focused through understanding its customers' changing needs and consistently delivering both existing and new services, such as bonus points, financial services and online shopping, to the highest possible quality. It also sees the importance of providing better parking spaces for families with young children and opening additional check-outs if a queue is developing. It reassures customers of its commitment to low prices through television advertising.

Nokia has also won over many mobile phone customers by being customer focused and by combining functionality and design with continual innovation. By responding to its customers' continually changing needs it has become a market leader.

Organisations exist because of their ability to supply goods, services and ideas to customers. They invariably go to great lengths to let everyone know that they are very aware of this, with slogans such as 'The Customer is King!' As we explain in Chapter 2, it is vital to know who the different customers are and what each customer expects.

Customer dissatisfaction

However not all organisations provide customer satisfaction. Our day-to-day experiences as customers of such organisations leave us with emotions ranging from delight and satisfaction with a product that performs well or a service that was delivered efficiently and without hassle, through to frustration and anger with a poor quality product or a service that did not meet our expectations.

Of course, the majority of our experiences as customers are routine, but think about the occasions when you have been genuinely delighted with a product or service. No doubt you have remembered these occasions for a long time, but we suspect that these satisfactory experiences are few and far between, and are far outweighed by the occasions on which you have been disappointed. If you are a critical customer you may frequently observe that your sandwich is too dry or too wet, your fries are not crispy and the bus driver is surly and resents giving you change.

1.2 ORGANISATIONS AND CUSTOMER SATISFACTION

While it may seem quite obvious to us as customers what we need and want, in practice organisations often get it wrong. In the fast-moving, **competitive environment** it is vital for organisations to provide customer satisfaction otherwise they risk losing their customers to competitors. The penalty for not providing customer satisfaction can be a steep decline in the organisation's performance, as Marks & Spencer, McDonald's and British Airways (BA) have recently found. For decades these three companies had a reputation for delivering customer satisfaction but all three have been presented in the media as having taken their customers for granted and having failed to react quickly, to changes in the market environment and, in particular, in their customers' attitudes and needs.

Marks & Spencer suffered as competitors, such as Next and Asda, overtook them in the perceived quality and design of clothing, value for money and in actively promoting strong brand names. For some of its customers, McDonald's no longer offers as good value as competitors, and, for others, it has responded slowly to the need for more health-conscious eating.

It was felt by some that British Airways failed to respond to the customer need for low-cost, value-for-money, no-frills travel. It was competitors, such as easyJet and Ryanair, that gave customer satisfaction by providing services that were wanted. In fact, easyJet and Ryanair went beyond providing customer satisfaction and meeting customer expectations. Before they were established, customers were not even aware that they could expect these levels of prices and convenience in airline flights. Ryanair and easyJet therefore redefined what customers might expect and so were able to take customers from the other airlines and grow very rapidly. Achieving high levels of customer satisfaction and exceeding customer expectations can therefore be a major reason for business success.

In Chapter 3 we discuss how the whole market environment changes and how it affects customer expectations and customer satisfaction. Often it is the simple attention to detail that customers want but that is overlooked by senior managers, as was shown by a series of BBC TV programmes (Spotlight 1.1).

Spotlight 1.1

Back to the floor

The BBC ran a series of programmes entitled *Back to the Floor*, in which the chief executives of major organisations went to work on the 'shop floor' alongside staff in customer-facing jobs. For example, the chief executive of Sainsbury's worked on a store check-out for a day. The chief executives were invariably unaware of the irritations to customers caused by executive decisions, often made without consultation with 'shop floor' staff. Frequently, the cost of actions to put things right was relatively low whereas the cost of losing customers and the disillusionment among loyal and hardworking staff was high. But is this a good use of the chief executive's time?

Source: Adapted from www.bbc.co.uk

In our personal capacity as members of society, employees, managers and future managers, it is essential to understand exactly what customers require and what will win the customers over, because our prosperity and that of the organisations we work for depends upon it. Of course, overall success in delivering, as against understanding customer satisfaction depends upon many other things, including developing ideas, manufacturing, distributing, **marketing** and selling products and services, managing huge and complicated organisational structures, human resources and finances. We have excluded these areas from our discussions in this book for two reasons. First, omitting these areas allows us to maintain a sharp focus on understanding and managing customers. Secondly, and more importantly, success comes from really understanding customers and their perceptions of quality, before deciding what products and services should be offered to them. Too many organisations think that, because they supply customers routinely, they know instinctively what customers want. They often have internal rules and make decisions that are completely illogical. They often take customers for granted and customers simply become part of some organisational process, as Spotlight 1.2 shows.

Spotlight 1.2

Flying service

There seem to be endless anecdotes about airline service. Here are two typical examples.

At Brussels airport the pilot announced to passengers sitting in the Virgin aeroplane waiting to return to the UK that there would be a 20-minute delay in order for passengers, whose Virgin plane had broken down, to join the flight. Twenty minutes later the new passengers came on to the plane and walked up and down saying 'but there are no seats for us'. They were turned off the plane, at which point the pilot announced there would be a further delay while their luggage was found and removed. It took a further 55 minutes to find and remove the luggage. Only then could the plane set off. With all the elaborate check-in procedures it seems surprising that Virgin did not know how many seats were on the plane and how many passengers they had loaded on to the flight. If they had known this, they could have avoided the inconvenience to passengers.

Sometimes internal rules seem incomprehensible. Travelling on BMI (British Midland) low-cost airline, a passenger was told that his case was the right size but too heavy to take on as hand baggage. When asked if there was anything that could be removed, a rather heavy book was the obvious candidate. Surprisingly, the check-in official then allowed the passenger to put the book back in the case, carry it to the plane on the understanding that it would be taken out and put on his knee while the bag was placed in the overhead locker. Of course, the book remained in the case, but the passenger then spent the whole flight wondering whether the extra weight of the book would cause the overhead lockers to collapse on top of him!

Source: Robin Lowe

Organisations often try to inflict on customers products and services that are not wanted or are inappropriate. They effectively say to customers 'trust us, we know what is best for you'. Even worse, as Spotlight 1.3 shows, they sometimes even insult the intelligence of their customers.

Spotlight 1.3

Insulting the customers

Perhaps the most dangerous thing a CEO can do is to make an 'off-the-cuff remark'. In the UK this is called 'doing a Ratner'. This recalls an incident in 1991 when Gerald Ratner, the CEO of the Ratners jewellery chain, joked at a meeting of the Institute of Directors that the company 'sold a pair of earrings for under a pound, which is cheaper than a prawn sandwich from Marks & Spencer but probably wouldn't last as long'. He followed this by saying a sherry decanter was so cheap because it was 'total crap'. Consumers do not like to be taken for fools and £500 million was wiped off the company value. In 1994 Ratner and his name were removed from the company.

In 2001 the boss of the Topman clothing brand gave an interview to trade magazine *Menswear* and, when asked to clarify the Topman target customer, he said 'Hooligans or whatever.' He added 'Very few of our customers have to wear suits to work. They'll be for his first interview or first court case.'

In 2003 Matt Barrett, the Chief Executive of Barclays Bank, the largest UK credit card company, giving evidence to a UK government committee, said that astute customers would do well to steer clear of credit cards. He and his four children avoided them because they were too expensive.

Source: bbc online

The fact that organisations frequently fail to deliver what customers want is evidenced by the many stories in consumer magazines, TV investigative programmes and in the press of products and services failing to deliver what customers expected from them. Even major companies, can suffer significant loss of sales due to failure to build up-to-date information on the market (as we discuss in Chapter 4) and failure to respond fast enough to the often-changing needs of their customers. While it is recognised that the underperformance of many companies can be the result of incompetent management and poor financial, marketing and operations management, it becomes clear that the road to success for companies depends upon them achieving customer satisfaction.

For this reason we are not focusing on how to sell, how to market and how to organise the business. This comes later. The first step is to identify and investigate customers, understand them, know what influences them and what has to be delivered to them in order to leave them satisfied.

1.3 THE CONCEPT OF EXCHANGE

Central to an understanding of customer satisfaction is the concept of exchange. Customers exist because an exchange takes place (see Figure 1.1). Customers receive something from an individual or an organisation and give something in return. What is exchanged between the customer and supplier is a physical good, such as a can of beans, a service, such as a haircut, an idea, such as a political manifesto, or money or the promise of money. Some examples appear in Table 1.1. In practice, the exchange usually involves a combination of these, for example, servicing and insurance (services) might be provided free with the purchase of a car (a physical good).

The exchange will be considered a success if both the parties, supplier and customer, feel satisfied because they have received something of appropriate value to what they have offered in return.

Barter

Perhaps the first exchange took place in the Garden of Eden when we can only imagine what Adam obtained in return for the apple he offered to Eve. History did not record whether or not each considered they had received good value in the exchange, but partners have argued what the deal should be ever since!

In the days before money was invented physical goods and services were exchanged by **barter** but there are some flaws. It only works if both parties are willing

Table 1.1   Some examples of what can be exchanged

Physical good	Computer, CD, Car components, Power Generation plant
Service	Training, Loan, Dry cleaning, Financial advice, Consultancy, Design
Idea	Political party, Environmentalism
Money	Cash, credit, Foreign currency, Shares in a company

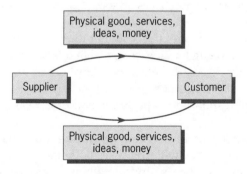

Figure 1.1   The exchange process

to accept what the other is offering in exchange at that particular moment. With bartering, such problems as how many chickens equal one cow could no doubt occupy a determined negotiator for days. Bartering in one form or another is still an important aspect of both local and world trade.

Money exchanges

The invention of money, of course, provided more flexibility in the exchanges by allowing the supplier of physical goods and services to earn money in return. The money could be stored and used to purchase other physical goods and services at a later date. The role of money in the exchange has evolved over time and is not limited to customers paying money to suppliers. For example, banks are prepared to supply money to customers in the form of a loan to buy a car or a house in exchange for a commitment to repay a loan over a period of time.

Money enables a precise, relative price to be placed on a good or service, which makes it clear and reasonably easy for a supplier to communicate a potential 'offer' to customers – what product, service or idea will be supplied on condition that the customer is prepared to pay a specific amount of money. It establishes a going rate for a good or service, enables customers easily to make comparisons between competing suppliers, and helps customers to realise if they are getting good value or being ripped off.

Customer expectations and competition

In return for the money paid out, the customer expects satisfaction from the product or service that has been taken in exchange. It is important to recognise that it is the customer who ultimately decides whether the product or service meets his or her expectations. If the customer is dissatisfied with a product or service and there are alternative suppliers available, then the customer will be unwilling to participate in a second exchange with the same supplier and is likely to switch to an alternative. If the customer is satisfied with the value obtained from the first transaction, it will be considered a successful exchange and he or she will be willing to engage in further exchanges with the same supplier. A supplier can build upon this and through a whole series of actions begin to build a relationship with the customer that will encourage repeat purchases. In today's competitive environment, however, even if the customer is satisfied, there are likely to be other suppliers competing to offer better value. This encourages the customer to 'shop around' and try one or more of the other suppliers, looking for an exchange that offers improved value and greater satisfaction.

The pressure is therefore on suppliers to aim to delight customers by adding unexpected extras that will exceed the customers' expectations. These levels of satisfaction in response to expectations and the resulting customer reactions are shown in Figure 1.2.

Of course, the idea is that if suppliers in even the most mundane businesses really want to, they will find ways to delight customers, as Spotlight 1.4 shows.

Customers do not just decide whether they were satisfied at the moment of purchase. They will constantly evaluate the whole experience long after the actual date

Figure 1.2 Customer expectation and satisfaction

Spotlight 1.4

Delighting dog lovers

Delighting customers can be very profitable for firms operating quite mundane services. Running dog kennels would appear to have limited scope for adding extra value for customers. However, a dog kennel in the north of England had a very profitable business with daily accommodation rates 50% higher than other dog kennels in the area. The kennels were always full. So how did they do it?

Owners who left their dog at the kennel while they went on holiday would arrive home to find a postcard from the dog saying 'I am having a lovely time at the dog kennel. I hope your holiday is just as good.' Moreover, while on holiday you could phone up the dog kennel and the assistant would take a mobile phone down to the dog. You could call its name, the dog would bark and you would know everything was okay.

This idea was topped in New York, as you would expect. There an investment fund manager gave up his job to set up a dog-sitting service just off Wall Street. Workers on Wall Street could bring their dogs into work with them, have them picked up by taxi and taken to the kennels. The kennels were fitted with web cams and so the investment fund managers could have part of their computer screen showing the dog happy in the kennel while the rest of the screen was focused on their multi-billion dollar deals. The owner of the kennel claimed to be making more money out of the dog kennels than he made from being an investment fund manager! What are the dog owners looking for from the dog kennels?

Source: Robin Lowe

of transaction. The potential for an exchange to be considered unsatisfactory by a customer starts well before the actual exchange takes place and finishes long afterwards. For example, a major civil engineering project, such as a new road, bridge or airport, requires considerable negotiation before the work is started in order to agree what should be delivered and long after the completion date problems may well need to be put right. Companies still make exaggerated claims as to how a product will perform, for example, it might take a few months after buying a car to find that it has a recurring fault that the dealers are reluctant to fix.

Supplier satisfaction and 'win-win'

To be fully successful, therefore, the exchange process depends upon agreement on what is acceptable for the supplier and what constitutes satisfaction for the customer when the exchange takes place. It also depends upon both the supplier and customer behaving responsibly. Customers can also be difficult! A customer may find trivial faults with a product or the delivery of a service in order to avoid or delay paying the full amount promptly, and for a small firm supplying a major customer not being paid promptly can be enough to make them bankrupt.

Reaching agreement on both customer and supplier expectations before the exchange takes place is vital for a 'win-win' satisfactory outcome for both and this usually takes the form of negotiation. Negotiation through haggling has formed the basis of street trading through the centuries and is completely opposite to the idea in other retailing where there is a fixed price – 'take it or leave it'. For complex deals involving many separate individual elements, negotiation to achieve customer and supplier satisfaction is essential.

Figure 1.3 represents the idea that both customers and suppliers need to be satisfied for the exchange to be considered a success. It is important to recognise that both customers and suppliers input into and receive something from the exchange process.

Dealing with external, uncontrollable factors

The final consideration in the exchange process is the effect of extraneous variables, which are the factors in the environment that affect the exchange but are not brought to it by the supplier or customer, as shown in Figure 1.3. The external, uncontrollable factors can have a significant effect on both the input and impact side of the exchange. For example, rain causing the abandonment of an outside sports event will have a serious effect on customer satisfaction and also the supplier's income from the event. Equally, an exchange between a customer and a supplier can directly or indirectly have a positive or negative effect on third parties, the community and environment in general. Charities not only help individuals but in doing so often improve the community and the environment in which the recipients live. By contrast, drug dealing can obviously have a harmful effect on the third parties to whom the drugs are sold, as well as the community in general by encouraging crime to pay for the drugs.

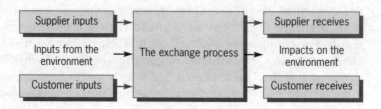

Figure 1.3 The exchange process and the environment

The competitive market and marketing

The primary focus of this book is on understanding and managing customers rather than how organisations proactively manage their business activity. For this reason it is our intention to only briefly discuss **markets** and marketing here. (See further reading at the end of this chapter for more information.)

In discussing the process of exchange we have introduced a number of players, such as customers and suppliers that are involved in the exchange. We have also recognised that there may be a number of suppliers, who offer similar products, services and ideas from which customers can choose. In a democratic society it is usually possible for customers to choose between alternative cars, fast food restaurants, airlines, banks and political parties. The different suppliers are in **competition** with one another. Other individuals and organisations have an interest in the exchanges that take place. Some are interested in how customers behave but, more particularly, how organisations behave when they act as suppliers in the exchange. These individuals and organisations are called stakeholders and include such organisations as the government, trade unions, pressure and consumer groups and the media. In total, all these players make up the market in which the exchanges occur.

Within the markets as we have described them, marketing is the range of activities of an individual or organisation that is concerned with managing exchanges between the organisation and its customers and other stakeholders. Many definitions of marketing can be found in marketing textbooks. Because the contexts in which marketing takes place vary so much it is difficult to find a satisfactory all-embracing definition, but we offer the Chartered Institute of Marketing's definition of marketing as a useful definition for our purposes:

> *Marketing is the management process responsible for identifying, anticipating and satisfying customer requirements profitably.*

It is worth noting that the emphasis in this definition is clearly placed on understanding what customers want and need rather than a selling approach in which the emphasis is placed on persuading customers to receive something that has already largely been designed or made.

1.4 THE CONCEPT OF QUALITY AND VALUE

Within the process of exchange, money has brought greater formality, precision and measurement to the part of the process that is concerned with what the customer offers in return for the goods, services and ideas. We now turn to consider whether formality, precision and measurement has been brought to the other side of the exchange, and specifically the quality of products and services. To do this it is necessary to consider customer satisfaction and value in more detail.

Satisfiers and dissatisfiers

Customers expect satisfaction and in doing so they distinguish between **dissatisfiers** and **satisfiers**. Certain elements of the exchange are necessary to avoid certain customer dissatisfaction. Dissatisfiers would include a car that will not start, a jacket that has been so badly stitched that the buttons fall off the first time it is worn, and a watch that does not keep the correct time. However, a car that works, a jacket that is well stitched and a watch that keeps time will not guarantee customer satisfaction and therefore are not satisfiers. The car may be an 'old banger', the jacket surgical green and the watch may have a cartoon character on the face, and so not ideal for the sophisticated reader wishing to make a fashion statement!

Dissatisfiers occur when the level of quality provided by the service supplier falls below the basic level that the customer expects. Customers have come to expect a basic level of product quality and service from any supplier as a right. However, they hope for additions to the basic level of product or service that will delight them. Of course, for organisations the key to this is understanding exactly what customers are looking for, what their responses to product and service offers are and understanding exactly why customers behave the way they do. We discuss this in greater detail in Chapter 5.

Spotlight 1.5 shows how understanding satisfiers and dissatisfiers can win or lose customers.

If the supplier delivers a basic level of product quality and service, it does not guarantee that customers will be satisfied because competitors may be offering additional value. For example, a customer taking an airline flight has a fundamental expectation that the aeroplane will arrive at the destination safely. Moreover, having paid the fare, the customer expects a seat, short queues at the check-in and the plane to run on time. If the plane is overbooked and cannot carry the customer, arrives late because of a failure of the airline or if there are long queues at the check-in, the customer will be dissatisfied. The customer expects these services to be part of the normal product in an efficiently operated airline but they will not create satisfaction for the customer. It will take something better to delight the customer. The customer may be delighted if she or he is offered better food than was expected, a seat upgrade, the opportunity to wait in the executive lounge or even if the cabin steward is prepared to chat to him or her in quiet periods during the flight. All these small events may make a boring airline flight more memorable for the customer.

The problem for suppliers, of course, is that customers get used to the free additions to the product and service that initially delight them and begin to take them for granted. Customers then start looking around for what extra value other suppliers are offering. All these extras ultimately have to be paid for and so suppliers find ways of increasing prices to cover their costs to the point where premium prices are being charged for over-elaborate products and services. One or two potential suppliers will then spot the opportunity to provide a 'no-frills service' at a low price. There will usually be plenty of customers who will wish to take up the offer and this kind of demand has led to success for easyJet and Ryanair in the airline industry and Netto and Aldi in food retailing.

Spotlight 1.5

Adding customer value in the caravan park

William has a caravan which the family uses for weekends by the seaside. He has no room to keep the caravan at home, but can keep it overnight on the road outside his house. He pays about £200 a year to store it at a caravan park in the next village, just outside Sheffield. A guard was on duty at the park to let the caravan owners in and out of the park from early in the morning until late at night. However, recently the caravan park was taken over by new owners who have decided to open a shop on the caravan site to sell caravan and camping equipment. To save money they have decided not to have the guard but instead use the sales assistants in the shop to let owners in and out. This means that now the caravan park will be open at the same time as the shop – from 9.00am to 5.00pm.

Unfortunately William works 20 miles away and, whereas in the past he could fetch the caravan out of the park after he got home from work in the evening, he now had to take time off work the day before his holiday in order to get the caravan out of the park and ready to go. Moreover, to ensure that he got the caravan back to the park in time for closing he had to set off from the seaside around 2.30pm, considerably cutting short his holiday.

Reluctantly, he has had to change to a new caravan park for storing his caravan. The park is another five miles away and is £50 a year more expensive. However, this park has a swipe card system for entry and electronic surveillance equipment for safety. He can now take his caravan into the park at his convenience, any time of the day or night and does not lose time at work or money when he wants to take his caravan out. Why is the old caravan park not offering what this customer wants?

Source: Robin Lowe

Organisations observe that out of the mass of potential customers they can identify groups or customer segments that have similar needs and expectations. For example, one group of customers simply wants low-cost basic food products from supermarkets, whereas another group wants a wider variety of food, perhaps with more exotic ingredients. We discuss the concept of customer segmentation in Chapter 6. Having defined these groups of customers with similar needs, the organisation can then clearly identify what each of the **customer segments** is looking for, and work out how their precise requirements can be delivered, and this is discussed in more detail in Chapter 7. The customer requirements take the form of **tangible and intangible benefits**. A customer might want a car that is spacious, fast and has been well designed. These are examples of the tangible elements. The customer might also want the car to be a status symbol that will impress his or her friends and neighbours, and these are the intangible benefits.

1.5 QUALITY

While the success of many exchanges is based upon customers applying subjective measures of **perceived value**, in practice more objective comparisons can be made between competing offers from the different potential suppliers and the reference point for these comparisons is the concept of quality. Quality can be thought of as having two dimensions: consistency and level.

Consistency

Consistency means that for each exchange involving the same product, service or idea, the customer can be sure that it will be the same every time. Of course, in customer satisfaction terms it might mean that the product is consistently good or bad, because of the customer perception. Achieving consistency in manufactured products is essential to success and organisations go to great lengths to assure and control quality, but things quite often go wrong, as evidenced by the number of product recall notices in newspapers, informing customers of a quality defect in a particular product.

Achieving consistency in services and ideas is a particular challenge because they are delivered and interpreted by individual people, who often have widely differing attitudes, beliefs and values that they inevitably apply to the delivery of services and ideas. Moreover, while customers cannot argue about the objective measurements of physical products, their attitudes, beliefs and values will lead them to have considerably different perceptions of the service experience. Visiting a fast food restaurant in different countries can show the difficulty of maintaining consistency in the quality of service and a music concert is unlikely to satisfy all the performers' fans in exactly the same way.

Level

By level of quality we are referring to differences or perceived differences in the specification of the product, service or idea. For example, both Audi and Skoda have similarly low levels of defects and are therefore quality cars in terms of consistency, but it may be perceived by some that the specification of the Audi would be expected to be higher than the Skoda in terms of refinement and comfort.

Certain elements of the product and service can be objectively measured and *proved* to be of higher specification and so at a higher level of quality. Other elements, however, may be *perceived* by customers to be of a higher quality. Again, this may be down to personal preference. For example, customers may perceive the Audi to have a superior design or better image than the Skoda and thus be a higher quality car. Given that both cars are made by the Volkswagen group, many components of both cars may well be the same. We discuss customer perceptions of the quality of products and services in Chapter 8.

As Dilemma 1.1 shows, appreciating and being sensitive to customer perceptions can be particularly challenging for organisations.

Dilemma 1.1

Saga Holidays – how to satisfy customer perceptions

Understanding customer perceptions is vital for firms so that they can tailor their products and promotions to appeal to customers. Customers not only have perceptions about products and services, but also have perceptions of themselves. Some customer purchase decisions might be made on the kind of products and services that meet their perception of themselves.

Older people have interesting perceptions of themselves. A friend's granddad, aged 80, enjoys taking lunches around to the homes of the 'old people' in the village where he lives. He would certainly not yet consider himself to be old. In fact, research suggests that people believe that others would estimate their age at 75–80% of their actual age, so there is a degree of self-delusion.

This presents Saga holidays with a problem. Its holidays are developed to meet the needs and wants of people over the age of 50 and they have achieved awards to suggest that they deliver satisfaction to their customers.

The dilemma is how should they appeal to their target customers? Such terms as 'senior citizens' are not going to appeal to their potential customers and the 'young-at-heart' elderly probably do not want to associate with people they would think were too old.

Source: Robin Lowe

1.6 THE DIFFERENT CUSTOMER SITUATIONS

While the word 'customer' has been traditionally used to relate to exchanges in which the receiver purchases something from the supplier, we have expanded the use of the word 'customer' to include the receiver in all exchange situations. The reason for this is that many of the exchanges that take place between a supplier and customer do not involve monetary payment and profit for the supplier but still demand the outcome of customer satisfaction. Parents of state-educated children do not have to pay for their children's attendance at school but still expect the highest standards of education and service quality throughout their dealings with the school and education authorities.

Customers have become used to many organisations providing high-quality products and standards of service and so expect this standard, no matter what the context of the transaction. The police force, for example, provides a service to the public and they are there for the protection of all sections of the general public. They also require the support of the public to do their job efficiently and effectively but this involves taking punitive action against certain members of the public. While the police force cannot guarantee that their exchanges will result in delight for their criminal 'customers', they must ensure that their dealings with the public in general will result in overall customer satisfaction. Over the past few years, however, there has been considerable criticism of the way the police have interacted with ethnic minorities, probably because of preconceived ideas, a lack of real understanding of the culture of these customer groups, and inaccurate or inadequate information about these particular customers.

In this book, therefore, we discuss 'customers' in a number of situations:

1. Those who are involved in 'for-profit' business, such as those commercial businesses that supply other businesses or individual consumers.
2. The 'not-for-profit' sector, which includes
   • those who are not directly paying for services at that time but may pay indirectly, for example, healthcare through government taxes and refuse collection and policing through payment of local authority rates; and
   • those who are not paying for the goods and services they receive, for example, the recipients of charities (see Dilemma 1.2).
3. Those that have a provider–customer relationship within the organisation (internal customers).

Dilemma 1.2

Shock tactics or compassion

The recipients of charitable work are customers of those charities. In return for the practical products, services and money that they are given, the recipients provide those donating money and time with the satisfaction that they are doing good, not only for individuals but for the community as a whole. There is not, however, an unlimited supply of people prepared or able to work for charities or unlimited money available for donation. The managers of charities of course wish to achieve great improvements in their area of interest and consequently compete with other charities for the donated pound.

It has been shown that stories (for example, of animal cruelty and human starvation) that shock, together with images shown on television and in the newspapers that are disturbing, often prompt the largest donations. However, these images, even with the best of motives, inevitably show the recipients of the charity very negatively, when they are most disadvantaged and often when they lack dignity.

The dilemma is whether charities should seek to maximise the donations, or generate fewer donations but preserve the dignity of their recipient 'customers' through their advertising. A second dilemma is whether charities should use donations to pay for professional management and marketing, which has frequently been shown to be critical for success in charities, when their donor 'customers' would prefer to see every penny raised spent on the recipients.

Source: Robin Lowe

The first two situations are discussed in some detail in the following chapter but it is to the third situation, internal customers, that we now turn.

1.7 INFLUENCING THE CUSTOMER

Customers are influenced by organisations in many ways in order to persuade them to continue to purchase. First, customers are influenced by the effectiveness of the organisation's operation and this, to a large degree, is affected by the way in which internal exchanges take place and how the organisation operates the internal customer concept, as this will be reflected in its external dealings.

Internal customers

In most organisations individual staff members or departments depend on being served by other staff members or departments within the organisation. The waiters and waitresses in Pizza Hut expect the chef to provide what they need to serve to the customer quickly; that is the full order attractively presented. Indeed, their tips will probably depend as much on the food served as the efficiency and the friendliness of their service! In this sense the waiters are the cooks' immediate internal customer and when all the contributions of internal exchanges between customers and suppliers are added together the result can be a huge success or a complete disaster.

Global companies, which operate across borders, face many additional challenges in achieving satisfactory internal customer exchanges. Staff from different countries and cultures have different expectations, standards and values, and communicate in different languages too. These companies often try to standardise their products, promotions and their new product launch plan in order to save costs. As discussed in Spotlight 1.6, a department in one country might be given the responsibility for planning a promotion or launch to be carried out by other parts of the company in their home countries. In the spotlight, the UK department did not fully understand the local French culture, and so failed to realise what was really important.

We address the concept of internal customers in more detail in Chapter 9.

Communications and relationship building

Through their external exchanges, organisations influence customers in their purchasing decisions. The communications that they send out (discussed in Chapter 10) help potential customers to know what they might expect from a product or service, what sort of organisation it is, how it differs from its competitors and what its standards and values are. As we shall see in later chapters, it is critical that organisations effectively manage the two-way communication exchanges that take place with customers in many areas of the business and though various media.

Often these two-way exchanges form the basis of relationship building that is critical for organisations in their efforts to manage their customers over a long period of time. It is through the knowledge and understanding that is built up

Spotlight 1.6

Understanding the French

One of the very largest US suppliers of mainframe computers was launching a new server to its business customers in 15 European countries. It decided to use the same product launch event and in 14 countries the launch was successful. In France the event was a failure. So what went wrong?

The company failed to understand the French psyche. The launch event was held in Marseilles, but the French believe that important events are held in Paris, so to them the launch could not have been important. The presentation was made in English, or at least in American English, with four slides at the end translated into French as a token gesture – what an insult! The worst mistake, however, was the food. The event was to have the same themed food in each country. The English branch of the company, which was handling the events, decided the theme should be an English pub lunch. The potential customers would be expected to eat standing up. The French could not take this seriously for a major event. For them it was essential to have a five course meal taking a couple of hours, complete with plenty of good quality wine – French of course! When should an international company adjust its product and service offers to customer needs and when should it keep the offer standard in all its markets?

Source: Robin Lowe

through long-term customer–supplier relationships that superior levels of customer satisfaction can be ultimately achieved and this is the subject of Chapter 11.

Finally, in Chapter 12 we look to the future and recognise that it will be vital for organisations to have a better understanding of the next generation of customers and their changing expectations. It will simply not be enough for organisations to try to keep up with the competition in offering similar new and interesting products and services but, in an increasingly competitive environment, they will have to influence their customers' purchasing decisions by creating and setting new customer expectations and then delivering the new products and services that will meet this new need.

SUMMARY

At one time or another all of us are customers. Also, as individuals and as employees of organisations, most of us need customers with which to exchange products, services, money and ideas in order to survive and prosper. The fact that many products and services that we receive on a daily basis prove to be less effective than we would like suggests that many organisations do not fully understand what customers want.

In practice, customers want quality in every aspect of their dealings with suppliers, but quality can mean different things in different customer situations. Quality is used in relation to the consistency of the offering and the level of quality offered, when compared to that of competitors.

Customers have expectations of receiving satisfaction and judge value from their own perspective. Whereas in the past the concept of customers was applied to 'for-profit' businesses, it is now necessary to think of customers in 'not-for-profit' situations too. We also discussed the supplier–customer exchanges that occur within the company, as the effectiveness of these transactions can affect the quality of the final product or service offered to consumers.

Discussion questions

1   Why do suppliers in (a) for-profit and (b) not-for-profit sectors often fail to provide customer satisfaction?

2   What are the criteria for success in a customer–supplier exchange involving the purchase of office equipment by a small business?

3   Detail the possible expectations of (a) a patient going to a hospital for treatment, (b) a football supporter going to see their favourite team, and (c) a customer buying a very expensive outfit from a fashion house. In each case identify what you consider to be the satisfiers and dissatisfiers.

4   Explain with examples the difference between quality as consistency and quality as level.

5   In what ways are customers under the age of 25 likely to assess value when considering the purchase of a two-week package holiday in Ibiza? How might this differ from customers aged 65–75 also buying a two-week holiday in Ibiza? What assumptions have you made?

Case study 1.1   Customer–supplier exchange at university

In the exchange that takes place between suppliers and customers it is important to recognise that customers evaluate not only the main elements of the supplier's product and service offer but all the elements in the total product and service offer. Moreover, when making their choice between competing suppliers and in assessing levels of customer satisfaction, customers will also evaluate certain factors that are outside the control of the supplier.

Universities offer courses to undergraduates that they believe they have the capability to deliver and will prove to be attractive to students. Students are able to shop around and choose between a range of courses and between universities in many locations. The Higher Education Funding Council (HEFC) controls UK government funding to universities and through the Quality Assurance Agency (QAA) operates a quality control process that is designed to maintain quality and provide guidance for students selecting between courses. The 'price' for entry to courses and the currency that students use to shop around and select a course are Universities and Colleges Admissions Service (UCAS) points which are earned through completing examinations at school or their equivalent.

As might be expected, university staff believe that the student's choice of course and place to study might be based on factors that they have some degree of control over, such as the reputation of the institution, the intellectual challenge of the course, the success of students gaining employment, levels of support given to students and the quality of accommodation.

Naturally, all applicants would consider these factors, but they might also consider other factors over which the institution has no control, such as whether the city or town in which the institution is located is close to the home of the student, has good sports facilities, good nightlife, good prospects for part-time work or has cheap beer. The student might also be influenced by parents' and their school teachers' preferences too.

A university or college course can take over five years to complete from the point of application through to graduation. The student makes a final, overall assessment of the exchange, including the perceived value of the course and the cost to the student. In addition, thousands of individual exchanges will also have taken place during the course. These might include handing in an assignment, obtaining accommodation or buying a meal in the restaurant, and each of these will be assessed in terms of satisfaction.

At the end of that period family and friends are likely to ask the graduate such questions as 'Are you pleased you chose that course?' and 'Did you have a good time at university/college?' The answers to these questions will be affected both by the factors that the university/college staff can control and those that they cannot.

Questions

1   What are the criteria that students might use in deciding which university and course is likely to suit their needs?

2 Chose three exchanges between university staff (not necessarily academic staff) and, using the model in Figure 1.3, identify the inputs from staff and students and the expectations of each that would lead to student and staff satisfaction.

3 After completion of the course, what are the criteria that will be used for the overall assessment? How will these differ between the various interested parties, such as students, parents and university staff?

Further reading

Dibb, S., Simkin, L., Pride, W.M. and Ferrell, O.C. (2000) *Marketing Concepts and Strategies.* Boston, MA: Houghton Mifflin.

Jobber, D. (2001) *Principles and Practice of Marketing* (3rd edition). New York: McGraw-Hill.

Website

For information on marketing, visit the Chartered Institute of Marketing on www.cim.co.uk

2

Who is the customer?

Isobel Doole

LEARNING OUTCOMES

After reading this chapter you should be able to:

■ **Understand the different types of external customer and their characteristics and be able to interpret the differences between customers**

■ **Recognise the individuals who make up the decision-making unit in any given buying situation and understand the components in organisational as well as individual/family buying situations**

■ **Appreciate the purchasing decision-making process and the types of purchasing decision made by individual and organisational customers**

KEY WORDS

Business-to-business
Business-to-consumer
Business-to-government
Buying roles
Client
Consumer
Consumer-oriented
Customer

Decision-making process
Decision-making unit
Not-for-profit organisations
Organisational customers
Problem solver
Supply chain
Total customer value

INTRODUCTION

As we learnt in Chapter 1, central to the success of any commercial enterprise is the organisation's relationship with its customer. If an organisation is to be truly **consumer-oriented**, then the analysis and understanding of their customers is of paramount importance. Without customers, businesses cannot operate. As was stated in Chapter 1, if commercial organisations do not provide customer satisfaction they will soon lose their customers. Meeting the needs of customers more effectively than competitors is central to a business if it is to achieve any advantages over its competitors and so survive in the market place.

In order to meet the needs of the customer a company needs to know who their existing and potential customers are and understand their current and emergent needs. In this chapter we seek to develop our understanding of the first of these by exploring in some depth what customers actually are.

2.1 ARE CUSTOMERS DIFFERENT FROM CONSUMERS?

Often the terms '**consumer**' and '**customer**' are themselves used interchangeably. Perhaps one of our first tasks, then, is to define exactly what we mean by these terms.

> *A customer is an individual or organisation who buys a product or service; a consumer is the person who uses the product and service or may be affected by its purchase.*

Customers are the ones who make the purchase and are therefore important to the buying decision. Sometimes the customer and consumer is the same person, sometimes not. The distinction between customers and consumers is important. Consumers, not customers, understand what they need from a product or service. However, it is the customer who usually makes the actual buying decision. When customers and consumers are different people, which is often the case in business-to-business (B2B) marketing, it may well complicate the buying process.

For instance, a business traveller who is taller than average, making a long-haul flight may prefer to fly with a carrier with more than average leg room between seats. However, the business traveller may not be the one actually purchasing the ticket, only the one using it. The manager in charge of the travel budget is usually the true customer of the airline and may well make the final decision as to which carrier is best for a company employee, the consumer, to travel on.

Customers, by definition, define value. Consumers, on the other hand, define what is needed from a product or service. When the people who define value and the people who specify the type of product or service required are different, they can disagree about priorities. This is because they are trying to achieve different objectives and are probably under different budgetary constraints. This can be illustrated in the case of televised football and the differing needs of the fans and the television networks, as in Dilemma 2.1.

Dilemma 2.1

Customers vs consumers

Football teams constantly have to jostle the demands of the television networks with the demands of their fans. The fans see themselves as the important customers and often prefer their football matches to kick off at 3pm on Saturday afternoons. The television networks, in trying to maximise live television coverage, may demand matches across many days of the week at many different times, rather than having all football matches across the country playing at the same time. Inconvenient times for fans may affect ticket sales but the club will be more than compensated by the payment from the TV networks.

Are they both important customers or is one a consumer and the other a customer?

2.2 ARE CUSTOMERS BUYING GOODS DIFFERENT FROM THOSE BUYING SERVICES?

The old distinction between product and service is becoming increasingly obsolete. This is why, as we saw in Chapter 1, businesses aim to provide **total customer value**, a combination of the tangible and intangible benefits experienced when a customer makes a purchase. Thus, whether customers are buying a good or a service they are primarily interested in the total value of the purchase on offer. Increasingly, even when buying goods, the value of the tangible benefits of the physical offering is augmented by the intangible benefits of the package of the services accompanying it. Consequently, the modern business has to be much more customer-focused. There is now the realisation that quality starts with the customer and not necessarily the physical product itself, and that the modern customer increasingly attaches values to the services as well as the good being bought. This means that business planning itself has to start from an understanding of who the customers are and how they can be most effectively serviced, irrespective of whether they are buying a physical good or a service. For instance, when choosing between two brands of a washing machine, if one has a five-year parts and labour free warranty, it may be more attractive to a potential customer than the competitive brand that has a greater number of features.

2.3 ARE CUSTOMERS DIFFERENT FROM CLIENTS?

Another area of confusion can be the distinction between the term 'customer' and the term '**client**'. While the purchasers of both goods and services are by definition customers, customers of services are frequently referred to as clients. In addition to this, in the not-for-profit sector, such as the National Health Service and certain government departments dealing directly with the public, consumers of their services are today usually referred to as clients. According to Murphy (2000), clients are driven by tension reduction whereas customers are driven by needs or benefits they are seeking from a product. Clients, however, usually require a service to help solve a problem that has created the tension. If the service is provided satisfactorily, the outcome is a reduction of that tension and the client happily goes on his or her way. If the service provision is unsatisfactory, there is usually an aggravation of that tension and the client then stays to voice his or her complaint. Murphy says this is why clients complain more then they compliment. Murphy identifies a number of important differences between clients and customers (see Table 2.1).

Table 2.1 Customers versus clients

Customers	*Clients*
Can be nameless to the supplier	Require personalised recognition by the supplier
Are often served *en masse*	Need to be served on an individual basis
Can be served by anyone available	Will require to be served by the professional they have chosen
Usually have no relationship with the provider	Perceive they have a personal relationship with the provider
Usually look for the best deal	Are often prepared to pay a huge premium to guarantee solution of the problem

Source: Adapted from Murphy (2000).

2.4 DIFFERENT TYPES OF CUSTOMER

In this chapter we shall consider two main types of customer, the individual/family customers, often referred to as **business-to-consumer (B2C)** and **organisational customers**. However, there are several different types of organisational customer, principally **business-to-business (B2B)**, **business-to-government (B2G)**, **not-for-profit organisations** and internal customers. Internal customers are those who buy products and services supplied by another department within the organisation or perhaps another subsidiary in a larger company.

One of the main differences between the different types of customer is the products and services they buy. Organisational and internal customers are mainly concerned with the purchase of capital goods, raw materials, finished goods and professional services. Government customers, in addition to the above, may well also buy buildings, administrative services and large-scale supplies and service.

Individual customers, on the other hand, buy products and services for their personal consumption and so will be more concerned with the purchase of consumer durables, consumables, impulse purchases as well as an array of services.

In the following section we will look in some detail at the individual/family customer – who they are, what they buy and how they buy. We will then examine these issues in relation to organisational customers.

2.5 THE INDIVIDUAL/FAMILY CUSTOMER

In the business-to-consumer market organisations are usually selling to the end user of the product or service. This could be a sole individual, a family or perhaps a household. The UK has a population of 58.8 million people who spend in excess of £600 billion a year on personal goods and services. Understanding who these customers are and how they spend their money is therefore of interest to many organisations. However, it is also important to understand the family as a **decision-making unit** as a large number of our purchases are made as members of a family. There have been a number of changes to the family structure over the past 30 years, many of which have impacted on children and their role as consumers. The fact that parents are delaying having children has meant that these parents are more affluent and have clearer views regarding such matters as healthy eating, educational priorities as well as ethical consumerism. Later and smaller families and the rise in the number of divorces have led to children having more spent on them individually and them playing a more prominent role in the purchasing decisions made by the family.

A major concern in quarters of our society is the pressure placed on children by advertisers to have the 'right' designer labels in order to fit in with their school friends. The issue of marketing and advertising to children is a controversial one. A number of companies now run high-profile schemes using brand sponsorship to raise money for UK schools, although this form of marketing has recently attracted controversy from consumer watch-dog groups and parents alike. The market place for products aimed at children is becoming increasingly complicated, with crossover marketing, brand extensions and character licensing all playing a part.

So what do UK individual/family customers look like today? Table 2.2 offers some interesting insights.

What does the UK consumer buy?

According to the UK Office for National Statistics, UK consumers spend £631 billion on personal items per annum. Nearly 18% of this is on housing, water and fuel alone. However, as we can see from Table 2.3, 37% of what we spend on personal consumption is spent enjoying ourselves either in recreation or eating and drinking, be it at home or out socialising. Little wonder then that so many television advertisements try to persuade us to part with our money in this direction.

Table 2.2 The UK consumer

Population

The UK has a population of 58.8 million

- 21% under the age of 16
- 16% over the age of 65
- By 2025 there will be 1.6 million more people over 65 than under 16

Households

There are 24.4 million households in the UK

- 64% have 1–2 persons
- 30% have 3–4 persons
- 6% have 5 or more persons
- 33% live in 3% of the land area
- 20% of children live with a lone parent

Wealth

UK households have a wealth totalling £4,573 billion

- The top 5% own 42% of the wealth
- The top 25% own 74% of the wealth
- The top 50% own 94% of the wealth, which means …
- The bottom 50% own 6% of the wealth

Spending

UK households spend £631 billion a year

- 65% of households now have mobile phones
- 40% have access to the Internet
- UK households take 39 million holidays overseas
- In 2002 we bought 41 million DVDs
- We spend 20 hours a week watching television

Source: UK Office for National Statistics 2002

Table 2.3 How UK consumers spend their money

Expenditure	£ billion
Housing, water and fuel	112
Transport	91
Recreation and culture	77
Restaurants and hotels	70
Food and non-alcoholic drinks	60
Clothing and footwear	37
Household goods and services	37
Alcohol/tobacco	25
Communications	14
Health	10
Overseas	23
Miscellaneous	75
Total UK household expenditure	631

Source: UK Office for National Statistics 2002

Increasingly, consumers are now buying through Internet shopping. A total of 10 million homes in the UK are now connected to the Internet, and this grew by nearly 4 million houses last year. This is not just the young middle classes. It is now estimated that at least 20% of the over 55 age groups are connected to the Internet and the growth in access is apparent across all the social groupings in society. However, despite the exponential growth in access to the Internet, consumers are still limiting their purchases to relatively few product lines. It is estimated that nearly 40% of all Internet purchases are for travel, another 26% for the purchase of tickets for events and concerts, and 45% is spent on books and CDs (UK Office for National Statistics). As access to the Internet has grown, so has the type of person accessing it. According to a survey by the Boston Consulting Group (BCG), there are now three types of Internet consumer, as Spotlight 2.1 discusses.

Spotlight 2.1

The Internet consumer

According to an e-commerce study carried out by the Boston Consulting Group (BCG), online consumers actually fall into three groups.

The first group, the *Pioneers*, has been online for at least three years and now comprises 29% of the online population. The *Early Followers* have been online for more than one year but less than three years and represent almost half of the current online population. The *First-of-the-Masses* are the most recent consumers to go online, having made the leap only in the last year, and represent 22% of today's online population.

With each successive wave, the online population is becoming more representative of the demographics of the mass market. While the demographics of Pioneers are consistent with the Internet-user stereotype of the young, male technophile, the *Early Followers* and the *First-of-the-Masses* are increasingly female, mature, less educated and less affluent consumers.

Consumers who have had a satisfying first purchase experience online are likely to spend more time and money online. However, a number of consumers find shopping online offers convenience fraught with compromise. Among both new and experienced Internet consumers, anxiety over credit card security was the main barrier to purchasing online. Purchase process breakdowns were also a major irritant, as well as a deterrent to further online shopping. To help the mass market move online, BCG advises retailers to remove access barriers – better search engines, information entry systems and site navigation are all important in smoothing the shopping experience and paving the way for purchasing.

Source: Adapted from 'Online shopping promises consumers more than it delivers', available at: http://www.sellitontheweb.com.

2.6 HOW DO CUSTOMERS MAKE THEIR PURCHASING DECISIONS?

As we have seen, in making purchases consumers make a staggering number of purchasing decisions. In Chapter 5 we will examine in detail the behaviour of consumers and the factors that affect their purchasing behaviour. In this chapter, in examining who the consumers are, we will briefly examine the **decision-making process** they undergo in making the above decisions. Figure 2.1 provides a framework by which we can consider this issue. As can be seen, a consumer will invariably go through several stages in making a purchasing decision.

Problem recognition

This first stage is when we sense there is a difference between our actual state and desired state. This means that the start of the buying process is something that triggers our desire to find a solution to a problem that we have become aware of. Perhaps previously there was no desire or perhaps no recognition that there is a purchasing need. This, then, is the very beginning of the recognition of the need and the start of the process the consumer undergoes to identify that in order for that need to be satisfied a purchase has to be made. This trigger could be an impulse, or it could be a growing realisation that in order for the need to be satisfied or the situation to be changed a purchase needs to be made. The stimulus for problem recognition can be external or internal. An external stimulus could come from one of many sources; it may be an advertisement, point-of-sale material in a supermarket or perhaps through chatting to a friend or colleague.

Advertisers are sometimes accused or creating unnecessary needs through their advertisements and making consumers feel pressured into thinking needs are real. This is a particular issue in advertising to children, who see products on television and then put immense pressure on parents that they really do need the product advertised. Equally, however, the stimulus could be the creation of an internal awareness. At its simplest level this could be the feeling of hunger or thirst which then requires satisfaction through a purchase or it could be a growing dissatisfaction with the products or services currently being used.

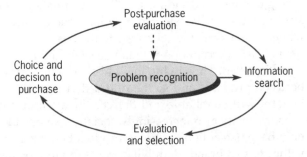

Figure 2.1 The decision-making process

Information search

Once a purchasing problem is recognised, it sometimes may stay unsatisfied, in which case it will remain a latent need. However, a consumer may go on from that position to either actively search for information or simply have a heightened awareness, and so be more receptive to advertisements or other external stimuli. In obtaining information on which to make purchasing decisions, consumers use a variety of sources, such as:

- personal sources – family, friends, colleagues
- commercial sources – advertisements, sales people, displays, dealers
- public sources – mass media, public information sources
- experiential sources – seeing the product or service being used, handling and examining the product or experiencing a similar service.

In Internet marketing, understanding how potential customers search for information is a critical success factor. The travel and leisure retailer lastminute.com sends more than 2 million emails to customers each week. The content of the email is tailored to fit the recipient's age, lifestyle and other factors. Carl Lyons, head of marketing at lastminute.com UK, says, 'Email is a different medium with its own culture so you have to know how to use it properly if it is going to be effective. What you are trying to do is convert lookers into bookers' (*Financial Times*, 05/02/03, 2003, p. 5).

Evaluation and selection

In searching for information, particularly on the Internet, consumers may be faced with a huge number of potential alternative solutions to their buying problem. Most consumers will not have the time or the energy to make an exhaustive evaluation of these alternatives and so will try to identify specific criteria, either subconsciously or consciously, to help them decide among the alternatives on offer. Consumers use several criteria to evaluate alternatives, for instance:

- *Product/service attributes*: when weights are attached to the various attributes to identify the key ones. Perhaps in making a more complex purchase, such as a car or a consumer durable, a consumer will list and rank the attributes needed to solve the problem identified.
- *Salient attributes*: when the decision is based on the attributes which most easily spring to mind. In deciding a holiday destination it may only be the most salient attributes that are considered – perhaps the quality of the night life available or whether a particular hotel is near to the beach.
- *Brand beliefs*: perceptions as to how each brand performs on the important attributes identified. Thus in buying a hi-fi system it may be difficult to differentiate between products and so the brand that is most well known is bought in the belief it will be reliable and deliver the attributes desired. However, modern consumers are also increasingly socially responsible consumers. They may not only have perceptions as to the product benefits but also be concerned with the values of that brand. Both Nike and Gap are global brands, but both have been under increasing pressure from socially responsible consumers concerned about

their usage of child labour in the manufacture of their products. As society has become more affluent, ethical considerations have become more important to us in choosing among brand alternatives (see Spotlight 2.2).

- *Utility/functional value*: an assessment of the expected value of the consumption of the product or service, depending on the alternative levels of each attribute. Thus, in choosing a car the functional value of a speedy acceleration may be regarded as more important than the functional value of alloy wheels by such customers.

Spotlight 2.2

How the ethical consumer makes decisions

Of course, ethical consumerism is nothing new – The Vegetarian Society was founded in 1847. Occasionally campaigns such as the Montgomery Bus Boycott in the USA in the 1960s, Caesar Chavez's California grapes boycott and boycotts of South African products during the days of apartheid have attracted widespread support.

Ethical consumers have helped to raise awareness of Third World debt and, as a result, prompted government action. Clearly, they tap into a latent anti-Americanism within some people.

Most consumers are moderate but their expectations of corporate social responsibility are being steadily changed by the issues these campaigners raise, and this, in turn, is influencing their purchase behaviour.

For example, concerns about animal welfare have fuelled demand for Freedom Food, organic meat and dolphin-friendly tuna while growing environmental awareness has prompted a massive growth in organic/quasi-organic and bio-dynamic products. Greater social awareness has led to the development of Fair Trade products and anti-child labour campaigns.

Of course, moderate ethical consumers are highly selective about what they will boycott: many vegetarians eat non-vegetarian cheese or wear leather shoes; people who openly claim to be concerned with the environment use their cars instead of public transport, 'fashionistas' buy Nike trainers if that's what the fashion pack dictates; and people resist paying a couple of pence extra for Fair Trade coffee even though they claim to be concerned about Third World labour exploitation. These new consumers are the 'selfish ethical'. They won't rampage down Oxford Street but they will listen to what the activists are demanding.

But good marketing is about anticipating consumer demands. So rather than waiting to see what will be the next big thing, marketers should be paying rather more attention to what the ethical consumers are saying. Their influence is probably greater than they realise.

Source: Adapted from P. Seligman, *Financial Times Information*, 11 July 2002.

The result of the evaluation stage is the ranking of the alternatives. Potential customers will develop a final shortlist for more in-depth evaluation to help the formation of the purchase intention. However, two factors can interfere with this process:

- The attitude of others, such as family, friends or perhaps personal contacts whose opinions are valued and respected.
- Unexpected situational factors – perhaps the supermarket doesn't stock the particular choice of brands or perhaps the price of the preferred alternatives is too high to pay.

Choice and decision to purchase

The choice made and the actual decision to purchase is the outcome of the evaluation stage. Sometimes the choice is easy to make if there is a clear alternative or perhaps if it is a simple purchase and so the risk of making a wrong decision is not costly. If a particular brand of shampoo is chosen, but it proves to be the incorrect solution to the buying problem, then buying a replacement does not involve huge cost. However, if the consumer is making a major purchase, the risk of a wrong decision is much higher. This means how consumers make their actual decision to purchase will depend on the perceived risk involved in the purchase, the type of risk and how they decide to resolve the risk. If the risk is high, consumers will involve more people to help make the correct decision. These could be people whom they believe have expertise in the area or, again, family and friends whose judgement is trusted. Marketers, recognising the difficulty consumers have in making decisions, will try to make this stage as easy as possible. Furniture retailers offer 24 months free credit to help you choose their alternatives, car manufacturers offer three years warranty to reduce our fear of buying an unreliable car, retailers may offer free delivery or perhaps a no-quibbles guarantee if we are dissatisfied with the product, all to reduce the risk and help us make this final decision go in their favour.

Post-purchase evaluation

Most consumers, having made a purchasing decision, will need to seek reassurance after the purchase that the decision made was the correct one and so they will make a post-purchase evaluation. In the case of low-risk purchases this will be when, having experienced the product or service, they can assess their level of satisfaction in its usage. For larger purchases, which have involved a higher degree of risk, consumers will seek reassurances that the decision was the correct one and avoid what is known as *cognitive dissonance*. This occurs when consumers experience some degree of discomfort that their purchase was the correct choice and so still have doubts. Car manufacturers spend millions of dollars with glossy advertisements in Sunday newspapers often targeting the recent buyers of cars to reinforce the benefits and attributes of their cars in order to reassure customers. They also know of course that their customers are their best ambassadors and will be sought out by other potential buyers for their advice.

The post-purchase evaluation stage is also important to ensure companies retain customers and ensure they return to make a repeat purchase. 68% of customers/

clients who stop doing business with an organisation do so because they are upset with the treatment they have received and yet on average only 4% of customers ever actually complain. This means that businesses never hear from 96% of their customers. Given that it costs three to four times as much to gain a new customer as to keep an established one, it is important for businesses to know who their customers/clients are and to keep them happy. This is why the post-purchase evaluation stage is as important to marketers as it is to consumers. Grizzard Performance Group, a US direct marketing agency, estimates that 60% of US companies devote most of their resources to customer acquisition rather than customer/client retention and yet they suggest that by successfully retaining as few as 5% of customers they lose these companies could improve profits by 100%. Spotlight 2.3 highlights the costs of not keeping track of customer needs.

Spotlight 2.3

Keeping the customer satisfied

Being a customer can be baffling these days. There is lots of choice, special deals and accessing services by the telephone, constantly being told 'your call is important to us'. Companies seem keener than ever to sell to us and despite all the talk of building relationships with customers, not many companies are successful in doing so. We often feel their efforts to be friendly are false and despite the information revolution, companies still do not seem to understand their customers.

Companies try to use the Internet and the rest of today's technological wizardry to cut costs, but at the same time to give people the sort of service that sends them away happy. Only happy customers will be loyal ones – and loyalty is something companies desperately need if they are to survive in today's difficult economic climate.

Already, many companies find it more of a struggle than they did to win new customers and to keep those they already have. Companies that do not respond can find that old loyalties evaporate quickly. The Internet has brought new competition into many established markets. Michael Dell, with his build-to-order manufacturing, has revolutionised the PC business. Manufacturers of cars, white goods and other products are now trying to do something similar, with the eventual goal of 'mass customisation'.

The arrival of new competitors and the spread of information have also raised the cost of acquiring new customers: more mail shots, more advertising, bigger welcome discounts. It thus takes longer for, say, a mobile telephone company to earn back its initial investment. Companies have always known that it can cost three or four times as much to acquire a new customer as to make a repeat sale to an existing one. In hard times, and with growing competition, that arithmetic makes successful retention all the more crucial.

Source: Adapted from 'Keeping the customer satisfied', *The Economist*, 14 July 2001.

Figure 2.1 above provides a framework for the consumer decision-making process and in this section we have discussed the decision-making process a consumer may traditionally go through. However, the complexity and length of that process will to a large extent be determined by the type of purchasing decision being made and the type of consumer making those decisions. In the following sections we will consider these two aspects of the consumer.

2.7 ARE THERE DIFFERENT TYPES OF PURCHASING DECISION?

The complexity of the decision-making process will be determined by the type of purchasing decision being made. Purchasing decisions fall into three principal categories: routine, limited or extensive problem solving.

Routine purchasing decisions

The majority of purchases a consumer makes fall into the category of routine purchasing decisions. These are the many repeat purchases made for a myriad of products and services that are frequently bought. In these types of decision consumers usually have a good knowledge of the attributes of the alternatives available and strong beliefs about the brands that can satisfy the purchase need. Their understanding of the alternatives is well established and they are already likely to be predisposed to one particular brand. Thus products that are low-risk, low-priced and frequently purchased tend to fall into this category. Usually it means that the energy involved in seeking out alternatives is not viewed as being potentially beneficial as the product or services we regularly use adequately meet our needs.

Limited problem solving

Limited problem solving tends to occur when the consumer is not able to fully assess the choice of alternatives and so some comparative information is sought. This could be in situations where the risk of making a wrong decision is higher, probably because the expense of the purchase is higher. This could happen perhaps in the case of replacing consumer durables such as dishwashers or other kitchen equipment. It may be some years since the previous purchase was made and so the consumer does not have an up-to-date knowledge of the alternatives available and so needs to do a more in-depth information search than if it was simply a routine repeat purchase.

Extensive problem solving

This is really when a consumer is making a major purchase and does not feel they have sufficient knowledge or understanding to make an informed purchase. The consumer will then seek extensive information concerning the alternatives available and probably involve others in the purchasing decision process. Usually consumers will put considerable effort into making sure the purchase decision is the correct one. This could mean a much more formal decision-making process. In the case of a routine purchase, the whole process could be quite instinctive and the stages hardly discernible. In an extensive problem-solving situation the consumer will be much more involved in the decision process, put a much greater effort into each stage of the process and take much longer in making the decision.

However, this may not always be the case as how a consumer goes through the decision process will also be determined by the type of consumer they are, as we will see in the next section.

2.8 TYPOLOGIES OF INDIVIDUAL CUSTOMERS

Not all individual customers will behave in a similar fashion. If you differentiate customers by the way they purchase products and services you can identify four different types: the economic/rational customer, the passive customer, the cognitive customer and the emotional customer:

- *The economic/rational customer*: This is the customer who makes decisions based on economic rationale alone. The customer has been able to access a complete understanding of all the other alternatives and has been able to fully evaluate those alternatives and so identify the best one. Many marketers view this as unrealistic as customers rarely have enough information to make a full evaluation, nor do they have the search and evaluation skills necessary. Furthermore, a lot of customers may be unwilling to spend the time needed to make such an evaluation.
- *The passive customer*: This customer is basically submissive and makes irrational decisions. Passive customers are seen as impulsive and easily swayed by marketing promotions. Thus they make decisions based on what information is readily available and do not actively seek to develop an understanding of the alternatives available and may skip whole stages of the decision-making process.
- *The cognitive customer*: This customer focuses on the purchasing process. Cognitive customers seek information and evaluate that information, and then evaluate their purchase in light of perceived risk. Therefore the customer is seen as an information processing system but accepts that it is an imperfect world so sets the objective of getting enough information to make an adequate decision.
- *The emotional customer*: This customer puts a lot less emphasis on the search for information. Current mood and feeling are the key determinant of the purchase decision. This customer views making purchases to satisfy emotional needs as entirely rational. Thus the emotive benefits of the alternatives are much more important than any rational attributes. Perhaps in the case of a car purchase this customer will be more concerned with the social recognition that the purchase brings than the mechanical attributes of the car.

2.9 BUYING ROLES

As we have seen, in any buying situation, be it for a service or a product, the customer is a **problem solver**. This is so whether the buyer is a single individual, a family, a business, an organisation or a government buyer. The customer is a complex decision-making unit (DMU). As customers go through the decision-making process they take information, process that information in the light of the existing information and then take an action to achieve satisfaction and enhance their lifestyle. In order for the process to be undergone, the persons involved in the purchasing decision will play a number of different roles which facilitate the process. All these **buying roles** may well be played by one or perhaps two people, however a number of purchasing decisions involve a number of people who will make up the DMU. Each of these will have distinct roles in the buying decision:

- *Initiator*: These are the individuals who first suggest the buying of the product or service (see Spotlight 2.4). They do so in their role of seeing such a purchase as the solution to the problem. This could be a mother seeking to buy new clothes for a child or perhaps the child himself seeking to buy a DVD to alleviate his own boredom.
- *Gatekeeper*: These people control the flow of information. It may be a parent or a secretary/receptionist in an organisational buying situation. Purchasing departments in organisations often act as gatekeepers as they are the department to which promotional material is often sent by potential sellers.
- *Influencer*: The advisors, whose opinion carries weight with the buyer, they inform or persuade at different points of the purchasing decision. The child may initiate the search for a DVD but the parents will have an important role in the buying process in influencing which DVD they think is a suitable purchase.
- *Decider*: This is the person who determines the buying decision – whether to buy or not and which provider to choose. In a B2C buying situation this could well be the same person as the influencer. However, in a B2B buying situation, while the purchasing department may act as the gatekeeper and have a role in influencing the decision, it could be a departmental manager who is the budget holder and who makes the final decision.
- *Buyer*: These are the people who make the actual purchase. In a B2B buying situation this person could have had little to do with the decision to buy. The buyer is the person who places the order and pays for the goods or service.
- *User*: The user is the consumer, the person who consumes the product or uses the service provided. Users may have had little to do with the buying decision process, but they are of critical importance. The satisfaction of the user (or consumer) is paramount if the service or product provider is to achieve customer loyalty over the longer term.

Spotlight 2.4

Egg

Egg, the highly successful online financial service provider set up by Prudential in 1999 now has 2.4 million customers. Their nearest rival, Smile, has 500,000 customers. Patrick Muir, Egg's UK marketing director, says:

> To build a strong credible consumer brand in a highly commoditised product-led market and to generate continuous awareness without a high street presence were major challenges. We did it by living our brand proposition and giving customers what they wanted. We have always been clear who our customers are. The Internet acts as a huge filter. What matters is that someone is willing to buy a financial product online.

Source: *Marketing Business*, April 2003 p.11

Although the actual customer can carry out all of these roles, often they are carried out by different people. An important part of marketing research, as we will see in Chapter 4, is to understand the roles in the buying situation for a product and service, who carries out the roles and who plays the key roles. Where the roles are carried out by different people it can be difficult not only to identify who the role players are but also, once they are identified, to reach them. This means it is sometimes necessary to develop different communication strategies targeted at different individuals. If the same person carries out the roles, different approaches may still be needed to cater for each stage of the buying process.

In Part Two of this book we will explore the different typologies of customers and the way they behave in much greater depth.

2.10 THE ORGANISATIONAL CUSTOMER

There are several different types of organisational customer, principally business-to-business (B2B), business-to-government, not-for-profit organisations and internal customers. A customer operating in an organisational environment can differ from the individual customer in a number of ways:

- They generally go through a more complex buying process.
- The purchases they make maybe infrequent or one-offs.
- The decision to buy can be postponed indefinitely.
- The demand for products and services is derived from their clients and the end users.

- Traditionally they have been highly concentrated either geographically or by industrial sector.
- Lead and delivery times are of paramount importance.

Let us now look at the different types of organisational customers.

2.11 THE BUSINESS-TO-BUSINESS CUSTOMER

B2B customers are usually concerned with obtaining inputs to create an added value in either goods or services that flow down the **supply chain**. In the purchasing of products this means B2B customers are usually either manufacturers or intermediaries in the supply chain who will either add value to the product or sell it to the next link in the supply chain. In the purchase of services, the B2B customer could be any of the parties mentioned above or perhaps another provider of business services.

Manufacturers as B2B customers

Manufacturers of original equipment are major purchasers of components and parts, which they then integrate into the products they are manufacturing. Historically, whole industries have developed in close geographical proximity as suppliers have endeavoured to beat their competitors by being as close as possible to their customers, for example the automobile industry around Birmingham and the steel industry around Sheffield. Today, however, the globalisation of manufacturing processes, together with growth of global sourcing and the development of global supplier Intranets, means manufacturers and their suppliers have a much more virtual proximity through e-business than actual geographical proximity.

Supply chain intermediaries as B2B customers

Intermediaries as B2B customers purchase goods to sell on to the next stage of the supply chain. These could be wholesalers and retailers, distributors and agents or perhaps franchisees or brokers. The key role for all of these intermediaries is to provide the route to the end-user market for the manufacturer and to help them get their goods to the right customers at the right time and in the right condition. However, they are also customers in their own right and, like end-user customers, the manufacturer needs to understand the motivations for buying the product and the needs they are hoping to satisfy by reselling the products. Manufacturers will endeavour to build close relationships with such customers as it is such intermediaries in the supply chain that have the skills and resources to reach the end-user market. It is also these intermediaries who are in constant communication with the final consumers and who may therefore have a greater knowledge of the market place than the manufacturer themselves. In Dilemma 2.2, Flybait considers that its relationship with these intermediaries is critical to achieving competitive success with its final consumers.

Dilemma 2.2

Flybait tries to remain competitive

Flybait produces and distributes a range of fishing tackle products specifically for the game and fly-fishing markets. The company employs 17 people and has an annual turnover of approximately £1,300,000. The company sells exclusively to retailers and specialist distributors. Its principal communication vehicle is by catalogue and website. It supplies a large number of product lines, including fly-fishing materials, tools and equipment, floatants and sinkants, fly boxes and tackle bags, and a range of rods, reels, lines, nets and fishing products. Its flagship product line is a vast range of over 1,500 exotically coloured fishing flies.

In all the product lines, the company attempts to provide added value through innovative product design. However, the products supplied by Flybait are simple and easy to copy and the market in which they operate is becoming increasingly competitive. Flybait is now wondering whether, to remain competitive, it should focus its limited resources on building closer relationships in the supply chain to its customers or whether it should invest more heavily in developing new products and extending the product range.

Flybait's dilemma is, as a small company, should it invest its limited resources in keeping its products ahead of the competition or should it use them to build close relationships to keep the competitors away from its supply chain intermediaries.

What are the advantages and disadvantages of Flybait building closer relationships within its supply chain as opposed to investing in new products? What do you think it should do to remain competitive?

Service clients as B2B customers

B2B organisations require a wide range of services to facilitate their operations and so are important as customers of services. These services are not just the financial, legal and management advisors they may need, but maintenance contractors for the whole range of office and production equipment as well as for building, facilities and other requirements. Such services are usually provided through contract providers. This means the service customer sets up a service level agreement, setting down clearly the expectations as to the level of service required. While the vetting process may not be as arduous for a contract service provider as for one who is providing technical goods, the penalty clauses for not meeting the conditions of the service level agreement can be punitive for the supplier. Earlier in the chapter we looked at the differences between a client and a consumer. In B2B markets, a provider may be servicing the needs of a client who also has customers. For the original service provider the question of who is really their customer is a difficult one, as we can see in the case of the provision of in-store credit cards in Dilemma 2.3.

Dilemma 2.3

Who is the customer?

As part of one of the largest companies in the world, GE Capital provides consumer credit in the form of Private Label Credit Cards (PLCC). In the UK these are commonly known as 'storecards', as they act as a credit card that can be used in a particular store or group of stores.

These cards are branded by the retailer, so you could be forgiven for thinking that it is Debenhams, House of Fraser or B&Q that is providing the credit facility linked to their card. In fact, the company that currently provides the consumer with credit to make purchases in these stores is GE Capital.

Retailers are often keen to provide this facility as it can lead to more frequent and larger purchases, and more consistent preference for the store. A crucial concern, however, is that this is achieved without damaging the core activities, services and brand image. The decision as to who is awarded the contract to provide consumer credit services is taken very seriously.

For GE Capital, the interest paid on store-based credit cards provides the main source of income, and links with cardholders provide opportunities to 'cross-sell' other financial services, such as insurance and personal loans. For the marketing team at GE Capital, therefore, it is vital that the needs of both retail clients and individual borrowers are understood, anticipated and satisfied in order to maintain the contract, generate income and build customer relationships.

This can often lead to complex dilemmas as all consumer research, promotion, product development and pricing activities must be approved by the retailer. After all, from their point of view, it is their core business, their brand and their customer base that is at stake.

So, a marketing plan that is seen to be critical to business development in GE Capital may be rejected by the retailer because it doesn't meet their core objectives. For example, personal selling of the 'storecard' by staff at the point of purchase may increase card usage, but cause long queues at the till, irritate customers and damage perceptions of the store. Similarly, frequent direct mail promoting insurance and personal loans, continuous market research and cards that offer inappropriate benefits may dilute the retailer's brand image.

So, GE Capital faces a situation whereby it must understand, anticipate and satisfy the needs of both retail clients and individual credit consumers. As we have seen, this can often lead to difficult and complex marketing decisions, at the core of which we find the critical question ... 'who is the customer?'

Source: Anthony Grimes, University of Hull

Whatever the type of B2B customer, we can discern from the above descriptions that B2B customers have a number of special characteristics. First, both B2B buyers and sellers are usually active participants in the buying process. The process is one of active negotiation on both sides. This can differ from the individual customer, where impulse purchases or purchases made in response to aggressive advertising are much more common. Secondly, B2B customers are much more likely to form a long-term relationship with their suppliers which can, in some cases, be sustained over a long period of time. However, the nature and the strength of this relationship may well depend on the characteristics of the buying problem itself. If the purchase is perceived as highly important to the buyer and they rely on the seller's capabilities to help them solve the buying problem, the relationship will be stronger and closer than more routine purchases which are not seen as problematic and where the buyer feels they have the capability of making the correct purchasing decision.

As we have discussed above, purchasing decisions are concerned with problem resolution. The nature of the decision-making process will vary with the seriousness and complexity of the problem being faced by the purchasing organisation.

Robinson *et al* (1967) cited in Jobber (2004) divide the different types of purchasing decision carried out by B2B customers into straight re-buy, modified re-buy and new task. A *straight re-buy* represents the bulk of the business buying. The buy signal is often triggered through information systems when stock levels reach a predetermined replenishment point. The *modified re-buy* indicates a certain level of information search and re-evaluation of products/services and supplies before the purchase is made. The *new task* represents an area of considerable uncertainty in which the company needs to make decisions about what it wants, about performance standards and about supplier capabilities. The new task, particularly if the purchase is of major importance to the company, will involve discussion with senior management and perhaps require a board level decision. It may also take a long time for the whole process to be completed.

2.12 THE GOVERNMENT AS A CUSTOMER

In many countries in the European Union, the government is the biggest buyer of products and services, far larger than any individual consumer or business buyer. Governments (B2G customers) buy a wide range of goods and services: roads, education, military, health and welfare.

It has been estimated that 20% of the gross domestic product of the European Union is controlled through purchases and contracts awarded by the government or public sector. In the USA approximately 30% of the gross national product is accounted for by the purchases of US governmental units. For some companies the main or even only customer may be a buyer in either local or national government. It is important, therefore, to understand how the government behaves as a customer.

The requirements of public accountability and the need to be seen to be equitable and fair has led to buying procedures in government becoming cumbersome and bureaucratic. It is sometimes only the stout-hearted companies that persevere through the arduous buying processes. The usual forms of procedure when government departments are buying is the open tender and selective tender. In *open* bid contracts, tenders are invited against a tight specification. Contracts are usually awarded to the lowest price bid. *Selective* tender contracts are offered to companies that have already demonstrated their ability in the area appropriate to the tender. Only those companies on the selective tender list will be invited to tender. As with open tender, the lowest price is often used to adjudicate the bids.

As stated above, the tendering process can be seen as making quite arduous demands on suppliers. As with B2B customers, close relationships are important with B2G potential buyers, if only to ascertain when contracts may be going out to tender so that advance preparations can be made. Once the bidding process has commenced it is unlikely that a new entrant would have the time to meet the procedural requirement of such tenders.

In the European Union specific rules have been drawn up in an attempt to remove the barriers for potential suppliers of government contracts from different countries of the EU. Suppliers from all EU member states should have an equal opportunity to bid for public authority contracts and public works contracts must be advertised throughout the EU. However, one of the main problems remains the poor response rate to EU tenders. In a bid to improve the response the European Union is investing heavily in e-procurement. This will ensure all forthcoming tenders are available on the Internet in an effort to widen the awareness of such opportunities throughout the EU member states. An example of how e-procurement can help even small companies win EU tenders can be seen in Spotlight 2.5.

Spotlight 2.5

EU tendering

Fox Safety Lamps manufacture and supply safety lamps for hazardous areas. They define their market as 'personal and portable safety lighting equipment for use in potentially explosive atmospheres'.

Changes in the European market came about due to the ATEX Directive, (Explosives Atmosphere Directive, and ATEX, 94/9/EC.) An important implication of this directive was the stipulation that every new safety lamp sold and supplied would need to be Conformitée Européenne (CE) marked in accordance with the ATEX Directive.

Fox were highly proactive in ensuring their products met the new requirements, and believed they were probably the first of the hazardous safety lighting producers to obtain the CE mark under the new ATEX Directive. This gave them a competitive lead in tendering for EU contracts which they very successfully exploited, particularly in the accession countries of Poland, Hungary and the Czech Republic. In preparation for membership of the EU, these countries were undergoing a process of ensuring their industries complied with EU health and safety regulations and, as such, required such lamps as part of their programme of upgrading safety equipment.

Source: Isobel Doole

2.13 NOT-FOR-PROFIT CUSTOMERS

Not-for-profit customers can be a range of organisations. Large institutions such as hospitals and universities are not-for-profit customers, although they are also large public bodies who, as customers, will bear many similarities to B2G customers. Equally, this category could include charities, churches or educational organisations. Such bodies obtain their funding from a range of sources both private and public and so will have a wide range of stakeholders who can potentially influence their purchasing behaviour. The major difference between these stakeholders and the stakeholders in a B2B buying situation, where the major motivation is to make a profit, is that the varying political, ethical and emotional motives for the involvement of the various stakeholders within the organisation can make the decision-making process in any purchase politically sensitive and sometimes highly complex.

2.14 INTERNAL CUSTOMERS

In examining who customers are we need also to consider customers who may be internal to an organisation. Many customers are internal to an organisation, for example where one department is supplying another department with products and services. For instance, the IT department in an organisation has many internal customers. Likewise, the subsidiaries of a multinational organisation may be internal customers of the head office, from whom they have to purchase all their supplies. In order to ensure such departments are customer-focused, many organisations find it useful to perceive the departments they serve internally as clients/customers.

In Chapter 1 we examined the importance of an organisation being customer-focused. A crucial element in achieving this is to ensure that all the internal departments work effectively as teams to achieve this end. A key premise in customer satisfaction is meeting the expectations of customers. While most companies have developed strategies to improve quality and external customer service, internal customer satisfaction is an area that is sometimes neglected. Organisations which highlight the importance of satisfying the internal customer would argue that total customer satisfaction can be attained only if all employees are devoted to external customer satisfaction, can work together and can assist each other to achieve the common objective. They argue that there cannot be total customer service unless all employees are supporting each other and working together towards common goals. In short, total customer service means meeting the needs and expectations of both internal and external customers.

This means that all departments in the organisation – sales, marketing, credit and receivables, manufacturing, distribution, packing and shipping, quality, production planning, etc. – have to work together and every individual in that organisation needs to understand that customer service is everyone's business. An organisation that works towards such goals sees customer service as an organisational responsibility. Quality customer service is the ability to create a climate of confidence, credibility and satisfaction for all parties in the 'chain' from product concept and design through manufacturing and distribution to payment or settlement. Along the chain, there is a continuous opportunity for the functional areas within an organisation to improve. Accepting that each of these functional areas is an internal customer is seen as an important first step in achieving this.

SUMMARY

In this chapter we developed our understanding of what a customer is by examining the different types of customer found in both business-to-business and business-to-consumer marketing. We have highlighted some of the confusion that sometimes surrounds the terminology used and explored the differences between consumers and customers as well as that between customers and clients. It is hoped that the reader has also gained an understanding of the buying process that customers undertake in reaching a buying decision and that the chapter has generated an awareness of the varying buying situations and their constituent components.

Discussion questions

1   What are the different types of organisational customer and how do they differ from each other?

2   What are the main differences between a consumer, a client and a customer? How do their needs and desires differ?

3   For a product or service purchase you have recently made, explain how you completed the different stages of the decision-making process.

4   A decision-making unit consists of various roles. Using specific examples, examine how these roles vary between an organisational customer making a purchase and a B2C customer.

5   How do the needs of the Internet shopper differ from someone purchasing through more traditional channels? What impact do these needs have on the decision-making process?

Case study 2.1 | Stadium Ltd

Stadium Ltd is a high-quality precision forger supplying precision forgings to aerospace engine manufacturers. Their clients are mainly major multinational companies with whom Stadium deal direct – there are no distributors or other intermediaries. Many of their clients operate on a global basis with subsidiaries around the world. Building and managing long-term relationships is therefore very important as business with a subsidiary in one part of world can often lead to new business with other subsidiaries.

The provision of a quality service in such an industry is of paramount importance and so the company invested heavily to ensure they met the requirements of ISO 9000. This was considered as imperative by the company if they were to achieve approved supplier status to many of their international clients.

The company also embarked on a process of internal reorganisation to enable them to be more responsive to customer demands and develop clearer communication lines to their customers. This meant a major shift in the way existing customers were handled; previously, the firm was organised to achieve a focus of managing the internal production process. Stadium worked to change this to an external focus of managing the process of a customer's order. Each customer was allocated a direct contact who was responsible for overseeing the progress of their order. This person reported to a customer services manager who was in charge overall. New technology was introduced to enable customers to make an input into the design process of their orders and for feedback to be easily relayed to them. A training programme was introduced to ensure all staff in the company were trained to deal with international customers and any enquiries that came into Stadium. Thus, the company worked extensively to build effective communication links with customers to enhance the building of closer relationships with them.

Five years ago, after 18 months of a sustained campaign and many visits, the company was successful in securing orders for aircraft forgings in Japan. The company viewed this as a major breakthrough in a difficult and competitive market. However, in the view of the company, the process of achieving the contract proved to be time-consuming and very exacting for Stadium. They had to undergo a complex process of quality assurance inspections, not only on product quality but also for the company procedures they had in place that guaranteed the delivery promises. Stadium had to make several presentations in Japan and the company was required to subject itself to a complete audit of its operations. However, the company viewed this as an important learning experience and a significant step in developing a presence in the Far East.

The first two years of the contract went smoothly and all parties were satisfied with its progress. However, the value of the Japanese yen then began a period of decline. At the same time UK sterling was increasing in strength. This meant that the prices agreed at the beginning of the contract were no longer seen to be appropriate by the Japanese client and so they sought to renegotiate terms when the contract came up for renewal. Stadium were asked to adjust their prices to a level they viewed as unacceptable. They made the decision that the demands of the Japanese would render the contract unprofitable and despite the strategic significance of the business, it would be better to lose the contract than tie the company into a potentially unprofitable situation for the next three years.

Questions

1 In view of their decision not to renew the contract when they came under pressure from their client, do you agree that Stadium were right to invest so much of their resources in becoming an approved supplier in the first place?

2 Fully assess how successful Stadium were in building a close relationship with their client.

3 What do you recommend Stadium should do now if they are to succeed in winning back this important client?

Further reading

Brassington, F. and Pettitt, S. (2003) *Principles of Marketing* (3rd edition). Harlow: Financial Times/Prentice Hall.

Frain, J. (2003) *Introduction to Marketing* (4th edition). London: Thomson Learning.

Little, E. and Marandi, E. (2003) *Relationship Marketing Management*. London: Thomson Learning.

References

Jobber, D. (2004) *Principles of Marketing* (4th edition). New York: McGraw-Hill.

Murphy, J.A. (2000) *The Lifebelt: The Definitive Guide to Managing Customer Retention*. Chichester: Wiley.

3

The marketing environment

Jeanette Baker

LEARNING OUTCOMES

After reading this chapter you should be able to:

- Understand why the 'environment' is important and what it can contain

- Identify some of the challenges a company may face and the effect these challenges may have

- Identify the role competitors can play in the market place

- Understand that different types of customer are influenced in a variety of ways by the marketing environment

- Understand how the marketing environment is experienced from the customer's point of view

KEY WORDS

Competitior analysis
Competitors
Customers
Environmental scanning

Macro-environment
Marketing environment
Micro-environment
PEST analysis

INTRODUCTION

Previous chapters have looked at who customers are and why they are important to companies. This chapter will deal with the **marketing environment** in which our **customers** and companies are located. This is important because unless companies understand the environment in which customers exist, then how can they hope to understand those customers? The market research tools used to find this information will be examined in Chapter 4, but here we will consider why the environment is important and also how it can be analysed to give companies the opportunity to understand customers. You will notice that we are using the phrase 'marketing environment' to represent the place in which companies operate.

It is also important to note that whatever events or issues arise in the marketing environment, the effects of these changes are felt by both customers and organisations – nothing happens in isolation. The outcome of any change, and how that change is managed, can determine whether an organisation continues to be a player in the market place or not.

This chapter will begin by looking at what the marketing environment is and why it is important. Then we will look at analysing this environment using a process called **environmental scanning** to identify factors that make up a current business situation. The next step will be to use the PEST model to organise the findings of this analysis into a 'list' of elements, sorted into four major categories – political, economic, social and technological – and gain some insight into what effect these factors can have on customers and businesses.

The role of the **competitors** will be examined in terms of the impact they might have on a business situation. This will be followed by a look at how the environment influences different types of customer and affects the customer experience (see Figure 3.1). Chapter 4 will concentrate on market research, that is the tasks that deal with how to gather the information.

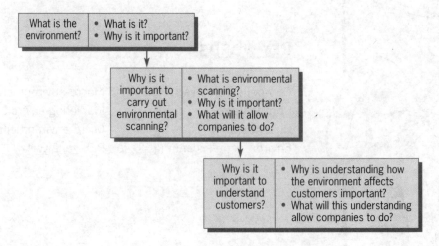

Figure 3.1 Chapter overview

3.1 THE MARKETING ENVIRONMENT

The idea that the marketing environment is undergoing change is not new. Organisations have realised for a long time that the only thing they can rely on is that change will happen. As we can see from Figure 3.2, the marketing environment was once seen as being easily managed with time available to develop understanding. Company personnel had time to get to know the industry, the market, the customers – knowledge that allowed them to compete effectively. Today the marketing environment is very different. Competitors are more numerous and customers have more choice. The result of this complexity is constant change at a rapid rate. Companies no longer have the luxury of time – time that previously gave them a competitive edge. They have to act quickly or they will find their competitors are already there.

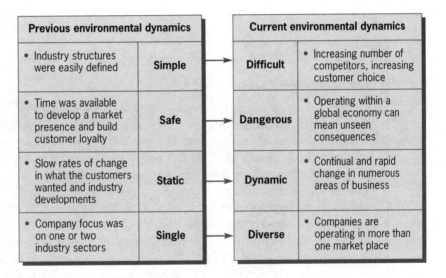

Previous environmental dynamics		Current environmental dynamics	
• Industry structures were easily defined	**Simple**	**Difficult**	• Increasing number of competitors, increasing customer choice
• Time was available to develop a market presence and build customer loyalty	**Safe**	**Dangerous**	• Operating within a global economy can mean unseen consequences
• Slow rates of change in what the customers wanted and industry developments	**Static**	**Dynamic**	• Continual and rapid change in numerous areas of business
• Company focus was on one or two industry sectors	**Single**	**Diverse**	• Companies are operating in more than one market place

Figure 3.2 The changing environmental dynamics
Source: Richardson (1989)

This market movement means the environment is no longer easily monitored and organisations therefore need to keep track of the changes that are of most relevance to them. To try to take notice of everything that is happening can actually be dangerous. Organisations could be spending so much time and energy on monitoring their marketing environment that the amount of information gained is huge, may result in all of it being ignored as the day-to-day business is attended to and the important information elements that could help are missed. As Richardson (1992) points out, we have moved from a simple, understandable environment to something more complex, with less chance of understanding anything.

3.2 ENVIRONMENTAL SCANNING

Any process that is used to look at a company's environment can be referred to as environmental scanning and involves the collection of information about an organisation's external environment. Organisations must be outward-looking to see what is going on around them. Whatever action they or their competitors take, an impact is felt in the environment by the customers. It is for them that businesses exist – in order to provide solutions for their problems. If an organisation is not aware of the changing needs and wants of these customers, while also taking into account what is happening in the marketing environment, then they are not in a position to compete.

The systematic monitoring of market indicators is required in order for businesses to identify the direction/rate of change. A regular view of the marketing environment can build a trail of events that the organisation can use to identify the directions in which a market may move (see Spotlight 3.1).

Spotlight 3.1

The Automobile Association (AA)

Products and services can be made that will give a competitive advantage to a business, for example something you provide that competitors don't. The Automobile Association (AA) has used its ability to text people that breakdown assistance is on its way and this has relieved pressure on its telephone system. Strategically, the service has been able to reduce the number of telephonists needed, thus also affecting the cost of this operation to the company while at the same time actually improving communications with customers. The savings incurred in this area of the business have provided an opportunity to redirect this financial commitment to developing the core service, that is car repairs. The likelihood of people having a mobile phone and seeing the growth of text messaging as a communication medium, has allowed the AA to capitalise on a market trend observed in the marketing environment.

Organisations do have to realise that having the system in place is not going to give them the marketing environment insight. It is *using* the information and *responding* that is where a competitive edge can be gained. To undertake such a task means devoting resources that could be otherwise employed. However, the warning is clear – some competitors will certainly be taking advantage of what they can learn from the marketing environment. The impact of their actions, and of you not scanning your environment, may be the taking of your customers.

It is important to cover all aspects of an organisation's marketing environment via systemised monitoring so a competitive response can be put together.

Organisations can respond in a number of ways and can do so using their 'marketing mix', that is what the company offers in the form of its product/service offering, promotion, price and place, etc. An organisation may need to adapt one of the marketing mix elements, for example promotion, so customers are kept up to date about any new product or service developments.

Without monitoring the marketing environment, organisations will continue to battle against competitors ignorant of information that could be used to develop a competitive offering.

Environmental scanning in rapidly changing market places is difficult due to the rate at which data and information go out of date. If companies find it difficult to keep up, there is a danger that they will be using obsolete information as a basis for decision making.

The findings from this activity are also used to forecast the direction of market movements in order to try to align company activities to meet the changes. If the changes are unpredictable, then forecasting also becomes less certain and therefore environmental scanning becomes less useful as a business tool.

3.3 ANALYSING THE ENVIRONMENT

To gain some understanding of a marketing environment we must look at what it typically contains (see Figure 3.3). The following 'list' is by no means comprehensive but it does provide a level of market understanding by suggesting a division of the marketing environment information into categories. Organisations must remember that if they are using this basis to analyse their marketing environment it is highly possible that their competitors will also be using it. If this is the case, how can an organisation compete successfully if everybody has access to the same information? As mentioned previously, the key is to use the information; companies can act on an information element which will allow them to meet the needs of the customers more effectively than a competitor.

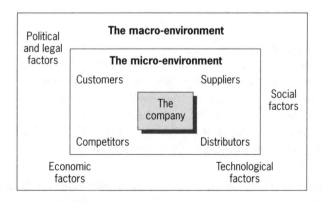

Figure 3.3 The marketing environment
Source: Adapted from Jobber (2001)

The first way to divide a marketing environment relates to how near, or far, the events in that environment actually occur in relation to the organisation. The **macro-environment** comprises events that occur at a distance, and will be looked at using the **PEST analysis**, that is the political, economic, social and technological factors that comprise the macro-environment. The **micro-environment** includes events that occur close to the organisation, and can be categorised as customers, suppliers, distributors and competitors. Basically, the macro-environment is not an area organisations have any control over, although companies can respond to meet both customer and organisational needs if they are aware of these types of issues. Events that happen in the micro-environment can be controlled, however, as these are concerned with issues that the company can influence directly, such as customers and suppliers.

The macro-environment

Political and legal elements

These elements are controlled by governing bodies ranging from central government to other regulating groups. Some of the output from these bodies is in the form of legislation which businesses have no option but to uphold. Other outputs may be in the form of recommendations or codes of practice that businesses may or may not 'buy into'. Legislation affecting how tobacco is promoted means that the industry has to identify how to communicate with its markets while also abiding by the law.

The following areas all come under the political and legal heading. The list is not comprehensive, but does give a starting point in order to survey what is going on at this level in the marketing environment.

Legislation

This gives all industries a degree of control under which they must operate by building in measures that point out the responsibility companies have for their activities. Government regulations can be imposed from central, regional and local government (Spotlight 3.2). In the UK businesses also come under the remit of some European legislation.

Regulatory bodies

Put into place by government to ensure legislation is upheld, regulatory bodies such as the Health and Safety Executive are organisations that have a responsibility to provide a workplace that will not endanger individuals operating there. Regulations are in place according to the type of business/industry, and organisations must comply with these. The Health and Safety Executive will carry out inspections to check good and bad practice.

Self-regulating groups – Advertising Standards Authority (ASA)

Self-regulating groups generally emerge within an industry to regulate and monitor the development of their members. They also act to reassure consumers that here is

Spotlight 3.2

Consumer privacy

This is an issue that is becoming more and more relevant in an information-driven society. The Data Protection Act (1984) began the introduction of control over an individual's details. Your information belongs to you and it is with your permission that organisations hold and use it. Organisations now operate under a combination of several pieces of legislation dealing with this issue. The Data Protection Act was updated in 1998 and now limits the acquisition and passing on of information by companies. The implications for the telecommunications industry were fairly drastic. They had large amounts of information and the threat was that they would not be able to do anything with it.

an authoritative industry body to protect them. The Advertising Standards Authority (ASA) is an 'independent, self-regulatory body for non-broadcast advertisements, sales promotions and direct marketing in the UK' (www.asa.org.uk). It administers the British Code of Advertising, Sales Promotion and Direct Marketing (the CAP Code) to ensure that advertisements are legal, decent, honest and truthful. Complaints are investigated to identify if there is an infringement of the CAP Code. The outcome can be the withdrawal of the message from the market place. For example, Benetton used a 'shock' tactic approach in its advertising and the ASA upheld complaints about the disturbing nature of Benetton's advertising.

Trade associations

These are bodies that represent particular industries. The Retail Motor Industry Federation is one such association. It aims to represent organisations and consumers in this industry. This association represents the UK car industry in its dealings with government, Europe and consumers, and will support consumers with information about how to deal with car companies. This is one trade association that does have legislation supporting its existence.

Other trade associations are formed by companies in an industry coming together in order to pool good practice, but there is no legislation in place to back up the trade associations. The British Association of Removers is one example. It has a Code of Practice and a quality standard (BS EN 12522, www.barmovers.com) which identifies what a 'quality removal service' should contain.

European Union

Originally started with six members, numbering 16 in June 2003 with a further ten included in May 2004, the principal objectives of the European Union are to work on behalf of all member states' populations in a worldwide market place (http://europa.eu.int/abc-en.htm) (see Spotlight 3.3).

Spotlight 3.3

The European Union

The European Union works to raise the living standards of member states. It developed an internal market (people, products and services can move around the European continent freely) and provided the structure of a large economic body that allows Europe to compete at a world level. The combination of member states means they have a louder voice and larger presence in the world economy, which gives each member an opportunity to compete at world level.

Economic elements

The economic elements are pertinent to the macro-environment and the micro-environment. The economic conditions include such things as the value of currency, the cost of raw materials, and whether customers are actually willing (and able) to purchase products and services. A downturn in a country's economy means there is less consumer money available for particular types of product and service. In turn, the fall in purchasing levels means organisations do not buy as much from their suppliers and so their suppliers suffer a fall in revenue generation (see Spotlight 3.4).

Let us now look at some examples of economic elements and how they impact on both consumers and organisations.

Spotlight 3.4

A possible effect on customers of economic elements

Economic movements will give customers more or less buying power in a market place. The decision by the Rover Group to move its production of a new MG Rover model from its Longbridge plant, Birmingham, England to India, means that demand on current UK-based production facilities is less and may lead to redundancies in the Birmingham area. This reduces the spending power of people living and working in that area and will affect local businesses negatively. Reduction in spending levels may mean the closing down of local product and service providers, people may leave the area, taking away any future spending power, and reduce the skills base of the local labour market.

Source: based on http://news.bbc.co.uk/1/low/england/2594697.stm

Economic growth

A basic definition of economic growth is 'the rate of change of real income or real output' (Begg et al., 2002 : 424). If an economy is growing, there will be an increase in Gross Domestic Product (this is the value of the total production output of a domestic economy) and/or Gross National Product (this is the total income earned by selling domestic produce). Organisations need to understand whether the growth is long-term, what the cause of the growth is and the effect of economic policies on that growth.

Unemployment

This is a factor affecting the ability of a population to purchase products and/or services. Levels of income are greatly affected by unemployment. If large numbers of a population are unemployed, the overall purchasing capability is severely limited. Items that are needed, such as accommodation, food and clothing, are generally the first purchases, which can leave little or no disposable income for other products and services people may want. The effect on a local economy can be that local retail outlets' sales fall, their viability is questioned and they may cease trading. The closing down of businesses means there is a reduction in the economic base of the area and the services it provides.

Inflation

Inflation is when the average price of goods and services changes on an annual basis. If inflation is high, products and services are more expensive and people can afford to buy less. If the price of oil increases, then the cost of importing oil also rises, the consumer pays more for the same quantity and this can result in falling consumption, reducing sales and purchasing levels.

Income

Regions of a country containing a large population, such as a city, will lead to a concentration of earning and spending in that area, and consequently the concentration of services and the development of facilities in that area. In the case of London, for example, there are a large number of theatres, airports and art galleries. People's income in this area means their spending power supports and sustains the provision of these services.

Resources

Organisations need resources to operate. Resources can be in the form of raw materials, the skills of people needed to carry out the business or a pool of potential customers. Without these elements a business cannot function. In today's competitive environment, organisations can compete effectively by using their resources to the full potential. Call centres which support financial services employ people to deal with calls for a range of businesses so each of the businesses is only paying for a share of that support resource but gaining the benefit of having access to a large, up-to-date facility. This leaves them to get on with running the core business.

International economic environment

Events happening on an international basis are very likely to affect continents and economies that are geographically remote from the source of change. More and more businesses operate internationally and even those that do not can still be affected by international issues.

Trading blocs

Countries working together in regional trading blocs based on regional trading arrangements offer benefits to members in the form of preferred suppliers, cheaper prices, etc. The European Union is an example of a trading bloc – the euro currency that European countries have adopted has the advantage that there are no fluctuations related to exchange rates.

Exchange rates

Dealing on an international basis can mean the exchange of products and/or services is done in a different currency from an organisation's domestic currency. Exchange rates fluctuate. The threat and opportunity of this is that a product or service may be expensive to international customers one day and cheap the next. Organisations need to react very quickly if they are to be able to take advantage of the positive outcome of this type of situation. British Telecom (BT) now sources cheap telephone calls from America. However, on days when the British pound is strong compared to the American dollar, BT pays more for calls than on days when the American dollar is stronger than the British pound. As these fluctuations are rapid, BT has to make sure it has sufficient margin of profitability on the charges customers pay to ensure the calls are not being sold at a loss. This affects BT's revenue generation and ultimately their profits.

Market structure

In some industries we find that there are a few major players which dominate, as in the games software market. In industries such as pharmaceuticals and retail, mergers are resulting in large 'mega-corporations'. There is also corporate activity in the widening of product and service portfolios. Tesco, originally a supermarket, added financial services to its offering and has also ventured into offering a pre-paid and contract phone service (Ritson, 2003 : 20). Organisations are using the attributes of their brand that customers know as a platform for offering additional products and services.

Taxation

The higher the tax rate the more of an impact it has on the consumer's disposable income. Purchasing products which have tax incorporated into the price inflates the price and can be a barrier to purchasing. In many of the UK goverment Budgets, we find the Chancellor of the Exchequer increases tax on cigarettes, petrol and alcohol. This increases the price and can have two outcomes: it may reduce consumption but can also increase the amount of revenue generated for the government.

Interest rates

An increase in interest rates is used as a monetary mechanism to slow down consumer spending. If consumers are paying more to borrow, then there will be a large number of borrowers whose level of disposable income is reduced. They in turn will spend less on other purchases, such as mortgages, as the interest rate increases and the outcome can be a reduction in overall consumer spending.

Social elements

Social elements, including cultural issues, look at how customers behave. It is the customers' attitudes and opinions that dictate what types of product and service they are interested in. Socially, one of the biggest changes in the UK is the change in tolerance of those who smoke. Large numbers of public places (e.g. stations, restaurants, etc.) are likely to disallow smoking inside their premises. This social change has been led by a change in attitude in which people see smoking as an anti-social activity. The outcome of this change of mind is that a large number of businesses have adapted their provision of smoking and non-smoking areas.

Culture plays a strong part in influencing how people view products and services. Culture can be said to be a combination of people's beliefs, knowledge, attitudes and customs that are formed depending on the society in which those individuals live. Let us now take a look at some social and cultural examples.

Religion

Religion and ethnicity give rise to people's values and can dictate a lifestyle. There may be particular foods that cannot be consumed or a type of behaviour that is not acceptable. Deeply-held beliefs are strong and can have a far-reaching influence on generations of consumer behaviour.

Class

Societies contain different classes of people. These differences arise from the views held by collections of people on issues such as education, work and sometimes political views. The issue of private and public schools is an area where people make a choice according to their view. People with the view that education should be provided by the state will not pay for their children to be educated privately. Others take the view that something that is paid for has more value and they will pay for education.

Regional differences

Within the UK we can observe regional differences that manifest themselves in the different lifestyles, foods, drinks and geography. For example, in the South West the weather is generally warmer, the climate is conducive to fruit growing, particularly apples, which has given rise to the regional drink being cider. Regional differences are important to the distribution of a product or service as they may, or may not, contain customers.

Demographics

By looking at the demographic profile of a country or region, organisations can identify potential pockets of customers. One product or service will not meet the needs of a whole population. The population trend in the UK shows that 2 million of the country's 59 million people are over the age of 50 but there are fewer than this in the 15–20-year-old category, showing a decline in this age group (Office of National Statistics, 2001). The implications of these two pieces of information are that the pool of employees for any company is ageing and there does not appear to be a plentiful supply of young people to take their place – who will staff their product or service provision? An opportunity for the travel industry is that a large number of people of 50 years of age have sufficient funds and time to take advantage of more holidays.

Attitudes

These are formed by individuals and influence their behaviour towards products and services. This can be positive, for example, a brand of toothpaste that will clean a child's teeth while not harming the environment with phosphates. However, attitudes can also be a barrier to a purchase – a consumer who has had a poor experience with a brand of car from a mechanical and service point of view will view that brand that way at all times.

Attitudes, once formed, are very difficult to change. Volkswagen (VW), the German car manufacturer, had a battle on their hands when they took on the Škoda range. Regardless of the VW reputation for quality cars, Škoda was not generally perceived to share this accolade. The danger was that Škoda cars would affect the VW brand in a negative way. While it has taken VW both time and energy to reinforce a positive message, consumers are slowly seeing that the original Škoda brand can now be linked to a quality product.

Ethics

More and more pressure is being brought to bear on organisations to adopt an ethical view in how they conduct their business operations. It is an issue that consumers are pushing as they feel that the lure of big business and profit making is blinding organisations to their ethical responsibilities. The case study at the end of this chapter provides an example of how demand for a consumer product, chocolate, has been combined with an ethical approach to dealing with suppliers of cocoa beans in a fair and responsible manner. The company, Day Chocolate Company, was formed in conjunction with the fund-raising body Comic Relief to ensure that the Ghanaian cocoa bean growers are no longer exploited. The Body Shop is another example of a company whose ethical responsibilities are a core business srategy (Spotlight 3.5).

Social responsibility

Seen as the reason for adopting ethical business practice, social responsibility is about organisations making sure they are not just taking from the environment, but also that they realise there are opportunities to put something back. The Body Shop is involved in a campaign to promote the protection of children – not just children in under-developed nations, but also those in our own society who, for some reason, are

Spotlight 3.5

The Body Shop

The Body Shop is a well-known example of a company with an ethical approach to business. Products are not tested on animals and raw materials are generally sourced from areas around the globe that encourage investment in the suppliers' community. The new product development process in this organisation stems from the sourcing of materials from areas of the world that need controlling, replenishing or that give the growers and producers some control over their environment. Anita Roddick, one of The Body Shop's owners, is about to launch an ethical clothes range to add to the already wide range of 'naturally inspired skin and hair care solutions' (www.bodyshop.com). Her message is that the products should be achieving two objectives: they provide much needed income for the producers and also let the consumer movement see that ethical business can meet consumer needs.

being failed by society. Emotive issues draw attention to themselves; more organisations are taking on a role that is addressing some element of social responsibility, a role that demonstrates to the world at large that organisations do care.

Environmental awareness

Ecological issues are an area of concern for industries the world over. Fora involving large numbers of different countries try to identify and address the scale of issues such as the greenhouse effect and global warming. Organisations are charged with adapting production processes so as not to contribute in a negative way to these processes. Conservation of nature is undertaken in a variety of ways, from the Eden Project in England (where they replicate all the known climate regions of the world and the flora and fauna found naturally there) to conservation projects in the Brazilian Rain Forest. Deforestation is taking away this vast source of wood and projects to control the removal and replenishment do happen to a certain degree.

Consumerism

As consumers have more choice and accessibility to more information, they have become a very well informed body of people. This means they are more discerning in what they know about products and services, and exercise that knowledge to make sure that they are getting what they expect to get. Consumer rights are protected by legislation (beginning with the Consumer Protection Act 1987), along with bodies like Consumer Protection departments provided by local authorities and magazines such as *Which?*, which campaigns and promotes consumer rights and information. Taking this battle into the mass medium of television means that consumer force grows as more people become informed.

Complaints are on the increase. The numbers of consumers who will approach organisations if they are less than satisfied with a consumer experience are growing. Companies now provide a means of contact that allows consumers to convey their disappointment with whatever element of the experience is felt to be wrong. An apology is no longer enough.

Organisations are finding that if consumers are not satisfied with the response to a complaint, then the Internet is the perfect vehicle for them to share this with thousands of other consumers. More and more consumers are exchanging views – consumers are sometimes in the situation of approaching a purchasing experience armed with information about what they don't expect and they are not reticent in telling organisations what they know.

It is difficult for organisations to understand and keep up to date with social and cultural influences. Consumers are constantly identifying issues that are important to them but that may not necessarily be appreciated by business. Organisations can use the customer view point on issues to help develop a competitive edge. Companies such as the Co-operative Bank, with its ethical investment stance, encourage customers to use their money in organisations that are not involved in arms dealing or exploitation.

Unless consumer social and cultural factors are taken into account, organisations can easily alienate their business life-blood. All aspects of products and services need to be tailored so as not to offend consumers or be seen to be trying to fool them. The change in work patterns is something organisations like IBM encourage and adapt to accordingly. IBM has a 'hot desk' facility in many of its buildings. People use a desk and connect to the organisation via their laptop computer so the concept of having one's own workspace is more flexible.

Technological elements

The impact of the technological revolution has added a speed to business processes that, from a competitive point of view, means we are doing things a lot quicker. As always, we must remember that this means the same thing for competitors. One of the ways that this has manifested itself is in the way products and services are developed and offered to the market place. The change is due to the dramatically increased rate of technology integration in the workplace. Organisations use it to do everything from word-processing and collecting customer information to distributing services and new product/service development.

Internet shopping

Although previously mentioned in this chapter, it must be realised that Internet shopping has neither grown to the degree organisations may have wished nor has it replaced the traditional way of shopping. Internet shopping is very much an activity that runs alongside other forms of shopping, such as telephone, mail and visiting the local high street. The Internet has provided an additional communication and distribution channel for companies and has added to the complexity of the competitive environment.

Speedier telecommunications

A social trend that has grown out of the advances in technological development is that of the widespread use of the mobile phone. There are very few people in the UK who do not have one. In 2002 there were 50 million users, with sales increasing to nearly 15 million handsets (Mintel Retail Intelligence, 2002) (see Spotlight 3.6).

Spotlight 3.6

Mobile phone customer segments

Different mobile phone customer segments have different needs and wants from the same product depending on how they want to use it (Mintel, 2001b). The 15–24-year-old category is the one that is most concerned with the 'want' aspect of this product, that is how trendy is the handset, whereas the 25–34-year-old category is concerned with using the product for contact purposes. As the technology combines more media in the mobile telephone, so the users are taking advantage of the facilities offered. Image-sending is now growing. While the take-up is less than that of text messaging, it is always interesting to see these developments become established as a part of everyday life.

Telecommunications developments

Interconnectivity between the telecommunication infrastructures of different countries can mean easier communications between them. Organisations with a worldwide company structure can operate as if all departments are located next to one another. But there can be a downside, as Spotlight 3.7 shows.

Spotlight 3.6

The Love Bug virus

There is a negative side to the international linkages resulting from the development of telecommunications. Technological communication development provides an opportunity for a divisive use of the connectivity – viruses can be easily spread. The occurrence of the Love Bug virus, which originated in Indonesia, took 24 hours to infect computer storage worldwide. If one opened the offending email, the virus wiped stored files from systems. Just 12 lines of syntax was all it took to reduce global corporations to a state of panic as information disappeared before their eyes.

Faster new product/service development

More and more we find computer-based systems speeding up the rate of new product/service development. New products can be easily simulated in a virtual reality application, allowing companies to speed up the development process while having something to 'show' customers.

Involving your customers in this process means customer views, usage and preferences can be incorporated at design stage. The impact on industry is that products are brought to the market place more quickly, reducing the time customers have to wait, the time competitors have to compete and the time a company has before it has to come up with the next generation of offering. In the personal computer market lead times are reduced to approximately 12 weeks – this is the time frame in which companies have to establish a new product/service before there is a new offering available.

Services are more easily offered via technology. As services are intangible, any changes that are required can be implemented by updating or changing information. An insurance policy can easily be adapted to individual customer needs. Information is kept about previous purchasing habits, which allows the company to foresee what the customer may require next time and 'next time' can be prompted by the electronic system actually generating the offer information before the customer has asked for it. This is something we all experience in our dealings with banks, insurance companies, etc.

Managing customers

The rise of new companies such as call centres has been a direct result of the progression of technology. Information systems support a huge industry, as we have seen in the growth of the 'call centre' industry. The estimate is that 350,000 people – more than 1% of the UK working population – work in these organisations, responding to customer calls dealing with banking issues, travel arrangements and pension advice, to name but a few (http://news.bbc.co.uk/1/hi/uk/637987.stm). Customer service is the role of the call centres and can be a dedicated in-house service or, as is more commonly found, a centre that provides customer service support for several companies. Ventura is one such organisation, providing out-sourced customer services for the customers of O_2, Northern Rock and Thames Water.

Technological developments in distribution and service delivery

Electronic distribution of services is easily carried out but what about products? Technology means companies can monitor where the products are in the distribution channel. Honda use technology to communicate what colour car a particular customer would like so the customer sees a car produced to their specification. It can also track the production process and say where in the production process a car is at any given time – a mass produced product with a degree of customer specialisation!

Service delivery is simplified as it is very easy to sort out a customer's insurance request, update personal details and automatically produce the relevant documentation which is then sent to the customer. Technology allows this service to be individually tailored and, importantly for the company, allows the information about the transaction to be retained so that future opportunities can be identified for other products and/or services.

Changes in business processes

Technology can be used to undertake traditional business processes such as marketing and promotion. Marketing has been able to benefit from the mechanisation of information gathering by allowing companies to have access to up-to-date, relevant market information. Promotion is being carried out in a new way – via the Internet. As a communication portal, the Internet can be used by companies to send promotion information to customers but, importantly, allows those customers to respond and enter into two-way dialogue (Spotlight 3.8).

Spotlight 3.8

Viral marketing

Viral marketing is one form of electronic promotion that is being used more frequently. Word of mouth is a most effective means of promotion because it is one people tend to trust. Imagine this on an electronic forum, the Internet for example. Viral marketing takes the message to whoever the original recipient emails. We know how easy it is to send a message to a group of people, so what better way for something to be promoted. British Airways used this form of promotion to give away free flights. If you sent the email to five friends you were entitled to a free flight in Europe, if you sent it to ten friends you could have a free flight to any destination in the world. Although limited in terms of time (you have to choose and take the flight within 12 weeks of the offer going out) it was very quickly over-subscribed. It was an opportunity for British Airways to sell what would otherwise be empty plane seats (www.britishairways.com).

Customer service

While an electronic system means companies can keep an information trail on customers, there has been an increasing demand for improved customer service. Good customer service is defined by your customers – if they feel an automated system is dealing with them in an automated manner, they are quick to realise this and dismiss a company's attempts at calling this 'customer service'. People want *people* to deliver their customer service. People going into a train station will see monitors that are constantly updated with train information, but what do people do? They seek out Customer Service Advisors to reassure them that their train is indeed arriving in 15 minutes at platform 2 – the information the monitor has already given them. So does technology run parallel to a person? Federal Express encourage customers to log on and see where their delivery is. In this way customers feel they are receiving a personal service when in fact it is an automated process.

Customer information

Customers are sensitive about information relating to their finances, health, family issues and gender so companies need to be very careful about who they pass customer information to and what they do with it (O'Connor and Galvin, 1997).

Dilemma 3.1

Data Protection as a legal issue

The Data Protection Act 1998 (updating the 1984 version) came into effect 1 March 2000 in the UK. The legislation limited the acquisition and passing on of information by companies. Companies were required to process all personal data 'fairly and lawfully'; the implications for the telecommunications industry were enormous. If they could not use their raw material of information, then their business offering would be severely limited. The introduction of the 1995 European Directive (covering European Union member states), which was to run alongside the Data Protection Act, brought with it another issue – which legislation was to be adhered to in order for companies to be conforming to the industry legislation? This depended on where the information originated from, where it was to be used, what was to be done with it and by whom. In other words, was it the original company or somebody else who had acquired the information? This was an issue because personal data was only to be used if that data had come directly from the individual concerned. Internationally, this data could only be transferred outside the European Union to areas that operated under the same level of legislation. In 2000 this limited the globe to Hong Kong, Quebec and New Zealand.

How can a company based in the UK share customer information with a supplier based in South America to develop a new product?

The micro-environment

Now we will consider the elements contained in the micro-environment – customers, suppliers, distributors and competitors – elements over which a company can have some control and influence.

Customers

How does the customer experience the marketing environment?

Different customers experience what is on offer in different ways. The different types of customer were discussed in detail in Chapter 2 so we already have an understanding of who they are and how they behave. Customers set and follow market trends for products and services. They react to social and technological developments – some of them are quick to adopt new ideas while others take time to get used to the offering before following suit. As consumers become more informed so they become more discerning.

Companies therefore have to make sure that the information they pass out to the market place leads to a positive purchasing experience or customers are quickly finding a loud voice with which to complain. Generally, the more choice that is available the more customers will move from one provider to another.

Customers are very discerning in how they make their choices. Companies need to understand that customers seek out the most convenient solution to a problem and make their purchase accordingly. Customers are looking for the point of least resistance. Barriers in any shape or form will divert customers from the path to your door and send them to your competitors.

Customers experience the business environment by being the 'demand' that products and services are provided for. It is the existence of their needs and wants that companies are striving to meet. If companies are continuously communicating that customers are the focus of their activities, then this is the experience customers will be looking for.

The power of customers

As people use various products and services their points of view are passed around the market place and opinions are formed about them. A powerful communication process goes on but the most important aspect that organisations must be aware of is that this is one communication customers will listen to! The American Pilsbury Company developed the Häagen Dazs ice cream brand even though lots of premium brand ice creams were around at the time of its launch. The target audience was identified as being quite narrow, rather than the traditional mass market that ice-cream products were generally 'targeted' at. Originally it was the domain of a chosen few, selected distribution, premium product and price with high-quality promotion. Word of mouth was used as the main method of promotion; customers spread the whisper and it became louder and louder, attracting more and more people to consume this product although availability was limited. Now distribution has been expanded and the mass market purchases Häagen Dazs. The lesson to be learned here is that customers listen to customers. Organisations know that to listen to them is one of the best sources of market information. It will tell them how customers judge whether current offerings are meeting their needs, how those needs might change and what customers expect to see next.

Suppliers

According to Kotler et al. (2001), suppliers are an important 'link' between what the company is offering and what the customer requires. Suppliers are the source of resources that are the bases of the product or service that is purchased. For example, suppliers to Marks & Spencer are wide-ranging, from food to clothes. Marks & Spencer do not produce these products; they source them from a range of suppliers and sell them to the customers via their retail outlets. The financial services offered by Marks & Spencer are provided by financial institutions but are sold under the retailer's name. What Marks & Spencer provide is access to these products and services, and access to customers that the suppliers might otherwise not have. Suppliers are obviously important to companies because without supplies, there can be no sales for anybody. Marks & Spencer have a reputation for using suppliers who conform to their standards, which are dictated by customer expectations of their clothes, food and other products in terms of style, price and quality. Suppliers who do not meet these standards are soon replaced.

Distributors

This is the part of the purchasing process that actually gets the products or services to the customer. Distribution to retail outlets, again using Marks & Spencer as an example, means delivering products so they can be sold to customers who visit the stores. However, we can also see Marks & Spencer as a distributor of a supplier's products – through the network of established Marks & Spencer stores.

Distribution is sometimes done by a supplier, for example Amazon, the online book seller. This company sells a large numbers of books over the Internet. The distribution of these products is undertaken by companies that have established distribution facilities, such as Royal Mail and Federal Express.

Competitors

Companies strive to deliver to the customer something their competitors cannot or will not provide in order to gain and retain customers. This means being aware of what the competition is offering to customers, who is buying this competitive offering and what exactly they get in return for their money. It could be that some small element of the product or service delivery is making the difference to customers; anything that eases their purchasing situation will be attractive to them. Let us take another look at Marks & Spencer in relation to competition. It was one of the first retailers to make its exchange policy a reason to shop there. If people purchased clothing that was just 'not right', it could easily be returned. It started an expectation in customers that they then demanded from other retailers. Marks & Spencer were not legally obliged to do this; they did it to reassure customers that the company had faith in the products sold.

It is important to remember that the environmental elements that are important to a business will also be important to that business's competitors. Organisations need to understand who their competitors are in order to gauge the degree of threat they pose to their being able to meet customer needs. In order to do this, organisations need to be aware of the market characteristics of the competitive arena and what influences need to be taken account of. It may be possible that the competition are able to offer the market something unique which is giving a competitive edge, and organisations need to know what this is and how they themselves can develop such an edge.

M.E. Porter (1980) suggests that there are five competitive forces putting pressure on market places that affect the outcome of all business operations. As the balance of power between these forces moves from one to another, so the market place changes and reacts to them. Here we shall look at what these forces are and how they can affect a company's customers in the market place. The five competitive forces that Porter suggests are:

1. *New entrants to an industry.* These increase the competitive pressure on existing companies. They may extend choice to customers by offering something new or cheaper than what is currently available.
2. *Substitute products/services.* These are the products or services that can be easily replaced by alternatives, such as tea and coffee or switching between insurance companies. Customers experience a wider choice and as such can exert this power in the market place in their purchasing behaviour.
3. *Bargaining power of buyers.* This will decrease if there is an increase in the number of buyers (companies not individual customers) in a market place. The buyer with brand leadership will have the most power as this company will have developed a loyal customer base. Customers are assured by brands they are familiar with as this reduces uncertainty in the purchasing situation.
4. *Bargaining power of suppliers.* This can affect a company's profitability. The more suppliers there are, the lower the cost of the raw materials and the better opportunity a company has to maintain a preferred level of profitability. If raw materials are limited, then prices rise and profits are reduced. A reduction in suppliers can mean customer demands are not met and they may look for alternatives, although this obviously depends on the product or the service being sought.
5. *Rivalry between existing industry competitors.* This can be affected by a number of factors, such as the number of competitors, how much difference there is between the products and services being offered and how easy it can be for a competitor to move its business focus elsewhere. Customers may benefit from this rivalry as sometimes the outcome is a fall in prices. However, they may lose an element of choice if a company ceases to offer a particular product or service.

Dilemma 3.2

Every little helps

Boots is not automatically seen as being in direct competition with Tesco. There is an overlap of the types of product each sells but Tesco has now made a move to increase that competition. It is applying its price reductions to baby care and health and beauty products. This is seen as an 'aggressive challenge to high street specialists such as Boots, Superdrug and Mothercare' (Bowers, 2004). Price reductions are what the large retailers use to attract customers in this highly competitive market. Customers may go to the 'specialists' for several baby care products unless there is an alternative closer to hand! Cheaper prices at Tesco could be that alternative – the convenience of doing one's whole shopping in one place, plus cheaper prices on products normally purchased elsewhere, benefits the customer and Tesco alike. Boots, the specialist, has to compete with its care products against Tesco, the general supermarket. Tesco has its risk spread over a much larger product range and does not rely on one type of product.

What do you suggest companies like Boots, Superdrug and Mothercare do to combat this issue of low prices? Do you think they are specialists? What would you suggest Tesco does if other supermarkets and the specialists reduce their prices?

Industry structure

An industry can comprise a large number of small companies or be dominated by a small number of large companies. It is necessary to understand how an industry is structured in order to see how it operates and thus competes. For example, there may be advantages in sharing resources such as suppliers. The car industry shares components which means they can be acquired more cheaply and easily than using specialist pieces.

Competitor analysis

Companies need to understand what their competitors are achieving in order to know where they sit in relation to them and, more importantly, why customers go to one or more of them rather than other providers. It is the customers' perception of a company that gives it its market position, not what the company thinks about itself. This can be achieved through **competitor analysis**.

What competes with your product or service?

Part of understanding the competition is asking questions about what it is that the competition is actually offering:

1. Is it something that can take the place of your product or service? For example, customers who want mobile phone handsets have several alternatives from which to choose – Nokia, Siemens, Sony Ericsson and Motorola.
2. What alternative products or services deliver the same benefit? If a customer needs transport to get from A to B what are the alternatives (air, road, rail or coach)?
3. What might also be vying for the consumer's spending? For the provision of recreational activities, for example, customers have a huge choice – a visit to Alton Towers, a video game used at home, or shopping in the local retail outlet.

SUMMARY

In times of vast choice, customers will seek out the point of least resistance to find a solution to their problems. Any company wishing to differentiate its offering from that of the competition needs to keep a very close eye on the marketing environment in order to understand those problems and identify customer needs.

As we have seen, the marketing environment is complex and contains a large number of constantly moving elements. These elements can be categorised in order to monitor change. PEST is a framework that allows the macro-environment to be analysed while we can use the four elements of customers, suppliers, distributors and competitors to understand the micro-environment.

Environmental scanning is the constant collection of this marketing environment information. A systematic approach to this task means companies can gather data and use it to respond to the marketing environment challenges. The danger of not employing such an important business operation is that companies operate on old or obsolete knowledge of their marketing environment. Failure to update this information means giving any competitive edge to competitors who will be updating their knowledge and working to meet customer needs more closely.

Customers are the people who consume the products and services produced. Unless companies understand the environment in which customers exist and what effects those environmental elements have, how can they understand and deal with customers?

There is also a role that suppliers and distributors play in the marketing environment which affects how and when companies can get their products/services to customers. Without considering suppliers and distributors, and the power they have in the marketing environment, a company can fail to meet the customer needs even if those needs are understood.

Competitors operating against one another shape what is on offer to customers. Competitor analysis is used to identify exactly what it is that a company (and other competitors) is competing against in terms of the product/service offer. To compete without this information, when there is a strong possibility that the customer has it, means you are giving your customers to your competitors.

We will now look at how companies can collect this marketing environment information and how they can analyse it to develop an understanding of what is happening in the marketing environment.

Discussion questions

1   What do you understand by the term 'environmental scanning'?

2   Consider the political category of the PEST analysis. What new elements can you identify that could affect the car industry?

3   What effect would the change in taxation on steel production have on the price of washing machines?

4   How might regional differences in the European Union affect the production and distribution of a children's story book?

5   What would you suggest are
    (a) a new entrant?
    (b) a substitute product for the mobile telephone?

Case study 3.1 | The Day Chocolate Company

Started in 1998, The Day Chocolate Company launched a new mass-market chocolate bar into the UK confectionary market. Organisations involved in the start-up of The Day Chocolate Company, along with Kuapa KoKoo (the farmers' co-operative), were Twin, The Body Shop, Christian Aid and Comic Relief. Finance was facilitated by the Department for International Development and banking to suit the company's need was offered by NatWest. Kuapa KoKoo sorts out the distribution for its members in as clear a way as possible. Transparency of the business processes is an important aspect of this situation as everything must be open and above board to fit in with the ethos of fair play. The company operates under licence from the Fairtrade Foundation. This ensures that acceptable 'fair' business practice is recognised and followed.

The chocolate market in the UK is valued at around £4 billion, which suggests there is a viable return to be made even if only a small market share is gained. Brand positions are built by companies investing large amounts of money to achieve and hold the top-selling positions.

The chocolate bar called 'Divine' has been produced to match the British taste in chocolate, as The Day Chocolate Company sees it competing in the main area of chocolate bar buying (www.divinechocolate.com). Trends in the UK support the fact that there is a high level of chocolate consumption and suggest the potential for a small market share to deliver sufficient returns to sustain the business.

What is Fair Trade?

Fair Trade looks to provide fair remuneration for developing country producers. This body works to make sure that producers receive a fair price for their products and also that there is an involvement in developing the producer's community. The Day Chocolate Company has taken this concept further. Kuapa KoKoo is a farmer's co-operative that produces cocoa for Divine chocolate and owns one-third of the company. This means that a supplier, located on the other side of the world from where the finished product is sold, has an active role in deciding how Divine chocolate is produced and sold. The supplier also gets a share of the profits. Success in the fair dealings of its members has meant that the organisation has grown to 35,000 members.

The product range

The product range consists mainly of chocolate bars but has recently introduced seasonal offerings such as mini eggs and Christmas themed chocolate. The cocoa content of the chocolate is 70% whereas normally a 55% content makes it a high-quality offering (www.cadbury.co.uk).

Market developments

Food with an 'ethical' element is seen as a leading differentiator from other products and services. Within the ethical food market Mintel suggests that there is a potential worth of £1,100 million (Mintel 2001a). In this sector, chocolate is seen to be worth an estimated £3,795 million. Fair Trade chocolate is seen to be growing with a suggested 85% increase in sales in 1998 over 1997 and a huge 119% increase in 1999 over 1998.

Target market and the ethical consumer

The Divine chocolate bar is a mass-market product that the company decided should be made to appeal to the everyday chocolate consumer. Other products have been introduced into the range for 'special' occasions.

The number of 'ethical consumers' is growing. Previously, people considered political issues as a reason to buy or not to buy a product, but now they are considering the content of the product and where the raw materials are from. As for being able to identify a target market, there are only a few factors that are associated with ethical purchasing and these factors do not point to any one customer segment.

The ethical view point is not taken into account by any particular age group, but there does seem to be a link between social standing and the purchase of ethical produce. Mintel found that generally regular purchasing of ethical produce is more likely to be done by those in the social category of AB and less likely by those in the social group of E. Mintel also found that the view held by consumers is that they do not want products associated with three main environmental concerns – child labour, animal testing and Third World exploitation (Mintel 2001a).

As most ethical producers are small concerns, it appears that consumer are more likely to patronise them in order to support their survival. Consumers also see that the quality of these products is on a par with other products (previously they were seen as being of a poorer quality than was acceptable because they were sourced from the Third World). Thus, as well as addressing the ethical issue, they are now delivering acceptable product quality.

Promotion

Promotion of ethical foods is undertaken predominantly by the large retailers who talk about the fact that they stock an 'ethical' food range. Mintel has identified an increase in the amount of money spent: £6.5 million was spent on ethical food promotion by all companies in 2000, whereas in 1999 the amount was £3.9 million. (Mintel, 2001a).

The companies that actually produce these Fair Trade foods have only small advertising budgets, which means it is not easy to communicate with the market place on any large scale or for any length of time. Fair Trade companies have therefore looked for alternative means of promotion, such as PR – the story of how these companies work and the ethical offering itself attracts consumers' interest and enhances their ethical view. As a result, individual product promotion is not undertaken by these companies (Mintel, 2001a).

Distribution

Supermarkets are the main outlets, stocking an ever increasing range of Fair Trade products, thus offering the consumer a choice of ethical produce. Produce can also be purchased from charity shops and catering outlets. Retailers, such as Marks &

Spencer, have ethical guidelines for suppliers and the sourcing of products. Waitrose uses its purchasing power to encourage the development and support of suppliers of produce, ensuring the provision of good working conditions for employees. The Ethical Trading Initiative (ETI) is the UK-based alliance of companies, non-governmental organisations and trade unions that work to promote good working practices and conditions for suppliers (www.eti.org). Organisations such as Marks & Spencer, Waitrose, Tesco, Co-op, Sainsbury's, Asda and Iceland are large retail industry representatives involved in the ETI. We also see other outlets such as health food and charity shops supporting the selling of these products to support their source communities. Ethical produce is also being used more frequently by catering companies in their food offerings, for example Costa Coffee and John Lewis Partnership.

The future

Mintel found supporting evidence that the growth of awareness surrounding ethical concerns is increasing. Findings from lifestyle research indicate consumers are willing to pay for this type of product, even if it is slightly higher than the everyday offering. The effect on the purchasing of ethical foods is therefore seen to be positive.

The Day Chocolate Company prices its products at the same level as the main competitors so people are not expected to pay more for their ethical beliefs. The number of charitable and ethical causes in the market place means that companies have to give clear messages about their particular issue. By making sure consumers know which of these ethical issues they are addressing through their purchasing habits, it is felt that ethical purchasing will grow along with awareness.

Source: Based on www.divinechocolate.com; www.eti.org.com; www.cadbury.co.uk; and Mintel (2001a) Attitudes Towards Ethical Foods (February). London: Mintel.

Questions

1   Choose three categories from Section 3.3 above and suggest how they will affect how The Day Chocolate Company operates.

2   Using the suggested competitor analysis, in which category would you place a company like Cadbury's?

3   Who are the customers for the chocolate bar and are they different from the customers for the seasonal products?

Further reading

Brassington, F. and Petitt, S. (2003) *Principles of Marketing* (3rd edition). Harlow: Financial Times/Prentice Hall.

Jobber, D. (2004) *Principles and Practice of Marketing*, (5th edition). New York: McGraw Hill.

References

Begg, D., Fischer, S. and Dornbusc, R. (2002) *Economics* (7th edition). London: McGraw-Hill.

Bowers, S. (2004) 'Tesco cuts target Boots', *The Guardian*, 5 January.

Jobber, D. (2001) *Principles and Practice of Marketing* (3rd edition). New York: McGraw-Hill.

Kotler, P., Armstrong, G., Saunders, J. and Wong, V. (2001) *Principles of Marketing* (3rd European edition). Harlow: Financial Times/Prentice Hall.

Mintel (2001a) Attitudes Towards Ethical Foods (February). London: Mintel.

Mintel (2001b) *Mobile Phones and Network Providers* (April). London: Mintel.

Mintel Retail Intelligence (2002) *Network Operators*. London: Mintel.

O'Connor, J. and Galvin, E. (1997) *Marketing and Information Technology*. London: Pitman Publishing.

Office of National Statistics (2001) *Key Population and Vital Statistics*. London: HMSO.

Porter, M.E. (1980) *Competitive Strategy: Techniques for Analyzing Industries and Competitors*. New York: The Free Press.

Richardson, W.R. (1992) lecture notes.

Ritson, M. (2003) 'Mobile branding flops create a market ripe for Tesco entrance', *Marketing*, 12 June.

4 Building information on the customer

Debbie Hill

LEARNING OUTCOMES

After reading this chapter you should be able to:

- **Understand the importance of collecting relevant, reliable and valid information**

- **Recognise that there is a variety of information sources available to organisations**

- **Critically appraise the different sources of information**

- **Utilise appropriate information sources in order to answer specific information needs**

- **Build information on customers by applying appropriate analytical techniques**

KEY WORDS

Customer information system	Qualitative information
External information	Quantitative information
Focus group	Questionnaire
Internal information	Reliability
Key customer values	Respondents
Moderator	Sampling
Observation	Secondary information
Personal interviews	Topic guide
Primary information	Validity

INTRODUCTION

Previous chapters have explored the rationale for putting the customer at the heart of a company's efforts. This means that the company must be united in its aim to create satisfied and loyal customers. However, we have also witnessed the dangers of the organisation having a myopic view of the customer; customers come in many guises and a business must carefully consider the range of customers it is serving. Finally, in the previous chapter, we have seen the importance of influences exerted by the external environment. Organisations do not conduct their business in a vacuum; influences on them, in their environment, will set the framework within which their business is conducted.

Putting the customer at the centre of the organisation's efforts, irrespective of who that customer is, assumes some knowledge of customers. Working with the environmental influences assumes the same. So, for any business aiming to be customer-oriented, the first step will be to acquire knowledge of its customers and its environment.

This chapter looks at how a company can properly understand and manage its customers by creating knowledge through the implementation of a systematic process of information collection and analysis.

4.1 WHY DO ORGANISATIONS NEED INFORMATION?

The importance of information

We have already seen that businesses do not operate in isolation and do, in fact, evolve as a result of (and sometimes in spite of) the influences surrounding them within their environment. Knowledge of these influences is of paramount importance to them since knowledge is a prerequisite to understanding and it is understanding that will help them to successfully navigate the difficult waters of their environment. So let's take this a step at a time.

A business needs to acquire knowledge, how does it do this? Well, knowledge comes from information and information comes from the facts accumulated about certain things. But facts about what? How would a business know what information it needs to acquire?

Spotlight 4.1 is from a press article written by a journalist. The journalist has collected information and acquired knowledge about the perfume industry in order to write this article. Take a look at it and respond to the suggestion at the end. It might be helpful if you review what you have learnt in Chapter 2 about the nature of customers and in Chapter 3 about environmental influences in responding.

Spotlight 4.1

FT **Product development in the perfume industry**

At the Manhattan headquarters of Ralph Lauren Fragrances, there is a sense of quiet but palpable jubilation. It is high summer, just a few months after the launch of Romance, Lauren's first major scent for women since 1996. The sales figures are looking good. In the US, Romance hit the number one spot in 98 per cent of the stores it was in. These are only the US figures, but since the US has 40 per cent of the 'prestige perfume' market, what happens there is crucial. 'You can usually tell within a few weeks if you have success on your hands,' says Andrea Robinson, general manager of Ralph Lauren Fragrances (RLF) worldwide.

The reason for the high tension surrounding this (and every) launch is that there's a thorny problem at the heart of the fragrance business. A fragrance takes a couple of years to develop (if it's done properly), costs a fortune to launch and promote (RLF had a war chest of about $20m to get Romance on the road), and yet the fashion cycles during which they can expect to sell are becoming shorter and shorter.

Claudia Lucas, buying manager of perfume and cosmetics at Selfridges, says that 15–20 per cent of the perfume business is now new fragrances. And much of that occurs in a narrow window of opportunity: Christmas. Harrods says that 40–50 per cent of all its perfume sales take place in the eight weeks up to Christmas, while one large distributor does 48 per cent of its annual business over this period, and 32 per cent in the last four weeks before Christmas. Nor is the market growing appreciably. Even at Selfridges the perfume side has grown by 9 per cent in the past year, compared with 33 per cent for skincare and cosmetics. 'As the launch markets get more and more aggressive,' says Lucas, 'fewer and fewer fragrances have much longevity to them.' Deborah Nadler, head of public relations for RLF, agrees. 'You used to be able to get a new customer and keep her for 20 years – now you'd be very lucky to keep her for five.' But to Ralph Lauren, whose fragrance division is estimated to contribute between 8 and 12 per cent to overall profits, all this time, money and effort will only pay off if Romance becomes one of the handful of new perfumes that are still around in 5 and 10 years' time.

The further problem is that the market seems to have reached saturation point, so that the only way to make bigger profits is to increase market share. Another worrying factor is that the nose of the consumer has changed in the past two decades. John Horvitz, president of Horvitz & Associates, a marketing consultant who specialises in beauty, cosmetics and perfume, is in no doubt that the industry is going through major changes. 'It used to be a very fragmented business with hundreds of players, and it was relatively easy to make and sell a perfume,' he says. 'Saks 5th Avenue or Neiman Marcus would take a punt on a small fragrance maker. Today, four companies – L'Oréal with 15–16 per cent, Unilever with

Spotlight 4.1 *continued*

14–15 per cent, LVMH with 13–14 per cent and Lauder with 10–11 per cent – control about 55 per cent of the worldwide fine fragrance business. Not only that, but department store groups in the US are consolidating, so that newcomers find there are just six main department store groups, and if they say "no", that's a very big "no" and it closes very big doors.'

It is fascinating to see how badly RLF seems to need a new fragrance. Why the endless need for something new? Says Robinson: 'We have to refresh the brand, slightly change the look of things if we're going to bring in new customers. The challenge is to be new and different enough to catch the attention and yet have staying power.'

Source: Adapted from Lucia van der Post (1999) Let Us Spray, *Financial Times*, Wecherd FT Issue 44, November and in Levela Rickard and Kit Jackson (2000) *The Financial Times Marketing Casebook* (2nd edition). Harlow: Prentice Hall, pp. 144–6.

Look at the article above and note how many different pieces of information the journalist would have needed in order to compile this piece. Remember not all information is 'hard' facts.

So Spotlight 4.1 shows that anyone wanting to develop an understanding of a situation needs to collect information from a variety of sources. However, given what we learnt about the dynamism, difficulty, diversity and danger of the environment in Chapter 3, a business cannot rely on acquiring knowledge as a one-off act as this would simply create a snapshot of its environment. Therefore, it needs to commit itself to a process of knowledge acquisition by gathering information on a continuous basis so that it is always aware of the current state of its environment.

Once the business knows that it needs to collect information continuously from a variety of sources to acquire knowledge, it must consider how the knowledge is converted into understanding. Simply collecting facts about particular aspects of its environment will be interesting but not meaningful. For example, a business might find out that its market share figure is 34%. This is interesting as it means that of all the customers who are buying a particular product, 34% are buying this business's offering in preference to that of a competitor. However, the market share information becomes more meaningful if the business can also find out what its competitors' market share figures are, that is how many customers are buying competitors' products. Continuing the example, if it becomes apparent that there are three other competitors in the market and their market shares are 38%, 25% and 3%, the business can see there are a total of four organisations in the market, that it is occupying the second place in the market (the market challenger), its position is quite close to the competitor with the largest market share (the market leader), there is one minor player at the moment but the third placed organisation could be a threat.

Knowing its market share figure was interesting but the information became more meaningful when comparisons were made. The information collected was converted into knowledge and understanding of the market from a competitive perspective. It is this understanding that would enable the company to take measures to, for example, ensure that it continued to satisfy its existing customers and attract the customers of competitors.

Finally, to summarise, information is important because it provides an organisation with the means to continuously acquire knowledge and understanding of customers, competitors and the market so it is better able to satisfy customers than its competitors.

How information can be used

We have already looked briefly at some of the broad areas of information a business might collect, for example, information on its customers, competitors and the market. In this section we will look at how the information will be used and how the 'raw' information is, in the first instance, converted into knowledge. We have also established that in order to be customer-oriented an organisation will need to be continuously aware of the status of its environment. So, one of the most basic functions of the information collected is to provide an audit or examination of its environment.

Any customer-oriented company will want to know what customers are looking for so that it can provide this better than its competitors. As a result, much of the audit will concentrate on aspects external to the organisation. However, knowledge of what customers are looking for to satisfy their needs and wants and how well competitors are providing these is only one aspect. To be competitively successful, it must be able to mobilise its operations to ensure a higher level of customer satisfaction than competitors. What this means is that a comprehensive audit will also look at aspects within the organisation's operations to determine how well its resources are organised to deliver what the customer wants.

Within the context of **external** and **internal information**, we will now look at some specific functions of information.

Information can be used to establish general trends in the environment. Businesses will be interested in determining the overall size of a market in terms of how many units are purchased by customers (the market volume) as well as how much the market is worth (the market value). One of the more critical pieces of knowledge sought is whether the market is growing or not since this will indicate whether the market is still acquiring new customers and whether customers are repeatedly purchasing what the market has to offer.

Information can also be used to scan the market for opportunities and threats. The scale of the market (in volume or value terms) and the overall trend (whether the market is growing, declining or stagnating) will be an indication of whether the market presents an opportunity or threat for an organisation. Markets that are growing, even in their infancy, present opportunities; competitive pressures are likely to be less than in markets that are declining or stagnating – there are enough customers for everyone. In addition, new markets offer opportunities to steal the lead. However, markets that are declining or stagnating present a competitive threat –

competitors will be aggressively seeking to defend their market share at the expense of other players in the market.

On a more general level, the macro-environmental issues identified in Chapter 3 can lead to market opportunities and threats. For example, in the UK not only are people living longer, but older people are more affluent than they have ever been and are an attractive proposition for companies wanting to satisfy their many needs. Conversely, our increasing reliance on out-of-town retail outlets for everything from food to mobile phones has almost extinguished the retail trade in town centres.

Information can enable the organisation to assess competitor activity. As well as market share comparisons, a business will also be interested in the precise offering of competitors in terms of the product, how it is priced, how it gets to the customer and how it is promoted (we call these aspects the marketing mix). It will also want to find out about a competitor's overall aims and ambitions (we call this its strategy) because it is this that will influence the composition and execution of its marketing mix.

Information can help the organisation to explore and examine consumer behaviour and help the organisation to design its approach to the customer. The desire to know and understand consumer behaviour is at the heart of a customer-oriented philosophy. How can companies achieve successful competitive advantage by satisfying customer needs better than their peers if they do not understand which customers buy, why they buy, what they buy, how they buy, when they buy, where they buy. Chapter 5 covers this area in more detail.

Information that will help it to gauge the extent to which its resources 'fit' with its ambitions. Is the company equipped to deal with the challenges of the environment and satisfy customers better than the competition?

There will be much internal information at the disposal of the business. For example, it will know how many people it employs, how much it pays them and what jobs they perform. As we saw earlier, this information is interesting (particularly to employees and accountants!) but it is how this information is used, within the framework of a customer-oriented philosophy, that matters.

Take the example of employees. First, rather than simply counting the number of employees, the customer-oriented business will want to ensure that it is employing the right people with the right attitudes. In short, the organisation will want its employees to demonstrate that they can embrace the idea of customer orientation so that customers matter as much to them as they do to the organisation.

Secondly, salary and wage levels are important but, to the customer-oriented firm, only as far as the fact that they should work within a reward system which motivates employees to work with them in their aim to achieve sustainable competitive advantage through customer orientation.

Finally, are employees performing the right tasks? Employees should be focused on tasks that will contribute towards customer satisfaction such as serving customers or handling their enquiries, not on internal tasks such as completing the 'necessary forms'.

The example above considers the knowledge a business will seek in terms of its human resources and it is by no means exhaustive. Furthermore, it will also be seeking information and knowledge in other aspects of its business, such as its operations and finance.

In summary, we have seen that there is a huge amount of information available but that it only starts to become useful when it adopts a functional approach because it is at this stage that the information becomes knowledge. We have also seen that information (and knowledge) can be collected from quite diverse sources both external and internal to a company. Finally, we know from the previous section that it is important for information to be collected continuously. How a business does this is covered in the following section because, ultimately, the functionality of information in the customer-oriented organisation is that it will help the organisation to build a **customer information system**.

The customer information system

Companies can take the approach that information is collected on an *ad hoc* basis – indeed many (unsuccessful) firms do. Unfortunately, those that take this approach tend to search for information when they hit an obstacle, and by this time the information will arrive too late to help overcome the obstacle – it will only help them deal with the aftermath. Companies like this are reactive. Take the example of what happened to the English football league clubs when ITV Digital went bust in the 2002/3 football season. The football league clubs realised far too late that they relied on money from television rights to support their balance sheet.

The customer-oriented (and wise!) firm realises that information provided on a continuous basis will help it to anticipate its environment. Such companies are better placed to deal with obstacles and, more importantly, take competitive advantage of situations within the market place. You only have to look at how the food retailers have responded to recent social changes in the UK. We travel more, we are a multicultural society, we have more demands on our time but we like to eat well – what is the food retailers' response? Well they provide in their chilled cabinets all manner of ready-made meals with accompanying breads, pickles, dips and so on, so that we can enjoy an 'exotic restaurant' meal in our own home, at our convenience and prepared with the minimum of effort.

In short, the customer-oriented business will embed a systematic and continuous process of information acquisition, analysis and dissemination within its processes. This will enable it to move forward proactively and be positively prepared for the future.

So what is this system called? It's called a customer information system (CIS). The CIS becomes the system by which companies can systematically (in other words regularly) collect information, turn it into knowledge and understanding through appropriate analysis and then 'distribute' it (in an intellectual as well as physical sense) to appropriate decision makers. In short, the CIS can be defined as:

> *An operational framework that enables an organisation to manage and structure the gathering of information from sources within and outside of it.*

Figure 4.1 shows a number of boxes, these are stages within the system. It also shows arrows linking the stages. Let's go through the diagram a stage at a time.

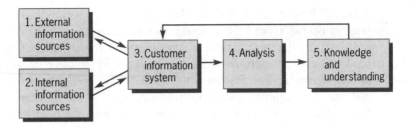

Figure 4.1 Customer information system

Stage 1. External sources of information are accessed and fed into the CIS. At this stage, information will be gathered on the general environment, the market, competitors and customers among other things. Table 4.1 (page 88) gives more specific details of the potential sources of this type of information.

Stage 2. Concurrently, internal sources of information are also accessed and fed into the CIS. Remember, here we are talking about information on the company's resources (which can include human, physical and financial resources) and its operations to name but a few. Consequently, not only many aspects of its activities, but many employees will be involved in the provision of internal information.

Stage 3. The external and internal sources of information are collated within the CIS. The CIS is not some form of computer software package (although software may be used in stage 4). What we're talking about here is the coming together, or gathering, of pieces of external and internal information within one physical part of the organisation. This 'coming together' may well be handled by employees within the company's marketing department who have the necessary skills to perform stage 4 (in smaller organisations this may be an individual with responsibility for marketing). These employees will probably be given the specific task of collecting different types of information on a continuous basis so that the information audit can be completed.

Stage 4. As we have said, it is likely that at stage 3 employees within the marketing department will have the specific task of collating internal and external information. However, we have also seen that this information must be translated into knowledge in order for the company to develop its understanding of its environment. So how is information translated into knowledge? Well, essentially, what we're talking about here, as a first step, is the process of analysis. This will be discussed in more detail later, but for the time being it is worth re-examining why this task is likely to be performed by employees within the marketing department.

The employees of the marketing department are likely to be those closest to the philosophy of customer orientation. Marketers truly believe that analysis of environmental information leads to knowledge and understanding and that it is a critical first step to identifying and pursuing sustainable competitive advantage. Furthermore, these employees will be the company's full-time marketers and, accordingly, are likely to have the necessary skills and abilities to undertake the task. Finally, in a truly customer-oriented business, the marketing department will be a focal point for customer-centred activities.

Stage 5. Once the analysis has taken place, the information is translated into knowledge and understanding. It is at this stage that the firm's decision makers will get involved. By decision makers, we mean senior management who are responsible for the business. The actions of the business are likely to come in two different guises, strategic and tactical. Strategic actions will happen over the longer term and be significant, for example, to enter a new segment of the market. These actions will be the result of the information and analysis that has been undertaken during the annual planning review (the once-a-year review in which the business reassesses where it is, where it wants to be and how it is going to get there). Tactical actions will happen on an *ad hoc* basis and are, generally speaking, of less significance, for example, increasing the number of staff in a call centre during a promotional campaign. These actions will still be the result of information received, but the information is likely to be of a more discrete/moment-in-time nature.

Finally, you will see that the CIS is a feed forward system – stages 1 and 2 feed into stage 3 that feeds into stage 4 and then stage 5. However, there are aspects that feed back into the CIS. It is likely that the decision makers involved in stage 5 will also want to influence the nature of the information collated within the CIS (stage 3). The information received will be constantly evolving, not just as a result of the demands of decision makers, but in response to changes within the external and internal environment. What this means is that there will be interaction between the CIS and the information sources.

So, in summary, we have seen how the CIS will not only facilitate the organisation's desire to have a continuous system of information collection, but will also provide the much needed knowledge and understanding.

Reliability and validity

The previous sections have demonstrated that information is the key to knowledge and understanding. However, any information collected must observe two basic principles.

Information must be reliable. **Reliability** is 'the quality of producing almost identical results in successive repeated trials' (Dibb et al., 2001: 181). In short, reliability of information is concerned with the extent to which the information is error free. If information is error free, it will produce the same results time after time. Take a look at Spotlight 4.2.

Information must be valid. **Validity** is 'a condition that exists when an instrument measures what it is supposed to measure' (Dibb et al., 2001: 181). In short, the validity of information is concerned with the extent to which the information collected is what it was intended to be.

Take a second look at Spotlight 4.2. The information collected would be valid if PetFood Inc were trying to establish why customers purchased Mittens, but what if they were trying to establish the relative importance of price, quality and brand in the purchase decision? In this case the question set out in Spotlight 4.2 would not be valid. To find out the relative importance of price, quality and brand in the purchase decision, PetFood Inc would have had to ask customers to show (perhaps in order of importance using a scale of, say, 1 being most important and 4 being least impor-

Spotlight 4.2

PetFood Inc

PetFood Inc, the producers of Mittens (a cat food), have undertaken a telephone survey among their customers. One of the aims of the survey was to find out why their customers bought Mittens. This aim was translated into the following question:

What is the main reason why you choose to purchase Mittens cat food?

Price ☐

Quality ☐

Brand ☐

Other ☐   Please specify ....

The response to this question showed that 48% of customers purchased Mittens because of the brand, 25% because of the quality, 25% because of the price and 2% said other things not associated with brand, quality or price.

The information collected via this survey would be reliable if a repeat of the survey under the same conditions (for example, using the telephone and asking the same type of people the same question in the same way) produced the same response.

tant), the extent to which price, quality and brand influenced their decision to purchase Mittens.

What we've just looked at is a specific example of reliability and validity but it is important to understand that reliability and validity permeate all information collected.

Consider the example of a company collecting sales information regularly in order to monitor the trend in sales. Information like this is likely to be freely available from its sales department. However, the company must be sure that the basis for the collection of the information is the same time after time. In this way it can be sure that in compiling trends, it is comparing like with like. The information would then be reliable. An example of validity would be that often decision makers, a company's senior management, get involved in directing what information is collected. Validity could be an issue here if the decision makers have not properly specified what information they want or if those involved in the collection of the information have not properly understood what was required. Finally, an example of reliability and validity would be if a firm has employed a market research agency to seek information from the public on its behalf. In such a case, it must be sure that each person involved in the collection of the information is asking the right questions in the same way and so the information is both reliable and valid.

In conclusion, information can be reliable but not valid and vice versa. It is therefore critical that businesses give themselves the best chance to collect reliable and valid information by recognising the importance 'good' information plays in securing a successful customer orientation.

4.2 INFORMATION SOURCES

Information is a generic term covering the facts from which knowledge and understanding can be derived. In reality, it comes in a plethora of guises. We've seen examples not just in this chapter so far but in Chapter 3 also. There are many different types of information available both inside and outside an organisation. Information can also come in different forms from 'hard' numerical facts to more in-depth details about a subject. Information is also available at many levels; information can be found at an individual customer level and it can also be found at a general environmental level. However, in principle, information can be divided into two distinct sources: **secondary information** and **primary information**.

Secondary information

Secondary information is information that has already been collected, initially for a specific purpose, but which is later used for a purpose other than the original use. Another way of saying this is that secondary information is information that is already in existence.

Uses

It is inefficient (and sometimes ineffective) for an organisation to embark on the collection of primary information without first considering the extent to which secondary information can satisfy its information needs. So secondary information has its uses:

- *Providing background information.* Secondary information can be used to help those involved in the information collection process by providing background information on unfamiliar areas. This might need to happen even before a problem has been properly recognised.
- *Problem definition.* It can help to define the organisation's problem or provide some exploratory information on a possible issue. In so doing, it can help the organisation to get beyond problem recognition and move towards specifying the purpose of information collection.
- *Aid the information plan design.* It can also aid the organisation in drawing up an information collection plan. With an evaluation of what appropriate secondary information is available, the organisation can then go on to identify areas for closer (primary) examination.

Advantages

Secondary information is also useful for three key reasons:

- *It is quick to initiate.* Secondary information is information that is readily available. It has already been collected and comes in a variety of easy-to-use formats (e.g. databases, the Internet).

- *Collection and analysis can be completed quickly.* The collection (and subsequent analysis) of secondary information can be completed within a short space of time.
- *It is cost effective.* Since secondary information is already in existence, collection and analysis is cost effective and, compared with primary information, it is relatively inexpensive.

Disadvantages

However, there are some drawbacks:

- *Relevance.* Secondary information can lack relevance because it is often of a general nature or has been collected as another organisation's primary information. Thus it may not be applicable to the organisation's information need. The organisation will therefore be particularly interested in the validity of any secondary information collected.
- *Reliability.* Because secondary information has been collected by another organisation, a company cannot be absolutely sure that it does not contain inaccuracies and is, therefore, unreliable. It is important in this case to use well-recognised sources of secondary information and be sure of how and what information has been collected.

Sources

Secondary information sources are vast and diverse and Table 4.1 gives some useful sources.

Primary information

Primary information is 'new' information collected for a specific purpose although, interestingly, it is information that may later be used as secondary information. A business will use primary information to bridge any identified gaps in its knowledge. For example, it may want to gauge customer reaction to its latest television promotion or it may want to determine how the price of its products compares to competitors. It is unlikely that the company will be able to access existing (secondary) information to find this out so it must consider collecting some additional information of a more specific nature.

Uses

We have seen that there are times when secondary information alone cannot provide the organisation with the information that will help it to satisfy its information collection objectives, there remains an information gap. It is the role of primary information to bridge such gaps. Having studied the rationale for and uses of both secondary and primary information, can you distinguish between the two? Take a look at Dilemma 4.1.

Table 4.1 Sources of secondary data

Global sources		
Global Market Information Database	*http://www/euromonitor.com/gmid*	International consumer statistics and information
Reuters Business Insight	*http://www.reutersbusinesinsight.com*	Global market research reports on various sectors
World Advertising Research Center	*http://www.warc.com*	Demographic and economic information on a range of countries
EU sources		
from Eurostat, the EU's statistical office	*European Economy*	Economics trends in member states
	Panorama of EC Industry	Trends in 100+ product groups
These and other publications are available	*CRONOS*	Economic and social trends in member countries
from Euro-info Centres and	*REGIO*	Demographic database
European Documentation Centres	*COMEXT*	Intra-EU trade and extra-EU trade data
Online sources	*http://www.europages.com*	European business directory
	http://www.eiv.com	Country report and news
UK government sources		
from the Central Statistical Office	*Annual Abstract of Statistics*	
	Regional Trends	
Other European Government Statistics Offices:	*Social Trends*	
	Monthly Digest of Statistics	
INSEE (France)	*Census of Production*	Manufacturing industry statistics
Instituto National Estadistica (Spain)	*Census of Distribution*	Retail and wholesale statistics
Central Bureau voor de Statistiek (Netherlands)	*Business Monitor*	Product market information
	Digest of Tourist Statistics	Statistics on the tourism industry
	Guide to Official Statistics	A list of all available UK government publications
Online sources	*http://www.dti.gov.uk*	Overseas trade and market information
Chambers of Commerce and Trade Associations	*Chambers of Commerce*	Local information and business contacts
	Trade Associations	Specialist reports and/or libraries for members
Commercial publications		
Published by Dun & Bradstreet	*Dun's Europa*	Information on top European enterprises
	Who Owns Whom	Information on which companies own other companies and brand names
	Key British Enterprises	Top British enterprises; similar publications available country by country
	Datastar	Online database of international companies

Table 4.1 *continued*

Published by Euromonitor	*Retail Monitor International*	Monthly report on retail trends and statistics
	European Directory of Retailers and Wholesalers	Information on 3,000 distribution companies across Europe
	European Marketing Data and Statistics *International Marketing Data and Statistics* *World Marketing Data and Statistics* *Retail Trade International*	
	Consumer Europe	Statistics on 250 consumer products across Europe
	The Book of European Forecasts	Data on lifestyles and trends across Europe
	Market Research Europe	Monthly journal
	Market Research International	Monthly journal
Published by Mintel	*Mintel Market Intelligence*	Monthly market research reports on various consumer goods
	European Lifestyles	Data about consumers in EU countries
Published by NTC Publications	*European Marketing Pocket Book*	Data and statistics about European consumer markets
	Retail Pocket Book	Data and statistics on UK retail industry
	British Shopper	Data and statistics on UK consumer shopping habits
Published by Key Note Reports	*Market Sector Overviews*	Research reports on consumer goods
	Industry Trends and Forecasts	Research reports on industries
Published by Newman Books	*Directory of European Retailers*	Lists 4,000 retailers
Published by Graham and Trotmans	*The Major Companies of Europe*	Lists 8,000 companies
Published by Price Waterhouse	*Guide to European Companies*	
Published by ELC International	*Europe's 15,000 Largest Companies*	
Published by CBB Research	*Directory of European Industrial and Trade Associations*	
Published by Manor House Press	*Store Buyer International*	Lists 9,000 retail buyers
Other Useful Organisations	*Kompass* *Yellow Pages* *Economist Intelligence Unit* *Financial Times Management*	
Other online sources	*http://www.dis.strath.ac.uk*	Summary of sites with business information

Source: Adapted from Brassington and Pettitt (2003)

Dilemma 4.1

ChildAid

ChildAid is a non-profit-making organisation trying to raise funds for underprivileged children. Their campaign so far has not been as successful as they had hoped. As a consequence, they have recognised they have a problem and have decided that they want to improve the performance of their campaign. This has led them to state the following objectives.

First, they want to find out how many people regularly donate to a charity. Secondly, they want to find out what the population's attitude is towards ChildAid. Thirdly, they want to identify those within the population who regularly donate to charity and would be well disposed towards ChildAid. Fourthly, they want to look at the likely response of this group towards a marketing initiative promoting the charity via direct mail.

Consider each of the above objectives and decide which would require the collection and use of primary information and why?

Advantages

The main advantage of primary information is that it aims to collect specific information. This means that is it likely to be more valid than secondary information. In addition, because the company controls how it is collected, reliability is less of an issue.

Disadvantages

However, there are disadvantages associated with primary information. It is expensive to collect because the company bears the full cost of its collection. It can also be time-intensive – the process of actually collecting and analysing primary information can be a time-consuming, often laborious, task. Finally, depending on what primary information is required, the information collection plan can be quite complex.

Internal and external information

From what we've already explored in this chapter, it is evident that some of the information will be found in sources within a firm. Examples include sales figures, details about customer complaints, product costs, productivity rates and so on. However, not all information needs can be satisfied with information located within the confines of the company. Consequently, the company must also utilise external sources of information. Examples include government population statistics, market trend information and information on competitors.

Quantitative and qualitative information

We have seen that some information comes in the form of 'hard', numerical facts, for example, market share figures (often expressed as a percentage (%)), productivity rates (again numerically expressed as a rate/hour) and the number of customer complaints (a simple numerical count), but this is not the only form of information. Information can also come in the form of an in-depth appraisal of a subject. This form of information will contain few, if any, 'hard' scientific facts but is still seen as information. It will still help a business to acquire knowledge and understanding and, most importantly, it can help to 'put the flesh on the bones' of the 'hard' facts. Let's think a little more about this using an example.

As you will see later in the book (Chapter 11), not only must companies ensure that they are customer-oriented to acquire new customers, they also have to ensure they are customer-oriented throughout the time a customer continues to do business with them. Sometimes during this time, the company will not get things right and the customer will want to complain. In the first instance, the customer-oriented business will want to ensure that it has an appropriate complaints procedure. It is also likely that it will want to collect 'hard' factual information about complaints, such as how many complaints are received. However, it will also be important for it to get more detailed information about the complaints by, for example, finding out what the complaint is about and how well the company's complaints' procedure worked. This is more in-depth information and the company needs a combination of 'hard' factual and in-depth information in order to get the best possible view of what is happening.

We call the 'hard' factual information **quantitative information** and the more in-depth information **qualitative information**. Let's look at each in turn.

Quantitative information is 'hard' information. It is often numerically or statistically based. It is principally concerned with providing a count of the number of times something occurs rather than exploring why it happens.

Qualitative information allows the company to find out why a particular situation exists. Qualitative information is particularly useful when it wants to examine behaviour, motivations, attitudes and perceptions. It is information which aims to describe and explore something rather than simply count the number of times it happens.

We return to the subject of quantitative and qualitative information later but before we leave this topic, take a look at Spotlight 4.3.

What we've seen in this section is that information can come from secondary or primary sources, it can also be found within or outside a firm and, finally, it can provide 'hard' facts or more in-depth details. Now what would be useful at this stage would be for the company to have some way of seeing how all of this fits into its ambitions of creating a continuous system of information collection, analysis and dissemination – the CIS. The next section seeks to do this.

Customer information systems revisited

Reconsider the customer information system we first outlined on page 82 and now revisit in Figure 4.2. We can see that in each of the information collection boxes (stages 1 and 2), the information can be collected using secondary and primary information sources and using a combination of quantitative and qualitative forms of information.

Spotlight 4.3

Qualitative and quantitative information

The table below takes two specific, randomly selected, issues, the geographical location of the population in the UK and awareness of an organisation's recent TV promotion.

The table has three columns, the first covering the issue, the second covering the type of quantitative information which could be acquired to resolve the issue and, finally, a third column which shows the type of qualitative information which could be acquired to resolve the issue.

Issue	Quantitative information	Qualitative information
Geographical location of population in UK	Breakdown of population by region by % from government statistics	Underlying reasons for population distribution such as industrial development, now and in the past
Awareness of an organisation's recent TV promotion	% of population aware of advertisement from journals such as *Marketing* magazine's Adwatch	Underlying reasons for awareness/unawareness such as the extent to which the advertisement has captured the attention of the target audience

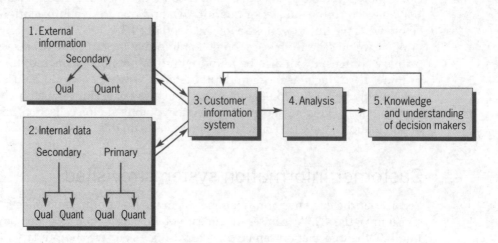

Figure 4.2 CIS revisited

4.3 THE PROCESS OF INFORMATION COLLECTION

If a company accepts that to achieve a sustainable competitive advantage it needs to be more customer-oriented than its peers, if it also agrees that this can be best delivered by having, and acting upon, a better knowledge and understanding of the customer through a continuous system of information collection, then this begs the question of not what the system looks like (because we've explored this when we looked at the CIS) but how such a system is operationalised. What is the process behind such a system? How does a company set about this task and, more importantly, how can it be sure that the information need it has identified at the outset is satisfied at the conclusion of the process?

Take a look at Figure 4.3. What we can see is a process that starts with an articulation of the information need and ends with an evaluation of the extent to which the need is satisfied. What lies in between are a number of stages aimed at achieving this. This process can also be called the research process.

It is probably worth pointing out that this process runs alongside stages 1, 2 and 3 of the CIS, when the organisation is involved in collecting and collating information. Given this fact, it is likely that the marketers involved in the CIS will also 'own' the information collection process. Let's now look at each stage of the process in turn.

Problem recognition

This is the first but perhaps the most critical stage of the process. It is vital that the organisation is open enough to recognise problems (or issues for investigation) in the first instance since this will facilitate its quest for customer orientation through sustainable competitive advantage – remember what we said at the outset of this chapter about proactivity versus reactivity. However, this stage is also vital for

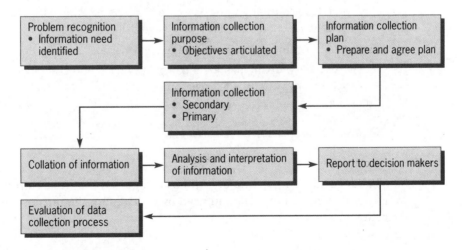

Figure 4.3 Information collection process

another reason. In recognising a problem, the company starts to identify an information need. It is only when it has identified this need that it can begin the process of collecting, and then analysing, information that will help to resolve its problems.

There are many types of problem that businesses can encounter and identify, but principally they can be classified by the extent to which they are investigative or resolutionary, although in practice some problems will be a combination of the two. This notion is explored in more detail in Dilemma 4.2.

Dilemma 4.2

Types of problem

Organisations may be aware of problems that they want to find a solution for. In this case, the information collection will be focused on *providing solutions* to the problems. Examples here include information that is concerned with looking at the behaviours, motivations, attitudes and perceptions of consumers so that the organisation can establish a basis for segmenting the market. It can also include information that will help the business to gauge the reaction of customers to a product or pricing change.

However, there are times when it will seek information in order to identify the nature of a problem. In this case, the information collection will be focused on *providing an outline of the problem*. Examples here include information that will explore the opportunities in a market or help the business to better understand why it is achieving a particular level of market share.

Take a look at the following scenarios and ask yourself whether the information collection is focused on providing (a) a solution or (b) an outline of the problem or (c) both.

Scenario 1: A company undertaking a process of information collection to establish the reaction of customers to advertising.

Scenario 2: A company trying to find out why its sales are at a particular level.

Scenario 3: A company has identified that of all of the complaints it receives, the vast majority are about delivery delays. It wants to correct this but first it must find out more.

So what does the company do after it has recognised that it has a problem? Well it translates this into an information need by articulating the purpose of information collection.

Information collection purpose

Once the business has identified a problem, it has accepted that it has a need for information. However, if the information collected is to be valid, then a clear and precise statement of the purpose of the information collection must be made. The business must seek to ensure that there is significant cohesion between the problem and the purpose for collecting information by articulating a clear set of objectives. Before we summarise the purpose of doing this, let's have a look at what we mean by an objective.

An objective is an aim or goal. What the business is trying to do is to say what information the process aims to collect. For example, if the problem identified is that the level of satisfaction with its customer service is decreasing, an objective of the information collection might be to 'establish why customer satisfaction is decreasing'. However, some other objectives might be to 'explore areas of customer service where customers are satisfied and dissatisfied' and to 'identify areas where customer service can be improved'.

To summarise, the reasons why companies must clearly state the purpose of information collection are two-fold: first, by articulating objectives it will give focus to the information collection plan, and secondly, associated with this, the information collected will be valid. Having done this, the firm can start to consider how it actually collects the information specified.

Information collection plan

The information collection plan contains the details of not just the objectives of the information collection process but also how the business aims to achieve them. Given that the marketing department is 'owner' of the CIS and information collection process, it will probably be the originator of the plan.

In terms of detail, the plan will document the background to the problem and from this state the purpose of the information collection and precise objectives. It will then detail what methods will be used in the collection of information and, subsequently, what type of analysis will be undertaken. Remember this is where information and knowledge become understanding. It is also likely to detail the costs of collecting the information and how long it will take, including stating when the analysis will be presented to decision makers.

Having documented the details of the process within a plan, the next stage is to actually collect information.

Information collection

It would be ridiculous for a company to gather via primary means all of the information it requires. This would be time-consuming, costly and totally unnecessary. Before even considering what primary information it needs to collect, it must look to identify what specific objectives can be satisfied by accessing information already in existence, that is, how secondary information can help the organisation resolve its problems.

Once the secondary information has been collected and some objectives achieved, the company is then in a position to identify the focus for the primary information collection.

Methods and tools

Figure 4.4 shows the methods and tools that can be used in the collection of primary information. The first decision to be made is whether quantitative or qualitative information (or even both) is required. Review what is meant by quantitative and qualitative information (page 91) before reading on if you need to remind yourself of the distinction between the two.

If quantitative information is required the organisation can choose to collect it via several methods. Each has its strengths and the final choice of method will depend not only on the nature and scale of the information required but also on how much time and money the organisation has to spend on the collection process. We will look at the range of methods now. The methods have been grouped according to their likely use:

- Methods that enable the company to collect information from individuals (commonly called **respondents**) on specific topics at a distance. The methods here are *by computer (via email)*, by *mail* or *by telephone*. These methods provide a relatively cost-effective and efficient means of collecting information – they are cheap and quick. They are particularly useful if the information being collected is not too extensive and the company has ready access to potential respondents.
- Methods that collect information from individuals by gathering it *in the street* or in an individual's *home*. These methods will involve a researcher directly asking

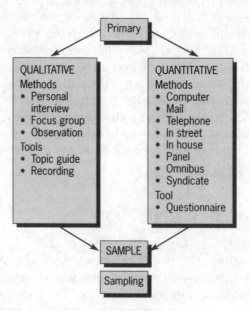

Figure 4.4 Primary information

an individual a series of questions about a particular topic. While these methods are more time-consuming and costly, they enable the firm to explore areas in more detail. Conducting the information collection in locations where there will be a high penetration of the individuals sought can contain costs a little.

- Methods that involve a company getting together with other companies to undertake a joint process of information collection, for example by research *panel*, *omnibus* or *syndicate*. Often the information is collected periodically so the information flow is continuous. These methods can provide a cost-effective method of acquiring information since costs are shared with other organisations. In addition, because the information provided is continuous, it is a quick method once the process has been set up. However, because a number of organisations get together to set up these methods, sometimes the extent of the information that can be collected is limited.

So far we have looked at the variety of methods for collecting quantitative information but have said nothing about the tool used. Well in each and every case, the tool is the **questionnaire**. While there are some standard questions to be found on every questionnaire (such as those about age, gender, income), the length and composition of each one will be dependent upon the method and that in turn depends upon the objective of the information collection process. Individuals are much more likely to respond to a short questionnaire on the telephone. We can't imagine anyone answering questions on the telephone for an hour but we can imagine them answering questions on the telephone for 15 minutes. Conversely, if someone was to be stopped in the street it is likely that they would be prepared to answer questions for longer than they would on the telephone.

If qualitative information is required, then the choice of methods for information collection are by **personal interview**, by **focus group** or by **observation**. We will now look at each one in turn.

The personal interview method involves a **moderator** (this is someone who has experience of collecting information – usually a trained researcher) sitting with an individual and leading them through a particular topic area via a series of predetermined prompts (these prompts are the tool). Often personal interviews are used when the topic is of a sensitive nature or the interviewee is more likely to discuss the topic if the discussion takes place on a one-to-one basis.

The focus group method involves a moderator sitting with a group of between four and seven people and encouraging them to talk about a particular topic by leading them through a **topic guide** (i.e. the tool). The moderator will be involved in controlling the progress of the discussion so that the discussion has validity and everyone in the group has an opportunity to get involved. Focus groups are now quite commonplace and are used, for example, in new product development and to test promotional techniques.

The observation method involves the researcher observing a subject in a particular situation at a particular point in time. The tool in this case is probably a video or tape recording of the situation. The subject is unaware of the observation. This type of method can be used to examine the behaviour of staff during the purchase transaction (here it is called mystery shopping) or the behaviour of consumers in the retail setting.

So we can see that although there are three different methods of obtaining quali-tative information, each has its own strengths. A business will choose the most appropriate method given the nature and scale of the information required.

This section has looked at the different methods and tools for collecting informa-tion. We have seen that the nature and scale of the information sought has a bearing on the method chosen. We have also introduced the term 'respondent', meaning the person whose views the organisation is seeking. These are the people who, the organisation feels, can provide some of the information it requires and who also influence the method chosen. The next section will look at how the organisation chooses respondents so that it gets the information it requires.

Sampling

We have already talked about the fact that primary research is undertaken with respondents. These respondents may be individual consumers, employees or repre-sentatives of businesses, charities etc., anyone really whom the organisation feels can provide it with the information it requires. Respondents are selected because it is their opinions that matter to the company.

Collectively, respondents are referred to as a sample. A sample will be a subset of a population that the company is interested in. Let's think this through. If a com-pany wanted to find out what the UK population thought about its latest TV advertisement, it could ask each and every member of the 58 million or so people that constitute the population. However, this would be extremely costly, time-con-suming and unnecessary. If it chose a smaller subset of the population that was representative of the whole population (perhaps in terms of age, gender and social class), then the same question could be asked of the subset and the response would be representative of the whole population. Look at Spotlight 4.4.

In summary, **sampling** enables a company to collect the information it requires in a cost-effective and efficient manner. Once the information has been collected, either by secondary or primary means, one could believe that the task is complete. However, right at the outset, we talked about how information in itself, while useful, does not help the organisation. It is the overlaying of analysis that adds meaning by converting information into knowledge and understanding. This is the next stage of the process.

Collation, analysis and interpretation of information

At this stage, it is beneficial to return to a point made at the outset of this section and that is how the CIS and information collection process are integrated. We can see this by examining how stages 3, 4 and 5 in Figure 4.2 merge with this stage of the information collection process where the focus is on collation, analysis and interpretation. The company will also want to assure itself at this stage that the information is reliable, that it can be trusted, has validity and really has provided the information intended.

In addition, the company will be involved in taking all the facts and in-depth detail it has collected and converting it into knowledge and understanding through

Spotlight 4.4

Stationery Express

Stationery Express Limited is a firm that has provided a wide range of stationery to offices in its locality for many years. It has remained a small company but has been reasonably successful. Brian Mason, the managing director, has become aware of the increasing use of technology in business: his bank now offers online banking, his daughters regularly order books and CDs over the Internet and his wife is a keen advocate of grocery shopping over the Internet.

Recently, Brian helped to staff his company's stand at a regional trade fair. He was pleasantly surprised by how many people wanted to take his catalogues but was quite alarmed by how often he was asked if orders could be placed online. He came back from the show quite committed to the idea of introducing online ordering. However, his marketing manager, Anita Overton, has suggested that they find out what potential there is to improve sales by offering this facility before embarking on the development. Together Brian and Anita have decided that primary information is needed from both existing customers and non-customers. However, there are many offices locally and they feel that the cost of undertaking research among all of them would be prohibitive. Anita has also advised that it is probably not necessary. She has suggested that they approach the local Chamber of Commerce for a list of offices in the area. Anita feels that they should then mark up the list according to whether the office currently does business with Stationery Express or not. She says that then they can take a sample of each, say every fifth business on each list. This she feels will help them to find out what potential there is to improve sales by introducing online ordering without putting too great a financial and resource burden on the organisation.

analysis and interpretation. Initially, this means returning to the problems and objectives articulated at the outset of the process. How do all of the strands of information contribute towards providing a complete picture of the problem or its resolution? Indeed, do all the strands of information come together to achieve this? It also means producing something for decision makers that is not a rambling and lengthy description of the information but an interpretation of the information within the context of the problem identified. To achieve this, analysis of the information needs to take place and, typically, this will involve an analysis of the market, the competitors operating within it and, critically, the customers.

Market analysis

Before a company can do any kind of market analysis, it must decide what market it is in. For example, there is no such thing as the pub market; rather, pubs are players within the entertainment or leisure market, as are cinemas, computer games and bowling alleys. You will find a further, more detailed, discussion about this in Chapter 3.

Once the organisation has decided what market it is in, at the very least, it will want to collect some basic information. For example, it will want to analyse the market in terms of its size – what is the scale in volume and value terms. In addition, the company will want to know what trend the market is demonstrating – is it growing, declining or just stagnating? Growing markets are attractive, declining markets are not and, like stagnating markets, can be both challenging and threatening.

Having analysed the market and gained a broad view of what is happening, discovering more about the players within it is critical.

Competitor analysis

Organisations do not operate in isolation and, inevitably, their fortunes are affected by the behaviour and capabilities of their competitors. At the very least, it is against these competitors that consumers make comparisons that eventually lead them to choose which organisation to patronise. It is therefore important for a business to have knowledge of and understand its competitors.

First, the company needs to understand who its competitors are. We have already had an outline discussion of this in Chapter 3 but, to recap, there are several levels of competition. The first level is that an organisation has competitors who offer a similar product to the same market. The second level is those competitors who operate in the same product category. These are the competitors who satisfy the same need. Finally, the third level is those competitors who are competing for the same spending power. Only when a company has analysed its competitors at these three levels will it really know who its competitors are.

Once it has a view of its competitors, the finer details become the focus. Some of the issues we are about to consider have already been covered in more detail in Chapter 3 so we will simply recap. First, the organisation will want to evaluate the state of the competitive environment. The competitive environment is influenced by a number of factors, for example, the number and strength of competitors, including new entrants, within it, and the business will need to establish an overall understanding of what is happening in the competitive environment. Secondly, having found out who its competitors are and how well they are performing, it will want to get a view on how these competitors see their future, that is, what their strategies are. It is not just important to know the current situation of competitors but also what their plans are for the future since the business will have, at some time, to deal with the ramifications of these.

Proactive organisations, organisations that are customer-oriented and want to achieve sustainable competitive advantage, will collect this information on a continuous basis. The organisation will need to establish another continuous information gathering and analysing system running in conjunction with the CIS. Such a system will involve selecting three or four key competitors (in the light of what we have said at the beginning of this section about levels of competition) and then considering what information is needed both internally and externally. Resources need to be committed to undertake the task of information collection and to formalise the procedures for information collation. Once this has been done, through a series of regular information returns, the business can use the CIS to pass the analysis through to decision makers.

This seems to make sense but where would an organisation find information on its competitors? Refer back to Table 4.1 on page 88 for some ideas of where to find competitor information.

Now having looked at the types of analysis a company might perform on its market and competitors, we will turn our attention to the analysis of customer information.

Customer analysis

The level of knowledge and understanding a customer-oriented organisation will want to achieve is infinite; it can never know too much about its customers and it can never understand its customers too much because, at the very least, customers are constantly changing their attitudes, behaviours, motivations and perceptions. The nature of customer behaviour will be examined in detail in Chapter 5.

In this final section, we will look at a single, yet quite critical, piece of analysis. The reason for choosing this piece of analysis is that it probably underpins everything the customer-oriented company does. If a company believes that the customer is the focal point of its activities, then it is vital that the company knows what it must do not only to satisfy customers but to delight them and ensure loyalty. Only then can it set about the task of creating a sustainable competitive advantage. Take a look at Spotlight 4.5.

Report to decision makers

In terms of the practical implications, the reporting of the information to decision makers can be in written or verbal form or both. Decision makers will be interested to hear a reaffirmation of the background to the problem and the subsequent information collection plan as well as the findings. In short, they will want to hear or see an eloquent summary of what has happened and why. In addition, they will be interested in how those who have been so involved in the collection, collation and analysis of the information see the problem and its possible resolution now. What do they recommend the organisation does?

Evaluation of information collection process

No process would be complete without some means of closing the loop and the information collection process is no exception. It will come as little surprise, given the emphasis on a continuous system of information gathering and processing, that there will be some evaluation of the information collection process itself. The business will be interested in the areas where it has performed well and the areas where it hasn't. In the case of the former, it will want to preserve things that have gone well, maybe a particular team of staff have been effective or a particular information source has worked well. In the case of the latter, it may want to change how something has been done, say a particular piece of analysis has not worked as well as it could have or aspects of the information collected have been unreliable.

Spotlight 4.5

Key customer values analysis

The following analysis is designed to illustrate the use of **key customer values** (KCVs) in assessing an organisation's, and its competitors', strengths and weaknesses as perceived by customers against criteria that have a critical impact on customers' (and potential customers') purchasing decisions.

Step 1. Identify the KCVs of the organisation's customers (and potential customers). These are the absolutely essential things that, *from the customer's point of view*, any competitor must get right to succeed. It is increasingly likely that these will be mainly service-oriented issues rather than product-oriented issues. Let's take an example. Say customers have said speed of service, convenience of access, pleasant and helpful staff, size of product range and price are the critical things that a food retailer must get right.

Key Customer Values

1. Speed of service
2. Convenience of access
3. Pleasant and helpful staff
4. Size of product range
5. Price

Step 2. Attach a weighting to each KCV (Column A). This weighting should be based on what the customer says about their relative importance. The total of the weightings should add up to 10. Let's say the following weightings have been allocated by customers.

Key Customer Values	Weighting (A)
1. Speed of service	2
2. Convenience of access	3
3. Pleasant and helpful staff	1
4. Size of product range	3
5. Price	1
	10

Step 3. Collect more information that allows the organisation to score customers' perceptions of its performance in each KCV out of 10 (Column B). Once this has been done, multiply (A) by (B) to give (C). (C) shows how the organisation is performing, taking into account the importance customers place on each of the KCVs.

Spotlight 4.5 *continued*

Key Customer Values	(A)	(B)	(C) (A × B)
1. Speed of service	2	5	10
2. Convenience of access	3	4	12
3. Pleasant and helpful staff	1	8	8
4. Size of product range	3	3	9
5. Price	1	7	7
	10	33	46

We can see that the organisation has scored 33 (out of a possible 50) in column (B) but, more importantly, we can see that in column (C), it is not scoring well in the areas which are most important to customers – convenience of access and the size of the product range – but it is scoring well in other areas (price and staff) which matter less to the customer. So this particular food retailer needs to reconsider where it concentrates its energies if it is to improve how it is perceived by customers.

This is quite an interesting analysis for the organisation but it can become even more meaningful if step 3 of the analysis is repeated for each of its key competitors. Then, not only will the organisation have a view of how customers perceive it, but also, more importantly, how they perceive the organisation relative to its competitors. Then and only then can the organisation be sure that it has identified the factors that will create a sustainable competitive advantage and has assessed the extent to which it is achieving this.

SUMMARY

This chapter has looked at how and why organisations need to build information on their customers. It has shown that it is important to begin this process by collecting relevant, reliable and valid information. It has also presented the view that there are a variety of information sources and that organisations need to utilise appropriate information sources in order to answer their specific information needs. Finally, it has shown the part played by a continuous system of information collection and analysis in enabling the business to use information to build knowledge and understanding of the customer.

This chapter concludes Part One of the book, Identifying the Customer. The situational analysis has been done, we've gone through the rationale for organisations being customer-oriented, irrespective of the precise nature of the customer, and we've seen how organisations need to fit this within the context of their environment.

Before moving on to look at how businesses respond to such information by influencing the customer, it is time to reflect upon the nature of customer behaviour. Part Two of the book looks at Understanding the Customer.

Discussion questions

1   Suggest four uses of information.
2   Why are reliability and validity so important when considering information?
3   What are the relative advantages and disadvantages of secondary and primary information?
4   What is the difference between qualitative and quantitative information?
5   Describe the different types of research problem.

Case study 4.1   Males boost use of cosmetics in Europe

Growing use by men of skin care products, fragrances and other toiletries and a return to colour cosmetics by women have contributed to the biggest growth in sales for the European cosmetics industry since the beginning of the 1990s. Sales of cosmetics and toiletries reached €43.7 billion ($45 billion) in the European Union (EU) last year, 6.4% up on 1997, according to figures published by Colipa, the European industry body.

Country-by-country figures provide material for those fond of national stereotypes. The French, for example, are the highest spenders per capita, buying €140 of cosmetics and toiletries a year, compared with an EU average of €117. This puts them on a par with Americans and only slightly behind the Japanese, who are the highest spenders globally. French consumers spend a higher proportion than the average European on perfumes, cosmetics and skin care, but they spend less than average on hair care and general toiletries such as soap, shower gels and deodorants. UK consumers also spend more than average at €121 per head a year but tend to spend more on cosmetics and toiletries and less on perfumes and skin care. Germany is the biggest European cosmetics market, with sales of €9.7 billion, which puts it third globally behind the USA and Japan. However, Germans spend a lower proportion on fragrances and decorative cosmetics than average, and more on general toiletries. Bottom of the league table are Portugal and Greece, spending an average €71 and €83 a year, respectively, last year. Scandinavian countries also spend less than average in the Colipa figures, which exclude duty-free sales, a fact that is more important in these high direct tax countries than elsewhere.

EU per capita spending on perfumes, cosmetics, skin and hair care products and other toiletries mirrors growth in income and has reached the same level as that on bread, says Colipa. Most consumers now see such purchases as essential items in their weekly shopping. Make-up – an eighth of the total – produced the biggest growth last year, up 11.3%, as fashion moved away from colourless, natural products back to colour cosmetics. The biggest category is toiletries, with more than a quarter of the market; it rose 5.2% last year. Growth last year was the highest since the start of the decade, when the reunification of Germany boosted sales. It was similar to the increase in the US market, which is now worth slightly less than the combined EU total. Own-label sales remain stable but are now growing in a market driven by the innovation offered by branded products.

The market is dominated by large companies such as L'Oréal of France, Unilever, Procter & Gamble and Wella of Germany. But the European cosmetics industries also include about 2,500 small and medium-sized enterprises (see Figure 4.5).

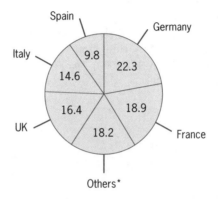

Figure 4.5   Market share of cosmetics and toiletries (%), 1998

Figure source: Colipa Statistics Task Force.
*The Netherlands, Belgium/Luxembourg, Austria, Sweden, Greece, Portugal, Denmark, Finland and Ireland.

Case study source: Adapted from John Willman (1999) Males boost use of cosmetics in Europe, *Financial Times*, 25 June, and in Levela Rickard and Kit Jackson (2000) *The Financial Times Marketing Casebook* (2nd edition). Harlow: Prentice Hall, pp. 31–2.

Questions

You are the marketing manager for one of the '2,500 small and medium-sized enterprises' operating within the European toiletries market. You currently specialise in the skin care element of the market that is not as popular in the UK as other elements of the market. Your organisation's aim is to improve the popularity of your skin care products within the EU. Although the case study offers some secondary information on the market, you need a more detailed picture of what is happening before you decide on your course of action.

1 What is your opinion of the market? Use the frameworks within Chapter 3 to review the secondary information given in the case.

2 Consider what primary information is required to give you a more detailed picture of what is happening.

3 Draw up a plan to show how you will collect the primary information.

Further reading

Chisnall, P.M. (1991) *The Essence of Marketing Research*. Harlow: Prentice Hall.

Crimp, M. and Wright, L.T. (1995) *The Marketing Research Process* (4th edition). Harlow: Prentice Hall.

Proctor, A. (2000) *Essentials of Marketing Research* (2nd edition). Harlow: Prentice Hall.

Malhotra, N.K. and Birks, D.F. (1999) *Marketing Research: An Applied Approach*. Harlow: Prentice Hall.

References

Brassington, F. and Pettitt, S. (2003) *Principles of Marketing* (3rd edition). Harlow: Financial Times/Prentice Hall.

Dibb, S., Simpkin, L., Pride, W.M. and Ferrell, O.C. (2001) *Marketing Concepts and Strategies* (4th edition). Boston, MA: Houghton Mifflin.

Rickard, L. and Jackson, K. (2000) *The Financial Times Marketing Casebook* (2nd edition). Harlow: Prentice Hall.

Understanding the customer

Within this section of the book we build upon the material presented in the first four chapters by focusing on ways in which organisations, having identified potential customers, can begin to understand the behaviour of their customers. We begin, in Chapter 5, with a discussion of the importance of understanding the behaviour of customers so that customers can be effectively managed. We go on to examine the process of decision-making and the factors that can influence the process. Following this we discuss the individual factors that influence customer behaviour.

Chapter 6 discusses how organisations can group customers together meaningfully. We examine the bases upon which customers can be grouped and the uses to which the results can be put. We also develop the argument that all methods of grouping are not of equal value. We then turn, in Chapter 7, to an examination of what the customer is looking for in term of products and services. We discuss product development and expand the concept of customer focus. The importance of branding, from a customer's perspective, is also developed.

This leads logically to an examination, in Chapter 8, of the importance of the delivery of quality to the customer. We stress the significance of understanding the quality factors that are important to the customer and examine methods to deliver this to the customer effectively. Ethics are also examined in some detail, together with arguments regarding the consequences for organisations that fail to deliver quality to customers.

5

Why organisations need to understand customer behaviour

Peter Lancaster

LEARNING OUTCOMES

After reading this chapter you should be able to:

■ Evaluate the scope and importance of customer behaviour to business organisations

■ Understand how customers make buying decisions

■ Assess the individual influences on customer behaviour

■ Appreciate how organisations use this knowledge to influence customers

KEY WORDS

Affective component	High/low involvement
Classical conditioning	Information search
Cognitive component	Instrumental conditioning
Cognitive school	Motivation
Connative component	Need/drive/want
Connectionist school	Post-purchase processes
Cues	Problem recognition
Decision-making process	Reinforcement
Emotional motives	Utilitarian motives
Gestalts	

INTRODUCTION

In the previous section we examined how to identify customers and how to collect information on customers. Now, in this section, we turn our attention to how to better understand customers in terms of why they behave as they do, how to group customers, and to understand what customers are looking for and how they perceive quality and services.

We begin this exploration by examining the factors that explain why customers behave as they do. In doing this, we first examine the importance of this understanding to business organisations, and then go on to look at how customers make buying decisions. We are then in a position to consider the factors, both environmental and individual, that affect that behaviour.

5.1 THE SCOPE AND IMPORTANCE OF CUSTOMER BEHAVIOUR TO BUSINESS ORGANISATIONS

The study of how and why customers behave as they do began when business organisations realised that customers do not always act or react as companies would like, or as theory suggested they would. Despite a sometimes, 'me too' approach to fads or fashions, customers often rebelled at using identical products that they felt everyone else used. Often they preferred products with a little more individuality that maybe reflected their own personality, special needs or lifestyle. This was, to a lesser degree, due to more similarity in needs, reflected among industrial customers. Here they also exhibited different preferences and less predictable purchasing behaviour. Of course, other factors contributed to this increased interest in customer behaviour, such as the increased rate of new product development, the rise of the consumer movement, increased environmental concerns and the opening up of international markets.

However, the field of customer behaviour is firmly rooted in marketing strategy that evolved in the 1950s when some companies began to realise that they could sell more goods, more easily, if they produced those goods that customers really wanted, rather than trying to sell goods that the firm had already produced. Hence customer needs and wants became the firm's primary concern and came to be known as the *marketing concept*.

The key assumptions underlying the marketing concept are that, in order to be successful, a company must determine the needs and wants of specific target groups of customers and deliver the desired satisfactions better than its competitors. In other words, the marketing concept focuses on the needs of the customer. Widespread adoption of this concept provided the impetus for the study of customer behaviour.

The study of *customer behaviour* focuses on how individuals make decisions to spend their available resources (time, money and effort) on consumption-related items. This includes what they buy, why they buy it, when they buy it, where they buy it, how often they buy it, and how often they use it.

For example, consider a simple product like a home telephone answering machine. Customer researchers want to know what kinds of customer buy answering machines for home use. What features do they look for? What benefits do they seek? How likely are they to replace their old model when new models with added features become available? Answers to these questions can provide the manufacturer with important information for design modification, product scheduling and promotional strategy. In addition, researchers are also interested in how individuals dispose of their once-new products. They are interested in this because companies must match their production to the rate with which customers buy replacements.

The study of customer behaviour was a relatively new field in the 1960s and because it had no history or body of research in its own right theorists borrowed heavily from concepts developed in other scientific disciplines, such as psychology (the study of the individual), sociology (the study of groups), social psychology (the study of how an individual operates in a group), anthropology (the influence of society on the individual) and economics to form the basis for this new discipline. Early theory, based on economics, put forward the notion that customers acted rationally to maximise their satisfactions. Later research discovered that customers are just as likely to purchase impulsively, and to be influenced not only by family and friends, by advertising and role models, but also by mood, situation and emotion. All these factors combine to form a comprehensive model of behaviour that reflects all aspects of customer decision making.

The **decision-making process** can be viewed as three distinct but interlocking stages: the input stage, the process stage, and the output stage. These stages can be seen in the simplified model of customer decision making (Figure 5.1).

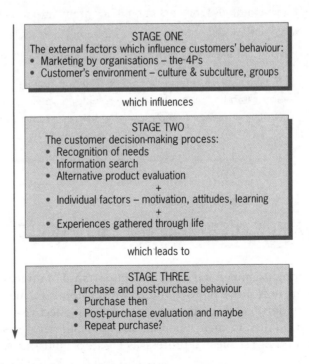

Figure 5.1   A simplified model of customer decision making

Stage one influences the customers' recognition of product need and consists of two major sources of influence: the company's strategy and the environmental influences. The cumulative impact of these two factors is likely to affect what customers purchase and how they use what they buy. Stage two focuses on how customers make decisions and how the psychological factors inherent in each individual affect the decision-making process. Stage three consists of interrelated post-decision activities: purchase, post-purchase evaluation and repeat purchase. However, repeat purchase is dependent upon the outcomes of the post-purchase evaluation. In turn these outcomes are fed back into experience, which will affect subsequent purchases. Hence we see the importance and the scope of customer behaviour to organisations. This importance can best be shown by an illustration of how one major company views this area (Spotlight 5.1).

Spotlight 5.1

Lever Bros approach to customer behaviour

Every week our researchers talk to more than 4,000 customers to ascertain:

- What they think of our products and competition.
- What they think of possible improvements to our products.
- How they use our products.
- What attitudes they hold about our products and our advertisements.
- What they feel about their roles in family and society.
- What are their hopes and dreams for themselves and their families.

Today as never before, we cannot take our business for granted, that's why understanding – and therefore learning to anticipate customer behaviour – is our key to planning and managing in an ever changing environment.

(Chief Executive, Lever Bros)

5.2 HOW CUSTOMERS MAKE BUYING DECISIONS

Having examined the scope and importance of understanding customer behaviour, let us now move on to examine how customers make buying decisions. This must be understood if companies are to develop effective strategies to deliver satisfaction and quality to their customers. The customer decision-making process can be viewed as a sequential process, as Figure 5.2 illustrates.

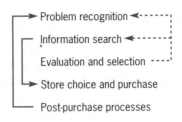

Figure 5.2 The customer decision-making process

Problem recognition

The initial stage in any decision-making process is **problem recognition**, which occurs when an individual senses a difference from what he or she perceives to be the ideal state of affairs compared to the actual state of affairs at any moment in time (see Spotlight 5.2). The most common cause of problem recognition is depletion in stock of goods, for example the weekly shop for groceries. Another common cause is disenchantment with goods due to evolving technology or changing fashions.

Spotlight 5.2

Influencing problem recognition

Take the example of high street banks. Part of their business comes from selling loans to customers. What concerns many people when thinking about loans is the interest rates, which determine how much the periodic repayments will be. So, if banks were to promote their product on the basis of interest rates alone, would they obtain as much business? The answer is probably no, they most certainly would not.

So what do they do? They stimulate problem recognition in the minds of customers by promoting the uses to which a loan could be put – a new car, a holiday, a home improvement. In fact they stimulate demand by getting people to recognise the difference between the desired state and the actual state and then giving them a way to rectify the situation. Once this has been achieved the product is almost certainly sold.

Information search

The next step is either an internal search into memory to determine whether enough is known about available options to allow a choice to be made without further **information search**. Should this not be the case, an external search of information sources, advertisement, the Internet etc. is required.

Alternative evaluation and selection

The prospective buyer will now examine the alternative products offered in terms of their attributes as compared with his or her own standards and specifications. In order to do this customers will use evaluative criteria – the standards and specifications used by customers to compare different products and brands. In other words, these criteria are the desired outcomes from purchase and are expressed in the form of preferred attributes. In turn, they are shaped and influenced by individual differences and environmental influences. In short, they become a product-specific manifestation of an individual's needs, values, lifestyle, attitudes and so on.

Store choice and purchase

Store choice is made in a similar manner to product evaluation. Purchase will often take place in some form of retail outlet, although there are many forms of in-home shopping which are growing rapidly. Often the customer will require contact with a highly skilled salesperson. This gives companies further opportunities to deliver a quality service to the customer. However, the point is that deliberation and evaluation is very often done before the customer comes to the counter.

Post-purchase processes

Due to a massive shift of emphasis, to customer satisfaction and retention, here it is important for companies to probe into the **post-purchase processes** of customers. The most significant question here is: Are customers' expectations being met? If expectations are met by performance, satisfaction is the outcome. A shortfall in this respect will not be met easily by customers, especially when the purchase has high perceived importance. The quality of post-sale service can therefore make a huge difference.

However, it is necessary to grasp that customer decision making is NOT a singular process, as Figure 5.2 seems to indicate. It is, in reality, based on two dimensions:

1. The extent of decision making necessary to select between alternatives. It is this dimension that distinguishes between decision making and habit.
2. The degree of 'involvement' in the purchase decision. It is this dimension that distinguishes between **high involvement**, where the purchase is important to the customer and is closely linked to the individual's self-image, makes a statement about the individual and involves some elements of risk (financial risk, social risk, safety risk or psychological risk), or **low involvement**, where the purchase is not very important, makes little or no personal statement about the customer and exhibits little or no elements of risk (see Spotlight 5.3).

These two-dimensional distinctions produce four types of decision process, which are illustrated in the Figure 5.3.

INVOLVEMENT DECISION MAKING	HIGH-INVOLVEMENT PURCHASE DECISION	LOW-INVOLVEMENT PURCHASE DECISION
Decision making Information search Alternative evaluation, etc.	**Complex decision making** Homes, cars, major appliances, etc.	**Variety seeking** Breakfast cereals, etc.
Habit No information search, one brand only	**Brand loyalty** Perfumes, cigarettes, etc.	**Inertia** Toilet tissue, paper towels, etc.

Figure 5.3 Types of customer decision-making process

Spotlight 5.3

Do high-involvement products have to be expensive?

Ask many customers to give you a description of a high-invoevment product and they will often begin wih a product that is expensive, such as a car or a new hi-fi system. This is simply because they very obviously appear to meet the criteria for high involvement, such as being personally meaningful, requiring an extensive search, etc. The problem is that they have overlooked other important criteria, such as purchase occasion, reason for purchase, etc.

Think about the last time you bought a birthday present for your mother or father. It probably didn't cost the earth, because your parents probably didn't expect it to. However, you probably gave it considerable thought, looked around a variety of shops and compared items before you made your final decision and purchase. This purchase also bears all the hallmarks of high involvement but was not particularly expensive. The moral of this tale is not to blindly assume that all high-involvement products will cost a lot of money.

Can you think of four or five other examples of high-involvement products that are not expensive?

Complex decision making

This introduces many of the key behavioural concepts relevant to the development of strategy, such as motivation, attitudes, learning, etc. Customers go through the full array of decision making before arriving at a decision of which product or brand to purchase.

Brand loyalty

The result of repeated satisfaction and therefore represents a strong commitment to a particular brand. It is not to be confused with inertia, where the emphasis is placed on 'can't be bothered to change'. Under brand loyalty there is a conscious move to buy the same brand time and time again.

Variety seeking

Boredom with a particular brand results in brand switching in order to alleviate that boredom. It is also linked to impulse purchasing where a customer impulsively tries out a new brand. It is not often linked with high-involvement products.

Inertia

This is buying the same brand repeatedly, simply because it is not worth the time and trouble to seek alternatives. However, companies are now attempting to increase the level of involvement in several of these product types, for example with the introduction of quilted, and even scented toilet tissue.

This concept of two-dimensional decision making can be shown diagrammatically (see Table 5.1).

Having examined how customers make buying decisions and also having examined in Chapter 3 the environmental influences on customers, we will now turn our attention to the individual factors that influence how customers behave as they do. In other words, those factors that are central to strategy development: **motivation**, learning and attitudes.

Table 5.1 Consumer decision processes for high- and low-involvement purchase decisions

	Low-involvement purchase decisions	*High-involvement purchase decisions*
Problem recogniton	Trivial to minor	Important and personally meaningful
Information search	Internal to limited external search	Extensive internal and external search
Alternative evaluation and selection	Few alternatives evaluated on few performance criteria	Many alternatives evaluated on many performance criteria
Store choice and purchase	One-stop shopping with substitution very likely	Multiple store visits with substitution less likely
Post-purchase processes	Simple evaluation of performance	Extensive performance evaluation, use and eventual disposal

5.3 MOTIVATION

Companies in Japan have recognised that what worked with young customers in the 1980s will certainly not work in the early twenty-first century. Research has shown that they 'don't like to be told', that they 'can make up their own mind'. Today's young customers put a big premium on individuality, rather than price tags or labels; they buy what they like, rather than the fads their 1980s predecessors snapped up. In fact, it can be argued that: 'You can't fool them. Instead you have to convince them – a tougher task in any market.' An interesting scenario, isn't it? It is a graphic illustration of what happens when companies fail to understand what motivates the customer. This section is to help keep you from joining the ranks of baffled companies who have only themselves to blame for their predicament.

People can be said to be motivated when their system is energised (aroused), made active, and behaviour is directed towards a desired goal. The company's challenge is to discover the primary motivating influences and to design strategies that both activate and satisfy felt needs. Companies that have managed this have prospered. This section explores some fundamental concepts and theories of motivation, beginning with a discussion of the dynamics of the motivation process and the central importance of need activation and satisfaction, moving ultimately to the primary implications for strategy formulation.

In the overview of the motivation process (Figure 5.4), you will notice that everything starts with need recognition (activation). A **need** is activated and felt when there is a sufficient discrepancy between a desired state and the actual state. As this discrepancy increases, the outcome is activation of a condition of arousal referred to as **drive**. The stronger the drive the greater the urgency of response. Alert companies do everything possible to provide products and services that are effective in reducing this state of arousal.

Over time, certain behaviour patterns are recognised as more effective than others for need satisfaction, and these come to function as **wants**. For example, you are walking through town with friends and suddenly you say, 'I'm peckish'. First, you perceive discomfort, you feel a need, that is recognised as hunger. This

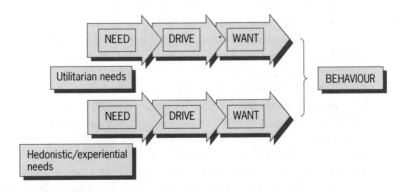

Figure 5.4 The motivation process

activated need leads to drive (arousal). A Mars Bar, your favourite snack, from the nearest shop is the thing you most want and you act accordingly.

Felt needs can be activated in different ways, either physiologically such as hunger or thirst, or sometimes purely by thinking about a person or object not present at that time. The thought process itself can be arousing. For example, we can feel thirst at times simply by thinking about our favourite beer. Or you feel a need for a new upgraded PC when you see advertisements for, say, Dell computers in the Sunday papers.

Figure 5.4 also illustrates that felt needs can be classified into two broad categories based on benefits expected through purchase and use. Utilitarian needs lead to consideration of objective and functional product attributes or benefits, for example processing speed or multi-tasking with a newer, more powerful PC, whereas hedonistic/experiential needs encompass subjective responses, pleasures and aesthetic considerations. These two types of need can function quite commonly together in purchase decisions. For example, a potential purchaser of a house in the country will look at such objective dimensions as number of rooms, size of rooms, number of bedrooms, etc. but will also include hedonistic benefits such as view, prestige of a good address, pleasure of sitting in the garden, etc. Any alternative evaluation becomes more holistic, focusing on the overall offering rather than on specific features.

Nothing presented so far should come as any great surprise, as all of us are aware that we are motivated by both objective and subjective considerations. However, a reading of much of the literature in this field from the 1960s to the early 1980s would have led you to the conclusion that customers were influenced by purely objective factors. This was a reaction to the excesses of the Freudian period. Fortunately, common sense prevails today and we have returned to the much more balanced perspective that customers are motivated by both **utilitarian** and **emotional motives** (see Copeland, 1924: Chapters 6 and 7).

You will recall from a discussion earlier in the chapter that the concept of involvement is of major significance in understanding customer behaviour. Dependent upon the extent that involvement is present, customers can be said to be motivated to act deliberately in order to minimise risks and maximise benefits gained from the purchase and usage of the product. Thus involvement is a reflection of strong motivation in the form of the highly perceived personal relevance of a product or service in a particular setting, and falls on to a continuum ranging from low to high. Involvement becomes activated when personal characteristics (needs, values) are presented with appropriate strategic stimuli within a given situation. The old adage applies here: 'You have a better chance of winning customers if you make them feel good.'

It is important at this stage to take a closer look at needs (sought benefits), and at how needs can be classified. Although theorists have been classifying needs for nearly 100 years, and have developed some lengthy and complex lists, perhaps the only contribution that has stood the test of time is the offering from Abraham Maslow (1954). Maslow purported that needs are organised in such a way as to establish priorities or hierarchies of importance among them (known as prepotency) (see Figure 5.5). He argued that each higher need in the hierarchy is presumed to be dormant until lower order needs have been satisfied (see also Katona, 1960).

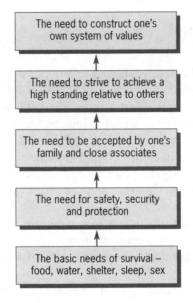

Figure 5.5 A hierachy of needs

Few theorists today would legitimately accept that lower order needs cease to function once they have been fulfilled, as Maslow originally implied. Actions can be impelled by a variety, or combination, of needs across the hierarchy. Also there is great variation in hierarchies across different cultures. Thus Maslow's theory is a more helpful general principle rather than a determining rule of behaviour.

A major criticism of many companies today is that they manipulate unwary customers by inducing them to buy things that they do not need. In other words, they create needs. I would rebut this contention and state that needs are not created by companies. Rather, needs do exist, although they may lie dormant and largely unrecognised. Skilful marketing can stimulate a want or desire for a product or service, but this will not happen unless a need already exists. Companies will find new and innovative ways to satisfy needs. The market place is full of such examples (see Spotlight 5.4).

Spotlight 5.4

Home entertainment

This need has been around for many years. Rich medieval lords employed jesters and musicians, the Victorians played parlour games and piano. More recently we have radio, television, video recorders, Hi-Fi, DVD players, etc. None of these innovations has really created needs; they have simply taken an existing need and provided customers with newer ways of satisfying an age-old need.

5.4 LEARNING

Learning can be defined as a relatively permanent change in behaviour as a result of experience. However, behaviour is also used to refer to non-observable cognitive activity as well as to overt actions. Thus it is possible for learning to occur without any change in observable behaviour. Students learn during the course of their education but no changes to observable behaviour may be apparent. In addition, learning results in relatively permanent changes in behaviour. Having learnt to swim or ride a bicycle, you never forget how to even if years pass between practising the activities. Theoretical knowledge is stored and can easily be resurrected from memory.

The above definition stresses experience. However, much of early learning is dependent upon the degree of physical development necessary to practise the activity. Much of customer behaviour is related to experience – of products, brands and companies.

There are three main types of learned behaviour:

- *Physical behaviour.* This involves responding to the many situations people face in everyday life, such as walking, talking and interacting with others. People tend to learn certain physical behaviour through copying the behaviour of others.
- *Symbolic learning and problem solving.* People learn symbols in order to think and communicate. Marketers in companies make great use of such symbols. For example, the 'Marks & Spencer' label means quality and value for money to many people. The large yellow M of McDonald's represents a place to eat. The rearing horse of Ferrari means speed, prestige and power. I am sure you can think of many more.
- *Affective learning.* People learn to value certain elements in their environment and to dislike many more, which means that customers learn many of their wants as well as what products satisfy these needs. Also people's attitudes are influenced by learning, thus customers will learn favourable and unfavourable attitudes towards a company and its products. These attitudes will, in turn, affect the tendency to buy or not to buy certain brands.

Why is learning important in understanding why customers behave as they do?

- Develop an advertising campaign that discusses those product characteristics that will lead to the formulation of favourable attitudes towards the product.
- Send a free sample to selected households.
- Offer a rebate upon proof of purchase.
- Distribute coupons offering a price discount.
- Develop an advertising campaign that pairs the product with other stimuli that are favourably evaluated by the target market.

What the above strategies have in common is that they are all designed to influence purchase behaviour among the target market. However, more importantly, they are all based on learning theory. Thus, an understanding of how customers learn is integral to the development of strategies.

Principle elements of learning

Learning has four main elements:

1. *Motives.* As was noted in the previous section, it is the motive that arouses individuals and thereby increases their readiness to respond. This arousal is essential as it activates the energy necessary to engage in learning activity. However, any success in achieving the motivating goal tends to reduce arousal. This is a reinforcement, and will create a tendency for the same behaviour to occur again in a similar situation. Hence, this is why companies attempt to have their products or their names available when customers' motives are aroused – it is hoped that customers will learn a connection between the product and the motive. For example, Ambre Solaire suntan creams, or Wall's ice cream during the summer; Heinz and Campbell's soups shortly before winter.

2. *Cues.* **Cues** are a weak stimuli, insufficiently strong to arouse customers, but strong enough to give some direction to motivated activity. In this way it can influence the manner in which customers respond to a motive. The market place is packed full of cues, such as colours and promotions. Customers use these to help choose between the response options in a learning situation. For example, if we are hungry, we are guided by restaurant signs or aromas of food cooking, simply because we have learned that these stimuli are associated with food. In contrast, colour can appeal or repel. Butchers' shops very often use blue in their decor because it is recognised as a cold colour and is associated with freshness; they rarely, if ever, use green as it is associated with rot in terms of meat and would likely repel customers.

3. *Response.* This is the mental or physical activity customers make in reaction to a stimulus situation. Appropriate responses to particular situations are learned over time through experience in facing that situation. However, as was noted earlier, it is not always possible to observe the response, although it does not necessarily mean that learning has not taken place. For example, prior experience of a particular store has not been good, so you tend to ignore the store in the future. There is no observable behaviour; you just do not go in, you walk past. To an observer it looks as though you make no response, yet learning has taken place, leading you to choose not to shop there.

4. *Reinforcement.* Probably the most widely accepted view of **reinforcement** is anything that follows a response and increases the tendency for the response to reoccur in a similar situation. Companies can attempt to provide reinforcement by reducing motive arousal. They can achieve this by removing a negative reinforcer, for example headache remedies which stress fast relief are removing the negative reinforcer, an unpleasant headache. Or they can stress a positive reinforcer, for example Pizza Hut advertisements show a group of

friends sharing a pizza and having a good time. However, it is also possible to apply a negative reinforcer to help people to learn to avoid certain behaviour patterns, for example the anti-drink driving campaigns or the safe sex anti-HIV campaigns have used negative reinforcement. The drink driving campaign stresses the mayhem that can result and the sanctions imposed by society provide the negative reinforcement, while death is the ultimate negative reinforcer in the HIV campaign.

Reinforcement can also take place very subtly by implied reinforcement, for example the nod of approval during a campaign from someone other than the main protagonist. Hence customers may be encouraged to develop attitudes or patterns of behaviour towards products without them being aware that such changes are taking place.

Learning classified

Several theories have been put forward in order to explain different aspects of learning. It is possible to group these theories into major categories in order to offer some focus to the discussion. The major division is between the **connectionist school** of thought and the **cognitive school** of thought. The connectionists stress that what people learn is connections between stimuli and responses, which can be subdivided depending upon the type of conditioning employed. The cognitive school, on the other hand, argues that people learn by discovering patterns and insights (see Figure 5.6).

Connectionist theories

The connectionist school maintains that people learn by developing the connections between a stimulus and a response. Hence, the association between a stimulus and a response is the connection that is learned. Reinforcement can be seen as a crucial part in the process of understanding customers' learning behaviour. However, reinforcement is employed with two fundamentally different methods of learning connections, **classical conditioning** and **instrumental conditioning**. Let us now examine each one in more detail.

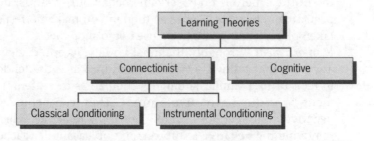

Figure 5.6 Schools of learning

Classical conditioning

Essentially, this method pairs one stimulus with another stimulus that already elicits a given response, over time, and with repetition the new stimulus will begin to elicit the same, or a very similar, response. This is illustrated by Pavlov's experiment (Figure 5.7). Evidence suggests that humans are capable of even further levels of conditioning.

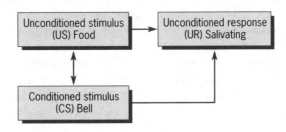

Figure 5.7 Pavlov's experiment

Instrumental conditioning

The method of instrumental conditioning (also referred to as operant conditioning) also involves learning connections between stimuli and response, but the process differs from classical conditioning in several important ways. Classical conditioning relies on an existing connection between stimulus and response, whereas instrumental conditioning requires the learner to discover an appropriate response, one that will be reinforced. This can be best illustrated with reference to the pioneering work of B.F. Skinner and his pigeons. The experiment is represented in Figure 5.8 and illustrated in Spotlight 5.5.

Instrumental conditioning is a common characteristic of customers. Customers often buy to try. Once they have found the product or brand they prefer (reinforcement), they buy time and again.

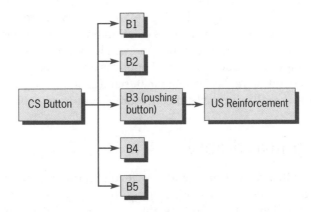

Figure 5.8 Skinner's experiment

Spotlight 5.5

One product versus another

Think about this the next time you visit the supermarket to do your food shopping. You decide to buy some tubs of yoghurt as desserts or snacks. There are several different brands available to you and the prices are very similar, so you decide to buy two of each brand rather than all the same brand. You justify this to yourself in that it makes sense to try the different brands but you only buy two of each because then if you don't like one brand, you haven't lost much. In effect, you are doing exactly the same as the pigeons in Skinner's experiment. You are learning by trial and error which brand or brands you like best. Tasting nice is the reinforcement, which will lead to repurchase in the future. Dislike is negative reinforcement which leads to you not buying again. Hence, like Skinner's pigeons, you have been conditioned.

Conditioning methods and their differences

Several differences are apparent between classical and instrumental conditioning:

- Classical conditioning is dependent on an already established response to another stimulus, while instrumental conditioning requires the learner to discover the appropriate response and as such involves the learner at a more conscious level than does classical conditioning.
- Classical conditioning is not dependent upon the learner's actions, but with instrumental conditioning a particular response can change the learner's situation. The response is instrumental in producing reinforcement, hence the name for this method of conditioning.

Because of these differences, each method is better suited to explaining different types of customer learning. Adapting to and attempting to control one's environment is better explained by instrumental conditioning due to the fact that it requires the learner to discover the correct response that will lead to reinforcement. Learning brand names or acquiring attitudes, tastes and opinions are probably much better explained by classical conditioning because the material learned in such cases can be associated with stimuli that already elicit either favourable or unfavouable experiences.

Cognitive theory

Rather than view learning as the development of connections between stimuli and responses, cognitive theorists stress the importance of the development of perception, problem solving and insight. They contend that much learning does not occur as a result of trial and error or practice but as a result of discovering meaningful patterns which enable customers to solve problems. These patterns are termed **gestalts**, and cognitive theorists rely heavily on the process of insight to explain the development of gestalts. A brief examination of the work of Wolfgang Kohler is useful to illustrate this view of how we learn.

An ape was placed in a cage with a box, and a bunch of bananas was hung from the top of the cage out of the ape's reach, even if the ape were to jump. After failing to reach the food, the problem was solved when the ape placed the box under the bananas, climbed on to the box and reached the bananas. Kohler suggests that this was not the result of trial and error but a result of thought and insight to solve the problem. The eureka situation with which we are all familiar.

Although in this case the ape did receive reinforcement in the form of food, reinforcement is not always as apparent in many cognitive learning situations. Do we get rewards when we solve that last clue to complete a difficult crossword puzzle? No, in this situation there is no tangible reinforcement. However, cognitive theorists suggest that the reinforcement comes from closure, the successful solution to a problem, and they argue that this concept of closure has significant reinforcing properties. An unsolved problem leads to tension and motivates a continued search for a solution. Solving the problem leads to closure. This reduces tension and, as such, is reinforcing.

Applying the learning concepts to why customers behave as they do

As we have demonstrated, cognitive theories stress problem solving and the learners' understanding of the situations facing them. This is not the blind behaviour as, perhaps, the learning of connections can be seen to be. These theories, then, can be applied to how customers learn which method of shopping, which shops and which products best suit their needs. It can take the form of learning about new products and their benefits, especially if they represent significant changes to previous products. It is linked to how customers see the problem and how to solve that problem.

Classical conditioning has already been shown to explain how customers acquire tastes and motives. Hence advertisers show their products in pleasant surroundings or otherwise positive settings. Here classical conditioning applies to the plan for repeated association of the product or brand with positive settings which will lead to customers developing a preference towards the brand.

Certain types of habitual behaviour can also be explained through classical conditioning. For example, many customers automatically purchase brands such as Heinz baked beans or Nescafé instant coffee because they have developed strong associations between the brand name and the generic product. This can be an advantage to companies who first develop a brand that dominates the market. For example, we often say hoover the carpet; perhaps in years to come we will say dyson the carpet. In other cases people still buy brands merely because their parents did. Many students coming away from home for the first time will buy brands their parents bought rather than giving any serious thought to their suitability for customers on a much lower income.

Instrumental conditioning is useful for understanding customer learning where the conscious choice results in positive or negative reinforcement. Favourable experiences resulting from the choice will lead to positive reinforcement of that particular choice. This is strong justification for the emphasis placed on satisfying customers.

Advertisements that depict satisfied customers can also result in learning a connection between a brand and favourable experiences. Other types of promotion, such as cash rebates, free samples, low introductory prices or trial periods, are forms of instrumental conditioning. The company's goal in these cases is to structure a situation so that customers are given a reward as a consequence of having performed an activity that is desired by the company, that is, having tried the product or new brand.

5.5 ATTITUDES

Earlier in the chapter we examined how companies can motivate customers and how customers learn. Now it is time to move on to what customers like and dislike. These likes and dislikes are called attitudes. They could also be referred to as an overall evaluation. These attitudes play a very important role in determining a company's and its products' standing among customers. They play an important part in shaping why customers behave as they do. Customers will invariably select the shop and products that are evaluated most favourably. Consequently, in attempting to understand why customers do or do not buy a particular product or brand or shop at a particular store, attitudes can be significant.

Attitudes can also be useful in judging the effectiveness of marketing activities. For example, in an advertising campaign designed to change customers' attitudes, if the advertisement failed to alter attitudes, it would need to be revised. Packing design is a further example. Establishing which pack design elicits the most favourable attitudes can prove useful in arriving at the final design. Thus an understanding of attitudes can be beneficial in many ways. Over the years studies of attitudes have yielded much valuable information upon which we can draw. However, this wealth of information would fill a complete textbook, let alone part of one chapter, hence we will restrict ourselves to an exploration of some of the fundamental issues that are relevant to attitudes.

What are attitudes?

- Attitudes are related to persons or objects that form part of an individual's environment.
- Attitudes form part of the way individuals perceive and react to their environment – they affect our perceptions of goals. In this sense attitudes are motivational.
- Attitudes are learned and are relatively enduring; they may change but usually gradually.
- Attitudes imply evaluation and feeling.

The components of attitudes

The traditional view is that attitudes have three components (the tricomponent model):

- The **cognitive component** – the knowledge component which is belief or disbelief.
- The **affective component** – the emotional component which embodies positive or negative feelings.
- The **connative component** – the behavioural tendency component which embodies a tendency for people to behave in a certain way (see Figure 5.9).

This model has a role to play in the marketing continuum which argues that customers move from unawareness through several stages to repurchase:

- The cognitive component is prevalent in the early stages of the continuum – unawareness, awareness and comprehension.
- The affective component is prevalent in the stages of conviction and preference.
- The connative component is prevalent in the stages of intent to buy, purchase, post-purchase evaluation and repurchase.

A more contemporary view of attitude components theorises that an attitude is best viewed as being distinct from its components, with each component being related to the attitude. Both the cognitive and affective components are seen as determinants of attitudes and are viewed together as feelings about the attitude object. Unlike the traditional view, the connative component is not seen as determinant of attitudes. Instead, the attitude is seen as determining the connative component. Thus customers' behavioural intentions will depend upon their attitudes. Consequently, customers' intentions to purchase a product should increase as their attitudes become more favourable (see Figure 5.10).

For products, attitudes will depend primarily on beliefs. For example, customers' attitudes towards a washing machine may be driven primarily by their perceptions or beliefs about how well it will perform or how easy it is to use, or other functional benefits. For other products, feelings may be the primary determinants of attitudes. For example, a rock concert or a football match are both valued for the feelings they evoke during consumption. It is also possible for both beliefs and feelings to influence attitudes. Take a car, for example. Beliefs about its reliability, residual value, fuel consumption, etc. will have a role to play in determining attitudes, but so will the feeling of being fun to drive and the prestige of ownership play their part.

Since behavioural intention lies closest to behaviour, this indicates that behavioural intention is expected to be more highly related to behaviour than attitudes,

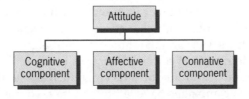

Figure 5.9 The traditional tricomponent model of attitudes

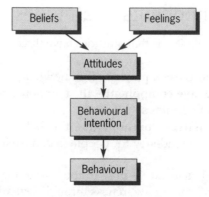

Figure 5.10   The contemporary view of attitude components

beliefs or feelings. For this reason, if one is interested in predicting behaviour, it is the behavioual intention that should be measured because it is likely to predict the most accurate results. Simply holding a favourable attitude will not guarantee behaviour. Antecedent factors, such as available funds, may prevent a purchase even when holding a favourable attitude. Many customers hold favourable attitudes towards Porsche cars, but not many can afford one. However, holding a favourable attitude at least gets the product into the consideration set of customers and, if all things come together, the customer may buy the product. However, the holding of an unfavourable attitude towards a product, or a company, will ensure that no purchase will be made. We will return to this later in the chapter.

The properties of attitudes

Attitudes exhibit several properties or dimensions:

1. *Valence*. This refers to whether the attitude is positive, negative or neutral. For example, a person may like Camay and Dove soaps, dislike Palmolive soap or be fairly indifferent to Imperial Leather soap.
2. *Extremity*. Attitudes can vary in their intensity of liking or disliking. In the example above, although the customer may hold positive attitudes towards both Camay and Dove soaps, he/she may be much more favourably predisposed to one brand or the other.
3. *Resistance*. This refers to the degree to which an attitude is resistant to change. Some attitudes are highly resistant to change while others are much easier to change. Manufacturers and retailers can find that some attitudes shift abruptly in line with whatever is 'trendy' at the time. Certain fads and fashions have fallen foul of abrupt changes in trends. Skateboards and hoola hoops are prime examples. Certain governmental campaigns have led to changes in attitudes to the detriment of certain industries (anti-smoking campaigns have led to a less favourable attitude towards cigarettes) and to the advantage of other industries (health campaigns have led to a more favourable attitude towards health foods, health clubs and exercise clothing). Businesses should therefore always seek to

keep track of customer attitudes as one way of anticipating potential changes in product demand and consumption behaviour.

4. *Persistence*. This reflects the idea that attitudes gradually erode as time passes. It therefore becomes important for businesses constantly to reinforce positive attitudes. Hence the constant advertising of well-supported products such as Oxo cubes, etc.

The functions of attitudes

Attitudes serve four major functions for individuals. These functions are the motivational bases of attitudes which help to shape and reinforce positive attitudes towards goal satisfying objects, and negative attitudes towards objects seen as goal threatening:

1. *Adjustment function*. This function directs people towards pleasurable or rewarding objects and away from undesirable and unpleasant ones. In other words, it serves the utilitarian function of maximising rewards and minimising punishment. For example, we are turned away from drinking and driving because of the punishment and unrewarding consequences of a driving ban, heavy fine, perhaps even injuring or killing a third party. However, similar attitudes hold for products or stores – some we see as maximising satisfaction and some as the opposite.

2. *Ego-defensive function*. Attitudes formed to defend our self-image from threats help to fulfil the ego-defensive function. Hence, customers form attitudes that they feel reflect their own self-image. Even when making poor purchase decisions they will often defend the decision by stating that it was the result of poor advice from a third party, perhaps a salesperson.

3. *Value-expressive function*. This function helps people to express their centrally held values. Hence, customers adopt certain attitudes in an effort to translate their values. Thus, a person who holds conservation as a centrally held value will often purchase only those products that are deemed environmentally friendly. Businesses should research values and design products and promotional campaigns to allow these self-expressions.

4. *Knowledge function*. People have a need for a structured and orderly world, and in pursuit of this they seek consistency, stability, definition and understanding. From this develop attitudes towards seeking knowledge. However, this need for knowledge can be quite specific, and as a result come attitudes about what we believe we need to know about and what we do not need to know about. For example, many first-year students have no intention of buying a house for several more years, and therefore are unlikely to seek information regarding property prices, etc.

It is perfectly possible for people to hold the same favourable attitude towards a product for very different reasons. For example, let us look at Chivas Regal, an expensive Scotch whisky:

1. It tastes nice – utilitarian reason.
2. It makes me feel good – value-expressive reason.
3. It makes me feel superior – ego-defensive reason.
4. I know that many people who drink this are successful – knowledge reason.

Also, attitudes tend to be clustered, which leads people to categorise people and objects, which leads to the forming of stereotypes and brand images.

Stereotyping is the human tendency to make oversimplifications about people and brands based on limited experience, for example, the woman driver, the foolish Irishman, etc. These are oversimplifications based on limited experience at best, some times on no experience at all. The same is true of brand stereotyping or the forming of brand images. Most people would say that Sony is a top brand in home electronics, and they produce top-of-the-range products. They are and do, but this attitude is an oversimplification based on limited knowledge. People are not making objective statements – brands stereotyped as inferior may have the same components as Sony and therefore are likely to be just as good. Also people do not always know of product failures that many reputable companies have had, and so their attitudes are oversimplified and stereotypical.

Attitudes and behaviour

It is often assumed that a customer holding a favourable attitude towards a company's product will lead to purchase behaviour. However, this is not always the case. While behaviour can follow from holding a particular attitude, it is by no means certain that it will. For example many of us hold favourable attitudes towards Ferrari or Porsche cars, but will never buy one due to lack of funds. This is the major problem in attempting to predict behaviour from attitudes held. Holding a favourable attitude is not the sole determining factor of behaviour, although it is an extremely important one. The products will remain in the consideration set of the customer and if all things come together, they may purchase.

Holding of an unfavourable attitude is a much more reliable predictor of behaviour. Customers who hold unfavourable attitudes towards a company's products are highly unlikely ever to buy these products. This shows why companies put such importance on creating favourable attitudes towards their products and brands (see Dilemma 5.1).

It is also true to say that behaviour can and does determine attitudes. A customer buys a new chocolate bar, on impulse, likes it, and so the behaviour has determined a favourable attitude that didn't previously exist. Thus the relationship between attitudes and behaviour can, and must, at best be seen as interactive (Figure 5.11).

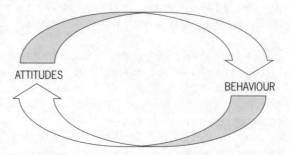

Figure 5.11 The interaction of attitudes and behaviour

Dilemma 5.1

Škoda cars

For many years the Škoda brand was the butt of comedians' jokes and viewed by some motorists as down market and poor quality. However, since the takeover by the VAG Group, Škoda simply has not put a foot wrong. Quality is now up to VAG standard and the Fabia range has won several awards from the motoring press. But still the ingrained attitudes of previous years tends to prevail, with some prospective customers still mistrusting the brand in terms of the image associated with it and its residual value upon disposal in part exchange.

Despite major advertising expenditure on television campaigns, Škoda has still not totally overcome the attitudinal problems it faces in respect of some of the motoring public.

How would you suggest Škoda attempts to overcome this problem?

However, certain variables exist that can help to establish the part played by attitudes in determining behaviour:

1. *The strength of the attitude.* The stronger the attitude the greater the extent to which it is likely to predict behaviour. A fanatical football supporter is much more likely to attempt to follow the team to as many games as possible, while a person with a passing interest in the team is likely to be content to sit and watch any games that are televised.
2. *The existence of other attitudes.* Stronger attitudes may inhibit or interfere with the behaviour tendency of weaker ones. You prefer Nescafé Gold Blend coffee, but don't mind Nescafé Original coffee. If Gold Blend is available you will choose that brand because the stronger attitude has won.

SUMMARY

In this chapter we have explained why customers behave as they do. Starting with an overview of why an understanding of this area is imperative to businesses, we looked at a simplified model of consumer behaviour in order to demonstrate the factors involved in an understanding of the subject area. However, having explored environmental factors in Chapter 3, the chapter concentrated on the individual factors of influence.

The chapter then went on to explain the individual buying model in terms of the processes that individuals progress through when making a purchase decision. We also explored levels of involvement in the buying process and explained the differences and some of the difficulties.

Next came motivation and an explanation of motives and the necessary factors to ensure that customers are motivated. This point is crucial to grasp if customers are to be attracted to a company's products. Learning theory was also explored and the different schools of learning were looked at in some detail. Business applications were also explored. Attitudes were defined and examined in order for a business to appreciate how to create favourable attitudes towards their products and activities.

Discussion questions

1   Will customer decision making follow the same process for all purchase decisions? Why or why not?

2   Can a case be made for the argument that all high involvement products are expensive? Fully argue the case.

3   Why is it important for manufacturers to achieve favourable attitudes towards the company and its products?

4   Can motivation be achieved through advertising? Present a balanced argument.

5   Describe and discuss the last time you were affected by some form of classical conditioning in your shopping behaviour.

6   Suggest ways in which organisations can use an understanding of customer behaviour to better satisfy their customers.

Case study 5.1   Tokai Guitars

The European market overview for electric guitars

The two biggest electric guitar markets in Europe are the UK and Germany; however, the UK market is the biggest single market in Europe with an estimated market size of £60 million per annum. The UK market has seen significant growth over the last 12 months with electric guitar sales reaching an all-time high. Suggestions for this growth are that older customers are coming back to something they did in their youth and significant growth has been seen in the play for pleasure market. A second factor is that electric guitars have never been cheaper in respect to income levels. It is possible now to buy an electric guitar manufactured in China for as little as £80. However, even the top-quality guitars such as Fender can be purchased for around the £700 price for an American-manufactured instrument. The top-priced guitars fall into the £2,500 price range for a brand new Gibson or Paul Reed Smith instrument.

These prices, when taken in respect of incomes today, represent a much lower proportion of annual income than the same guitars purchased by customers in the 1960s, when a Fender could have represented the equivalent of a full year's salary. There is, however, a significant collectors market for classic guitars and prices in this sector can be in excess of £50,000 for certain models. The market place contains a plethora of brands all fighting for a share of the market.

History of Tokai and birth of Tokai UK

Tokai was founded in 1947 in Hamamatsu, Japan, and produced all forms of musical instruments and had a large piano section. Tokai first appeared in the UK in the early 1980s, imported by a company called Bluesuede Music. At that time the two biggest names in electric guitars were those produced by the American companies Fender and Gibson, who both produced high-quality electric guitars but at a price that was prohibitive for the average amateur guitarist. Tokai took on Fender, with products that replicated the Fender quality and also closely resembled Fender guitars but for half the price. Not surprisingly, the Tokai product stood alone in the market place and competed with Fender by making quality instruments available to customers who couldn't afford a genuine Fender or Gibson guitar. Tokai's biggest seller at the time was the ST50, which resembled the famous Fender Stratocaster. However, Fender issued writs against Tokai which forced them to change the designs slightly so as not to infringe Fender's copyrights. Imports continued for a further three years and Bluesuede Music did remarkably well with the product, using sales agents out on the road selling guitars to retailers. Unfortunately, one of the partners in Bluesuede Music left, owing the company and Tokai money, and import supply ceased. Tokai guitars were then not really imported into the UK in any numbers for over 20 years.

At the beginning of 2002 Nick Crane, a British entrepreneur, went to Japan to see Mr Shohei Adachi, the managing director of Tokai, and agreed a deal to import the company's guitars once more into the UK. This started as a small operation and the products began to trickle into the UK. Shortly afterwards Nick Crane approached Bob Murdoch, who had 25 years' experience in the music wholesale and retail business. Bob Murdoch saw the potential to make a large company again and offered help in terms of both time and money. He became a partner in Tokai UK in early 2002. The company began by working from the garage of one of the partners, but over the subsequent 18 months turnover increased by 200% and Tokai UK now operates from premises on an industrial estate at Dinnington, South Yorkshire. Six months ago Nick Crane left the company, amicably, to follow other interests in Spain. Bob Murdoch bought out his partner and is now in overall control of Tokai UK and employs a staff of four people.

Objectives

Bob Murdoch's objectives for Tokai UK are:

- To expand the business each year over the next few years.
- To develop new guitar models with Tokai Japan.
- To expand the dealer network.
- To maintain and improve quality at a price that remains affordable to customers.
- To keep the business within a size so that it is not imperative to turnover £ multi-millions simply to pay overheads.

Tokai product range and policy

Tokai offer a wide range of electric guitars within their product portfolio, catering for every genre and playing style. Still within their range is the ST50, supplied in a single model, which was the top-selling model during the early 1980s venture into the UK. This is supported by the ATE55, supplied in two models plus a left-hand version. Both of these models are Fender-type guitars. However, today the Loverock model, in one of its many forms, has taken over as best-seller and currently out sells the ST50 by five to one. The Loverock is a Gibson Les Paul style guitar and is extremely popular among rock guitarists. Tokai UK supply this model in five variations plus a left-hand version.

Tokai also produce bass guitars and semi-acoustic electric guitars. The semi-acoustic ES model is produced in two model variants. An innovative guitar produced by Tokai is the Talbo aluminum-bodied guitar, which produces a quite unique sound, although perhaps this is a little ahead of its time and has not proved to be a best-seller in the European market. However, the Talbo is also supplied in a wooden version with a hollow maple body. The range consists of three aluminum-bodied instruments and two wooden-bodied instruments.

Tokai UK has also designed two new models of electric guitar that were both unveiled at the 2002 Frankfurt Music Exhibition: the Tsunami (Big Wave) and the Loverock 2, a double cutaway version of the standard Loverock. Response to the new models has been very good, especially towards the Loverock 2, with the next three months production of this model all being pre-sold.

Tokai UK are also working in conjunction with Trevor Wilkinson, of Wilkinson tremolos and guitar bridges, to produce new models and to strive to improve the quality of existing models. This demonstrates the company's commitment to design, innovation and quality. The custom shop in Japan also manufactures two semi-acoustic guitars: the ALS320 and the UES320 in very small numbers, essentially to special order, and these represent the ultimate in Tokai quality for the enthusiast.

Some guitars are also produced in Korea but are of lower quality and do not feature in the Tokai UK portfolio.

Production

Tokai guitars are still produced in the same factory in Japan as 25 years ago and quality has been improved. The factory employs 60 people and guitars are produced in several formats:

- The solid-body bolt-on neck is where the neck is bolted to the body by several bolts.
- The solid-body set neck, where the neck is glued to the body to give a permanent fixture.
- The hollow-body semi-acoustic set neck.

The cheapest format is the solid-body bolt-on neck and the most expensive the hollow-body set neck. The extra expense is due entirely to the extra manufacturing costs because of the increased workmanship that is necessary. The output, however, has increased three-fold over the last 18 months. Tokai UK takes every set-neck guitar the factory can produce, but demand still remains unfilled, especially on the semi-acoustic models.

Pricing

Tokai UK prices for electric guitars range at RRP from £399 to £800 approximately. These prices compare very favourably to competitors' products of similar quality.

Gibson prices start at around £800 and Fender start at £409 for the Mexican product, the exceptions being the custom shop ALS320 for £1,800 and the UES320 for £2,500. These prices attract buyers but still allow retailers to make reasonable profits on the instruments. Of course discounting exists, but discounts come off the retailers' margin. Tokai UK maintain that this policy is better for dealers as it gives them a feeling of allegiance to Tokai UK, and causes the dealers to feel honour bound to react quickly to any problems customers might have, no matter how small. Tokai UK are also unique in that they do not charge a premium for left-handed guitars. They feel that it is wrong to discriminate against a customer simply because he/she happens to be left-handed. All other companies charge a premium.

Distribution

Tokai UK distributes its instruments throughout the UK and Ireland, and also to limited numbers of outlets in Spain and Italy. Germany was part of the distribution network but was dropped due to objections from the main Gibson agent in Germany. This led to court action which was resolved in Tokai's favour but at a financial cost, and so Tokai UK backed away to follow more profitable markets without the threat of legal action.

When Tokai UK was founded in 2001 the company started with 15 active accounts, that is these accounts would buy from every shipment. To date the company has 60 active accounts and a further 25 accounts buying from every third shipment. The accounts are shops of all sizes, ranging from the very large multi-outlet music mega stores, through the middle-of-the-road large one-off music shops, to the very small owner–operator music shops. Tokai UK prefer the middle-of-the-road shops because they feel the brand gets greater exposure and sales attention form these types of outlet.

Because of the commitment to quality given by Tokai UK, the dealers tend to reciprocate by paying invoices on time and handling customer problems quickly and efficiently.

However, Tokai UK wants to grow and expand its network over the coming years.

Promotion

Tokai UK advertise in the specialist media aimed at guitar enthusiasts such as *Guitar* magazine, etc. Their major exposure to the trade is, not surprisingly, via exhibitions. They exhibit at major exhibitions such as the NEC Birmingham, UK, which is the major music exhibition for the trade in the UK. They plan to be there in November 2003. They will continue to exhibit at the Frankfurt exhibition and plan to launch new models there in 2004. They also plan to exhibit at numerous other trade fairs across Europe in the forthcoming years, but plan to concentrate on the smaller, more intimate ones. They hope to take orders from these and expand their dealer network.

They produce a full-colour catalogue for dealers and customers. The next one is due to be released in July 2003, and features the new Loverock 2 on the front cover. They have produced a website (tokai-guitars.co.uk) for the benefit of dealers and end customers. Numerous Tokai enthusiast websites also exist, consisting of chat rooms were enthusiasts can exchange anecdotes or just chat about guitars in general, and Tokai in particular, and web forums exist for Tokai players where views can be sought or exchanged. Tokai guitars have built a following which dates back to their previous foray into the UK and enthusiasm was still present when Tokai UK announced it was about to return.

The future

Tokai UK's expressed aim is to expand over the next few years but to keep its ethos of maintaining quality. The major inhibiting factor to the growth of Tokai UK is the level of production possible at the factory in Hamamatsu. There appears to be little scope to expand into Europe in a big way unless the factory expands, as demand for the product remains unfulfilled in the UK.

Questions

1 Discuss the likely customer decision process for the purchase of a new electric guitar.

2 Suggest how Tokai UK could ensure favourable attitudes towards their products.

3 How might Tokai UK use learning theory to overcome consumer resistance towards their range of products?

4 What might motivate customers to buy a Tokai guitar as opposed to the products of their major competitors?

Case prepared by Peter Lancaster, Senior Lecturer in Marketing, Sheffield Hallam University, UK (2003).

Further reading

Engel, J.F., Blackwell, R.D. and Miniard, P. (1995) *Consumer Behaviour* (8th edition), London: Dryden Press.

References

Copeland, M. (1924) *Principles of Merchandising*. Chicago: A.W. Shaw.
Katona, G. (1960) *The Powerful Consumer*. New York: McGraw-Hill.
Maslow, A. (1954) *Motivation and Personality*. New York: Harper and Row.

6

How customers are segmented and organised

Chris Dawson

LEARNING OUTCOMES

After reading this chapter you should be able to:

■ **Define market segmentation**

■ **Understand why market segmentation is used**

■ **Appreciate the requirements necessary for segments to be viable**

■ **Recognise the methods used to identify consumer and industrial market segments**

■ **Determine the relative attractiveness of various groups of customers**

KEY WORDS

ACORN
Atomisation
Behavioural variables
Brand cannibalisation
Concentrated marketing
Critical events segmentation
Demographic
Family life cycle
Geographic
Industrial markets
Just-in-Time
Lifestyle analysis
Likert scales
Loyalty segmentation

Market aggregation
Market segmentation
Mass marketing
MOSAIC
Pinpoint
Profile variables
Psychographic analysis
Psychographic variables
Self-actualisation
SIC codes
SMEs
Standard Industrial Classifications
Supply chain management

INTRODUCTION

In Chapter 5 we explored how and why customers behave as they do in the market place. Now we turn our attention to how business organisations can group customers together to make viable target markets for the products they offer to the prospective customers, and to ensure that customers not only receive what they require, but receive it effectively and efficiently.

From a consumer's point of view we see ourselves as individuals. However, by our age profile, where we live and our behaviour patterns, organisations can categorise us into segments which make it easier to sell products and services to us (see Spotlight 6.1). In doing this, we must first look at why we bother to divide the market up, and what are the advantages and disadvantages of doing this, for both the customer and the organisation. We then examine the requirements for such an exercise to be viable, consider the criteria by which consumer and industrial markets can be subdivided before finally looking at methods of analysis to determine which subdivision(s) are most attractive for further company action.

6.1 PRINCIPLES AND PROCESS OF MARKET SEGMENTATION

Without any shadow of doubt, the UK market place is a very different world from what it was 50 years ago. After the Second World War consumer disposable income was very limited. Products and services were also limited, and consumerism was product-led and based upon Maslow's basic needs (see Chapter 5). Nowadays the UK is made up of people with very different backgrounds, countries of origin, religions, age groups, needs and wants, interests and lifestyles, and disposable income is higher.

It is this very diversity that makes market segmentation not only viable and profitable but also desirable as a business strategy. The conditions necessary for

Spotlight 6.1

Readership of this book

The readers of this book will tend in the main to be students in university or college. They will probably be between 18 and 23 years of age and in full-time education. They may live away from home in sponsored accomodation or rented housing, sharing the costs. If they live away from home, they will also live near other students.

There will be an almost even split between male and female (and the female segment will probably score higher on average in any examination or assignments associated with this book.)

segmentation are a population of sufficient size, with sufficient affluence and with sufficient diversity to lend itself to division on the basis of demography, psychological or some other strategic variable. These conditions exist in the UK and also in all other countries in the developed world, and in some emerging nations also. Hence these markets are attractive not only to home-based companies but also to global organisations.

The provision, by businesses, of alternative product offerings with alternative strategies are designed to better satisfy customers' needs and thereby increase their satisfaction and, at the same time, increase the companies' profits. Hence market segmentation is a positive force for both customers and companies.

6.2 WHAT IS MARKET SEGMENTATION?

Market segmentation can be defined as the process of dividing the market up into distinct subgroups of customers who display common characteristics and then selecting one or more subgroups which company action targets with a unique strategy. In earlier years, before the widespread acknowledgement of market segmentation as a business strategy, the prevalent way of doing business with customers was via **mass marketing** (or **market aggregation**), that is offering the same product to all customers with the same strategy – a 'one size fits all' approach. Mass marketing could be seen in the early strategy of the Ford Motor Company under Henry Ford and his Model T: 'You can have any colour you like as long as it is black.' One product, one colour was offered to all customers. The sole benefit of such a strategy in today's market place is cost saving as it obviously costs a company less to produce one product and offer it to all comers with a single strategy. The key drawback to such a strategy is that it allows competing companies to gain a competitive advantage over the firm practising mass marketing because the rival companies are in a better position to satisfy customers via market segmentation. However, it can be equally dangerous to view the market place as a vast collection of potential subgroups and attempt to be all things to all people. By offering a vast array of products with a huge selection of strategies companies fail to satisfy any subgroup sufficiently and may pay the ultimate penalty of closure.

Other factors, such as environmental issues and legislation, can also be an influence on changing needs. This can be seen in Spotlight 6.2 on the power generation market.

Market segmentation also has levels of strategy within it, ranging from **concentrated marketing**, which concentrates on only one subgroup of the market to the exclusion of all others (e.g. Rolls Royce, which concentrates on the very high-income, luxury-loving, status-seeking segment), to **atomisation**, which treats every customer individually and uniquely (e.g. an architect designing a one-off building for a client or a bespoke tailor making a one-off suit of clothes for a customer). However, in reality, most companies choose to concentrate their efforts on a number of segments.

Spotlight 6.2

FT **The USA: finding new niches in a saturated market (1)**

In the face of one of the biggest turndowns in orders for some time, equipment manufacturers in the USA, which accounts for about half the global market for electricity generation systems, are less pessimistic than one might imagine. While demand for new equipment has dropped dramatically in recent years, companies are keeping busy, responding to opportunities for servicing arrangements and demand for new equipment and upgraded technology to meet carbon emissions standards. They are also exploring renewable energy sources such as solar power, wind energy and fuel cells.

Caterpillar, which makes diesel engines, focuses on distributed generation, supplying smaller equipment of between 5kw and 100mw that is not connected to the main electricity grid. The company is also capitalising on servicing arrangements and equipment rental.

James Parker, vice-president of engine divisions at Caterpillar, attributes the success of this side of the business to the extensive distribution network the company has built up for its earth-moving machine operations.

GE (General Electric) is among the US operators to have seen an opportunity in the service market. About two-thirds of the company's sales are now accompanied by contractual service agreements and the numbers are increasing.

Source: Extracted from Sarah Murray, 'The US: Finding new niches in a saturated market', *FT.com*, 30 April 2003.

6.3 ADVANTAGES AND DISADVANTAGES OF MARKET SEGMENTATION

Clearly, because market segmentation more closely matches supply to the demands of customers, and also because the segments contain fewer and more similar customers, the business is able to obtain much more detailed information about customer characteristics. This leads to a number of benefits or advantages:

- Businesses are able to develop strategies that more truly meet the demands of customers, and hence overcome the lack of competitive advantage that is so obvious under mass marketing. For example, Mercedes-Benz developed the Smart car, which meets the demand for an environmentally friendly urban runabout, while their S series meets the demand for the luxury executive car. Neither of these models would be particularly successful if aimed at the mass market with a single strategy.

- Trends that arise in the market place due, perhaps, to changing tastes among customers can be more quickly detected and strategies adapted accordingly. For example, Sony developed the Walkman to capitalise on the taste for music on the move. This was much copied over the years but, as taste and lifestyles changed, so did music on the move, from portable CD players to mini-disc players, to MP3 players (see Spotlight 6.3).

Spotlight 6.3

Sony Walkman

The Sony Walkman was developed in 1979 and since then 150 million units have been sold worldwide. Sony and the development of the Walkman is an example of meeting the needs of customers. When the product was originally developed it did not have a target audience in mind. However its launch coincided with the rise in jogging and was rapidly taken up.

If customers had been asked in 1979 before the launch of the Walkman if they would use it the majority would have said no. It is an example of product led development.

- Product launches can be better timed, as can the releases of promotional campaigns. For example, hot snacks can be launched and promoted more readily from autumn, while cold drinks are launched and promoted more from spring.
- Because of the greater knowledge businesses are able to build up regarding their chosen segments, financial budgets can be allocated more exactly where and when they are required. Companies can move budgets from segments that are responding especially well to the strategies to segments that require more support.

However, a number of costs or disadvantages also arise:

- Costs will inevitably rise due to the investigation of more segments and the development of a variety of strategies to meet the segments' requirements.
- Overlapping segments can lead to **brand cannibalisation** as one product within the company steals sales from other products within the company. Breakfast cereals and margarine-type spreads can have particular problems in this area and some companies have begun to rationalise their product lines in view of this.
- Due to producing multiple product ranges, sometimes for smaller segments, manufacturing costs can rise due to shorter production runs. Also, similar costs can occur as a result of losing media quantity discounts due to advertising in more varied media to reach more diverse market segments. Thus market segmentation can result in greater sales for the company but frequently at higher costs. The ultimate goal, however, is for the resulting increased sales to lead to increased revenue and profit, which should outweigh the increased costs, which is illustrated in Spotlight 6.4.

Spotlight 6.4

FT **The USA: finding new niches in a saturated market (2)**

Most US machinery suppliers agree that pressure to reduce emissions will be a strong market driver.

The potential business emissions regulation could generate was illustrated when Dominion, the Virginia power company, agreed to spend $1.2 billion on emissions-control equipment on its largest coal-fired generating units in Virginia and West Virginia as part of an agreement with the Environmental Protection Agency. Part of the environmental agenda is being driven by the need to keep coal (accounting for more than 50% of US power generation) as an option.

In February 2003, the Department of Energy announced FutureGen, a $1 billion initiative to construct the world's first fossil fuel, pollution-free power plant that will serve as a prototype of carbon sequestration technologies and produce electricity and hydrogen.

'The long-term trend we see into the next decade is how to keep coal availability', says Hank Courtright, vice-president for the generation and distributed resources sector at the Electrical Power Research Institute 'And the key is going to be moving from coal combustion to coal gasification, because it's much more effective in capturing CO emissions.'

As in other markets, many equipment suppliers are examining the potential of renewable energy technologies. GE (General Electric) has secured a big chunk of the wind market with its acquisition of the wind energy operations of Enron, the failed energy trader. 'We're optimistic that we'll have a $1 billion wind business this year', says Mr Little, vice-president of energy products for GE Power Systems. 'That's an incredible thing for us, coming from nothing.'

Fuel cell technology is regarded by most as a longer-term proposition and one that will remain a niche market, even once it has developed. 'The cost of fuel cells is still too high to be competitive, so all the suppliers are on a learning curve to get the cost down', says Mr Zwirn of Siemens, which has a fuel cell division in Pittsburgh. 'But it has tremendous potential.'

Source: Extracted from Sarah Murray, 'The US: Finding new niches in a saturated market', *FT.com*, 30 April 2003.

6.4 THE NECESSARY REQUIREMENTS FOR VIABLE SEGMENTATION

There are several requirements that need attention if the segmentation process is to be viable.

The segment needs to be identifiable

It must be possible for the business to identify relevant characteristics to be able to subdivide the market into subgroups on the basis of shared needs or common characteristics. Some segmentation variables, such as **geographic** (physical location) and **demographic** (sex, age, ethnic groups, etc.) variables are easy to identify and may even be observable, while others, such as income or marital status, etc., can be determined via questionnaires. However, other variables, such as lifestyle or benefits sought, are much more difficult to identify. It is here that knowledge of consumer behaviour (discussed in Chapter 5) is especially useful to the businesses that wish to use such intangibles as a basis for their market segmentation.

The segment needs to be measurable

This does not simply relate to measuring numbers of customers, but to measuring the nature and behaviour of the segments. In order to formulate viable strategies it is necessary to be able to measure the people who exhibit similar behaviour. It is, for example, insufficient to measure the number of young adult males between the ages of 18 and 25 as x million, and then develop a strategy based on this figure, if the largest part of that number would never behave in the way you want and buy your product. Much of the study of consumer behaviour is about measuring behaviour.

The segment needs to be accessible

This relates to the reachability of segments. Companies must be able to reach their chosen segments effectively and economically and, as such, are always looking out for new ways to reach segments with the minimum of waste and the maximum of competitive advantage. The growth in usage of the Internet is the latest medium to attract businesses in this way. It allows the use of personalised emails to keep prospective and existing customers in their segments informed of new products or special deals.

The segment needs to be substantial

This very often means the size of market segments. While generally larger market segments are more attractive due to economy of scale factors, smaller niche segments can also be very substantial in terms of profitability. Rolex has a relatively small segment in the overall wristwatch market but because of its niche at the very top end of that market it remains a profitable company. In fact, the main concern is not the basic physical size of the segment, but the substance of the segment in terms of profit after the cost of segmentation has been considered.

The segment needs to be appropriate

The segment should be appropriate to the organisation's objectives and resources. The cost of changing the offering may make the segment non-viable as the costs outweigh the potential benefit, for example, a steel producer considering going into car production as a means of securing an outlet for its core product. The common problem here is also identifying market segments that will respond favourably to the specific strategy designed for them. There is little to commend the development of a unique strategy for a segment unless enough members of the segment respond to it. Segmentation has to reflect the competitive advantage of the organisation. It does not take place in a vacuum but in conjugation with the organisation's strategy.

Dilemma 6.1

 Chocolate fingered

Britain has the fastest-rising obesity rates in Western Europe and its increasingly chubby children could undoubtedly do with a bit more exercise. But Cadbury's offer of £8.8 million worth of sports equipment for British schools comes with a sweet, sticky string attached: you have to eat 161 million chocolate bars to get it.

Predictably, the British media have lambasted the company for the perceived absurdity of its proposition. Do you really make children fitter by giving them a basketball, if they have to consume more than 38,000 calories and 2 kg of fat before they can bounce it?

Cause-related marketing, of which the Cabury's promotion is an example, has become popular in the past decade or so because it offers companies the opportunity to tackle modern concerns about corporate social responsibility while simultaneously increasing sales. However there is a serious question whether it is appropriate hence the media backlash.

Source: Extracted from 'Leaders and Letters: Chocolate fingered', *Financial Times* (3 May 2003).

The segment needs to be stable

The segment should be stable over a period of time in order to recover the costs. Some markets are too volatile for organisations to respond to them.

Should the above criteria be fulfilled, market segmentation is an attractive proposition. Should any remain unmet, then the costs may well outweigh the benefits.

6.5 RECOGNISING THE CRITERIA USED TO IDENTIFY CONSUMER AND INDUSTRIAL MARKET SEGMENTS

Many methods or variables can be used to segment markets and there is no single prescribed way of segmenting a market. The first step is to select the most appropriate method(s) on which to segment the market. Several categories of consumer characteristics may be found that form the methodology for segmentation, although some categories could be classed as splitting hairs. A practical division of segmentation categories could be the three major divisions of **profile variables**, **psychographic variables** and **behavioural variables**, each broad category containing several subdivisions within it. There are also certain hybrid forms of segmentation in existence, such as geodemographic segmentation, which use a combination of several segmentation bases to provide richer and more comprehensive profiles of customer segments (see Table 6.1).

Table 6.1 Market segmentation type and selected variables for consumer markets

Profile	Psychographic	Behavioural	Critical Events	Hybrid
Age	Lifestyle	Benefits	Marriage	Geodemographic
Sex		Usage rate	Birth	
Income		Usage situation	Death	
Social class		Purchase situation	Unemployment	
Geography		Loyalty	Illness	
Family life cycle			Retirement	
			Moving house	

6.6 PROFILE SEGMENTATION

Age

Customers' needs and interests in products will often vary with age. For instance, adults of all ages buy clothes primarily to conform to social norms, but there are other motivations which set adult consumers apart with regard to this fundamental purchase. Younger adults will buy clothes to follow fashion or make themselves 'look good', while older adults are less likely to be influenced by the pure 'fashionability' of clothes but may buy to reflect status, or on a more functional basis.

Because of these age-motivational differences marketers have found age to be a particularly useful demographic basis for market segmentation. Many marketers have concentrated on specific age groups and in so doing have carved a viable niche in the market place. For example, McVities aimed its mini packs of Jaffa Cake biscuits at young children and later followed up with mini packs of chocolate digestives and ginger nuts aimed at adults.

However demographers have drawn two significant differences in the age variable: age effects (occurrences due to chronological age) and age cohorts (occurrences due to growing up during a specific time period). An example of the age effect is the greater propensity of retired people (both single and married) to take extended holidays abroad during the winter. This trend is an example of age effects because it seems to occur as people reach a particular age category. In contrast, the age cohort effect is demonstrated by the idea that people hold on to the interests they grew up to appreciate. For example, the fact that many of the audience at rock concerts are 40+ is not because many older people have suddenly altered their musical tastes but because these people grew up with rock music (Meredith and Schewe, 1994).

It is important for marketers to be aware of these distinctions. One stresses the impact of ageing and the other stresses the influence of the period in which one is born and the shared experiences with others of the same age (e.g. same history, same music and emerging technologies (Bickert, 1997).

Sex

Sex is frequently a distinguishing segmentation variable, and the differentiation starts very early – blue baby clothes for a boy and pink for a girl. Men have traditionally been seen as the main users of DIY and shaving products, women the main users of cosmetics and hair care products. However, this distinction is blurring, brought about by changes in society, the growth of dual income households, role reversal and a higher divorce rate. To the marketer this means that sex is no longer an accurate method of distinguishing consumers in some product categories. For example, women are now significant purchasers of home improvement products and the market for men's cosmetics has grown. It is now more common to see advertisements that depict both women and men in roles traditionally reserved for the opposite sex (e.g. childcare). This blurring has also led to the growth of unisex products such as Calvin Klein's CK1, a unisex eau de toilette. Media coverage for the sexes has also changed and marketers have been forced to explore more avenues of direct marketing, such as catalogues and the Internet, to reach many time-pressured working women who use these to shop for clothing and household accessories as well as many family needs.

Income

This has long been an important variable for identifying market segments, due to marketers' beliefs that income level is a strong indicator of the ability to purchase a product. For example, marketers of lower-priced PCs (under £600) felt that the main target market would be a household with a fairly modest income. However, they have also proven to be attractive to higher-level income households who want additional PCs for children. To make the best use of this variable it is common to combine it with other variables to give a more clearly defined segment, for example with age in the case of the affluent retired, or with age and occupation as in the yuppie segment. University students are also a sought-after segment which combines age, education and also occupation and income.

Social class

This is a variable that is measured in different ways depending upon the country taking the measurement. In the UK, occupation is traditionally used in the form of the Registrar General's Classification of A, B, C1, C2, D and E. In other European countries a combination of variables is used.

The extent to which this variable is a useful predictor of buyer behaviour is open to question. Many consumers in the same occupation exhibit different lifestyles, hold different values and show dissimilar purchasing patterns. However, some studies have shown that social class can be useful in discriminating between ownership of certain product classes (O'Brien and Ford, 1988).

Geography

In its simplest form geographic segmentation refers to regional differences between areas of the same country such as taste differences (northern versus southern beer, or English preference for pork sausage versus Scottish preference for beef sausage). In its wider sense it takes in cross-country boundaries with the incumbent cultural differences, language differences and taste differences. While there has been an increased level of globalisation and strategies have been sought that will be useful worldwide, many companies have found that some degree of adaptation is essential if they are to become successful on a pan-European basis. For example, McDonald's have had to adapt their product range to country tastes, and Nike found that their 'in your face strategy' did not sit well worldwide.

While the European Union has opened boundaries to freer trade among member states, the regional taste and value structures, as well as differences in consumption patterns, are ignored at the marketers' peril (Euromonitor, 2002).

Family life cycle

Family life cycle is a useful variable for marketers because purchasing requirements and disposable income are likely to vary according to life-cycle stage (young and single versus young and married with children). This variable is likely to be of greater value to marketers for more precise segmentation because consumption is more affected by family responsibility than by simple chronological age. For example, a married 19 year old with a child is likely to exhibit very different consumption patterns from a single 19 year old. Likewise 'empty nesters', whose children have left home, are viable target markets for expensive household items due to their greater affluence compared to young married couples starting out and building a home for the first time.

The financial services sector in particular have found life-cycle analysis of great use in better targeting their services. Financial advice for retirement and income tax preparation were relatively more important for older consumers than those in the bachelor or 'full nest' stages (Javalgi and Dion, 1999).

6.7 PSYCHOGRAPHIC SEGMENTATION

Lifestyle

Simple profile variables of segmentation simply describe consumers and tend to be based on bare statistical information in as much they tend to lack depth and richness in their descriptions. As a result marketers have embraced psychographic research in an attempt to address this problem. This type of applied research is referred to as **lifestyle analysis** and can be a valuable tool in aiding the identification of consumer segments that are likely to be responsive to specific marketing messages.

Lifestyle research measures *activities, interests and opinions* or, simply, AIOs (Reynolds and Darden, 1974: 87). Activities measure how consumers spend their time, interests measure preferences and priorities, and opinions measure consumers' feelings about a wide variety of events, political issues, etc. Examples of each category are shown in Table 6.2. Demographics are also included in most psychographic or AIO studies, as lifestyle segmentation does not replace profile studies but enhances them.

AIO studies may be general or specific. In general studies marketers seek to classify the consumer population into groups based on general lifestyle characteristics, with the intention that consumers within each group have similar lifestyles. The danger here is of stereotyping and generalisation. From a customer view point

Table 6.2 Lifestyle dimensions

Activities	Interests	Opinions	Demographics
Work	Family	Themselves	Age
Hobbies	Home	Social issues	Education
Social events	Job	Politics	Income
Holidays	Community	Business	Occupation
Entertainment	Recreation	Economics	Family size
Club membership	Fashion	Education	House type
Community	Food	Products	Geography
Shopping	Media	Future	City/town size
Sports	Achievements	Culture	Stage in life cycle

Source: Plummer (1974)

individuals may feel varying emotions, from humour at being so labelled to anger. However, stereotyping serves the purpose of highlighting certain behaviour, which may help the marketer.

The specific approach seeks to understand consumer behaviour in relation to a particular product or service. The AIO questions must be tailored to make them more product-specific. The advantage of this method is that groups emerge which are much more sharply defined in terms of their usage of a particular product or service.

In either type of study, customers are usually presented with **Likert scales** in which respondents are asked whether they strongly agree, agree, are neutral, disagree, or strongly disagree with the statements in the questionnaire. Under normal Likert scales, ranged on a five-point scale, a mid-, or neutral, point exists. It is possible to get more accurate results if a six-point scale is used as this forces respondents to be either side of neutral. Psychographic studies are used to develop an in-depth understanding of market segments. Psychographics can be used to define segments, although it is better practice to avoid defining the segments through AIOs in favour of using AIOs to provide a better understanding of segments previously defined using more traditional variables.

Cross-tabulations are used to analyse AIO statements on the basis of variables that are believed to be valuable for developing market segmentation strategies, such as sex, income, age, religion, etc. Factor analysis is commonly used to group the statements into a much reduced, and more usable, format. Factor analysis is a mathematical technique for examining the intercorrelation between statements in an attempt to determine common factors that explain observed differences (Hair et al., 1998). Such techniques often reveal factors such as the 'traditional' segment or the 'natural' segment, or the 'health-conscious' segment, or perhaps the 'modern' segment, etc. within a segment defined by other variables.

Several companies have identified a health-conscious segment of consumers through psychographics to either reposition or launch products. Sales of Café Hag, the decaffeinated coffee, took off when repositioned to the health-conscious segment. Olive oil and sunflower oil margarine, and low fat spreads, are all aimed at the health-conscious segments. Gillette targets its male razors to the young moderns with the line 'Be the best a man can be'.

Psychographic analysis allows marketers to better understand the lifestyles of those considered to be core customers, and thus marketers are better able to communicate more effectively with consumers in that segment. It also allows better positioning of new products within that segment, due to its ability to look beyond simple demographics and to position the product in line with hopes, fears, activities and dreams of the products' customers.

The objective of psychographic segmentation is to develop strategies that are consistent in all their elements with the AIOs of the target market. Hence advertising often stresses lifestyle elements rather than product attributes and uses models consistent with that lifestyle when viewed by the audience.

6.8 BEHAVIOURAL SEGMENTATION

Benefits

Marketers are constantly striving to identify the one key benefit of a product or service that will be most meaningful to consumers. There are many examples of such benefits but some of the more common ones include: *pain relief* (Nurofen); *white teeth* (Pearl Drops); *clean-smelling clothes* (Radion); *financial security* (Scottish Widows); *safety and longevity* (Volvo).

The process of benefit segmentation involves:

- Developing a complete list of the benefits that could be of value in segmenting the market. Not all benefits will elicit a favourable response from consumers.
- Developing sensitive and reliable scales to measure major attitude dimensions towards the benefits.
- Developing a quantitative measurement of the market which results in the clustering of respondents by their attitudes.
- Identifying those segments whose needs (sought benefits) remain largely unmet.

Changing lifestyles can play a major role in determining what benefits consumers will respond to and present marketers with opportunities for new product development in order to capitalise on new, emerging benefits. Supermarkets are now realising the benefit of home shopping and delivery required by many shoppers, hence the development of growing numbers of supermarkets offering Internet shopping. Similarly, by opening stores for 24 hours, supermarkets are offering consumers who work different hours an added benefit.

Benefit segmentation can be used to position various brands within the product category (Haley, 1995). A classic case of successful benefit segmentation in many countries is the market for toothpaste: the Signal brand is targeted towards parents because it stops the formation of cavities in children's teeth; the Colgate Complete brand encompasses several benefits in its approach to adults as it reduces plaque (health benefit) and removes tartar (cosmetic benefit); Sensodyne reduces pain in sensitive teeth (health and social benefit); and many home brands offer similar benefits to the branded products plus the additional cost benefit.

Usage rate

This method differentiates between heavy, medium, light and non-users of a specific product, service or brand. However, research has consistently shown that Pareto's Law (the 80/20 rule) applies in some degree or other. For example, approximately 25–35% of beer drinkers account for approximately 70–75% of all beer consumed. It is for this reason that marketers target their advertising towards the heavy users rather than spending considerably more attempting to attract the light-user segment.

Dilemma 6.2

 Doubts on Hutchison target for 3G units

Hutchison 3G is offering handsets capable of live video calls and has sold 20,000 units in the UK.

The figures will be watched by the mobile industry because Hutchison 3G is the first operator in Europe to sell phones running on the latest third-generation technology. This allows users to download data to their mobile phones at speeds several times faster than existing 2G networks. Sales show the mobile operator, marketing itself under the brand '3', is capturing the imagination of some consumers with services such as video clips of football match highlights and news from broadcaster ITN.

It looks increasingly unlikely that Hutchison will meet its target of attracting 1 million customers in the UK by the end of 2003. The phones are being sold at more than 1,000 outlets in the UK, including branches of Carphone Warehouse, Comet, Dixons and the Link. The operator's flagship videophone costs £200.

According to people at Hutchison 3G, the handset's most popular service is the live video call, with video calls accounting for almost half of all usage. Video calls, at 50p a minute, are one of its most expensive services.

Average customer spending on the phones is also high. About two-thirds of customers have opted for one of two 'all-inclusive' monthly tariffs at £60 and £100. By comparison, average customer spending on mobile phones in the UK is about £30.

Hutchison spent £8 billion on the purchase of 3G licences and has increased its network, analysts said it desperately needed to generate above-average revenues per customer.

The dilemma here is how can the company increase usage rate so that prices can come down thus attracting more customers to generate profit. What segmentation process would be most applicable?

Source: adapted from an article by Robert Budden, Telecommunications correspondent, *Financial Times*, 5 May 2003.

The same analysis can be applied in a wide range of other markets both in the consumer and industrial markets. Hence, targeting heavy users has become the basis of the marketing strategy of many companies. It should be noted, however, that medium and light users can be effectively targeted if marketers take note of the gaps in market coverage. Also non-users of a company's brand should not be ignored. Research can highlight reasons for their apparent dislike of a brand, and repositioning can then be effective.

Usage and purchase situation

It is often recognised by marketers that the occasion or situation can often determine what consumers will purchase. For this reason the usage situation can be focused upon as a segmentation variable. The following statement perhaps reveals the potential of situation segmentation: 'I always buy my wife flowers on St Valentine's Day.' On other occasions or under different circumstances the same consumer might choose differently. Circumstances can also influence choice, for example the day of the week, time, who the product is for, and so on.

Marketers have tried to suggest the suitability of products for certain occasions; others have tried to break consumer habits. Kelloggs, for example, have advertised cornflakes as more than a breakfast cereal. They suggest it can be eaten anytime, as a snack, for supper, and it can be made into cakes.

Many products are promoted for special usage occasions. The greeting card industry stresses special cards for a wide variety of occasions (Christmas, Mother's Day, Easter, etc.). The wristwatch industry promotes its products as a coming of age or retirement gift. The diamond industry promotes diamond rings as anniversary gifts or as a symbol of engagement. The chocolate industry promotes chocolates as suitable for Christmas, Mother's Day, Easter, etc. (see Spotlight 6.5).

Spotlight 6.5

Thorntons

Thorntons, the chocolate manufacturer, have taken to heart the situation of purchase of their products. They have specialised in personalising their products for special occasions, using St Valentine's Day, Easter, Mother's Day, Father's Day, Halloween, Christmas, etc. Thus their products can be used as a treat for the buyer or as a demonstration of feelings to another. These special occasions have become more important over the past 15 years as retailers and manufacturers have increased their promotonal spend (thereby increasing our guilt if we forget them).

See the website at http://www.thorntons.co.uk/

Loyalty

Loyalty segmentation involves marketers identifying differences in characteristics between brand-loyal customers and non-brand-loyal buyers so that they can direct their marketing effort to people with similar characteristics in the wider population with the objective of increasing the size of the loyal population. However, consumer innovators, almost by definition, tend not to be brand loyal. Increasingly, companies are rewarding brand loyalty in order to increase the brand-loyal segment. These rewards often take the form of 'club' membership, for example store loyalty cards that give discounts from a variety of member stores, or British Airways' frequent-flyer bonuses. These relationship programmes offer a variety of benefits to keep the loyalty of the frequent or regular customers.

6.9 CRITICAL EVENTS SEGMENTATION

Our lives are composed of major events which cause stress, happiness and other emotions, and affect our subsequent behaviour. These include:

- Marriage
- Birth
- Death
- Unemployment
- Illness
- Retirement
- Moving house.

These critical events offer companies opportunities to specialise and thus to provide products and services which meet not just our basic needs but also help us to achieve **self-actualisation**, in Maslow's terms, to give expression to the outside world of who and what we are. Marketers call this **critical events segmentation**.

6.10 HYBRID SEGMENTATION

Geodemographic

Geodemographic segmentation is the combining of location information and demographic information. Emerging in the early 1970s for public sector applications, but given the central nature of segmentation to marketing strategy, it was rapidly picked up as providing a major step forward in consumer segmentation (Mitchell and McGoldrick, 1994). The first company to offer a geodemographic system in the UK was CACI, with its **ACORN** (A Classification of Residential Neighbourhoods) system. It is based around census data and offers 38 neighbourhood types aggregated up to 11 neighbourhood groups (Mazur, 1993). Its major premise is that people who live in similar areas are likely to have similar lifestyle, behavioural and purchasing habits. In the UK, census data such as household size, ethnic origin, number of cars, family size and occupation are used to group small geographic areas into segments that share similar characteristics (see Table 6.3). As the industry has grown, other systems have become available, such as **MOSAIC** (CCN), PIN (**Pinpoint**) and Superprofiles (CDMS).

Table 6.3 ACORN User Guide

Index – Categories and Groups

Category 1 – Wealthy achievers

Group A – Wealthy executives
Group B – Affluent greys
Group C – Flourishing families

Category 2 – Urban prosperity

Group D – Prosperous professionals
Group E – Educated urbanites
Group F – Aspiring singles

Category 3 – Comfortably off

Group G – Starting out
Group H – Secure families
Group I – Settled suburbia
Group J – Prudent pensioners

Category 4 – Modest means

Group K – Asian communities
Group L – Post industrial families
Group M – Blue-collar roots

Category 5 – Hard pressed

Group N – Struggling families
Group O – Burdened singles
Group P – High rise hardship
Group Q – Inner city adversity

Source: Caci Ltd. (http:www.caci.co.uk)

The information obtained can be used to select targets for direct mail campaigns, to identify locations for retail stores and to identify the most effective poster sites. This is made possible because consumers are being identified by postcodes. Advertising spots on television can also be bought more precisely by linking information from viewership panels with postcodes to enable certain geodemographic groups to be targeted.

A major strength of geodemographics is to link buying behaviour to customer groups. Buying behaviour can be obtained from large-scale syndicated surveys, such as MORI or Target Group Index. Respondents are then geocoded and then geocoding those ACORN groups that are most likely to purchase a particular product or brand can be identified. Hence merchandise mix decisions can be made with greater accuracy. Supermarkets use drive-time maps to identify customers within a certain driving time (usually 10–15 minutes) to help select the product range for each store.

Geodemographic databases are becoming more sophisticated but should not be viewed as a panacea to solve all marketing problems. Before selecting a database marketers must identify exactly what it is they require and select the database that best fits their needs. They also need to recognise that databases are only as good as the information contained within them (O'Malley et al., 1995).

Geodemographic analysis is likely to become more prevalent in pan-European studies in an attempt to identify groups of 'Euro-consumers' living in separate countries but demonstrating similar socio-economic and demographic characteristics.

6.11 SEGMENTING INDUSTRIAL MARKETS

To a great extent, **industrial markets** can be segmented using similar variables to the ones just discussed. The difference, of course, is that instead of using the characteristics and behaviour of the individual customer, the segmenter uses characteristics and behaviours of the organisation. For example, in the case of microprocessors, different industry types, from consumer electronics manufacturers to military hardware manufacturers, may buy them. Order sizes may differ from light to heavy usage. Geographic location may vary from domestic purchasers to international purchasers, and organisational size may differ from huge multinational to small regional manufacturer. The type of purchase may differ from straight repurchase to new task purchase, and different benefits may be sought, etc. Figure 6.1 shows that business customers may be segmented on the basis of geography, organisational characteristics, purchase behaviour and usage patterns and organisational predispositions or policy.

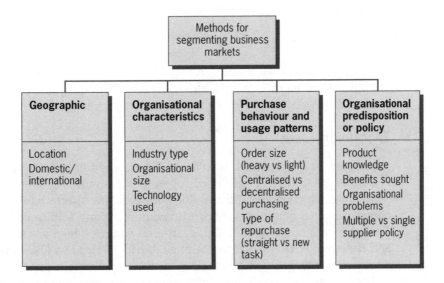

Figure 6.1   Selected methods for segmenting business markets

Geographic

Location

Delivery times for perishable goods can be a limiting factor in the selection of customers. Examples will include milk and local produce for farmers' markets. In ethical pharmaceuticals, distribution (prescription medicines to local pharmacists) relies upon a national network of warehouses or regional distributors.

Domestic/International

For business-to-business marketing the decision whether to serve the domestic market (UK only) or go international will depend upon delivery charges, exchange rates, tariffs (different VAT rates, etc.), regulatory requirements (although these tend to be reduced within the European Union), and hidden costs such as translation costs of documentation.

Organisational characteristics

Industry type

The **Standard Industrial Classifications** (SIC) index is an international method of identification for all industries. **SIC codes** are useful in the selection of segments for business-to-business marketing. When companies register at Companies House (www.companieshouse.gov.uk) they have to describe the main business and give the appropriate SIC code. Organisations can look at their customer base and analyse the SIC codes from their records at Companies House. Mailing list companies such as Dun and Bradstreet and Thomson Directories will produce mailing lists of similar companies.

Organisational size

This can be defined either by number of employees or by turnover. Segmentation can therefore include SIC code, number of employees and turnover or a combination.

Technology used

A company selling business software will only need to identify customers who use computers. A company selling nitrogen freezers will only need to identify those companies which use that technology, for example sperm banks, pharmaceutical companies, etc. Norcool is a Scandinavian company selling commercial fridges. Their product range includes glass-fronted fridges which are used in pubs, clubs and restaurants. They also have a range of fridges that can take panels, and kitchen designers use these.

The potential of e-commerce in business-to-business marketing in reducing costs is enormous. However, the use of EPOS systems means that only suppliers who can interface with the technology can take advantage.

Purchase behaviour and usage patterns

Order size (heavy vs light)

In a production line organisation, the longer the production runs the cheaper the unit cost. This saving can then be passed on to customers. This will only be profitable if the customers can take advantage of larger orders.

Organisations using price as an incentive will look for customers who can take larger orders. They do this by having minimum order sizes. This leaves smaller-order customers who cannot meet the minimum order size requirement to have their needs met elsewhere.

Centralised vs decentalised purchasing

Organisations with multiple sites may have different policies for their services. For example, legal services will be contracted out on a centralised basis whereas other services, such as window cleaning, may be decentralised but with a budget allocation.

Type of repurchase (straight vs new task)

Repurchasing, that is re-ordering, is essential to long-term profitability. If the repurchase is a repeat order, the set-up costs may have been covered by the first order, so repurchasing can be very profitable. If the orders are unique and not identical, then there will be set-up costs involved. Sometimes standardising processes can overcome these problems.

Organisational predisposition or policy

Product knowledge

In a business-to-business situation specialised product knowledge may be required in order to get the maximum benefit out of the product or service. Customers who already have these skills can be selected to avoid training costs. An example would include suppliers of energy-efficient boilers looking for customers who already use this type of equipment.

Benefits sought

Corgi developed an energy-efficient boiler which met the energy reduction requirements being introduced by the European Community in the early 1990s. Their initial customers were heating engineers who supplied replacement boilers.

Organisational problems

Some organisations in their normal business have a requirement for specialised needs. This can include health and safety requirements, for example disposing of asbestos or other toxic by-products.

Multiple vs single supplier policy

Companies using modern **supply chain management** techniques, including **Just-in-Time**, tend to have a single supplier policy. The selection of the company will depend upon a number of issues, including past experience and quality as well as price. Other companies use multiple suppliers to avoid being dependent upon a single supplier and to allow trade-offs between competing suppliers.

6.12 CUSTOMER SEGMENTATION IN THE BUSINESS-TO-BUSINESS AREA

The reality of segmentation in the business-to-business area may not be as scientific as that suggested above. Customers tend to arise out of buyer/supplier relationships rather than being sought out as in consumer activities, see Spotlight 6.6. This is looked at in more detail in Chapter 11 on relationships.

Spotlight 6.6

Who wants to be an accidental millionaire

In business-to-business areas it is often the customers who find the business organisation rather than the other way.

A survey was carried out on behalf of Parcel Force Worldwide. Its findings were published in the report, 'UK Small Businesses Admit Export Success is Accidental'. Researchers who quizzed 200 smaller companies, which were happily selling their products overseas, found that about 130 had never planned to do so. Foreign customers had simply drifted in, discovering their new suppliers through chance conversations or Internet trawls.

Every year David Storey, a professor of small business at Warwick University, compiles a list of the 100 fastest-growing businesses in the UK. Revisit it after three years, he says, and you will find that 90% of the original names have dropped out.

The dilemma is that manufacturing industry has been in steady decline, although UK plc needs an engineering and manufacturing base for its long-term strategic development. This means exports.

Source: Adapted from Jonathan Guthie's article 'Who wants to be an accidental millionaire?' in *Financial Times*, 6 May 2003.

SUMMARY

The reality of segmentation in 'real-life' may not be as simple as suggested in this chapter. The segments will appear blurred. Many organisations have been around for some time (and surviving and maybe thriving) without a formal segmentation process. Many **SMEs** (small and medium enterprises) say that they just get on with it. Their customers are anyone who will pay for their goods. However, if we analyse their customer profiles we very often find that the more successful organisations are focused upon a narrow segment. This is especially true in the case of not-for-profit organisations such as charities where their segment is clearly defined.

As customers we are becoming more eclectic, taking our lifestyles from more than one source. As customers we are also becoming increasingly more difficult to pigeonhole. From an organisation's point of view we appear, as individuals, to be in more than one (or even two) segments. In Chapter 12 we will look at how changes in customer profiles are forcing organisations to have a major rethink.

Organisations segment their customers so that they can position their products and target their marketing activities to produce a cost-effective solution – one that benefits customers (giving them the products they want/need) and the organisation (by maximising their profit).

Discussion questions

1   Spotlight 6.3 showed Sony Walkman as an example of product-led innovation. Would such a product developed with no prior consumer research be as successful today?

2   Taking into consideration the techniques and methods of looking at customers in earlier chapters, what new customer types are likely to arise when we consider lifestyle segmentation?

3   Spotlight 6.5 showed Thorntons as an example of how marketers can use a purchase situation, such as Easter, Christmas, St Valentine's Day, to commercial advantage. Is this an example of increased commercialisation or are we being miserable Scrooges for even suggesting it?

4   Spotlight 6.6 showed that many small business exports come from 'web surfers':

   (a) Should small businesses trust to 'luck' when setting up a website?

   (b) How can small businesses use their existing customer base to identify potential new customers?

Case study 6.1   Levi's leaps into the mass market

If you can't beat 'em, join 'em. The news that Levi Strauss is planning to sell cheap jeans through supermarkets suggests that brand manufacturers want a slice of the mass market.

It was not that long ago that Levi's was hauling Tesco before the courts to stop Britain's biggest retailer selling its jeans at bargain prices. The jeans had been bought on the so-called grey market, bypassing approved retail chains set up by brand owners to exploit the different pricing of the goods in different markets.

But last week Levi's announced that its Signature jeans, about to be sold in the US through the discount group Wal-Mart, would be coming to the UK and that it was in talks with mass-market discount retailers. For that, read supermarkets.

Brand owners, which have long spurned the advances of mass-market retailers keen to stock their goods, are having radically to rethink their approach. The fastest-growing segments of the consumer products markets are super-premium and discount. While some manufacturers are committed to remaining solely in one camp, many, like Levi's, are determined to see if they can straddle both. At the top of its range Levi's sells jeans for £175 a pair. The new Signature trousers will sell for £25, against an average price for its products of £45.

For supermarkets, selling branded goods cheaply – often half the recommended retail price – helps to bring more customers into their stores. Tesco and Asda have also targeted such areas as perfumes, sunglasses, watches and jewellery. It is part of a drive into non-food, something that will come under scrutiny by the Competition Commission under its current investigation into the Safeway bid battle.

Tim Mason, marketing director at Tesco, says the move by Levi's is a recognition that the group was missing out on a channel to market that was selling a lot of jeans. 'They are only trading in part of the available market', says Mr Mason. He says Tesco has sold 1 million pairs of its own-label jeans at just £6 each. 'We have value jeans already that sell very well', he says. 'We will talk to Levi's again, but I think this may be a Signature without a flourish.' David Miles, head of speciality retailing at Asda, agrees. 'Signature is not what our customers tell us they want', he says. 'They do not want a value version. They want the right version at the right price.'

But both men are sure that the decision by Levi's is part of a recognition by brand manufacturers that the times are changing. 'Brand owners are just not fighting us any more in the way they used to', says Mr Miles. Mr Mason says it is a victory for the mass market and its way of doing business. 'Whether people like it, or like it not, the mass market is a discount market. You can be in that mass market, or the branded end, both of which are doing very well. The risk is getting caught in the middle.'

Johanna Waterous, a leader of the European retail practice at McKinsey, the consultancy, agrees that Levi's is not alone in seeing that retailing is changing. She predicts that the group will be just one of a number of consumer product manufacturers that are forced to analyse their retail partnerships. 'Across all sectors of retailing in the US the theme of the year is competing in a value-driven world and how primarily Wal-Mart, but other players as well, are beginning to reshape the industry in terms of supply chain and supplier behaviour', says Ms Waterous. 'At the end of the day, distribution matters and the traditional middle-market channels

– department stores and other mid-market branded retailers – just cannot deliver the volume.'

Whatever their decisions, making the move into the mass market will not be easy for branded manufacturers. To meet the scale demands of the likes of Wal-Mart, many groups will have to re-engineer their supply chains, overhaul sourcing and review design. 'It is difficult to see what they won't have to change', says Ms Waterous. 'To do that for any company is quite challenging.'

According to McKinsey, companies can go one of two ways. They can improve their existing infrastructure, looking for economies of scale, and then fine-tune on the margins. Or they can start from scratch by building an entirely new and dedicated part of the business.

Whichever way they jump, it is clear that life is changing for the brands. Jo Middleton, Levi's European president, in effect admitted as much last week. The group, he says, could no longer afford not to tackle directly the growing ranks of value-conscious consumers. 'The whole value channel in clothing has become extremely large in recent years, and is becoming bigger', he says. 'It really cannot be ignored by anybody in our industry any more.'

Source: Extracted from 'Levi's leaps into the mass market' by Susanna Voyle in *Financial Times*, 1 May 2003.

Questions

1   Are supermarkets and clothing shops selling to different segments?

2   Can Levi's have a two-price structure in different types of outlet?

3   Can Levi's alter the quality of their product to justify a price differentiation?

Further reading

Hassan, S.S., Craft, S. and Kortam, W. (2003) 'Understanding the new bases for global market segmentation', *Journal of Consumer Marketing*, 20(5): 446–62.

Ah Keng Kau, Tang, Y.E. and Ghose, S. (2003) 'Typology of online shoppers', *Journal of Consumer Marketing*, 20(2): 139–56.

Lilly, B. and Nelson , T.R. (2003) 'Fads: segmenting the fad-buyer market', *Journal of Consumer Marketing*, 20(3): 252–65.

Ringberg, T. and Forquer Gupta, S. (2003), 'The importance of understanding the symbolic world of customers in asymmetric business-to-business relationships', *The Journal of Business and Industrial Marketing*, 18(6): 607–26.

References

Bickert, J. (1997) 'Cohorts II: a new approach to market segmentation', *Journal of Consumer Marketing*, 14: 362–63.

Euromonitor (2002) *Consumer Europe 2002/2003*. London: Euromonitor.

Hair, J.F., Tatham, R.L., Anderson, R.E. and Black, W. (1998) *Multivariate Data Analysis* (5th editon). Chicago: Prentice Hall.

Haley, R. (1995) 'Benefit segmentation: a decision-oriented research tool', *Marketing Management*, 4 (Summer): 59–62.

Javalgi, R.G. and Dion, P. (1999) 'A lifestyle segmentation approach to marketing financial products and services', *The Service Industries Journal*, July.

Mazur, L. (1993) 'Growth springs from ACORN', *Marketing*, 27 May.

Meredith, G. and Schewe, C. (1994) 'The power of cohorts', *American Demographics*, 16, 22–31.

Mitchell, V.-W. and McGoldrick, P.J. (1994) 'The role of geodemographics in segmenting and targeting consumer markets: a delphi study', *European Journal of Marketing*, 28 (5): 54–72.

O'Brien, S. and Ford, R. (1988) 'Can we at last say goodbye to social class?', *Journal of the Market Research Society*, 30 (3): 289–332.

O'Malley, L., Patterson, M. and Evans, M. (1995) 'Retailing applications of geodemographics: a preliminary investigation', *Marketing Intelligence and Planning*, 13 (2): 29–35.

Plummer, J.T. (1974) 'The concept and application of lifestyle segmentation', *Journal of Marketing*, 34 (January).

Reynolds, F. and Darden, W. (1974) 'Construing life style and psychographics', in Wells, W.D. (ed) *Life Style and Psychographics*. Chicago: American Marketing Association. P. 73–95.

7

What the customer is looking for

Mark Godson

LEARNING OUTCOMES

After reading this chapter you should be able to:

- Understand why an organisation should strive to be 'customer focused' as opposed to 'product focused'

- Recognise the different product needs of 'industrial' customers

- Appreciate how a customer's experience of a 'product' differs from that of a 'service'

- Reflect upon the different levels of a product/service and how customers' needs may be met through differentiation at these levels

- Appreciate the significance of branding and why customers form relationships around and loyalty to brands

- Understand the concept of innovation and how customers' expectations change over the lifetime of a product or a service

KEY WORDS

Augmented product
Brand equity
Brand stretching
Branding
Continuous innovations
Core product
Customer-focused
Differentiation
Expected product
Inseparability

Major innovations
Manufacturers' brands
New to the market products
Own brands
Perishability
Potential product
Product-focused
Services
Tangibility
Variability

INTRODUCTION

The previous two chapters have shown that customers have many reasons for behaving in the way they do, and that every customer is an individual, with his/her own set of motivations, needs, hopes and aspirations. As such there will be a demand for multitudes of different products and product combinations – each customer looking for something which will suit his/her requirements exactly. This presents a challenge for organisations, as understanding this myriad of requirements and designing products and services to suit will be the key to success.

7.1 MEETING CUSTOMER DEMANDS

From a cost point of view, organisations would like to produce the same product or service day in, day out, as once they have paid for the original set-up or tooling of their operations, they can run their operations to maximum efficiency without the expensive disruption of stopping and changing to accommodate different products all the time. This standardisation of products is the basis of 'mass production' and enabled factories in the nineteenth and early twentieth centuries to make products quickly and cheaply. One of the most famous pioneers of mass production was Henry Ford (see Spotlight 7.1). However, although mass-production techniques were able to meet basic needs, once customers had a choice (i.e. there was competition in the market), they would place their business with the company that offered products which most closely met their needs.

In order to ensure that their products meet these needs, organisations have to listen to their customers. This might sound obvious, but it is surprising how many companies do not pay enough attention to what their customers actually want.

This brings us to a second important concept in this area. Companies can produce excellent products, but if they do not match up with what the customer actually needs or wants, they are not likely to succeed. British inventor Clive Sinclair found this out to his cost when he launched a futuristic, low-slung electric tricycle, called the C5, in the 1970s. Billed as a product which would avoid traffic jams, cut fuel costs and be friendly to the environment, the C5 was a huge flop with customers who weren't ready for such a huge step change away from the traditional car or motor bike.

Product-focused

There is a risk that companies can become so engrossed in producing an ever better product, that they lose sight of what the customer actually wants. This is known as being **product-focused**.

Companies that have a tradition of technical excellence often fall into this trap. For example, Rolls Royce in the years after the Second World War was known for producing some of the finest aviation engines available. Buoyed by this reputation,

Spotlight 7.1

The impact of customer choice

In 1907 Henry Ford recognised the need for a low-cost, rugged and practical car, which would meet the needs of the basic population. Prior to Ford, cars had been hand made, one at a time. With such a system, the requirements of individual customers could easily be incorporated, for example different body shapes, engines, running gear, even the size of the cars was non-standard. The problem was that this came at a cost far above what the average person was able to afford. This is why in the early days of motoring, only the very rich could afford to own a car.

Henry Ford changed all this. He made cars available to the masses at low prices. But in doing so, he sacrificed the individual elements of the cars' designs. Every one of his Model Ts was identical, even the colour, hence his famous quip 'You can have it in any colour you want, as long as its black ...'.

Ford's policy was successful. The Model T became the world's best-selling car – a record only beaten many years later by the VW Beetle. But his policy would only work as long as there was no competition in the market. The customer had no choice – the motor car was still a relatively new phenomenon and they were just grateful for the chance of owning one. They didn't care what it looked like. However, once Ford's rivals started bringing out their own models, the customer did have a choice. They no longer had to settle for a black saloon car. They could get yellow coupés, red cabriolets, large cars, small cars, fast cars, slow cars. The more manufacturers who entered the market, the more the choice increased until Ford were forced to bring in product variations themselves.

their engineers concentrated on perfecting ever more clever designs. However, with the rise of the passenger jet aircraft industry, aircraft manufacturers were more interested in low-cost, basic but reliable engines which got the job done and no more. Rolls Royce, despite their technical excellence and reputation, ended up in receivership.

Additionally, companies that have enjoyed great success with a product can also become product-led, by assuming that they have found the winning formula and sticking too closely to it without looking at what is happening in the market. A good example of this is jeans manufacturer Levi Strauss, whose 501 jeans became an icon of youth and style in the 1980s. The mistake Levi's made was not keeping their eye on the market. As one youth generation gave way to another, the traditional Levi 501 product no longer met the needs of the new generation. What they wanted was baggy jeans and dockers, which Levi did not produce. Levi was perceived to be oblivious to this, confident instead that the market would beat a path to its door because of its past glories. Retailing giant Marks & Spencer fell into a similar trap when they stayed too long with their tried and trusted retailing formula and ended up losing customers to newer and more customer-focused rivals.

Customer-focused

The alternative to being product-focused is being **customer-focused**. Both Levi Strauss and Marks & Spencer have now re-evaluated their strategy and become much more aware of what the customer wants. Levi has introduced Dockers, Engineered Jeans and the Nevada brand. Marks & Spencer have abandoned many of their long-held policies, such as not accepting credit cards, and have introduced new ranges like Per Una.

This is the secret of success – listen to customers and give them the products they want.

Richard Branson has made a virtue of this. He has successfully entered a diverse number of well-established markets with redesigned products that meet customers' needs more closely than competitors. For instance, by listening to customers of financial services products, he found that many were put off by the complexity of the products. When he launched his financial products company, Virgin One, the products were easily accessible over the phone, clearly defined and free of jargon. James Dyson used a similarly customer-focused approach when he entered the fiercely competitive market for vacuum cleaners (see Spotlight 7.2).

Spotlight 7.2

Being customer-focused

James Dyson has built a multimillion pound business and become one of Britain's richest men by listening to customers and designing a product which meets their needs better than those of established competitors. When it arrived in the early 1990s, the Dyson Dual Cyclone revolutionised the vacuum cleaner market.

The product overcame many of the criticisms which customers made of traditional cleaners. For a start it worked better. The dual cyclone technology meant that it picked up dirt and dust much more efficiently than ordinary vacuum cleaners. Furthermore, it did not require a dust bag – a feature which removed the need for the messy operation of removing and replacing bags.

The front of Dyson's cleaner was clear perspex, revealing how much dirt it had gathered. This not only showed when the cleaner needed emptying, it also had the psychological benefit of showing that real dirt had actually been removed from the customer's carpet, engendering the satisfaction of a job well done!

Traditional vacuums tended to be heavy and difficult to lug around the house. The Dual Cyclone was lightweight, making it easy for most people to carry. The bright and funky colours of the Dyson were another novelty. Research showed that many customers did not want the drab greys and beiges of the old style cleaners.

Despite being a relatively expensive product, Dyson's sales have grown to over £3 billion worldwide, proving that when you give customers what they want, price is not an overriding factor.

Of course there are times when listening to customers and being customer-focused produces conflicting views. First Direct argue that by moving towards telephone and Internet banking, they are giving customers what they want. They point out that customers want the convenience of being able to conduct their banking at a time and a place that suits them.

On the other hand, Nat West has taken the line that customers want to be able to visit their own branch and discuss their banking affairs with their own bank manager. Nat West's advertisements underline this message with the strap line 'Another way', and the emphasis that their branches are not becoming 'trendy wine bars', like many other banks.

So who's right? Both are valid responses from customer-focused companies – it's just that they are focusing their products on two different customer types. This underlines the importance to an organisation of understanding its customers and designing their products to target the needs of specific customer segments (see Chapter 6).

The above examples show how important it is to listen to customers and the customer-focused organisation will use market research when developing products and services. There is a difference, however, between being customer-focused and being customer-led. A customer-led organisation will do what ever the customer wants, which might sometimes be detrimental to the organisation. For example, a few years ago, a large university Students' Union attempted to win business back to its Union bar. The elected Student Union Executive asked the students what they wanted and were told that beer at £1 a pint would sell. The inexperienced Executive actioned the students' request with the result that the Union made a large loss over the financial year. Being customer-led helps no one in the long run (even the customers will lose out, as pushing an organisation to bankruptcy will ultimately reduce the choice of products available). The customer-focused organisation, on the other hand, will gear itself to satisfying the needs and wants of customers, within its own capabilities – in other words, it retains control.

7.2 PRODUCTS AND SERVICES FOR INDUSTRIAL CUSTOMERS

When we talk about customers, we don't just mean members of the public. Companies or organisations can be customers too, because they buy things in order to be able to carry out their operations. For instance, the Ford Motor Company will buy steel, plastic and glass to make their cars. A hospital will buy medical equipment and drugs, and a Local Authority will buy all sorts of things, from road salt to computers.

This is known as business-to-business sales or B2B, as opposed to business-to-consumer or B2C. It is just as important to understand what business customers are looking for as it is to understand what people like you or I are looking for when we buy things. Generally speaking, business-to-business products fall into the following categories.

Raw materials

These are products in their very basic form. Little, if anything, has been done to them before they are delivered to the customer. Examples include timber, iron ore or sand. Organisations buying raw materials tend to be lower down the supply chain (see Chapter 9), because they will usually perform further operations on the materials in order to move them towards a finished product (e.g. smelting iron ore to make iron and steel, sawing timber to make building materials, etc.). Customers for raw materials therefore tend to have basic needs in terms of product features and will usually buy on price and elements of customer service (e.g. quick delivery).

Semi-finished products

Many manufacturing organisations will buy semi-finished products. These include things like sheet steel and rod, timber planks, glass and plastic. In other words, some processing will already have been undertaken, but the product is not yet in its final form (e.g. a container of plastic granules will already have been refracted from crude oil, but will finally end up as a child's plastic toy).

The producer must therefore understand what the customer is going to do with the product. Will a sheet of glass be used in the manufacture of low-grade greenhouses or for decorative, high-quality mirrors? As a result of this, producers of semi-finished products tend to be much more closely involved with their customers, and will often tailor their products to suit customer needs more closely than producers of raw material.

Components

Components are items which are specifically manufactured to form part of a larger product. Often, it is not economic or practical for a company to manufacture every single part of its product, so it will buy in components from other manufacturers. For example, Lucas Industries manufacture headlamp units which they then sell on to the car producers like Ford and Vauxhall, to be incorporated into their cars.

Producers of components often design their products specifically for one customer (e.g. a Lucas-made headlamp for a Ford Focus will not fit a Vauxhall Astra). For this reason, the manufacturers of components will often work in partnership with their customers. It is vital that they pay very close attention to their customers' needs as the customer's reputation often relies on these component products (e.g. if a Ford headlamp unit fails, the end customer will blame Ford, not Lucas). Very often, component products will be designed in conjunction with the customers' own design team.

As can be seen, industrial products become tailored more towards specific customer requirements as they move from raw material, semi-finished and component form. In addition to these, there are two further types of product that are bought by businesses.

Capital equipment

Most businesses need to buy products which help them to produce an end-product or service. These are usually high-cost items which will last the business over a lengthy period of time. Examples include computers, machine tools, factories, warehouses, fleets of lorries and vans, etc. Although some of these products are standard (e.g. a machine tool or a van) the producers must be flexible in terms of being able to modify them to suit a particular customer's needs. Many of them will also require high levels of associated service (such as the installation of a computer system, training of customer's staff and ongoing back-up maintenance).

Consumables

Every business needs consumables – stationery, floppy discs, even food for the canteen and toilet paper for the staff lavatories. It is unusual for business consumable products to be sold in exactly the same format as their consumer-based cousins which are sold in shops and supermarkets. Very often these are bought in large quantities, so they need to be packaged in bulk. Sometimes they will be designed for heavy use (e.g. carpets) or be made in a very basic way to keep costs low (e.g. toilet paper). This gives rise to the term 'industrial grade' which is often used in a derogatory way. Yes, they are designed for the customer, but here the customer is a business whose primary interest in buying consumables is in keeping costs down and not the business's employees whose primary interest might be comfort.

Many of these business-to-business selling situations require a much closer relationship between the supplying organisation and the customer and very often the two parties in this relationship become reliant upon one another. The implications of this are explored in greater depth in Chapter 9.

7.3 THE DIFFERENCE BETWEEN PRODUCTS AND SERVICES

Although the word 'product' is used interchangeably throughout this chapter when referring to goods and services, there are some significant differences in the way in which customers purchase and use **services** and these need to be understood. These relate to the concepts of tangibility, inseparability, variability and perishability, each of which has a bearing on how a service is provided.

Tangibility

Some services have tangible elements (e.g. a restaurant has the food and drinks it serves and the tables and chairs at and on which the customers sit). Other services have very few tangible features (e.g. a solicitor or an insurance broker). However, whatever the service, there will always be a large intangible element. In a restaurant, this is the way in which the food is cooked and served. It will also include the location, ambience and general surroundings. In other words, it is something which the customer experiences.

Therefore the big challenge for organisations developing services is not only including features that people want (e.g. good food), but also representing the intangible feelings that these provoke – an enjoyable night out, a special occasion, etc.

The same is true of other services – a haircut helps provide glamour and style, an insurance policy provides security and peace of mind, an amusement park provides thrills and excitement. In developing a service, therefore, an organisation must provide some level of **tangibility** to indicate to customers that they will meet their requirements (see Dilemma 7.1). This explains why banks were traditionally built in very solid, imposing styles. It was to suggest to prospective customers that they were strong and secure.

Dilemma 7.1

Shoe repairs and dry cleaning

Mister Minit's success has been built around a core business of shoe repair and key cutting. However, towards the end of the 1990s it was clear that both these services were in decline.

Stiletto heels and leather soles (the staples of a shoe repairer) were not as common as they had been. In addition, the falling price of new shoes and the trend towards a 'throw away' rather than a 'repair and mend' society led to a fall in demand for shoe repair.

Key cutting was not faring much better. The advent of magnetic, keyless security systems in many offices and hotels and the introduction of sophisticated, rolling-code transponder keys for cars meant that the traditional high street key cutter was unable to help.

As a result, Minit decided to add additional services to those it already provided. Dry cleaning was selected because it was another 'convenience' service which we all need from time to time. It was a relatively easy market to enter because all that was needed was an agreement with a local contract dry cleaner. The Minit shops would take the clothes in. These would be collected each day by the contract cleaner and returned after they had been cleaned.

The advantages seemed obvious. With no dry cleaning taking place in the premises, Mister Minit was able to continue using their existing small shops and avoid the expensive overheads of dry cleaning machinery. Additionally, their central, convenient locations made it easy for a customer to use the service.

However, early results were disappointing. Although the quality of the dry cleaning provided was excellent, customers were reluctant to use a shoe repair shop for dry cleaning.

Why might this be and what could Mister Minit do to overcome this?

Inseparability

When a service is purchased the customer has to interact with the service provider in some way. Many services actually require the physical presence of the customer (e.g. a haircut or a meal in a restaurant). Others require the presence of a customer's possessions (e.g. car repair or house painting). Even distantly provided services like insurance or online banking will require interaction at some stage between the customer and the service provider. This is **inseparability**.

Inseparability doesn't often happen with physical products. It is unlikely that someone buying a tin of baked beans will ever have any contact with Heinz. Customers will have contact with the supermarket where they buy the beans, because the actual retailing of the beans is a service, not the beans themselves.

This means that people or systems are a very important part of a service. In a restaurant, the customer expects the waiter to be clean, polite and attentive. When a customer takes her car to be repaired, she expects courteous and efficient service. She will expect to be told how much it will cost and how long it will take. When a customer wishes to change a standing order on an online bank account, he expects the Internet or telephone-based systems of the bank to work quickly, simply and efficiently.

This means a challenge for the providers of a service, for not only do they have to make sure that the basic product lives up to expectations (e.g. the food in a restaurant, the standard of a repair in a garage), but also that the people or systems delivering it are up to scratch. These all form part of the 'product' as it is experienced by customers.

Variability

The fact that a customer experiences a service personally leads us to the next big difference between physical products and services. Physical products can be standardised, but it is very difficult to standardise a service. For instance, if you buy a Mars bar every week for a whole year, every single one will be identical to the next. Production techniques will ensure that exactly the same amount of chocolate, sugar, caramel, etc. goes into every one, and every bar will be produced to the same dimensions using the same recipes and processes. On the other hand, if you visit a restaurant every week for a whole year, it is unlikely that the experience will be exactly the same each time. There will be variations – sometimes slight, sometimes quite large. Many things could cause the **variability**. The usual chef might be on holiday, the waiter might be in a bad mood, the fresh lobster might be out of season, the people on the next table might be drunk and rowdy. The following week, the opposite of all these could be true. How many times have you recommended a restaurant to friends, only for them to go and have a poor experience?

Some services are easier to standardise than others (e.g. banking and insurance), but people-oriented services in particular are difficult to standardise. This means that the service provider has to pay much more attention to staff training, systems and procedures. It means that the service provision has to be flexible (so that if the fresh lobster is out of season for instance, an equally attractive dish can be offered instead). Once again, this requires a clear understanding of what the customer is looking for and being able to provide it in different ways if necessary.

Perishability

The final big difference between physical products and services relates to production and consumption. A service has to be bought by a customer at the moment it is produced. It has **perishability**. It cannot be produced one day and sold the next.

Think about the restaurant again. Let's say it opens at 7.00pm and closes at 11.00pm. In order for it to open, all the staff will need to be present, the tables must be made up and the kitchens stocked with food. The lighting, heating and music will also need to brought to the right level and the reception staff or *maître d'* prepared. This, in effect, is a large part of the 'production' part of the service. If no customers come through the door, or half of the tables are empty all night, this production will be wasted. Once the restaurant closes at 11.00pm a whole evening's production is lost for ever.

Unlike a physical product which can be stored, sometimes for long periods before it is sold, the service must be sold when it is produced or it will be lost for ever. In other words, it is perishable. Once again, therefore, the service provider must design flexibility into the service. This means managing customer demand so that as much of the service production as possible is taken up at any one time. Thus pubs and restaurants will have 'happy hours' to encourage consumption at quiet parts of the day. Hotel and travel companies have 'off-peak' special offers and theatres, cinemas and sports clubs will sell season tickets to try to generate a consistent take-up of service over a period.

7.4 THE DIFFERENT LEVELS OF A PRODUCT

A more in-depth way of considering a product is by asking what it offers to customers at different levels. This is illustrated in Figure 7.1.

The **core product** is the first level, representing the basic reason why the product is purchased in the first place. This defines not only what the product is used for, but how it meets more specific needs and differs from other products in the same category. A Ford Fiesta and a Ferrari Maranello represent two quite different core products. One provides practical, economical, everyday motoring, while the other provides head-turning looks, race-bred engineering and high-speed performance.

Both the Ferrari and the Ford fall into the product category of 'cars', but they are easily distinguishable at the core product level because of the different customer needs they satisfy. However, when two products both meet the same basic customer needs, they can be said to be in competition with each other. For instance, a Ford Fiesta and a Fiat Punto can both be said to provide practical, economical, everyday motoring in a small car. It is difficult to separate them at the core product level.

The next level up, the **expected product**, describes what the customer expects from the product. In a small hatchback car, the customer will expect certain levels of comfort, performance, reliability, build quality and styling features. In the past, this was often an area where two products differed, so some customers would have expected one car to be better than the other. These days, however, cars are built

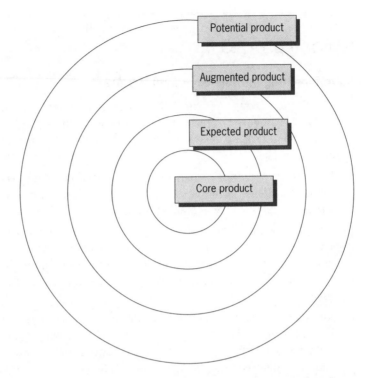

Figure 7.1 The different levels of a product

along standardised procedures, using similar componentry. Thus standards of build quality and reliability are similar across all small cars. Additionally, many equipment and styling features have now become common to all (e.g. air bags, CD players, high-level rear lights). As a result, there is little for the customer to differentiate between the products at the 'expected' level.

The third level can be described as the **augmented product**, and it is at this level that many organisations now seek to make their product stand out from the others, by exceeding customer expectations. This usually involves building in associated services, or features which enhance the core and expected product (see Spotlight 7.3).

The key to successfully augmenting the basic product offering is understanding exactly what the customer will value. Thus a hotel might offer business services, such as modems and ISDN lines for personal computers, teleconferencing links, printers, travel booking facilities, etc. This would be ideal if the hotel's principal customers were business people, but little more than an amusing diversion in a tourist hotel.

In the rush to outdo their competitors, many organisations have augmented their products in inappropriate ways. For instance, a university Students' Union provided a free bus service to and from its night club events. The service was withdrawn after just three weeks because students were not using it. Many of the buses were running completely empty. What the Union had failed to recognise was that transport was not an issue for students when choosing where to go for their night out – the venue was more important. In addition, most students preferred the

Spotlight 7.3

Augmenting the service at Sytner BMW

The Sytner Group is a top UK retailer of prestige and specialist cars. It has become a hugely successful operation by 'augmenting' its 'core' business of selling and servicing cars with a range of additional features which are of value to the customer.

To begin with, Sytner recognises that many of its customers are busy people. It therefore offers the choice of being able to deal direct with local dealers or through a central, fully interactive website.

All cars brought in for service are given a full valet inside and out and customers are able to wait for their cars in comfortable waiting rooms with television, reading materials and refreshments. A children's play room is also available. Some dealers even provide hairdressing and beautician studios for their customers!

For customers who don't want to wait at the dealer, Sytner can book them in to local sporting facilities for golf, keep fit or swimming. Alternatively, cars can be collected from the customer's workplace and returned later, thus causing minimum disruption to the customer's day.

In addition to these features, all Sytner customers are offered corporate or personal finance and company car operators are given advice on tax calculations. Customers can even locate and buy their own personalised number plates on Sytner's website!

All of these features show that Sytner is offering more than the average car dealer and it is these little details that keep customers coming back.

flexibility of moving around a number of different clubs and bars and did not want to be bussed in to just one location at the start of the evening. The free bus service did not therefore add any value to or augment the core product in any way.

An organisation, therefore, has to understand its customers fully in order to start separating itself from its competitors at the augmented product level.

Differentiation at the augmented level

British Airways is making a name for itself in the business market through the provision of executive lounges with business facilities and the introduction of fully reclining seats which act as beds on transatlantic flights. This is something which business travellers value, because it helps them to do their jobs more efficiently. Boots stays ahead of rivals by developing a reputation as a source of advice on fitness and health (through its in-store and online information services). It also offers customers the opportunity to shop online, or through mail order catalogues if preferred. American motor cycle manufacturer Harley Davidson has built up a huge members' club called HOG, which offers owners special insurance rates, tailored holiday packages, clothing and accessories, as well as the opportunity to socialise with fellow Harley Davidson owners. This is something which customers value and sets it apart from competitors.

All of these examples demonstrate how organisations can augment their basic product offering by providing additional features which the customer does not necessarily expect, but nevertheless finds extremely useful. As a result, these organisations are able to remain highly competitive without resorting to price cutting.

The problem with augmentation is that features like these can be copied by competitors. If this happens, the augmented features no longer convey any advantage – they move back down to the 'expected' level.

Perhaps the most difficult 'augmented' features for competitors to copy are those associated with a strong brand, like Harley Davidson, or those which rely on personal service. The way customers are greeted, enquiries are handled and complaints are dealt with tend to be unique to individual businesses as they rely on the personal touch. As a result, it is in areas like these where lasting product augmentation has occurred.

There is a final level which some commentators believe a product can reach, which is known as the **potential product**. This lifts the product away from its core function into something altogether different. Thus, in the example above, Harley Davidson might become a principal provider of financial or travel services. It is difficult for an organisation to design in 'potential' product features, as it generally requires long-term vision and commitment. Instead, the 'potential' product tends to evolve over time.

7.5 BRANDING

One of the concepts which lifts products from the core and expected levels to the augmented and potential levels is **branding**. Branding is nothing new and we are all familiar with brands (see Table 7.1).

What is a brand?

Brands are nothing new. Centuries ago, men would mark their possessions to prevent them from being stolen and to help them to identify which was theirs. An obvious example is the branding of cows and sheep and other livestock. Later, branding came to be associated with companies which wanted to reassure customers that what they were buying was the genuine article.

The world's very first commercial brand was the red triangle used by Bass to identify their beer. In the days before consumer protection laws, customers had no way of knowing what they were buying. Beer was often watered down or produced in unsafe conditions. Bass introduced the red triangle on to their bottles to tell

Table 7.1 The world's biggest brands, 2002

Brand	Sector	Approximate value (£bn)
Coca-Cola	Soft drinks	42
Microsoft	Computers	39
IBM	Computers	31
General Electric	Electrical appliances	25
Intel	Computers	18
Nokia	Telecoms	18
Disney	Entertainments	17
McDonald's	Fast food	16
Marlboro	Tobacco	14
Mercedes Benz	Automotive	13
Ford	Automotive	12
Toyota	Automotive	12
Citibank	Banking	11
Hewlett Packard	Computers	10
American Express	Finance	10

Source: Interbrand

customers that this was a beer of consistent and genuine good quality. After a while, publicans started to display the red triangle on their pub signs to show customers that they could rely on genuine good Bass beer being served on those premises.

Why is branding important today?

Nowadays, most products are produced under a brand name for the same reasons – so that customers can distinguish one product from another and can form expectations around a particular brand. We have seen in Chapter 5 how the buying situation will affect the customers' decision process and ultimately influence their final choice of product.

Low involvement products

Some products will be of relatively low importance to customers in terms of risk or personal involvement with the product. Typically this would include things like the groceries we buy in a supermarket each week. (These types of goods are known as fmcg – fast-moving consumer goods.) Often the customer is faced with a bewildering choice and, as there is little risk associated with the purchase, may be tempted to try out different products each week.

Under these circumstances manufacturers do their best to make their product stand out from the others and often use the attraction of special offers, free gifts and so on to entice the customer. The overall goal of an organisation developing a product in this area is to win customers and then to keep them. Customer loyalty is therefore an important objective for the producers of low involvement products.

High involvement products

Other products will mean more to the customer because their purchase entails an element of risk (e.g. buying a car). In these situations the customer can feel vulnerable and therefore needs to be able to trust the product. The challenge for an organisation here is how to build in an element of trust.

Another reason why a product might be classed as 'high involvement' is when customers adopt them as part of their lifestyle. In this case they shift from a purely functional level to an emotional level. Products which fall into this latter category include things like cigarettes, clothes, drinks and cars – in fact anything which it can be said says something about its user or owner. The organisation developing a product in this area therefore has to do more than just make sure that the product fulfils its core function – it has to imbue some sort of personality into the product, to which the customer can relate.

Branding is a tool which can be used in all of these situations, as it helps create loyalty and trust and provides the product or service with a 'personality' (see Spotlight 7.4).

Spotlight 7.4

James goes to university

When James went to university, it was the first time he had lived away from home. One of the things he had to get used to was doing his own food shopping and, although he did not have a lot of money, he often found himself buying products which his mother had bought and he had grown up with, such as Marmite, Heinz Baked Beans and Kellogg's Coco Pops. He knew what products he liked and he was loyal to the brands.

One of the first things he needed was a computer. He had never bought anything so complicated before and he was worried that if he made the wrong choice, or the computer kept going wrong, he would have wasted his money. He had heard about Dell computers – his elder sister had bought one and he knew she was very pleased with it. There were cheaper computers available, but Dell was a brand he trusted, so this is what he bought.

As he made new friends and developed a new social life, James was keen to fit in and show people what sort of person he was. He always wore Nike training shoes and was keen to stick to brands like Firetrap and Ted Baker when he could. He would not have felt right in a pair of Wrangler jeans because they were what his father wore – James was choosing brands to *reflect his personality*, so the brand was very important to him.

Differentiating products through branding

We have already seen that in customers' eyes, many products are very similar and will fulfil the same basic functions. This does not just apply to fast-moving consumer goods. Even products like cars can be indistinguishable from each other. Branding is a way for manufacturers to separate their products from those of competitors. This is called **differentiation**. Imagine things like colas or chocolate bars. Take away their packaging and how many of us would honestly be able to tell the difference between them?

When cars have been presented to members of the public without their badges, many have been mistaken for much more prestigious marques. Škoda makes a big play on this in their advertising – 'Honestly, it's a Škoda'. In Škoda's case they are trying to play down what has traditionally been a very poor brand image in the UK.

How does a brand add value?

At one time, two shops, Gullivers and Next, both sourced women's handbags from the same factory in the Far East. The bags were identical except that one had a lining and a clasp which bore the name Gullivers and the other had a lining and a clasp which bore the name Next. The Gullivers bag was priced at £11.99, whereas the Next bag sold for £22.99. Why the difference? The simple fact was that most young women thought that Next was a more attractive and fashionable name. They were happy to carry a Next bag on a night out, where fashion mattered, and they were thus willing to pay a higher price for the bag. Taken to its extreme, we can see that top-branded handbags like Gucci or Hermes can sell for thousands of pounds. This is far above their intrinsic value – no matter how good the quality of the leather or the fittings on the handbag are. What people are paying for is the name or brand. When this happens, a product is said to have **brand equity**.

Brand equity is a very valuable thing for an organisation to possess. Not only does it mean that it can charge more for its products, but it can often be transferred to new or different products to give them instant appeal. Thus, when Mercedes Benz launch a new car, customers automatically know what to expect (because they value the brand) and will often be willing to place orders for the car even before the first one has rolled off the production line.

Sometimes companies can use a strong existing brand name to move into a different market. For instance, Marlboro has launched a successful range of fashion clothing and accessories. This is known as **brand stretching**. It is particularly common among famous fashion names like Pierre Cardin or Ralph Lauren, whose move into new areas has given rise to the term 'designer labels'.

In many cases brands have become more valuable than the products they adorn. When BMW bought the Rover group in 1995 for £80 million they were more interested in the famous brands like Mini and Land Rover than the factories and the models that were in production at the time. When BMW sold Rover in 2000, they kept the 'Mini' brand and have since turned it into a hugely successful product.

A strong brand, which customers know, respect and even love, is often therefore an integral part of a good product.

Developing strong brands

There is no slick formula for developing a strong brand. Most good brands have developed over time. Much of their success lies in how customers perceive them and the 'personality' which customers attach to them. When BMC launched the Mini in 1959, they had no idea that it would turn into the phenomenon it did. It was the customers who took the little car to their hearts that made the legend.

In order to develop and maintain strong brands an organisation must understand what the values of the brand are and continue to communicate these as much as possible. This can entail advertising, sponsorship, good public relations, associations with celebrities, etc. Organisations can work hard to position a brand where they want to see it (a bit like spin doctors who try to package and present politicians in a certain way), but customers are canny, and it is they who will ultimately decide the fate of a brand.

The owners of many successful brands go to great lengths to protect them. One of the biggest threats is counterfeits, which illegally trade on the success of a brand with a usually cheap and inferior product (e.g. fake Rolex watches).

Owners of expensive brands will also try to maintain their exclusivity and cachet by controlling the way in which they are sold. Perfume brand Chanel wants its products to be sold in the correct surroundings and with dedicated sales staff. It argues that selling at cut prices in a discount retail environment, such as Superdrug, devalues the brand in the eyes of the customer.

Own brands and manufacturers' brands

This brings us neatly to another hotly contested issue surrounding products and branding. Many shops have introduced their **own brands**. These can go under the shop's own name (e.g. Gap or Next) or a different name (e.g. Matsui at Dixons, or Jonelle at John Lewis).

Controversy has arisen over **manufacturers' brands**, when manufacturers like Kellogg's or Coca-Cola have accused retailers of copying their brands by adopting similar packaging or brand names. There have been many court cases (e.g. Coca-Cola versus Sainsbury's Classic Cola and McVities Penguin bars versus Asda's Puffin bars).

However, shops' own brands have been very successful – in the UK they account for over 40% of grocery purchases. One of the reasons for this is that groceries fall into the low involvement category (see p. 176) so customers are willing to try out different things. This has led to something of a crisis for many manufacturers (see Dilemma 7.2).

Dilemma 7.2

Can a manufacturer rely on its brand any more?

It is very much in a supermarket's interest to stock products which are own branded. Not only do they have more control over these, in terms of their manufacture and supply, but they also make more money out of them. From the customer's point of view, own brands are usually cheaper and there is a wide-held belief that supermarkets' own brands are made by the big brand manufacturers anyway.

Manufacturers have fought back hard, arguing that customers want more choice, not less, and they have spent millions of pounds promoting their brands to try to maintain their place in customers' affections. This usually means that their products are more expensive, so only a brand with a very strong customer appeal will be able to maintain its position.

Manufacturers now have a choice. Do they agree to make products for the supermarkets to sell under the shop's own brand, or do they continue to fight as independents? Heinz has taken the view that they will maximise their sales by producing shops' own brands alongside their own Heinz-branded products. In this situation, they must be careful to ensure that the product they make for the supermarkets differs slightly from their own, otherwise they will end up undermining their own brand.

Kellogg's have taken a different view and refuse to make shops' own brand products. They have even made a virtue out of this with the strap line 'If it doesn't say Kellogg's *on* the box, it isn't Kellogg's *in* the box'.

7.6 NEW PRODUCT DEVELOPMENT AND INNOVATION

We have seen throughout this chapter how today's most successful products are those which 'delight' the customer. This is because customers have become more demanding in what they expect and it has become more and more difficult to differentiate a product through its basic features. Innovative product features which give a company differentiation are soon copied by competitors and become expected by customers. As a result, differentiation is now increasingly achieved at the 'softer', augmented levels, such as offering a superior customer service, or weaving psychological benefits around the product through branding.

In order to start developing products at the augmented level, organisations must be clearly aware of the wider need that they fulfil for customers. For instance, for many owners, a BMW car does more than just get them from A to B. It provides them with a status symbol.

So what exactly is a new product and how does an organisation know if it has a new product which delights the customer? The bald fact is that the majority of new products will fail and be withdrawn within a short period of time. Even large organisations, spending millions of pounds on research, still get it wrong. Cadbury's did not get the success it was looking for with Ticket or Banjo, and Kellogg's failed to make an impression with Skanda Krisp and Skanda Brod. After the hugely successful Ford Granada, the failure of its replacement, the Scorpio, has seen Ford withdraw from the executive car market in Europe.

There can be a number of reasons why new products might fail:

- The product might be ahead of its time. Many Internet retailing services fell into this category because customers weren't ready to make a big change in the way they shopped.
- The product might not offer anything new to the customer. Many fmcg goods fall into this trap, as they are simply launched as 'me-too' products to match something that a competitor is already offering. This highlights the importance of being first to the market with a new product.
- The product fails to win customer acceptance, either by not meeting their expectations or not giving them what they want. This was the problem with the Sinclair C5 electric tricycle. Although customers liked the idea of cheap, personal urban transport, the C5 did not meet their desires in terms of street credibility or perceived safety.
- The product might struggle to find distribution channels. This happens to many products from small suppliers. The large existing suppliers will tie up the distribution outlets to keep them off the shelves, for example many of Britain's micro-breweries are denied access to pubs by the big distribution chains who prefer to handle large, low-risk, existing products. If this happens, customers lose out because they are denied choice.

With this last notable exception, all of these reasons for failure can be attributed to the organisation not fully understanding the customer. This can be a particular problem when the people designing the product are far removed from the customers who will actually consume the product. Products aimed at children or teenagers can be very hit and miss, as the adults who design them do not always understand how these customers think in terms of what is 'in' and what is 'out'. The actual users of a product are often the best people to drive new product development (see Spotlight 7.5).

Not all new product ideas come from customers, however. The head of Sony came up with the idea for the Walkman for his personal use, while 3M's Post-it note began life as a mistake, as the glue was originally developed for a much stronger purpose. It was very nearly rejected, until some enterprising member of the design team used it to mark the page of his hymn book in church.

Types of new product

We have already seen that customers have to accept and value a new product if it is to succeed. However, products can have different degrees of 'newness' to a customer.

Spotlight 7.5

Products developed by the people who use them

Many successful products have been designed by people who saw a need in the market through their own experiences. For instance, the folding DIY workbench was developed by Ron Hickman, a designer with Lotus cars, after he had struggled to saw a piece of wood by balancing it on a chair.

The JCB digger was invented by Joseph Cyril Bamford, who saw the potential to find an easier way to excavate large amounts of earth. He used hydraulics on a converted tractor, which he developed in his garage, to come up with a world-leading product (in this country, JCB has almost become a generic name for a mechanical digger).

Owen Maclaren was a former test pilot and aeronautical engineer who had designed aircraft landing gear. He invented the folding baby buggy after experiencing difficulties getting his granddaughter's unwieldy pram on to and off a passenger plane, thus sealing the fate of the old traditional pram design.

Like many drivers in the 1930s, Percy Shaw found driving at night dangerous because, even with headlights, it was difficult to see the road ahead. However, he noticed that when illuminated in the beams of his lights, a cat's eyes shone brightly. He took this idea and developed small glass reflectors which were built into the road surface, thus showing drivers the route ahead. Even today, we refer to these reflectors as 'cats' eyes'.

New to the market products can be described as ideas or concepts which the customer has never seen before. Examples include the first microwave ovens and the Sony Walkman. Predicting the success of products like these is difficult and any organisation launching such a product must ensure that it offers clear-cut benefits to the customer at a price which they will be willing to pay (no one would have paid £2,000 for a Sony Walkman!).

Major innovations are big leaps forward within an existing product (e.g. the DVD over the video tape). Again, the benefits to the customer must be clearly apparent, otherwise why should they move to the new product? However, the risk involved in launching products like this is less than it is for completely new products because demand for what the product does has already been established by the old product. For instance, when music companies launched the CD, they already knew that customers wanted to buy music to listen to in the home, but when Sony launched the Walkman, there was no real proof that customers wanted to walk around listening to music on headphones!

Continuous innovations are much smaller advances from an existing product. They would include things like the launch of new washing powders or tinned foods. New cars would also fall into this category. In fact, most products are being innovated continuously. How many products can you think of that are exactly the same as they were 20 years ago?

Sometimes this continuous innovation is to keep up with competitors (e.g. when Barclays Bank introduced hole-in-the-wall cash machines, all the other banks soon followed). At other times it might be to take advantage of new technology (e.g. many cars now feature airbags and anti-lock brakes). Then again it might be to expand the organisation's portfolio of existing products (e.g. when Mars launched an ice-cream bar). Or it could be just to freshen something up and strengthen a brand (e.g. the characters Snap, Crackle and Pop on Kellogg's Rice Krispies packets were redrawn in 2000).

The risk here is that organisations launch new, or revamped products which are not necessarily what the customer wants. In other words, they lose sight of the customer, or even worse, take the customer for granted. Coca-Cola underestimated the strength of customer feeling when it changed the recipe of its product in 1985 and brought out 'New Coke'. The public outcry that followed caused them to bring back the 'old' product within nine months.

It is vital therefore for any organisation launching a new product (no matter how great or small the level of innovation) to understand the customers and try to predict how they will receive the new product and how many of them will buy it.

Customer adoption of new products

Different customers react in different ways to new products. Some will rush out and buy them because they like to be the first to have them. We all know people who must be the first to have a mobile phone with the latest features, or who were the first to have a DVD player. These customers are known as 'innovators' and organisations rely on them to get the product established.

Other customers will be interested in the product, but will hold back just a little while to see how the product goes before they themselves buy it. These people are known as the 'early majority' and they will be watching the experiences of the 'innovators' with interest.

More cautious customers will wait until the product is firmly established before committing themselves. By this stage any early problems with the product will have been ironed out and the product will have proved itself. These people are known as the 'late majority'. They are not risk takers and are not interested in being the first to have something.

The final type of customer will not buy the product until it has been on the market for a long time. In fact, it is no longer a new product – it might even be close to being replaced by a further new product. This customer is known as the 'laggard'. Thus, people who are only just buying their first mobile phone would fall into this category. These four stages of product adoption are illustrated in Figure 7.2.

Understanding the nature of this curve helps organisations to monitor how successful their new product is. For instance, if the product sticks at the 'innovator' level and is not adopted by the 'early majority', then it could be that the product is ahead of its time and needs to be modified to fall within the bounds of more mainstream acceptance.

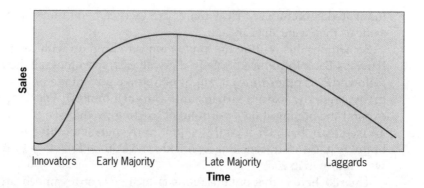

Figure 7.2   The four stages of product adoption

The shape of the curve in Figure 7.2 is interesting because it is similar to the way in which a product sells over its lifetime. Starting from zero just before the product is launched, customer demand will rise steadily until a plateau is reached. Then, as customers get bored with the product, or another, better product comes along, demand will tail off (see Figure 7.3).

The shape of this demand curve will vary depending on how quickly demand for the new product develops, how long this demand lasts and how quickly it tails off. Some products will remain popular over many years (e.g. KitKats or Corn Flakes), while others will enjoy a brief spell of intense popularity before customers get bored with them (e.g. the child's toy Tracey Island, which was in demand several Christmases ago).

Once demand starts to tail off (or, ideally, just before) organisations should aim to have a new replacement product ready to take over. This explains why new car models are constantly being launched (e.g. the Volkswagen Golf has been replaced with a new model four times since its launch in the 1970s).

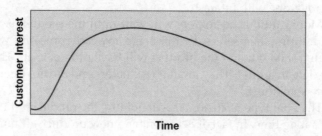

Figure 7.3   The demand curve of a product

SUMMARY

Customers buy products and services to meet their own personal requirements. Once there is a choice in the market, they will naturally gravitate towards those organisations whose products most closely meet these requirements. It is important, therefore, that an organisation is customer-focused, as opposed to being just product-focused.

If one product is going to attract customers over another, it is no longer sufficient to meet just the basic core requirements. Instead it must incorporate features which customers will value at higher, augmented levels. Customers see products in a unique way and branding is a means of imbuing the product with a personality to which the customer can relate. If this happens in a positive way, it can impart a huge advantage to the organisation that owns the brand.

But no matter how much a customer values a product, there will come a time when they grow tired of it or their requirements change. For this reason, organisations must strive to keep up with changing customer requirements and ensure that they update or replace products before this happens.

Discussion questions

1   The Managing Director of a large manufacturing company was overheard at a conference to say 'our products are our life blood. I'm proud to run a product-focused organisation!' Discuss the possible risks that such an approach might lead to. Taking the opposite view, should a customer-focused organisation ignore its products?

2   Imagine you are visiting a large theme park. How might the concepts of tangibility, inseparability, perishability and variability affect the way the park presents itself to you?

3   Thinking of individual product categories (e.g. soaps/shampoos, breakfast cereals, clothes, drinks, perfumes/after-shaves, etc.) draw up a list of brands that you buy or use on a regular basis. Try to think why you buy these particular brands and not others. Now draw up a list for your friends, family and other people you know. How would you explain any differences between the lists?

4   How would you describe the difference between product/service development which is: (a) new to the market; (b) a major innovation and (c) a continuous innovation? Can you think of three retailers which would fall into each category?

Case study 7.1   Driving the past

Morgan cars are renowned for their traditional build and appearance – the quintessential English sports car. See one on the road and you might think it was an old classic, lovingly restored from an earlier age of motoring, but you'd be wrong. Morgan cars are still being built in the small factory in Malvern, Worcestershire, where they have been based for the last 80 years.

Until recently, little had changed over the years. The cars were constructed with a separate chassis, made of ash timber. The basic design of the 4/4 (so called because it had four cylinders and four wheels) and the Plus 4 models had remained unchanged since the 1940s. Features which we have come to expect on even the most basic modern car, like power steering and electric windows, had no place in a Morgan.

But there has never been a shortage of buyers. People queued up to buy Morgans. During the 1970s and 1980s the waiting list was seven years long! This has since been reduced to just one year, but for many the allure of owning a distinctive, hand-built sports car makes the waiting worthwhile. Indeed, many thought that it was this shortage of supply that was fuelling demand.

Recently the company has launched a new model – the Aero 8. With luxuries like air conditioning and a state-of-the-art engine and running gear from BMW, this car is mechanically up to date. But it is still built around a wooden frame and the styling includes traditional Morgan features such as the long tapering bonnet, the large, bulbous front wings and separate running boards along the base of the doors. In other words, it still looks like a sports car from the 1930s. The long-running 4/4 and Plus 4 remain in production alongside the new Aero 8.

The Morgan Motor Company, which has made a virtue of slow incremental change, increased production from about eight cars a week in 1990 to nine cars a week by the late 1990s. Following the introduction of the new Aero 8 model and an expansion of the factory, production is now running at a heady 13 cars a week.

Orders for cars are taken by dealers. Customers pay a deposit and join the waiting list. Every deposit handed to a dealer is recorded by the factory and an order number is allocated so potential buyers can be traced should a dealership change or go out of business during the waiting period. Morgan is scrupulously fair about the waiting list and it is not possible to 'buy' one's way up the queue.

Part of the appeal is the car's simplicity. It stands for a set of values that have all but disappeared. With no refinements like power steering (on the basic models) or automatic gearboxes, the cars appeal to those who enjoy driving and want something different.

However, advancing technology, rising development costs and saturation in the market are leading to a consolidation among the world's car manufacturers. In the race to find new customers, many (e.g. Chrysler and BMW) are introducing 'retro'-styled models and the customer now has a bewildering choice of hi-tech, hi-style cars at affordable prices. In such a climate, whether Morgan can remain virtually unchanged for the next 80 years remains to be seen.

Questions

1. Morgan cars exist because the company understands its customers. Discuss.

2. Given that the company's products are produced in low volume, do they have the scope for increasing profits by: (a) increasing production or (b) increasing the prices? How will this affect the brand?

3. Is the Morgan experience relevant in a modern customer-oriented business situation?

Source: Based on the *Financial Times*, 18 April 1999. Also in L. Rickard and K. Jackson (eds) (2000) *The Financial Times Marketing Casebook* (2nd edition). Harlow: Financial Times/Prentice Hall.

Further reading

Cagan, J. and Vogel, C. (2002) *Creating Breakthrough Products*. Upper Saddle River: Financial Times Prentice Hall.

Hart, S. and Murphy, J. (eds) (1998) Brands. *The New Wealth Creators*. Basingstoke: Palgrave.

Interbrand (2000) *The Future of Brands*. London: Macmillan Press Ltd.

Riezebos, R. (2003) *Brand Management. A Theoretical and Practical Approach*. Harlow: Prentice Hall.

Seybold, P. (2001) *The Customer Revolution*. London: Random House Business Books.

8 Customers' perceptions of quality

Robin Lowe

LEARNING OUTCOMES

After reading this chapter you should be able to:

- **Describe what quality means to customers and assess what judgements they make about quality**

- **Specify what contributes to the total customer experience and therefore will determine whether the customer is satisfied with the product or service**

- **Discuss the quality perceptions in B2B markets and how they differ from B2C markets**

- **Explain why customers expect organisations to behave ethically as part of their approach to assessing the quality of an organisation's offering**

KEY WORDS

Business-to-business sector	Investors in People
Conformance to requirements	ISO 9000
Counterfeiting	Product or service specification
Ethics	Quality
Government regulators	Stakeholders
Grey marketing	Value for money

INTRODUCTION

In Chapter 7 we explored what customers are looking for in terms of the products and services that are provided. Now we turn to what **quality** means to customers and the different perspective that customers have of the quality of the products and services that they receive. Against the background of the discussion of the augmented product in the previous chapter, we consider the various dimensions of quality that determine whether customers receive satisfaction from their total experience of dealing with the organisation. In doing this we first look at the different quality judgements that customers make, both personal and subjective, and rational and objective, and then go on to examine the whole experience of dealing with the organisation and its staff. We also consider the perspectives of quality within the **business-to-business (B2B) sector** and in other market sectors before finally looking at customer judgements about the ethical behaviour of the organisation.

8.1 WHAT QUALITY MEANS TO CUSTOMERS

Over time there have been evolutionary changes in what might be considered to be a 'good quality' product or service because customer expectations have changed and evolved. As customers have become more knowledgeable and choice has increased, so other measures of quality have come into play. People over the age of 50 will remember that when they were at school trainers were called plimsolls and there was choice – you could either have black canvas or white canvas! The only measure of the quality of plimsolls (because they were all exactly the same) was how soon they wore into holes. You might like to think what measures of quality a customer might use today when purchasing a pair of trainers. The quality evaluation may not stop at the product design, expected performance and durability, but it may be important whether they have been advertised, if a sports personality endorses the brand, where the trainers are available to be purchased, and the appearance and attitude of the staff in the shop.

This simple example illustrates some of the many quality perceptions of customers applied to the product and the purchasing process. In fact, customers use the word quality to mean quite different things:

- quality as **conformance to requirements**;
- quality as superior **product or service specification**;
- quality as a standard, a badge or a league table;
- quality as **value for money**;
- quality as innovation and added value;
- quality as a personal evaluation, perception or experience;
- quality based on trust.

Essentially, however, these different dimensions can be categorised as quality in terms of consistency, introduced in section 1 below, quality in terms of level, introduced in section 2 below, and quality in terms of customer perception, introduced in section 4 below.

1 Quality as conformance to requirements

Perhaps the fundamental view of quality is the idea that every product that is made and delivered should conform exactly to the customer requirements. We expect that every can of Coca-Cola or Heineken lager will appear and taste exactly the same. To ensure that this happens, a set of specifications that exactly describe the properties of the product is drawn up, so that when the product is manufactured to that specification it will meet the customer requirements. The product is then made to the specifications, and the properties of each product, or a representative sample, are measured against the specification to ensure that every can is exactly the same. The customers know what they want and expect to receive it every time. They also expect defective products to be withdrawn from distribution by the manufacturer before they reach the factory gate.

This definition of quality is concerned mainly with the consistency, with no deviation of any product from the specification. By this definition, of course, a Ferrari and a Ka car can both be described as quality products if they conform to their own, individual specification. Equally, *The Sun* and the *Daily Sport* are quality newspapers by this definition because every issue delivers exactly what their readers expect.

As can be seen from Spotlight 8.1, Japanese car makers during the 1960s and 1970s exploited the failure of many Western car manufacturers to deliver consistently reliable and durable cars, but over the years many customers have changed their views about what constitutes quality.

Of course individuals have different requirements. Some people prefer other lagers than Heineken and other colas than Coca-Cola. Clearly, the manufacturer, based upon their customer knowledge and research, makes decisions about the precise nature of the specification. This inevitably will not appeal to all cola and lager drinkers. Even loyal customers of Heineken and Coca-Cola actually receive different specification products in different countries. For example, the sweetness of Coca-Cola is changed to suit different tastes in different countries.

For services, particularly those that are dependent for delivery on people, quality that is defined in terms of conformance to requirements can be a problem as different people deliver the same service with different levels of skill, knowledge and attitudes to customers. Every delivery of the service will be different, therefore, and an independent person cannot comprehensively measure quality objectively as they can with a product, because many of the measures are subjective. For example, how often are customers of a hairdresser totally satisfied? The stylist creates the cut and style accurately but at home the customer's partner has to respond to questions such as 'Does it make my face look fat?', 'Is the fringe too long?' and 'Should I have had it dyed darker?'

The success of a service in conforming to customer requirements can ultimately only be assessed by the customer, based on his or her experience, and the deliverer in terms of what he or she was aiming to provide. For example, a teacher might con-

Spotlight 8.1

The customer's changing view of quality

For decades following its birth, the British car industry had a good reputation with customers for making high-quality cars such as Rolls Royce, Jaguar, Mini and MG. During the 1960s and 1970s customers found that many British cars were of poor design, neither reliable nor durable (they rusted) and fewer people bought them. During this time the British car companies had frequent disputes between the management and workforce and insufficient money was invested in new production plant and models. Because many US and European car manufacturers were facing similar problems Japanese car makers were able to fill the gap. They offered value-for-money cars that consistently offered quality (conformance to requirements), durability and reliability. The contrast was that at this time the better-performing European and US car firms saw quality as a way of differentiating their product from their less competent competitors, whereas Japanese manufacturers believed that quality should be taken for granted by the consumer.

The European car industry then began to consolidate and many car brands were bought by more powerful car manufacturing groups: Rolls Royce by Volkswagen, Jaguar by Ford and Mini by BMW. Moreover, the better US and European car makers were starting to achieve a similar quality to that of the Japanese car makers.

By the 1990s, however, customers had become bored with cars that were reliable but were starting to look all the same. A succession of more imaginative cars were introduced by European manufacturers, which were designed to appeal to customers' self-image and fit their lifestyles. This has led to a revival of some of the old brands, such as Jaguar and Mini.

Source: Robin Lowe

sider a lesson at school to be a success on the basis of the efficient delivery of the material to the pupils or the 'fun factor' but, ultimately, the success of the lesson is dependent on the effectiveness of the learning of the pupils and may be measured by their ability to pass an examination in the subject.

2 Quality as superior product or service specification

This first view of quality as conformance to requirements does not take into account the different specifications of what appears to be the same product. The readers of *The Times* and *Financial Times* (*FT*) are unlikely to refer to *The Sun* as a quality newspaper. For them, *The Times* or *FT* would be a quality newspaper, perhaps because longer words are used, more complicated concepts and wider knowledge is assumed along with greater intellect on the part of its readers. In this case, quality refers to specification. In the same way a Mercedes may be considered to be a quality car when compared to a Fiat because of perceived superior build quality, better performance and greater passenger comfort. The Mercedes might also be expected to last longer without showing signs of wear and so is likely to hold its second-hand resale value too. This is of little comfort to those purchasers who cannot afford to buy and run the Mercedes. Equally, the relative sales figures would suggest that a large percentage of newspaper readers find the *FT* and *The Times* unsuited to their tastes.

3 Quality as a standard, a badge or a league table

There are many quality standards used for different purposes. Some of them, such as **ISO 9000**, are essential for firms engaged in many B2B supply situations. Others are very much for the benefit of consumers. For example, ATOL in the tourism business or Corgi for domestic gas appliance installations ensure the customer will be guaranteed delivery of the service and the provider of the service can be expected to have a certain level of service delivery competence. In many cases, however, these standards are not all they might seem to customers. Quite often the standards are written very specifically to cover certain aspects of the service and are not a complete guarantee. A plumber may have been awarded the Corgi standard, but this only covers work concerned with gas and not other plumbing services. Even ISO 9000 has been criticised as a guarantee of quality control in management procedures rather than an indicator of high specification and product quality.

The UK government has strongly promoted the **Investors in People** (IiP) award for firms that have demonstrated a commitment to develop their staff. The inference is that customers can be assured that they will receive good service from an organisation with the IiP award because of the commitment of staff. In the early years, many of the companies and departments that undertook the programme of preparation prior to assessment by the government agency managing the IiP award found the process very bureaucratic as lots of paperwork was required as evidence. This was particularly onerous for small firms which questioned the value of the 'badge' compared to the effort required to gain it. More recently, the paperwork has been reduced and, as a result, a wider range of organisations have been encouraged to undertake the preparation and have gained the award.

In some situations the achievement of standards is linked to league tables which compare the performance of organisations. However, these are often incomplete and superficial indicators of the relative quality of the organisations that are compared. The league tables published for public services have led to considerable debate. For example, the league tables of school exam success have been criticised because they only measure final results and do not measure added value. A school that obtains good results from pupils who entered the school with poor previous results and a lack of motivation will be thought by some to have achieved more than schools which only have pupils who are high academic achievers and would be successful in exams anyway.

The QAA (Quality Assurance Agency for Higher Education) of teaching in higher education focuses on the efficiency of teaching processes and procedures rather than on the content of the course. The ratings that are published in newspapers can therefore be misleading to potential students as some very large five-star research departments in the leading universities have been rated lower on teaching quality than some small research-inactive departments in newer universities.

4 Quality as value for money

Typically, a higher specification would suggest a higher price, or a higher price would suggest a higher specification and a superior product, particularly when the product is supported by a strong brand. This is the case with 'supercars', such as Ferrari and Lamborghini and with fashion clothing brands. In this case the brand is guaranteeing quality.

This idea was used by Stella Artois in their famous advertisement, which claimed that Stella was 'reassuringly expensive'. In practice, Stella was routinely discounted in the UK and was not regarded as a product of superior quality by others in the market. However, advertising activity created a customer perception of quality. In this case the brand appeared to be compensating for quality. Customers are prepared to pay premium prices for products and services that they perceive to offer more added value than their competitors, but if they feel that a less well-known brand is just as good, taking into account the tangible and intangible value, then they will buy it.

This concept of quality as value for money underpins much of the growth in own-label sales, particularly in food retailers, such as Sainsbury's own-brand corn flakes, which competes with Kellogg's. These supermarket own-label products claim to be exactly the same as the branded product but much cheaper. A significant percentage of customers do not believe that certain own-label products are equivalent and remain loyal to their favourite brand product. Many customers are still prepared to pay two or three times as much for a can of Heinz baked beans, rather than buy the other 'value brand' alternatives.

Lidl, Netto and Aldi have a 'no frills' approach to food retailing and this is maintained throughout their business, as can be seen from just looking inside their stores. Consumers are assured that the whole organisation avoids unnecessary cost and waste. By contrast, a higher specification product or service raises higher expectations among customers. If, for example, customers pay a high price for a fashion garment, then they expect the product to be sewn, finished and displayed better than lower-priced products.

5 Quality as innovation and added value

One of the most significant ways in which a product or service can be made more attractive to customers is through improved and more 'up-to-date' design. When products move beyond being merely functional, then they have greater appeal. Continuing with the car example, as we saw in Spotlight 8.1, the way that the Western car producers fought back against the Japanese producers was through developing better and more innovatively designed cars to appeal to different purposes and customer lifestyles, with models such as the Ford Ka, the Range Rover, the Renault Espace and Renault Scenic, and so on. Companies develop images that customers are expected to associate with the cars and this becomes apparent when watching television advertisements.

Customers now expect design to be a core aspect of any product's features, even for products bought largely to carry out some basic functions, such as garden tools for cutting or digging and office equipment for copying, printing or communicating. Both examples can be designed to avoid causing strain or fatigue, to reduce injuries and to be more attractive to the user.

We have said that customers' perceptions of quality include not just the product itself but also where the product is displayed, or the service that is delivered. Designers such as Terence Conran have applied their talents not just to furniture but also to interior decor for restaurants and the fashion houses, which must not only display well-designed clothing, but make the displays attractive too. The Christmas decorations in department stores such as Harrod's in London and Macy's and Saks Fifth Avenue in New York are tourist attractions in themselves.

6 Quality as a personal evaluation, perception or experience

As we have seen throughout this book, specific products will appeal to different customers in different ways, and the different dimensions of the product and service offering may take on greater significance. Consequently, what one customer segment or individual might consider to be a quality product can be very different from what another segment or individual might want. You will hear a veteran or vintage car enthusiast talking about the quality of the design and manufacture of an Aston Martin or E-type Jaguar, but this is a very individual appeal. Most car drivers prefer the benefits of a modern car. Some consumers are equally passionate about their favourite brand of cola or beer, or their favourite clothes designer, while others simply cannot tell the difference between the brands.

The customers' experiences of using a particular product might also vary, either because they were unfortunate in getting the one product in ten thousand that did not conform to requirements and slipped through the quality control net, or because it did not suit their requirements, even though it conformed to the specification. For example, a customer might buy a stereo system that seemed to perform all the functions that were required and sounded perfect playing the carefully selected CD in the shop but, at home, the sound might appear to be quite different and unacceptable.

One of the more interesting aspects of customer perception of products and services is the country-of-origin effect, as Spotlight 8.2 shows.

7 Quality based on trust

Customers are frequently not technically competent to judge the quality of many products and services that they require: their specification, their suitability for the job, and their safety in use. Few people are equipped to judge the competence of a

Spotlight 8.2

The country-of-origin effect

Customers have certain beliefs about the quality of products that originate from particular countries. For example, we expect German products to be well engineered, Italian products to be well designed with 'flair', and American products to be typically big and brash. You might like to think what stereotypes you associate with products from other countries such as Japan, China, France, Russia and the UK, and the effect of your own perceptions of the country of origin on your purchasing decisions of products originating from those countries.

A number of companies and their products have very strong associations with the USA and its heritage. Obvious examples include Coca-Cola, McDonald's, Microsoft, Marlboro and Harley Davidson. While many customers would believe the US heritage of these brands to be a guarantee of quality, other customers, who are less favourably disposed to the USA, would see the association as very negative.

Source: Robin Lowe

---

hospital consultant who carries out complex surgery or medical treatment, of a lawyer dealing with an obscure area of legislation, of the MMR vaccine used to protect children from a number of diseases, or the safety of food that might contain genetically modified (GM) cereals. Consequently, customers expect to be able to trust the relevant regulatory authorities, such as the General Medical Council, the Law Society, the Health and Safety Agency, to ensure quality on their behalf. Customers also trust that **government regulators** such as Ofsted (education), Oftel (telecommunications) and Ofwat (public utilities) ensure that customers obtain value for money from public sector services, monopolies or recently privatised services.

However, there is a feeling among customers that such regulatory authorities have often failed to protect customers from inappropriate decisions, secret negotiations and unscrupulous or misguided business activity, such as appeared to have occurred in the case of the BSE crisis in the UK. Customers should be able to trust politicians to protect customer interests, but it is even more difficult for customers to judge these issues based on government statements, often because complex arguments are reduced to 'sound bites' which reflect only one side of the argument and are usually politically biased. When these one-sided statements are reported later to have been 'only half of the story' and perhaps untrue, the customers lose trust in politicians. Other sources of information, such as newspaper reporting, are frequently proved to be equally biased and untrue.

Because customers cannot judge the quality of the work of the professionals they tend to find other observations which might act as indicators. A coffee stain on the foldaway tray on the aeroplane or unusual in-flight sounds might make customers question the maintenance standards of the airline and wonder if the engines have been serviced properly. Equally, the cleanliness of the hospital ward, the ease of getting through on the telephone, the difficulty of parking, the unhelpfulness of some staff and the arrogance of some consultants might result in criticism of the 'quality' of a hospital because it is difficult for patients to assess objectively the effectiveness of the treatment. As Dilemma 8.1 shows, however, crude measures that are introduced to improve quality do not always produce a satisfactory result.

Dilemma 8.1

National Health Service waiting times – customer quality or political spin

For the last two decades successive governments in the UK have attempted to improve the efficiency of the National Health Service. Few people in the UK have cause to question the skill and dedication of the staff, or the effectiveness of the treatment they receive, but many would criticise the efficiency of the service and especially the length of time it takes to obtain treatment or even a first consultation in hospital.

The Blair government placed NHS reform high on its agenda and set targets to reduce waiting times. The justification for this was that this would demonstrate the improvement patients were looking for. Because the achievement of targets was the measure by which hospitals would be judged and funded, hospital managers were forced to put the achievement of targets as a higher priority than patient care.

Priority was given to patients with minor problems who had been waiting longest above those patients with the greatest need. So in BBC television and newspaper reports a trauma surgeon explained that younger patients with smashed hips should be treated within two weeks in order to have a strong chance of making a full recovery, whereas they were now being made to wait longer than that because of waiting time targets.

In practice, too, waiting time figures are being manipulated and, in some cases, staff have 'cheated', being in fear of losing their jobs. Extra staff have been brought in to help improve figures when the waiting time figures were being measured.

With the next election approaching, the government faces a dilemma. It needs to prove it is succeeding in improving NHS efficiency, but it cannot risk being accused of reducing the quality and the effectiveness of patient care.

Source: Robin Lowe

8.2 SERVICE QUALITY AND THE TOTAL CUSTOMER EXPERIENCE

So far much of our focus has been on the quality of the core benefit and the augmented product, as discussed in Chapter 7, and in doing this much of our discussion has been of products. But now we turn to the quality of services. In thinking about this it is important to include service quality both from:

- the perspective of the augmented product, for example, the after-sales service and technical advice that might be offered in conjunction with a product, or the design, delivery and installation of equipment or an appliance, as might be involved in the purchase of a new kitchen;
- and the services themselves, particularly those that include a high 'people' content, such as hairdressing, garage services, personal financial management or training.

The augmented product and after sales-service

We said earlier that the conformance to requirements of a tangible product could be measured precisely and independently, but customers view the overall quality of a product offer not just by the physical product but also by the augmented product and the associated marketing services. This includes how customers are treated when they are seeking information prior to purchasing a product or service, how they are helped to make the decision and how they are treated after purchase when they have a problem with the product. For example, customers get a good indication of the quality of the service from an organisation by how complaints are dealt with.

The effectiveness of delivery of these services can have a serious impact on the customer's perception of product quality. For example, call centres have been a particular source of irritation for many customers. At times when the centre is busy customers might be kept waiting for 20 minutes or more for a call even to be answered in the first place. Many centres operate a complex menu system, requiring the customer to categorise the nature of their enquiry or complaint according to how the firm's internal departments are organised rather than how they perceive the problem. Quite often this is confusing and customers choose the wrong option only to find that they have to go back to the start of the menu system or even have to dial another number.

Most customers are realistic and do expect things to go wrong occasionally. It is also accepted by many organisations that if they deal well with a customer's complaint the customer will often become a loyal advocate of their products and services.

Services

As we have seen earlier, services tend to be individually delivered and the success of the service is usually determined by the specific experience of the customer. For example, a men's hairdresser that is located on a relatively low-income estate in Doncaster charges higher than average prices but the shop is usually full because the owner provides a better customer-oriented service than any of his local competitors, and customers enjoy going to the shop. He and his staff take an interest in the customers and remember their likes and dislikes.

Organisations offering services often try to manage the expectations of customers by explaining the standards that customers might expect from the service offering. Of course, having been led to expect a particular standard, customers will be very aware of and sensitive to poor performance. By promising home delivery within one hour, Domino Pizza set expectations of their own service. Moreover, in fast food outlets, for example, customers might compare the speed with which the order is served in different restaurants. Customers also make service quality comparisons across sectors, for example, between the speeds with which the cashiers check off goods in a do-it-yourself outlet compared to a food supermarket. Organisations therefore put considerable effort into achieving consistency to meet the standards they have set by, for example, thorough and intensive staff training.

Customers want organisations that are easy to deal with and expect the 'process' that they are taken through to be a satisfactory experience. A large charity recently realised that it was making it extremely difficult for potential donors to make donations using a credit card, because it was insisting on various checks despite the fact that there was no risk of financial loss to them. One of the largest suppliers of computer systems realised that because the organisation was split into many divisions, each with its own salesforce, the purchaser of a major hardware and software installation would be visited not only by account managers and senior executives, but also by up to nine salespeople to handle different hardware, software and services that made up the package and up to four more salespeople, who would try to sell financing packages for the different products and services as well. It is hardly surprising that customers could be put off by the army of people that were likely to visit.

It is bad enough if the organisation makes the customer experience unsatisfactory because of its own failings, but things can get much worse in situations where the organisation cannot control all the aspects of the overall customer experience. Quite often the process that a customer goes through in receiving a particular service can be affected by many outside (extraneous) variables over which it has little or no control, as Spotlight 8.3 shows.

In thinking about all these different dimensions of quality it is clear that customers expect satisfaction, as measured by their own personal standards, throughout their interactions with any organisation. You might like to think about your own experiences of the services that you have received recently at the supermarket check-out, the petrol station, the bank, from the bus driver, from your mobile phone service provider, or from the shop assistant. Was your experience determined by the service provider or did outside factors have an effect?

Most importantly, there is often a gap between the service levels that the organisation would like customers to receive and the level of service customers felt they actually received. A number of research studies have been carried out in this subject (e.g. Parasuraman et al., 1988; Payne et al., 1995). Parasuraman et al. (1988) found that customers have expectations of service and they also know what they want from the service encounter (i.e. their desires). Between these two there is a zone of tolerance. Above this zone of tolerance the customer will be pleasantly surprised, while below it the customer will be dissatisfied, frustrated and unlikely to stay loyal.

Spotlight 8.3

The total customer experience

For a fan, the visit of his favourite band to the local venue was the highlight of the year. The venue was 20 minutes along the motorway but five minutes into the journey the traffic came to a halt. The traffic jam lasted 45 minutes, by which time the car park near the venue was full. The overflow car park was 15 minutes walk away. Unfortunately, there was a thunderstorm at the time. By the time the fan reached the venue, completely wet through, the concert had already started. The seat that the fan had booked turned out to have a rather limited view of the stage. Moreover, the acoustics in the hall were poor. Alongside another fan sang along very loudly to all the songs, completely out of tune. At the interval there was a long queue for the toilet, the cold lager turned out to be warm and the burger was cold. At the end of the concert it was still raining, there was another traffic jam on the motorway on the way home. Going into the house the family asked 'How was your evening? Did you enjoy it?'

Now, unknown to the fan, the band played the concert of their lives. Everything worked and they were sensational. But unfortunately the group had little control over the fan's total experience and satisfaction with their performance that evening.

Source: Robin Lowe

Customers expect satisfaction throughout

Customers have increasing expectations of not just the products and services they receive in terms of quality and consistency but, in fact, all of their interactions with the organisation because customers are making judgements, either immediately, based on instinct, or after careful consideration, about the products and service that they have received or are receiving. These interactions, of course, include not just the planned-for information but also news stories, rumours, personal experiences and other informal information that helps customers to build up a picture of the organisation.

You should think about the large number of interactions that you might have in just one transaction, for example, arranging accommodation for a holiday, or buying or renting a house. We have discussed earlier the help that customers might want in obtaining information, in making decisions and in getting reassurance after making a purchase, and you should think about how the organisation performed in providing this. In this section we discuss the quality expectations that customers have of organisations, which ultimately leads them to a purchasing decision, or which may be the basis of their loyalty to a company and its offerings.

Customers expect:

- reliable and useful information;
- something over and above the basic quality of the core product or service;
- the experts to get it right and organisations to control the experts;
- organisations to deliver what they promise.

Customers expect reliable and useful information

Customers are subjected to many messages from suppliers providing information about the products and services that they are offering and, of course, the accuracy of the most important information is protected in law, for example, by the Trades Description Act. Much more information is provided in many different ways by suppliers which, when put together by customers, gives them an impression of the quality and reliability of the organisation.

One of the most significant changes over the last few years, driven particularly by the Internet, is the increased access to information that will enable customers to make more informed purchasing decisions. At a simple level it allows price comparisons to be made, allowing customers to challenge company claims to be 'offering the cheapest prices'. By researching prices on the Internet customers have been able to make substantial savings on, for example, cars, airline flights, videos and books.

More information is freely available, particularly through the Internet, and increasingly customers can have more knowledge than the supplier of the products and services that they receive, as Spotlight 8.4 shows.

When customers believe they have received incorrect information from a supplier they begin to question the reliability or even the ethical standards of the organisation. When organisations also make what appears to customers to be illogical product or service offerings, customers often conclude that the organisation is deliberately misleading or 'conning' them rather than simply making a mistake. But the complexity of organisations and their systems can lead to unexplainable situations. Recently an airline was charging £360 for a flight from East Midlands airport to Frankfurt and £240 from East Midlands to Cologne. This might seem unsurprising until it is pointed out that the flight to Cologne involved taking the same flight to Frankfurt in each direction and then taking an additional return flight from Frankfurt to Cologne for £120 less!

Spotlight 8.4

The knowledgeable patient

A consultant was taking a group of students around the ward when he came to a woman lying in bed. The consultant turned to his students and said 'Mrs Smith has an interesting and unusual condition. In fact there have only ever been two research papers written on her condition.' Mrs Smith leaned over to the doctor and whispered to him 'Excuse me doctor, there have actually been three papers written on my condition. I have looked them up on the Internet.' In practice, this presents a significant problem for the NHS because recommended treatments are also available on the Internet. If a doctor administered a wrong treatment, or one that was a little outdated, his or her competency could perhaps be challenged by a patient and a complaint might follow.

Source: Robin Lowe

Customers expect something over and above the basic or core product or service

Increased competition has led to a proliferation of products from which customers can choose and, as a result, customers often make choices between products that appear to be broadly similar. Many products have been around for a long time and might be considered by customers to be commodities with very little to differentiate one product from another. In this situation customers simply expect the core product to be of an acceptable quality. They take quality for granted.

One of the basic ways in which customers differentiate products from each other is branding. It is true that branded products can command premium prices by conferring additional intangible benefits to customers. For example, wearing designer clothing or a Rolex watch might improve the customer's self-image, status and self-esteem. However, this assumes that to justify a higher price the branded products must be perceived by customers to be of higher value. A brand that promotes itself only as providing high-quality products and services is probably wasting its advertising costs. Customers want something more.

Brands do distort the relationship between quality and price. As we saw earlier, Stella Artois was able to justify premium pricing based on largely intangible benefits. The same can be said of many fashion items and luxury goods, where the same factory production line and same raw materials will be used to produce similar products that will carry different brands and so very different price tickets. Luxury brands allow prices to be set purely on the basis of what customers are prepared to pay, and many customers of luxury goods simply want to purchase products that are exclusive and priced beyond what the mass market can afford.

As we also saw earlier in this chapter, increasingly the firms that compete with the leading brands can and do offer product quality that is very close or equal to that of the leading brand. Supermarket own-label products are examples of this. Consequently, customers expect more from the leading brands if they are expected to pay a brand premium. They expect, for example, better design, new products, continual innovation, more eye-catching advertising, sales promotions and exemplary customer service to keep them interested. Sony, for example, offers a continual stream of product modifications and improvements on its home entertainment systems; the lager and beer companies, such as Boddingtons, Carling and Fosters, have used humorous advertising; and the budget airlines, such as easyJet and Ryanair, repeatedly use low-price promotions.

Customers expect the experts to get it right and organisations to control the experts

Customers believe that by accessing professional services the responsibility for providing solutions should pass to the expert service provider. The customer assumes that the service provider is qualified, competent and equipped to provide the service. If the expert service, for example, requires medical, legal, scientific or technical knowledge, it is unlikely that the customer will have the necessary knowledge and skill to assess whether the hired expert is delivering the desired service effectively, solving a problem efficiently or providing the correct advice. If in doubt, the best that the customer can do is to obtain a second opinion. But the expert is rarely challenged and mistakes can occur. In most professional services there have been a number of high-profile cases of incompetence.

Typically, customers have no alternative but to trust the expert. Customers may look for clues that indicate competence, safe working and so on. They also expect that official regulators are in place to ensure that professionals are trained, perform their services effectively and safely, and behave ethically. When the regulators appear to fail to protect the individual, customers, frequently supported by the media, reach the conclusion that there has been a cover up by the establishment and suspect that the regulators are not working independently. The companies in the financial services industry, their regulators and the government, for example, have received considerable criticism for the bad advice given to customers and the mis-selling of pensions and endowments.

We have already discussed many factors that customers expect the organisation to control, and although customers accept that they may not be able to understand the work of the experts, they do expect the organisation to be able to understand and control its experts. In the late 1990s there were a number of scandals in the National Health Service, for example in Bristol, where hospital consultants were able to continue to operate on babies and children despite having unacceptably high death rates among patients, and in Hyde in Cheshire, where the health authorities failed to detect the notorious murderer, GP Harold Shipman, despite the high death rates on his patient list. Because of the specialist knowledge and high degrees of trust upon which medicine is based, the health authorities had relied largely on self-regulation by colleagues to identify dangerous consultants and doctors rather than using statistical information and routine management controls.

Customers expect organisations to deliver what they promise

Customers expect organisations to deliver on the promises made in advertising and product and corporate literature. It seems obvious that there are many reasons why this should be taken for granted. However, frequently customers fail to get what they believe they were promised, or the actions that the organisation has taken causes them to feel cheated. There are a number of reasons for this, including:

- factors that appear to be directly within the management's control;
- factors that are partially or indirectly within the organisation's control;
- factors that are outside the organisation's control.

As we discuss these factors it is worth reflecting on the difficult decisions that managers must face. Dilemma 8.2 shows some factors that can make it difficult for Network Rail to satisfy all their customer expectations simultaneously.

Dilemma 8.2

Should safety or punctuality come first?

In the early 1990s the railways in the UK were privatised. The previously publicly owned British Rail was sold off to private owners in the form of Railtrack (now Network Rail), which operated the track and stations and charged the service operating companies, such as GNER, Virgin Rail and Midland Mainline, for their use.

Before privatisation the railways in the UK had suffered from years of under-investment, resulting in very old rolling stock, outdated signalling systems and poorly maintained stations, etc. It had been expected that the privatisation would lead to new investment in track and trains, better management, better services and performance. In fact, service punctuality did not improve, the fragmentation caused by having many operating companies and their contractors made communications between organisations difficult and a blame culture developed. Things came to a head with a series of fatal crashes caused apparently by poor track maintenance and poor working practices. At the same time the operating companies, and particularly Railtrack, were being criticised by the service operating companies, rail users and the government for poor service and poor punctuality. All the organisations were accused of putting performance and generation of profits before customer safety.

Source: Robin Lowe

How can customers ensure that their needs for both punctuality and safety be balanced and managed?

Factors that appear to be directly within the management's control

When extreme levels of failure in the delivery of products and services occur, of course customers can and do take legal action, and there is evidence of a greater willingness of customers to complain. This has been accelerated by the number of lawyers seeking to represent potential complainants through advertising and offering no win–no fee representation. But there are also many occasions when customers do not feel it is worth the effort of complaining, often because the organisation has kept within the letter of the law, but appears to have been devious. Does your favourite chocolate bar seem smaller than when you were a child? Is it because it just seems smaller in your larger hand or has the manufacturer gradually reduced the size? Often fast moving consumer goods (fmcg) have particular price points, such as 99p. When costs go up manufacturers sometimes decide to reduce the contents of the pack slightly so that they do not have to break through the price point and go to £1.05. They keep the bag size the same so that it appears that nothing has changed, except that, in small print, the weight of the pack contents is less.

More serious problems can occur when something goes undetected in the production and distribution process accidentally, through bad management, or deliberately, as a result of actions by disaffected employees or individuals unconnected with the company.

Factors that are partially or indirectly within the organisation's control

There are factors that are not seen to be the responsibility of a single organisation but rather are the result of accepted custom and practice of organisations within the industry. However, often widely adopted but rather questionable industry practices can rebound. For example, the reputations of respectable organisations operating within industry sectors that are offering valuable services (e.g. timeshare, double glazing and consumer energy selling) have been disproportionately damaged by stories of mis-selling, the use of undue and disproportionate pressure on potential customers and inappropriate incentives. It can be argued that the organisations affected should work together to set better standards for such industry practices in order to build customer confidence.

In a rather different, way when members of a supply chain are not effectively working together customers can make negative judgements about the products. **Grey marketing** (for a fuller discussion see Doole and Lowe, 2004) can affect the way a customer perceives the image and reputation of an organisation. Also referred to as parallel importing, grey marketing is the use of distribution channels across country borders that an organisation has not approved. As was discussed earlier in the book, Tesco accessed a limited quantity of Levi Strauss 501s from a foreign Levi Strauss distributor which had excess stock, and sold them in its shops at huge discounts. Levi Strauss did not approve of Tesco as a retailer of its products because Tesco was not prepared to sell the full Levi's range, and the heavy discounting gave customers the impression that other Levi's retailers were overcharging for the products. In a similar way, grey marketing has shown that customers are charged much higher prices for cars in the UK than in other parts of Europe, lower prices for alcohol are available in France than in the UK and perfume sells at much higher prices in department stores compared to some discount drugstores and food retailers.

Factors that are outside the organisation's control

There are also a number of additional factors that affect the customer's perception of an organisation and its products and these are largely outside the organisation's control. For example, unsubstantiated complaints and criticisms are hard to combat, particularly when they are communicated through the Internet and by certain pressure groups. **Counterfeiting**, or making unlawful copies and passing them off as the originals, not only takes away revenue from an organisation but can also damage its reputation. Even though customers often know that the branded products they have purchased at unrealistically low prices cannot be genuine, they may still subconsciously associate a counterfeit product that fails or underperforms with the brand that it is claiming to be. Many times grey marketing and counterfeiting become interlinked and it is sometimes impossible for customers to determine whether the branded product sold at a very low price is genuine, obtained through an unauthorised distributor or a fake.

8.3 QUALITY ISSUES FOR CUSTOMERS IN BUSINESS-TO-BUSINESS SECTORS

The emphasis of the chapter so far has been on customer perceptions of quality in consumer markets and, although many of the issues that have been raised are relevant for B2B markets, this section focuses on the more formal arrangements that B2B customers make to assess the quality of their suppliers' products and services. Consumers of retail products do not have the knowledge and resources to measure quality and make judgements in a formal way and instead look for indicators and in-depth information from other sources, as we have discussed above. By contrast, B2B customers do have the resources. It is also vital that B2B customers make cost-effective purchase decisions. Failure to do so will ultimately lead to bankruptcy. However, before that, the failure of another supply chain member to deliver quality components or services upon which the organisation depends will lead to:

- damage to the B2B customer's reputation and lack of confidence among its customers, due to its poor product or service quality;
- losses due to the cost of putting right the suppliers' defects, product rejects, or losses incurred because a product line had to be stopped;
- delays in the launch of new products.

Consequently, B2B customers make formal assessments of the quality of every interaction between the supplier and themselves. As we discussed earlier, whereas in the consumer market the purchase decision and consumption of the product or service will be the responsibility of an individual or small group, such as partners, friends or family, B2B buying is the responsibility of a team. Each member of the buying team will:

- have specific responsibilities within the purchasing process;
- set quality assessment criteria for their aspect of the process;
- establish formal measurement of the quality measures;
- take corrective action if the supplier fails to meet the criteria.

An example of the B2B purchasing process, and the associated responsibilities and measures of quality, is included in Table 8.1.

Table 8.1 B2B purchasing responsibilities

B2B Buying team member	Examples of quality responsibilities
Chief executive	Negotiation of major purchasing contracts to ensure delivery of quality products and services
Finance manager	Effective management of payments and financing of major contracts
Purchasing officer	Administration and negotiation of supply contracts
Technical manager	Control of specifications of new and existing products
Quality manager	Managing conformance to specification
Production manager	Ensuring that components and services contribute to efficient and effective production
Logistics manager	Delivery scheduling and stock control
Receptionist	Control of access of supplier salespeople to the organisation's managers

Formal quality assessment

Distinctions can be drawn between the objective measures and subjective measures by which a B2B customer will assess the quality of suppliers. Objective measures might include, for example, assessing delivery efficiency (average days, fastest and slowest delivery, etc.), the number of rejects and the number of complaints. Subjective measures might include assessment of the cleanliness of a factory, the helpfulness of staff and the effectiveness of training. As Spotlight 8.5 shows, this can sometimes be problematic.

Subjective measurement of quality

Subjective assessment can be affected by many things. We have already covered many of the factors in previous chapters, such as the reputation of the supplier, bad image, the lack of innovation capability, and the attitude and helpfulness of staff. But there are again quite irrational reasons, too, such as the managing director dislikes or distrusts the managing director of the supplier company.

Objective measurement of quality

By contrast, objective measures of component performance, safety and cost-effectiveness are based on scientific and technical measurement and the aim is to make the tests robust and reliable. Considerable time is spent by B2B customers and suppliers on reaching agreement on the most appropriate tests, carrying them out and monitoring results. But it is not just product performance that is measured, but many other aspects of the associated services, such as the efficiency and effectiveness of logistics, stock control and administration.

Spotlight 8.5

Assessing the quality of training

Attempts are made by organisations to assess the effectiveness of their management training. It is difficult to think of any reliable objective assessments and so organisations attempt to make their subjective assessments quantitative in order to increase their validity. A multinational company contracted with trainers to provide management skills programmes and, as is normal with these courses, at the end of the programme asked the delegates to fill in a questionnaire rating trainers on a scale of 1 (poor) to 5 (excellent) as a measure of satisfaction.

They added up the scores, calculated the average and agreed to pay the training companies £800/day for 80% satisfaction, £1,200/day for 90% satisfaction and £1,400/day for 95% satisfaction. As you might imagine, the trainers plied the delegates with drinks in the bar, made sure the delegates had time off in the evening to watch *Big Brother* and important soccer games, avoided difficult subject areas and avoided making any criticisms at all of the delegates' contributions. As a result, the training was rather ineffective and not exactly what the organisation wanted.

Source: Robin Lowe

Much of the US$600 million estimated cost of developing new pharmaceuticals from the initial chemistry through to the drug being prescribed by a doctor is concerned with proving efficacy and safety in clinical trials. Despite the huge amounts spent, scientific testing is not infallible and, even using these methods of measurement, quality cannot be totally guaranteed. Complex scientific testing and the results produced can be open to considerable debate and misinterpretation, and there have been examples where such testing has failed to guarantee quality. Perhaps one of the highest profile cases was Thalidomide, which was prescribed during pregnancy and led to babies being born with physical deformities.

8.4 CUSTOMERS EXPECT QUALITY COMPANIES TO BEHAVE ETHICALLY

In this section on customer perceptions of quality, we broaden the discussion to include the wider range of **stakeholders** and their expectations of the organisation's quality, particularly in terms of its **ethics**.

Customers may seek to purchase or receive value-for-money products and services, but customers are also becoming increasingly concerned that they should buy from reputable organisations. Again, while customers may be able to make assessments of product quality, they are dependent on being given information by other stakeholders with specialist skills and knowledge to evaluate the firm's ethical behaviour. Other stakeholders, such as Greenpeace and investigative journalists, produce reports, news stories and other communications about the organisation's relationships with employees, customers, politicians and the local community, and customers use these to form judgements about the organisation's behaviour.

Customers make subjective judgements about the organisation and whether or not they think it is a quality organisation in the sense that it is reputable, its behaviour is ethical and it has a genuine concern for its customers and its wider stakeholders in the community. There are many ethical concerns and customers tend to focus on those closest to their heart. Consequently, different customers have different views about which companies behave ethically. Their concerns might include the organisation's attitude to:

- honesty and reliability in dealing with its own customers;
- the 'green' environment (including pollution, waste dumping and deforestation);
- employment policies (including child labour, exploitation of deprived groups and exploitation of its own employees);
- animal testing (including toiletries, pharmaceuticals and other medical treatments);
- espionage activities (including spying on competitors and poaching expert staff);
- criminal behaviour and fraud (including misappropriating staff pension funds and the manipulation of share prices to defraud shareholders);
- bribery, lobbying and inappropriate payments to politicians and civil servants.

It can be argued that any company can contribute to the community and Spotlight 8.6 is one example.

Companies that are in industries where there is a high risk of causing environmental damage or companies that adopt unacceptable working practices spend

Spotlight 8.6

Tea and trees

Betty's and Taylor's of Harrogate is a company that combines traditional tea rooms in Harrogate and York with marketing Yorkshire tea that is sold nationally through supermarkets. The company ran an on-pack promotion in which consumers could collect six tokens in return for which the company donated £1 to a tree planting project run by Oxfam. Tokens were placed on 8 million packs and nearly 60,000 customers returned tokens. As a result, 1.2 million trees were planted in developing countries, especially where Betty's and Taylor's teas were grown.

The funds donated by the company amounted to 2% of its after-tax profits, which is not insubstantial. In the process, however, it helped to build its reputation with its environmentally conscious customers.

Source: Adapted from http://www.crm.org.uk/case7.html

considerable sums of money in trying to manage their activities and image so as not to be criticised for their behaviour as a 'corporate citizen'.

Many global companies, such as Exxon, McDonald's, Gap, Nike, Nestlé and Shell, have been criticised by some for what are perceived to be unethical practices. For example, Exxon has been criticised for not doing enough to explore renewable sources of energy; McDonald's for causing environmental damage and adopting unacceptable employment practices with its young staff; Gap and Nike for using contractors that employ child labour and pay extremely low rates to its workers for products with extremely high retail prices; Nestlé for promoting powdered baby milk to mothers in poor countries; and Shell for being too close to an unscrupulous government in Nigeria in the mid 1990s.

A number of multinationals, including some of those mentioned above, are working extremely hard to develop ethical policies. Certain organisations, such as The Co-operative Bank, have adopted an ethical stance as a point of differentiation in its offering, as far as possible trying to limit its investments in unethical organisations and thus attract customers who are particularly sensitive to these issues.

Frequently, when organisations are criticised for unethical behaviour they provide counter-arguments for the criticisms and are often shown to have fully evaluated the options available to them. Sometimes the behaviour is the result of an accident or unanticipated event. Most frequently, however, it becomes apparent that the cause of the unethical behaviour is the result of different perceptions of the event from the different expectations and interpretations of different cultures.

SUMMARY

Over time customers have become more sophisticated in their needs and wants and, as a consequence, a number of different views have emerged about exactly what quality is. Essentially though, quality has two dimensions, consistency and level. Therefore, quality ranges from universally recognised and measurable conformance to requirements right through to a very personal, individual perception: 'I know quality when I see it'. Inevitably, customers have ever greater expectations of the products and services that they are offered.

Customers have much greater expectations of organisations to provide quality products and services and deliver on their promises. This means that many organisations offering complicated products and services must take the responsibility of solving problems that customers cannot even articulate. They must also have a duty to behave ethically in all their activities and especially in those areas, such as production, where customers cannot evaluate the organisation's activities directly. Committing to deliver high-quality products and services can also cause problems for firms because the quality of their service might be affected by factors outside their control.

Finally, the assessment of quality in business-to-business situations is carried out much more formally and with greater structure because organisations have more to lose from accepting poor-quality products and services and also they have much greater resources to carry out in-depth measurement.

> ### Discussion questions
>
> 1. Explain the different customer perceptions of quality, using examples to illustrate your view.
> 2. 'Customers take quality and good service for granted – an organisation has to offer something extra to get them to buy.' Explain whether or not you agree with this statement and justify your view point.
> 3. Identify five situations in which the majority of customers do not have the expertise or knowledge to decide whether a service or product being offered is of satisfactory quality. In each case identify the methods that are in place that are designed to assist customers assess quality. How effective do you think these methods are?
> 4. How does the assessment of quality differ when it is a business buying from another business compared with a consumer buying from a business?
> 5. In what ways does the unethical behaviour of organisations affect the customers' perceptions of the quality of the products and services they offer?

Case study 8.1   New-style quality is just a fiddle

When Marks & Spencer were going through a bad patch a few years ago with falling profits, they still maintained they were offering 'attractive prices and unbeatable quality'. But the word 'quality' is one of the most overused and most abused words in business today. Our grandparents would have been in no doubt that quality meant excellence and the best of its kind. You know quality when you see it and a Stradivarius violin had quality, a tinker's fiddle did not!

An alternative definition was offered some 50 years ago by an American statistician, W. Edwards Deming, who said quality meant consistency and a lack of defects. But a defect is simply a result that lies outside a specified range. The resulting product that is specified can still be rubbish but at least it is consistent rubbish. Someone said about the Spice Girls' film *Spice World*: 'That was perfect, girls, without actually being any good.'

When did things change? When the US journalist Negley Farson visited Britain in the early years of the twentieth century he noticed that a brass column or banister in Britain would be solid brass, whereas in America someone would have worked out how to hollow it out in order to save a few nickels.

Fifty years later, a group of investment analysts visited a world-famous British engineering company and started asking questions about margins, stock holding, profit and balance sheets ratios. The company executives were puzzled why they were nit-picking about numbers. After all, their products were the finest in the world. The company, Rolls Royce, went bust in 1973. So over-engineered products and old-style quality could no longer be the norm for companies wishing to please the market. Of course, there is still a market – a relatively small one – for master-pieces and luxury goods where there are no compromises made on cost.

The new definition of 'quality' gained further credibility as Japanese manufactur-ers followed the principles of Edwards Deming and produced cars that did not break down, as European and American cars did.

Going back to Marks & Spencer, the question is which definition of quality can they be pursuing? Their goods cannot be described as masterpieces as they are not offering quality at any cost. Neither are they offering merely consistency of size, cut-ting and stitching, as you would expect clothes to have a degree of style and be satisfying to wear – in fact a little of the old-style quality definition.

This leads to the third definition of quality as value for money. This does not mean cheapness, because consumers expect all goods to be of a certain acceptable standard. McDonald's offers what it claims to be high-quality food, including the 99 cent or 99 pence hamburger. Whether or not this is considered by consumers to be high quality is questionable. So the problem with value for money is that different customers will have different perceptions of what value for money actually is.

Questions

1. What techniques may be employed to ensure that a product achieves maximum possible customer satisfaction?

2. How does a brand identity help or hinder the search for customer satisfaction? Identify situations from both sides of the discussion.

Source: Adapted from T. Jackson, 'New Style Quality is just a fiddle', in L. Rickard and K. Jackson (eds) (2000) *The Financial Times Marketing Casebook* (2nd edition). Harlow: Financial Times/Prentice Hall.

Further reading

Hooley, G., Saunders, J. and Piercy, N. (2004) *Marketing Strategy and Competitive Positioning* (3rd edition). Harlow: Financial Times/Prentice Hall, Chapter 16.

Website

For further information on Investors in People standards (IiP) visit www.investorsinpeople.co.uk and for ISO 9000 visit www.iso.org or www.bsi.org.uk.

References

Doole, I. and Lowe, R. (2004) *International Marketing Strategy* (4th edition). London: Thomson Learning.

Parasuraman., A. Zeithaml, V.A. and Berry, L.L. (1988) 'SERVQUAL: a multiple item scale for measuring customer perceptions of service quality', *Journal of Retailing*, 64 (1): 12–40.

Payne, A., Christopher, M., Clark, M. and Peck, H. (1995) *Relationship Marketing for Competitive Advantage*. Oxford: Butterworth Heinemann.

Part Three

Influencing the customer

Within this section of the book we build upon the material introduced in the first eight chapters by focusing on the ways in which organisations might influence the behaviour of their customers. In doing this, we begin, in Chapter 9, with a discussion of how the organisation needs to be structured if it is to serve its customers effectively. We examine the idea of the service culture and illustrate how a gap can develop between service expectations and service delivery. Against this background we then discuss some of the approaches to customer care and how any gaps in service delivery might be reduced.

Chapter 10 focuses on the ways in which organisations communicate with their customers. We examine the structure of the communications process and the sorts of factors that tend to inhibit effective communication flows. We then turn, in Chapter 11, to the ways in which customer relationships can best be managed for long-term effectiveness and results. This is an area that has been the subject of a considerable amount of research in recent years and the lessons that have emerged from a variety of sectors are used to develop a series of insights and guidelines.

Finally, in Chapter 12, we turn to the idea of the new consumer. The idea of the new consumer is based on a recognition of the ways in which the marketing environment has changed over the past decade, and has led to what we refer to as 'the new marketing reality'. This new reality is very different from the conditions of the past and, as we demonstrate, this demands very different insights and patterns of marketing behaviour.

9 Organising internally to serve external customers

Andy Cropper

LEARNING OUTCOMES

After reading this chapter you should be able to:

- **Define both 'internal' and 'external' customers and understand the importance of the relationship between the two to the effectiveness of a business**

- **Appreciate the impact of customer–supplier relationships within an internal organisational supply chain and be able to recognise the impact each stage of the chain can have upon customer satisfaction**

- **Understand the contribution that each employee is able to make to the 'quality' of any product or service delivered by an organisation**

- **Identify the benefits to an organisation of adopting a service-based culture**

- **Understand how culture might be created within an organisation**

KEY WORDS

Corporate capability
Customer complaints
Customer perceptions
Customer service
Distribution chain
Internal customer
Pre-conceived idea
Service culture

Service encounter
Service expectations
Suppliers
Supply chain
Value added
Value chain
Waste

INTRODUCTION

So far in this book we have focused on the concepts of customers and quality as they affect the external customers involved in exchanges with an organisation. Similar concepts, however, can and should be applied to the exchanges that take place between departments or individuals within an organisation. At work, a colleague or other department might be seen as a customer, supplier or both at different times of the day.

In this chapter we consider how applying the principles of 'customer' and 'quality' to these internal organisational transactions can lead to an improvement in the overall quality offered to external customers and the increased performance of the organisation. In doing this we discuss:

- What constitutes a 'customer' or a 'supplier' and how this concept can be applied across all aspects of the business.
- The relationships, involvement and expectations of customers and of those who supply them.
- Creating an environment within a business where 'doing the job' is replaced by 'ensuring that all customer expectations are understood, recognised and met'.
- The impact upon the way an organisation needs to operate in order to create an environment where employees are informed, encouraged and supported in maintaining a customer focus.
- The demands on the organisation in ensuring that all customer expectations, both internally and externally, are met.

Business chain

To bring this into context, we will start by looking at the concepts of **supply**, **value** and **distribution chains** and their relevance to an organisation.

Consider a simple product, an ice-cream, and think about what happens to get that into your hand on a summer's day. You might have purchased it from a shop, where it needed to be stored and maintained at the right temperature and under the right conditions. In order to get there it will have passed through the control of more than one person. It would have been transported to the shop, possibly by a transport company or in the back of the shop van from a wholesale warehouse, where it also needed to be stored. To get there it will have arrived via another transport company, who would have collected it from the manufacturer.

From the perspective of the manufacturer, the process of getting the goods from the factory to the end-user represents their 'distribution chain' and clearly if the ice-cream had been mishandled, badly stored or subject to inappropriate temperature changes during that process, your eating experience and impression of that company's products might be severely impaired.

In order to produce the ice-cream the manufacturer will have created a production process that starts with raw materials coming into the factory and ends with the finished product. They would also have tried to ensure that it would appeal to your tastes (see Chapter 5), to ensure that it was available at the shops you visit and that you would want to buy it (see Chapters 4 and 5).

The company is not just taking the raw materials and creating tasty ice-cream, therefore, but also encouraging you to select their ice-cream over competitor products. The production process is relatively straightforward, but the quality of the end product for the consumer is not just a product of the manufacturing process (see Chapter 8), it is also linked to the overall effectiveness and efficiencies of the organisation. The manufacturer effectively 'adds value' to the raw materials in order to create the finished product and be able to profit from it, and the internal process and management elements of the company make up its 'value chain'.

If we now consider the products and services that the company uses in order to add that value, and follow the supply of milk as an example, this might have been transported from a dairy, which will have received it from dairy farms. Each farm will have had to manage, care for and milk its herd of cows.

At the farm the quality of the grazing will affect the quality of the milk, so the nutrients and minerals added to the soil are also an important aspect of ensuring quality – including the manure! This aspect of the company suppliers makes up the 'supply chain' and again you can see that the quality of goods produced will be influenced by the quality of processes adopted and materials used by all of the suppliers. The elements of business chains are shown in Figure 9.1.

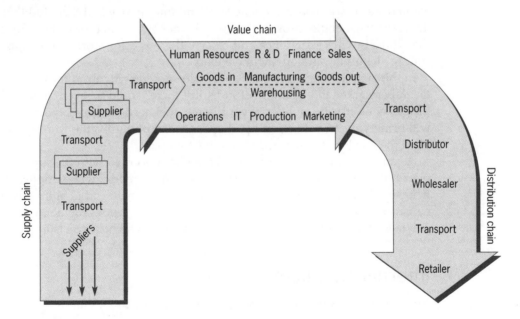

Figure 9.1 Elements of business chains

9.1 SO WHAT DO WE MEAN BY THE 'CUSTOMER'?

As you will have seen in Chapter 2, a *customer* is essentially someone who will buy your goods or services and a *consumer* is someone who consumes or uses them. In the case of the purchase of weekly groceries for a family, for instance, the person who undertakes the shopping could be both a customer and a consumer but family members will also be consumers.

From the perspective of both the customer and consumer, the quality of the goods purchased and their ability to satisfy immediate or future needs are paramount but there is more to the experience than that. For example, if you need to buy the ingredients to make a meal for some friends, you will have a specific list of ingredients and a set of criteria to which they need to adhere. Perhaps price, make or type (e.g. demerara, not white, sugar). You will seek out appropriate **suppliers** and their accessibility and the time and effort it will take you to acquire the goods are important considerations as well.

To complete the shopping and to find that some of the goods are damaged, perished or past their sell-by dates would be disastrous if you ultimately had to make the meal either without these ingredients or even with them. Consider as well the experience of shopping. Did you need to make two bus journeys to get to the supermarket and visit the bank to get the correct change to pay the fare? Did the shopping trolley seem to have a mind of its own? Were staff not around when you wanted assistance? Did you queue for 15 minutes to pay and then find that the plastic carrier bag handles broke on the way home? What can be seen here are aspects of the whole buying experience and clearly there is a lot more to the equation than simply identifying and buying the goods.

In this simple example there are six main suppliers involved for you – four buses, the supermarket and a bank, but in reality there would be even more. What about the gas or electricity supplier to your home, fuel needed to cook the meal, a taxi that will bring your friends or, and perhaps more importantly, the wholesaler that supplied the goods to the supermarket in the first place?

As an individual consumer you will not be concerned with the supermarket supplier but as a business you might well be influenced by who supplies the people who supply you. Using this example it is easy to isolate and identify who the external suppliers might be, but the concept of a supplier goes further. For example, if you need help to prepare the meal, are the people who help you 'suppliers' as well?

Internal suppliers

We now come to the *basic building blocks of a company*. In simple terms these are likely to be:

- buildings and facilities;
- equipment (e.g. desks, machines and computers);
- materials (e.g. operational goods such as notepaper and software, raw materials, work-in-progress and finished goods);

- money;
- people.

The first four of these are simply the tools required to provide whatever it is the company is there to deliver, but the process, production and delivery is undertaken by the final element, *people*. Regardless of the levels of automation involved, it is the people that make things happen, automation simply impacts upon the number of people required.

Developing this further, if we look at the basic construction of a company it will typically be by function (see Figure 9.2), with each having its own aims, objectives, duties, priorities and management. Logically, therefore, in order to perform the function of converting the supply chain inputs into the distribution chain outputs the **value added** by the company has a great deal to do with the contribution of the people within it and how effectively the various areas of the organisation co-operate.

Look at Figure 9.2 and instead of the company think of the meal you are preparing. Instead of the functions that appear, replace these with the supermarket, bus company and your other immediate suppliers. In essence, this is what the company is, a conglomerate of functions and sub-functions which support each other and are both the customers, consumers and suppliers of each other's products and services. If we now think of the company in Figure 9.2 in terms of how it operates rather than how it is structured, it would be appropriate to re-draw the model as illustrated in Figure 9.3.

Figure 9.2 Stylised company structure

Figure 9.3 Company functional relationships

Accepting this wider view of the way in which an organisation works, clearly the *operational processes*, *relationships* and *communications* between staff are of major significance and it is important for a company to not only recruit good staff but to ensure that they are well trained, motivated and effectively managed in order to prevent any work or priority conflicts occurring.

The employee

As an individual employee, it follows that in order for the organisation to gain the maximum benefit from your contribution it has to recognise that you will not simply perform a functionary role but will perform that role in the context of all the other people you come into contact with, either directly or indirectly. Consequently, you not only need the training and support required to perform your role, but would benefit from an understanding of the underlying aims and objectives of that organisation, the standards it strives to achieve, what it feels is important to its customers, what it is trying to deliver, not just in terms of the specific product or service but in terms of fulfilling the benefits sought by customers, and how the various elements of the organisation contribute to the delivery of those benefits. This provides you with an understanding of how your contribution fits in with the other functions of the business and helps you ensure that in dealings with others, both inside and outside the organisation, you can contribute effectively to delivering those benefits.

9.2 CUSTOMER AND SUPPLIER INTERACTION

We have now built a picture that is made up not of one company interacting with others in the various business chains but of individuals operating together, in work units, and then interacting with other individuals and units of people both inside and outside their own organisation – a much more complex environment.

Taking the stylised company structure shown in Figure 9.2, if we now take those broad departmental areas of Sales, Marketing, Operations, Finance, Production and Human Resources, consider the contact each department might have with any one of the company's key suppliers.

Marketing has responsibility for promoting the company and any of the communications activities it undertakes could be seen by anyone within the supplier company. The *Finance* department will be responsible for handling the payment of invoices and so might well deal with Operations, Sales and Finance staff as the supplier. *Operations* staff might be responsible for dealing with sales staff in arranging the order and managing delivery. *Production* staff might liaise with production staff to manage particular product specifications.

The degree and extent of contact between companies can be quite extensive (see Figure 9.4) and take place at many different levels for a myriad of different reasons, from a telephonist redirecting a call to the tone of a letter, the content of a website, the condition and state in which goods arrive and face-to-face staff contact.

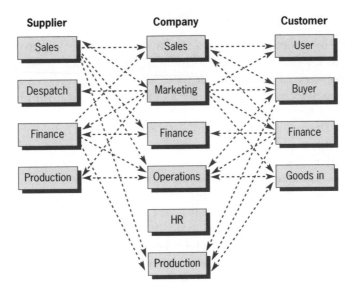

Figure 9.4   The many levels of contact

In addition to the functional purpose of those contacts, therefore, whether it is between a member of staff or between staff and customers or suppliers, every time interaction takes place, verbally or otherwise, it will either increase or decrease the impression held by each party of the other. It follows, therefore, that the efficiency and effectiveness with which employees operate and interact both with their colleagues and with suppliers, distributors and end-users will dictate the ultimate effectiveness of the organisation as a whole and also impact upon the degree of satisfaction experienced by those they deal with.

Employees and customer service

Consider the role performed by the check-out clerks at a supermarket. Their job is to check through the items, calculate how much is owed and take the money. That is the function of their role and it can be easily discharged as you, the customer, place your goods on the belt and then pack them once they have been recorded. From your own experience, think how this has differed and reflect on what may have caused this.

The functions of the assistant will have remained constant and on each occasion you will have left with your purchases. But the way in which the role was performed will have varied and that will have reflected upon your *level of satisfaction* with that transaction. A reflection you will also place upon the organisation itself. What we, as customers, are experiencing is the **customer service** aspect of the transaction, at the point at which we come into contact with a supplier. When and how that contact is managed will impact on our satisfaction with the transaction, how we perceive that organisation and whether or not we will choose to deal with them again.

The impact of 'pre-conception'

As a customer, it would not be unreasonable for us to expect, before joining a check-out queue, that the assistant would be efficient, courteous and helpful. So we start our **service encounter**, or point of contact between customer and supplier, with a **pre-conceived idea** that will inevitably vary from supplier to supplier and circumstance to circumstance.

These will also vary from individual to individual, as we apply our own social, cultural and experiential values to those **service expectations**. Our ultimate level of satisfaction, therefore, will be measured against these pre-determinations.

Curiously, if our expectations are met, then we might not even consciously register this experience and feel especially satisfied. Our expectation of service quality is simply representing what is acceptable to us. Effectively, therefore, in meeting expectations the impression might be little better than satisfactory regardless of how 'special' it actually might have been. Consequently, the challenge for any supplier in delivering a quality service is in exceeding the expectations of its customers, not just in meeting them. And not just once, but consistently, time after time, for the last experience is the one we tend to remember most clearly and the one that will have the greatest influence on our next choice.

Poor service perception will encourage customers to look elsewhere, while exceeding their expectations can turn them into loyal customers. Expectations are variable though and as our experience and exposure grows, so do our expectations. For the supplier, this is where the delivery and management of customer service becomes difficult. What may seem 'excellent' to one customer may simply be considered average by another. Conversely, what may repel one customer may actually attract another.

As an example, have you ever waited in a check-out queue while the assistant carried on a conversation with the customer in front of you? For those with time to spare supermarket shopping might be a social event, for others speed might be paramount. Consequently, marketers are not only faced with trying to anticipate and fulfil varying **customer perceptions** of what the service experience should consist of and how it should be delivered, but they are also faced with the prospect of those expectations changing and, potentially, with them varying diversely between customer groups.

Matching customer expectations

The impact upon an organisation that gets this wrong can be easily anticipated and the challenges of getting it right can be many.

Customer expectations may not be realistic and thus can never be effectively delivered in the first place. The challenge here, therefore, is to build an understanding of what those expectations might be and then to manage, guide and influence customers through the organisation's communications activities and service encounters in order to encourage them to re-evaluate and amend their expectations to a more realistic level. Alternatively, if expectations are achievable, while the aim is to exceed these, care has to be taken to ensure that customers are not led to believe that the organisation will over-deliver to a degree that it is actually unable to achieve. By raising expectations and then failing to meet them, it is possible to do more damage to the customers' loyalty than by not making any service promises. And sometimes this can happen without specific intention.

For example, Midland Bank (now HSBC) went under the strapline 'The Listening Bank' during the 1980s, yet it could never have anticipated that this simple statement would enrage certain groups of customers who felt that decisions were being made about their banking requirements without, what they considered to be, appropriate levels of 'listening' to them as individuals. In reality, it lifted expectations to the degree that people expected that they should be considered as individual cases and there were neither the systems nor the resources available to manage customers at this level. In practice, if a decision was made with which the customer disagreed, for example a loan was refused on sound financial principles, then the customer would simply claim they were not being 'listened' to and become dissatisfied with the service irrespective of any reasoned argument for refusal.

The task, therefore, is to monitor and understand expectation levels, to manage these through marketing communications activities (see Chapter 10) at an achievable level and then to ensure that the service promise to customers addresses those expectations and, at the same time, that service delivery is maintained at a level that is consistently above those expectations.

Service delivery

The issue of service delivery is complex. Customer service is an aspect of the contact between customers and suppliers and thus the most crucial element of this are the people involved. Regardless of any 'policy' decision about how service is to be delivered, ultimately the delivery falls upon the individual at that point of contact.

With this in mind, it is not surprising to learn that for many organisations it is the lower-paid, lower-grade staff who have responsibility for the vast majority of customer contact activities. For example, it is the supermarket check-out staff and shelf stackers who handle a lot of general enquiries. In banks it is counter staff or call centre staff. For others, such as the new 118 directory services, these are outsourced to a third party. How, in these circumstances, can the organisation manage the service delivery effectively?

There is an assumption that the desire to deliver high levels of service is a given; yet organisations can be focused in different directions and other factors may inhibit service quality. For example, there is a clear *link between cost and service*, with the increasing levels of service quality requiring greater time, resources, training, people, monitoring, etc. Organisations that are driven more by financial considerations than marketing ones, where the focus is on fulfilling customer needs, may underfund these areas and thus create a gap between what needs to be delivered and what can be delivered.

In addition, establishing what these levels should be requires an understanding of customers (Chapter 5) and an organisational structure focused on addressing those needs. This means starting with the customer and then driving the organisation from that perspective. Many organisations actually start by seeing themselves as manufacturers or retailers first and then consider their customers – a different perspective and one that can cause them to lose sight of customer needs and concentrate on selling what they have rather than producing or stocking what people wish to buy.

This brings us on to an aspect of service that is easily overlooked. The customer–supplier relationships do not simply exist between an organisation and the customers of that organisation but also between individuals, departments and divisions of the organisation. Consequently, all of the observations here also apply internally as well. If one department of an organisation has limited confidence in the quality of work provided by another, and they have the option to source outside, instantly you can see that there will be implications in cost, efficiency, management and control.

The concept of the internal customer

This idea of the **internal customer** developed alongside the programmes that many companies introduced in an attempt to improve the quality of manufacturing and operation, during which time it was found that many larger firms were wasting huge amounts of money due to a combination of factors, including:

* defective work that has to be rejected;
* having to use additional materials and resources to re-do jobs in order to correct mistakes;
* workers being poorly directed and thus performing their role inefficiently;
* machines lying idle because no one had ordered the necessary components to keep the production line going.

In addition, it was also found that problems did not occur just in the production area. For example, if a secretary could not read a scribbled note, or a boss's instructions were unclear, the secretary would then have to waste time asking the boss what they meant.

Poor communication often appeared to be a key cause of problems and it was realised that if everyone treated everyone else as either a supplier or a customer, then it would be much easier to establish exactly what the requirements for each transaction were.

As an employee, you can be a purchaser and a supplier at different times of the day, for example, the secretary and boss referred to above are both suppliers and customers of each other. The natural development of this was that if mistakes occurred in the transaction, then the internal customer should not accept them but insist that they be put right. In the same way this would happen with an external supplier.

The objective was not simply to fix problems and address immediate issues, but to understand the reasons why the transaction had gone wrong initially and enable an ongoing process of improvement in quality and efficiency of operation. This would enable the internal supplier and internal customer to get to the root of the problem, which could be in an entirely different department!

These problems and the solution in terms of the concept of internal customer and suppliers led to the development of business management concepts within organisations such as Total Quality Management (TQM) and Customer, Quality and Innovation (CQI).

Spotlight 9.1

Showing that we care

For many, telephone banking offers a number of advantages such as 24-hour availability, ease of access, no trips to branches, no long queues and speed, but all of these elements are just features and benefits of this way of banking. So what makes one telephone bank more attractive than another?

Many of the products and services offered are similar. Credit cards, cheque cards, savings accounts, mortgages and financial packages, so why do customers choose a particular supplier and, equally important, what makes them stay with that supplier?

Up until the 1990s, moving bank accounts was a complex and time-consuming business, so many customers remained where they were regardless of their satisfaction with a provider. During the 1990s movement became easier and consequently customer migration increased.

At that time, one major development was the introduction of telephone banking, followed rapidly by the introduction of Internet banking. Both of these new delivery methods offered financial benefits to the banks, particularly in relation to economies of scale and reduced operating costs. This was accompanied by a rise in consumer awareness and an equivalent rise in consumer expectation. For example, if the banks are saving costs and thus making more money out of me, then surely I should be getting more out of them as well?

With such similarity in products and services the logical area for banks to concentrate on was enhancing the quality of each customer's banking experience, using customer satisfaction to differentiate one bank from another.

Both telephone and Internet banking are grounded in the ability to gather good quality data on customers and with such detailed knowledge comes the opportunity to enhance the customer contact experience by tailoring the content of that contact more specifically to the individual customer. Consider this observation by a telephone banking customer:

> A few days ago I telephoned my bank to check if some money had arrived. The young lady I spoke to took me through the security check to make certain it was me and then checked my accounts. The money had just arrived that morning and on hearing this I thanked her. She then asked if I needed anything else and I said no, so she thanked me for my call and then, just before hanging up,

Spotlight 9.1 *continued*

said 'Oh, and by the way, Happy Birthday, Mr Cropper'. I was both surprised and impressed at the same time.

A cynic would observe that, having the customer details, the telephonist had simply responded to a prompt on a computer screen. But the point is that the bank took the trouble to build a system that identified this in the first place and also that the telephonist delivered the line in a cheery and pleasant way.

As customers we expect the features and benefits of the goods we buy as a standard element of that purchase. Those extra elements that support the purchase enhance that experience and when taken together these are what make up the total customer satisfaction experience.

Identify three places you shop at regularly, either in person or by mail, telephone or Internet. Why do you use these outlets? List the aspects of the shopping experience you like and any that you find less satisfactory. If a similar supplier were to set up in competition, what would encourage you to switch?

9.3 ADOPTING A SERVICE CULTURE

We can now see that a supplier cannot simply be defined as someone from outside the organisation, nor can a customer be seen in that way either. In reality there is a continual supplier–customer relationship in force between individuals working within the same organisation running alongside the more discernable supplier–customer relationships that exist between the organisation and those with whom it does business.

If we now take a closer look at organisations themselves and the way in which they operate, perhaps the clearest image that comes to mind is one of an organisation as a big machine that takes goods and supplies into one end, processes them systematically and then delivers the finished product or service at the other (see Figure 9.5).

In Figure 9.5 we have a view of how goods get processed and we can also see that in order to operate effectively there are a number of functions that need to be undertaken, but what we have effectively done is build a picture of the organisation based upon a functional view that tends to encourage us to compartmentalise the differing departments and to see their purpose and contribution aside from that of other departments. This is a view that can draw us away from what the organisation as a whole is trying to achieve.

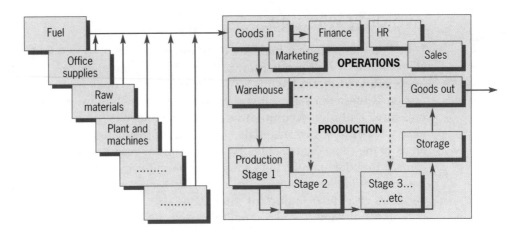

Figure 9.5 The organisation as a process and functions

Essentially, any organisation within the business world exists in order to make a profit; to generate sufficient funds to enable it to pay employees; to buy new materials and equipment; to cover operational expenses; and also to provide a return for investors. There are organisations, for example charities, whose aim is not to make a profit in the financial sense, but even for them survival depends on the same performance criteria. So while they might be 'non-profit making', their definition of profit has simply been restricted to that of generating sufficient revenue to enable their work to continue.

The value added by the organisation

With this in mind, consider the value chain and look at the output of the organisation from the perspective of the value added by the organisation rather than the way in which it produces its products or services and, in so doing, consider the relationship between departments and individuals and how that impacts upon the efficiency and quality of what is produced. Look at the effectiveness with which the organisation, outlined in Figure 9.5, converts the goods and materials it takes in into the products it manufactures and assume, for illustrative purposes, that these are dairy products.

Of the raw materials purchased, one of these would be milk and that has to be stored prior to processing. Storage will be governed by stringent health regulations involving temperature control and sterilised equipment and, as a perishable liquid, it can only be stored for a pre-determined time. A combination of factors, including production delays, servicing, maintenance, operational difficulties and spillage will inevitably lead to some of the milk being wasted and this same broad consideration applies to the other raw materials as well.

Avoiding wastage

Let us now assume that there are eight more production stages and a final storage stage in the overall production process, making ten stages in total that the raw materials move through while being converted to the final product.

Across these ten stages, just a 2% rejection at each point due to quality control measures will give accumulative **waste** of almost 19% of raw materials. This is nearly one-fifth of raw materials wasted and if this pattern is reflected across other areas of the same organisation, be it materials or resources of any description, you can see that the manufacturer might not be in business for long. Clearly, if a competitor can manage their operation so as to reduce this to 1% per stage, it quickly becomes clear how important internal quality management is when evaluating potential, profitability and competitiveness.

Now take this simple model and think of a complex organisation where there are many levels of operation. With so many variables it is clear that it is not just poor process management that can affect poor company performance or failure. It is also the effectiveness with which people and departments interact.

Waste should not just be applied to spoiled goods but also to all organisational resources. Elimination or minimisation of waste is not the only way of improving overall company performance though. Value can also be added through the internal supplier–customer relationships.

If you have ever held a part-time job or been in full-time employment you will appreciate that it is much more satisfying to work in an organisation where tasks are done efficiently. You are happier in your work and are also more effective in what you do. This, in turn, can help reduce error, and be under no illusion that internal mistakes can have a direct impact upon external customers. At a simple level, how many paperboys and girls have been unfairly criticised by *Daily Mirror* readers for correctly delivering an incorrectly addressed (by the newsagent) *Daily Telegraph*? At a more complex level, consider the impact on the organisation of the example in Dilemma 9.1.

Dilemma 9.1

24-hour helpline

'The concept is simple, we have customers using our products travelling around the world in differing timezones so we need the ability for them to contact us in emergencies in the case of equipment or service failure. As a small company we cannot afford a call centre so the solution was easy, a 24-hour phone number routed to the UK and linked to a mobile phone that support staff hold on a rota basis. If they have to put the phone on voicemail at any stage, the arrangement is that they check the voicemail at the earliest opportunity and call the customer straight back.' So went the rental manager's explanation. '... However, we forgot about the variables – staff arranging with each other to cover for them and less

Dilemma 9.1 *continued*

experienced staff having to manage complex calls, the mobile being left in the office in the evening, forgetting to switch it to voicemail while leaving it in the car, answering a call while sitting in a rowdy pub. The list goes on and the customer problems increased rapidly during the first six months of operation before we discovered what was going wrong.'

This highlights the need for staff to have a proper understanding of the cause and effect of their actions and the challenges that face line managers in controlling the quality output of their staff.

Employee contribution

A commonly used term within business is the 'Strategic Business Unit' (SBU), which is a convenient way of compartmentalising a large business and creating what are effectively independent profit centres, often with independent objectives as well. The positive effect of this is that it can increase the ability to manage efficiencies and costs as it encourages each unit to manage its 'business' within very specific parameters. However, if we view a distinct unit within the organisation without consideration for the others, then by looking inward in this way we risk losing sight of the mutual dependencies that exist and can take action that may benefit one unit but harm another.

The point this raises is that in order to ensure that the organisation as a whole operates effectively and efficiently then the various arms of the business do not just need to understand the business objectives and how their objectives fit in with these, but must also have a good understanding of the aims, objectives and priorities of other business areas as well, and understand how all of these need to work together. In addition, all employees also need to understand how they contribute to the overall profitability and future of the organisation so that they can appreciate the value of their contribution and understand the impact that their individual efficiency has on the long-term security of their employment.

Rather than thinking of the operational activities of the organisation in the way illustrated in Figure 9.5, therefore, we can now see that a major factor of organisational effectiveness is the *individual employees* – their individual skills, the clarity of their direction and the way in which they perform their roles. Consequently, the organisational model should, perhaps, be more akin to the movement of a finely tuned watch, with the cogs and wheels, no matter how large or small, being mutually dependent upon each other for it to function properly.

Encouraging employee co-operation

This brings us around to thinking about how an organisation can actually secure employee involvement and co-operation and the ways in which that organisation can ensure that its goals and purpose are sufficiently clear and understood and that the external customers' needs and expectations are met. To address this, it is necessary to consider where the key barriers to performance might be and then look at the way in which employees can be managed in order to overcome them. The implications can be modelled as follows (see Figure 9.6):

1. The fundamental 'marketing' approach to business is to start with understanding what the customer needs and then work towards fulfilling those needs, particularly in terms of service and quality expectations. In so doing, customers are more likely to be attracted to products or services and the chances of them remaining customers are improved. The challenge here is not just to build that understanding, but to communicate it internally to all who will contribute to it being fulfilled so that they understand what is expected of them. To misunderstand at the outset brings obvious difficulties, but to gather that understanding and then, through ineffective internal communication, misinform the management and staff responsible for delivery of what is expected can be disastrous.

2. Once this understanding is established, the next question is to what extent is the organisation capable of meeting those quality and service standards? In order to answer this we are not just trying to establish the **corporate capability** but also establish whether the management belief that it can be achieved actually matches the operational ability to achieve it.

3. The next question is to what extent can we actually achieve the standards when we have to? What we are capable of doing, as in 2 above, does not necessarily equate to what we might do. It is possible that the actual service delivery might fall below capability, perhaps as a result of poor staff motivation, direction or understanding.

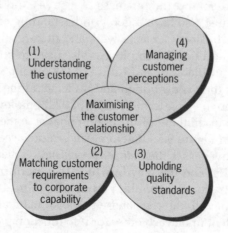

Figure 9.6 The elements of customer relationship

4. The final element is to do with the perception of customers as to how well the service and quality standards achieved by the organisation actually fulfil their needs. An organisation communicates with its customers in many different ways (Chapter 10) so there is a need to ensure that as a result of these, key customer service/quality expectations are appropriately addressed.

In order to focus the workforce upon the effective servicing of the external customers there is a need to:

- ensure that there are *effective and efficient internal communication* procedures in place to ensure that employees understand the organisational goals and priorities, the customer expectations, the expectations upon them and how their role forms a part of those performed by others in the organisation;
- have *clear rules of engagement* between departments and staff so that they manage the internal supplier–customer relationships in the most effective way;
- *be seen to value the contribution* of employees and encourage and motivate staff, in particular empowering staff within clear guidelines so that when dealing with customers they may do so in a positive, structured and flexible way without the need for procrastination, indecision and passing customers from person to person.

Spotlight 9.2

A sticky end

The production line was straightforward. Two people unpacked the empty glue tubes and placed them on the racks, four others placed them on the conveyor system in slots with the open end upwards. The conveyor took these to a glue hopper where each tube was filled. Then they continued past two people responsible for quality control to another machine which sealed them. Two more people placed them in boxes. The eleventh member of the team was responsible for the glue hopper. She removed damaged tubes before they entered the carousel and monitored the glue level, using a foot pedal to add more glue.

This whole process ran efficiently and an ability to fulfil orders quickly gave the company a competitive advantage. Two days ago a large export order was secured and if all went well a long-term contract was on offer. The message came down that 'all the stops should be pulled out' for this order. An extra performance bonus was offered if the deadline could be met.

Conscious that this was important, and that there was an attractive bonus, the eleventh team member had been at work all week despite having a bad cold. To clear her head she had bought some flu treatment on the way to work and it seemed to be working as she was finding it easier to concentrate and her head had cleared.

Spotlight 9.2 *continued*

Unfortunately, as she later recalled, she had not read the label on the bottle. She remembered pressing the pedal to add more glue to the hopper but her next memory was of being woken by the alarm to find that she was resting on the side of the hopper covered in glue. The bottle was marked 'Could cause drowsiness' and it had!

This short sleep led to a two-week cleaning up period, two weeks lost production, failure to deliver the Australian order and no bonus.

Who, if anybody, is to blame for the problems caused by the two-week downtime and why? Was the operator right to come to work despite having the flu? Do you think anything could have been done to reduce the risk of this type of accident happening?

9.4 BUILDING AND MANAGING THE SERVICE CULTURE

We have now built up an understanding of the need to adopt a quality and service orientation within an organisation, we have established the importance of the internal customer–supplier relationship and we have identified the need for effective internal communication, that is managing the relationships between employees and empowering them to perform their role. Let us now consider what can be done to create an environment where a **service culture** is integral to the organisation. This develops the elements shown in Figure 9.6.

Understanding the customer

This requires a robust and proactive approach by the organisation to gathering market information. As discussed in Chapter 4, this needs to be focused upon understanding and interpreting customer needs and requirements and should be gathered, collated and recorded in an effective management information system. But the simple gathering of information is not enough. The findings then need to be accessible to those who will need to act upon them and there has to be effective communication of the data to all the various levels of management.

Matching customer requirements to corporate capability

This requires an appreciation, acceptance, orientation and commitment by the management towards incorporating quality in all that they do. It can be achieved through a combination of organisational policy and training, introducing quality-based, measurable procedures and incorporating quality performance goals. With regard to operating procedure, this might well include the use of standardised systems or processes in order to improve overall consistency.

With this combination, it should be possible to ensure that management has a realistic understanding of what the organisation is capable of, thus ensuring that they are better able to address any shortfall between customer expectations and corporate capability.

Ensuring quality standards are upheld

With the benefit of building both an understanding and an effective delivery platform, the focus is now upon ensuring effective delivery. For this, we need to consider:

- recruitment
- training
- the individual's role
- productivity measurement and quality control
- the tools for the job
- inter-employee relationships.

Recruitment

Recruiting the right person for the role might seem to be an obvious step, but it can be extremely difficult to do and on occasion organisations can transfer or promote people into positions or extend the responsibility of an existing position simply because there is a vacancy to fill and the individual concerned is available to fill it. If, as the employee, the role is unsuited to you – perhaps it requires skills you do not possess, means you have to work shifts you would prefer not to work or is simply uninteresting – the quality of your work and contribution to the organisation will suffer. For example, if you have ever held a part-time job, did you take this because you were really interested in the work or because you wanted some extra money and the job was offered to you?

Training

Providing role-related training and ensuring this is oriented towards a quality/service culture is a vital element of the mix. Training staff does not simply involve addressing skill shortfalls though. It needs to incorporate education into the organisational goals and culture, so as to ensure clarity of expectation of performance. It also needs education into how the organisation operates, the interdependencies between the various functions and the importance of quality in ensuring longevity and growth. In addition, guidance and insight into the customers' expectations and the policy for managing those expectations is required.

The individual's role

As an employee, you would be concerned with the conditions under which you work, the relationships with fellow employees, the nature of breaks, work hours and your remuneration package, which you might initially view in terms of take-home pay. All of these elements are important, but job satisfaction and quality of performance is made up of a combination of factors and remuneration alone can go far beyond the sum of money you receive. For example, payment for your services could include holiday entitlement, performance or annual bonuses, flexible work hours, training and education opportunities, pension and medical insurance packages and guaranteed employment terms, all of which can be used to reward and motivate you.

Other elements that can affect the ability to perform your role effectively include the clarity of the role itself and the time allocated for tasks. You may have seen reports in the press about UK office workers taking short lunch hours and eating a sandwich while they work. Or perhaps about the trends towards starting early and regularly working later than the normal work hours – unofficially and without overtime payments. If you constantly feel under pressure to do more and the expectations of the employer are unrealistic, then your quality performance and motivation will decline.

Consider as well how employees perceive their specific roles alongside those of the others in the company. Might there be conflicting priorities that can cause confusion, or ambiguous direction that might result in decisions being made that might cause duplication of effort or counteract or conflict with those being made elsewhere? See Spotlight 9.3 for an example.

Spotlight 9.3

Matching functional priorities with business ones

Sometimes you receive no real advantage by having extra features associated with your products or services but, if you did not have those features, then you could be disadvantaged. This was at the root of the marketing of mobile phones in the early 1990s when international roaming was being promoted as a major feature and it was felt by users that the more countries in which you could use your phone the more attractive it was to own, despite the fact that many of the countries could be quite obscure and the vast majority of phone owners would never go there.

As this market developed and the world markets opened up, a number of niche marketing activities arose and one of these was the rental of equipment to cover

Spotlight 9.3 *continued*

short-term needs. These needs could be many and varied, but for most companies rental equipment was brought in to cover specific needs over regular intervals.

The world market for cellular phones is such that the technology in some countries is incompatible with that used elsewhere. This is the case in Japan and one rental company discovered that while trying to attract new business, a common question from potential clients was 'Do you offer a Japanese solution?' It transpired time and again that there was no immediate need for this service but, as a competitor rental company offered a solution, this had become a key factor in selecting contract suppliers.

To address this they secured an agreement with a Japanese supplier and while any rentals would generate little revenue, the ability to offer this service quickly helped secure new customers.

The first Japanese rental happened nine months after the service became available. It was trouble-free and the customer was satisfied. Two months later the rental company received a phone call from the Japanese partner. It appeared that although they had passed the invoice to the company so that the client could be charged, the Japanese supplier had not been paid.

When this was checked with the Financial Controller it was discovered that the invoice had been received and that the client had paid it, but as it was not considered of any great financial value it had been placed at the bottom of the pile and had not yet been processed. Promises were given that it would be paid immediately, but six weeks later another call from Japan confirmed it still had not been paid. It also signalled a breakdown in co-operation and a subsequent withdrawal of the 'Japanese solution'. The consequences were that several large contracts, with clients who had never used the service, were cancelled as soon as they became aware it was no longer available.

The Financial Controller was adamant that it would cost him more to process this invoice than it was worth and maintained that his responsibility was to prioritise his staff workload towards achieving the best financial return for the company. Is he right in taking this attitude? Why do you think that this problem arose and what do you think could have been done to avoid the subsequent loss of business?

In addition, to what degree are employees given the authority and responsibility to make decisions for themselves and not have to refer to others for direction? This is empowerment, allowing employees a degree of latitude in their approach to their role. An empowered employee is better able to develop and enhance a customer relationship when dealing directly with a customer while an unempowered employee has to rely on following the rules and this inflexibility can prove damaging.

Finally, while we have already identified a large number of factors that can contribute to employee satisfaction and motivation, it is appropriate to consider reward systems as well, that is those incentives introduced by the employer in order to encourage and motivate staff to continue to perform at a high level. These can be in the form of personal rewards, for example holidays, goods and bonus payments, or perhaps more substantive, team or department-related rewards such as recreational equipment or parties.

Productivity measurement and quality control

Regardless of all other factors, without effective monitoring and control systems to ensure that objectives and targets are being achieved and standards met, it becomes impossible for the organisation to control and maintain quality standards effectively. Operational processes also need to be in place, focused upon efficient delivery to prescribed quality standards. Attempts to incorporate such systems have seen the growth of Total Quality Management (TQM) and standards such as the ISO 9000 series.

The tools for the job

If you are doing some DIY and need to hammer in a nail, you will take a hammer from the toolbox. Like many people you probably only have one hammer, so regardless of the size of the nail you will use it. Clearly, the job might be easier or more effectively completed if you used the correct tool, and this same analogy is true of a business. Having the correct tools for the job, which are accessible by the appropriate people when required, can ensure that activities are performed in the most effective and efficient way.

Consider the area of technology, both computer-based technology and areas such as production machinery, communications equipment and bar coding. New technology is expensive to introduce and understandably organisations will try to get the most out of their investment. They will keep old technology for as long as they can before upgrading. Consequently, the capability of the organisation at any one time might well be limited by the technology employed. A thorough understanding of what is used and what is available can therefore help organisations manage their quality standard expectations.

Inter-employee relationships

As highlighted throughout this chapter, the interaction between employees is a vital element of the quality mix. The need to work with colleagues rather than in isolation of them is critical in ensuring that the organisation continues to pull in the same direction. Thus a strong sense of teamwork is necessary.

In order to create an environment where this develops it is necessary to incorporate the values of teamwork across all the aspects of this section. Recruiting people who work well in teams becomes vital, company expectations and culture need to be incorporated within the training programme, teamwork becomes a core element of an individual's role and co-operation becomes a key aspect of the management and process approach.

This issue of teamwork is also important with external suppliers and customers. Look at the supply and distribution chains and you will see that if you can create an environment where you work with external parties rather than just consider them as functions in the chain, you will be better able to overcome potential problems, remove barriers to delivery or influence the overall quality levels.

Managing customer perceptions

The final element to consider is the effectiveness with which the quality levels achieved by the organisation equate to those expected by the customers. In reality, if you, as a customer, believe that the quality you receive is good, then you will be satisfied. The important word here is 'believe', thus a key role of the organisation is to ensure that the customers' perception of the quality received meets or exceeds their expectations, regardless of the quality levels actually attained.

Effective communication is the key to managing that perception and it is necessary to ensure that this is both consistent and reflects the capability and output of the organisation. Thus, at whatever level the customer communicates with the organisation, consistency of message is vital. Care has to be taken to ensure that what is communicated does not go beyond the capacity of the organisation to deliver. To underpromise and overdeliver invariably results in a satisfied customer, but to overpromise and underdeliver can result in dissatisfaction and customers going elsewhere.

9.5 MANAGING THE EXTERNAL CUSTOMER RELATIONSHIP

We have now built up a picture of the internal supplier–customer relationship and established the importance this has in ensuring that the goods and services supplied by a company meet the necessary quality standards of customers. To bring this chapter to a close it is appropriate to take a brief look at how the interaction with external customers can be managed and how customer dissatisfaction can be identified and corrected.

At the centre of Figure 9.6 is the aim of maximising the customer relationship, and ultimately that is precisely what internal customers are working towards in serving external customers. With this in mind, let us remind ourselves of the many levels at which customers might come into contact with an organisation (Figure 9.4) and then think through the contact that occurs during the quote-to-order process.

We have established that customers can find themselves communicating with a multitude of different departments and people within an organisation and can also be exposed to a range of communication activities, such as promotional advertising and press reports. This exposure will not necessarily occur just when a transaction is taking place, but it will nevertheless create an impression in the mind of the customer as to the capability and attractiveness of the supplier.

The impact of ongoing customer contact

Think about the contact during an actual transaction and consider the process of seeking a personal loan. This will probably be that you:

1. Identify the need for a loan and gain an idea of just how much you will need to borrow.
2. Look around to see what is on offer, e.g. via the Internet, newspapers and high street banks.
3. Armed with an understanding of the cost, terms and your potential suitability you will approach suppliers to make a formal enquiry and obtain a quote.
4. With the benefit of having something tangible you will then make a decision as to whom you are going to borrow the money from.
5. Then you will complete and submit a formal application.
6. Receive a loan agreement form to sign.
7. Eventually receive the funds.

Think now about how this will be managed by the lending company. To begin with, in order to provide you with the information you need and encourage you to approach them in the first place, the data they provide has to be accessible to you and include the type of information you are seeking. Or else you might look elsewhere. How can the company ensure that it does this effectively?

Next, when you make a formal enquiry it has to ensure that the information you receive is appropriate and that your experience of dealing with them is equally attractive. Once again, how can this be monitored to ensure that your experience matches their intended service?

You then move into the formal paperwork stage, which will involve time delays and potentially confusing forms. Is this dealt with effectively or could the company have done more?

Finally, upon receipt of the funds you will no doubt be happy, regardless of the experience. But if there were aspects of it you disliked that might encourage you to look elsewhere for future requirements; how will the company know what they were so that it can overcome any barriers to your dealing with them again?

Managing customer contact

There are two key elements. First, the need to *monitor the internal activities of the company* in order to ensure that the required quality standards are met, that the communications are consistent with requirements and that the processes and procedures followed are in line with those set down. Secondly, the *external monitoring of the delivery*, that is the experience of the customer – you.

In order to manage the level of customer satisfaction and ensure that it is in line with what the company strives for and achieves, it is necessary to seek feedback from the customer and this can be gathered in a variety of ways.

To begin with, throughout the process highlighted above you will have had direct contact with company employees. If properly trained and guided, they will be able to gain an impression of your expectations and satisfaction. But if there is no internal process of gathering that information centrally so that it can be monitored and interpreted, then this valuable opportunity is lost. An alternative approach will be to seek direct feedback from customers, perhaps in the format of a customer survey.

With this approach you have to consider how many customers might actually fill these in, the nature of the questions you ask and how they are presented. For example, you could ask how satisfied a customer was with the service on a scale of 1 to 10. However, if they say '7', you will not learn why it was not higher, only that they are relatively satisfied – but not what aspects they are relatively satisfied with.

The value of customer complaints

A third approach is to provide customers with a point of contact for ongoing questions and concerns. Commonly referred to as a Customer Service Department, it not only deals with **customer complaints** but also provides a place to go to in instances of dissatisfaction, confusion or frustration.

Dissatisfied customers can be the source of valuable insight into the way an organisation operates and, while distressing to learn that they are unhappy, encouraging them to complain and then effectively managing that complaint can result in a more loyal customer. An unsatisfied customer will not only go elsewhere, but will probably convey their dissatisfaction with the company to friends and acquaintances, potentially resulting in more business being lost.

For the organisation it is important to encourage customers to complain, but it is equally important that a process exists for these complaints to be recorded, evaluated and acted upon, not only in relation to the specific complaint but also in relation to the way in which the business is conducted.

Addressing a specific complaint from one customer in isolation is simply the equivalent of placing a plaster upon a cut. It addresses the cut but not what caused it. It is important that a process exists to convey the nature of complaints to the key business areas that can take action across the business as a whole if necessary, for example planning, operations, human resources, communications and control (see Dilemma 9.2).

Dilemma 9.2

Tell customers to complain and they will

During the 1980s, the concept of keeping customers satisfied was taking on greater prominence within the financial services sector as it was recognised that it is easier to sell more goods and services to happy customers and that unhappy ones not only stop buying but they go elsewhere and can be difficult to get back.

Dilemma 9.2 *continued*

As a consequence, 'customer service' became the buzzword and departments were set up specifically to deliver this aspect of the business.

While this tended to functionalise the role of customer service, suggesting service was the premise of one department rather than of the business as a whole, this move was usually accompanied by a staff-training scheme rolled out across the organisation. Programmes such as this, however, took time to make an impact when the employees of each institution could number in thousands.

For many organisations the underlying reasoning for centralisation was that they operated branch networks and thus customers had personal access to named individuals for their normal business. What they lacked was an official, higher authority to be able to go to in order to express any unsatisfied concerns or dissatisfaction. In a wave of brilliant descriptive titling, therefore, the 'Customer Complaints Department' was born.

Customer complaints are an important element of business. These need to be identified, addressed satisfactorily for the customer and lessons learned that can help instigate positive change to the organisation. However, announcing to the world that you have a special department just for customer complaints could send out a message that if you need to have dedicated staff dealing with these, then there must be a lot of them. What, therefore, does that say about the overall standard of service the organisation delivers to potential new customers?

An inevitable consequence was that many departments began to receive phone calls and letters by the score, covering complaints from fairly significant service failure issues to the trivial. Many customers, it seemed, just needed someone to listen to them and it became clear that customer expectations were not properly understood and that the service being delivered fell short in many different ways. Clearly there was a demand for 'service' and if nothing else, the customer complaints departments identified this.

Within a couple of years these departments were quietly renamed 'Customer Service' departments and the service ethos was instilled more widely across the organisations as a whole.

What do you believe are the advantages and disadvantages of creating a Customer Services Department? What are the benefits to an organisation of encouraging customers to complain about aspects of their products or services with which they are dissatisfied? Do you believe that 'the customer is always right', and that all complaints are valid ones?

SUMMARY

Throughout this chapter the focus has been upon the contribution made by the staff of an organisation to its quality delivery levels. We have seen that within organisations there is an ongoing customer–supplier relationship between staff and departments and that it is vital for this to be recognised in order to ensure standards will be maintained. We have also explored the importance of service to customers and gained an understanding of how their impression of service quality is formed from every contact with an organisation, no matter how insignificant it might seem. In addition, we have considered ways in which a service culture might be developed.

Finally, we have considered the impact of pre-conception and matching the service levels delivered with those desired by the organisation and those expected by the customer. At the route of this sits knowledge, discussed in Part One of this book, and resolve, which is in Part Two. The other key element is making the customers (both internal and external) aware of what you are offering, and that is communication.

Discussion questions

1   What are the main differences between the various 'chains' associated with a business and in what way are they mutually dependent?

2   In trying to meet customer expectations, what are the major barriers faced by any organisation?

3   Discuss the key elements of developing a customer relationship. Why are these important?

4   What actions can an organisation take in order to ensure that a service culture can be effectively integrated into its operation?

Case study 9.1   Who lost the sale?

Penny is a very experienced saleswoman. With 15 years sales experience, she has been with her current employer for almost ten years and is now their most senior salesperson, responsible for staff in three countries. She currently deals with senior, international clients and has just returned from abroad. She is not, it has to be said, in very good humour.

Having spent four months tracking down the person to speak to within a major multinational and following two months negotiating, she managed to arrange a meeting in New York at short notice two days ago. Prior to the meeting she asked one of her colleagues to prepare a dossier on the company with a profile of their current business activities. At the same time, a secretary was asked to arrange the flight and hotel. Assistance was also sought from the marketing department to help prepare a presentation, to arrange for this to incorporate web links to launch pages from the company website during the presentation and to liaise with the person preparing the dossier. Following this she travelled to Germany to see another client and returned to the UK one day before her flight to the USA.

She then discovered that the presentation was incomplete. Marketing had been waiting for information from Sales, but as they had not asked for it, it had been placed in a file for Penny's return. Consequently, it was not completed until an hour before Penny was due to leave when it was then loaded on to a company laptop, provided by the technical services team.

On arriving in New York the day before the meeting Penny discovered the hotel was close to the client's Head Office but two hours' drive from the meeting venue. Because of the timing it was too late to switch hotels but she booked a car for the next day to get her there in good time. That night she ran through the presentation. Horrified, she discovered the file to be light on information, particularly regarding current client activities, so had to spend much of the night filling in the blanks and adding key information that really should have been incorporated already.

The following day, tired but confident, she drove to the meeting venue to discover that the meeting time had been brought forward an hour, but that the message had not been passed on from her office. Rather than arrive on time, therefore, she was 15 minutes late.

Determined to make a sale, she completed the initial introductions and started her laptop presentation. Reaching a point where she needed to bring up a website link a message came back that the page was no longer available. Despite several attempts it did not boot-up and she later discovered that the Webmaster had instigated some changes that morning and had replaced some pages.

Things took a further turn for the worse when the client stopped her mid-flow and announced that in anticipation of the meeting he had arranged for one of his colleagues to do a mystery shop a month earlier. The experience wasn't a good one. While the equipment arrived promptly and in full working order, a charger was missing and upon phoning the '24-hour helpline' all they received was a recorded message. Despite leaving a voicemail request, nobody returned the call and it took four more calls to reach someone who calmly told them not to worry because 'this is always happening'.

In addition, that morning a letter had arrived from Penny's Finance Department requesting payment of the outstanding bill. As the client explained, this was paid two weeks previously and the cheque had already been cashed.

Perhaps fortunately, the meeting then came to an end. Fortunately, that is, because following the revelation about the cheque Penny's computer died. The battery would not hold a charge and up until the meeting she had been operating it from a mains connection so this had not been spotted.

Questions

1   Identify the various customer–supplier relationships that this case highlights within Penny's company.

2   Who do you think was responsible for the failure to gain this new client and why?

3   What should have been done differently to avoid some or all of the problems encountered?

4   How do you think the company could prevent this from happening again?

Case study 9.2 Outside, looking in – a customer experience

With the spread of technological change and the inevitable improvements in personal computers, there comes a time when your existing PC can no longer be upgraded. So, in order to use the latest software you have to invest in a new machine. Consider this tale of someone who faced this very situation and started to look around for a replacement.

A new specification machine always seems to retail at around £1,000, so he was determined to choose carefully and spent a few weeks considering options and suppliers. He rationalised that the technology was fairly stable and thus price differentials related to capacity or manufacturer rather than reliability. A specification was selected and a 'good deal' was identified from a large high street operator.

A visit to one of their outlets was accompanied by a discussion with a relatively well-informed, non-pushy and personable assistant who introduced the appropriate piece of equipment, explained the current package and the shortcomings of the bundled accessories. Clearly, this was included simply to increase the perceived feeling of good value.

Following what could be described as a very pleasant 20 minutes, a deal was struck and money changed hands. The particular configuration was factory assembled to order, which cynics would equate to a clever way of reducing stockholding and encouraging a positive cash flow, but this was reflected in the price – £200 less than elsewhere. Delivery was assured within 14 days. As a result of this experience and feeling that the agreed deal represented good value, a happy customer returned home to await delivery.

Fifteen days later and disappointed at the lack of delivery and thinking that perhaps the initial belief in good value might have been misplaced, a phone call was made to the shop to ask what the problem was. The same assistant answered the telephone with the same pleasant voice, but clearly one without knowledge or power. 'It's Saturday' was the essence of the response, '...there's nobody at Head Office to check this with. I will phone them on Monday and get back you.'

Disappointed at a lack of solution and the realisation that 14 days was now to be stretched to 17, an unhappy customer waited. Monday came and went. No telephone call.

On Tuesday, day 18, and with disappointment rising further, another call to the shop was made. The same assistant assured him that the computer had been dispatched over a week earlier. Then came the first inkling of a problem in the distribution chain: 'The courier must have it.' The conversation developed. 'Hold the line and I will give them a call.' Then there followed a few moments of farce as the assistant tried to get the courier to speak to the customer by holding the telephone handsets together. Then came a promise that the courier would phone straight back.

For the customer, the feeling of lack of control at this point was overwhelming. All he wanted was his goods and for somebody at the company to take control. He felt as though he was being passed around and the disappointment and regret at the choice of purchase grew.

Over an hour later the phone call finally came and it appeared that non-delivery was actually the customer's fault. Someone had tried to deliver the computer eight days earlier but no one had been in. It was now sitting at the depot awaiting instructions for re-delivery.

Asking why a notice had not been left so a delivery time could be arranged the response was 'We never leave notes until after the third try.' Posing the question as to how they were going to know when to make the second try fell on deaf ears and the regret, disappointment and frustration grew further. Delivery was arranged for the following day and at 5.30pm in the evening, having waited in all day for delivery, it arrived – 19 days after purchase.

Prepared to write the previous few weeks off to experience, the customer carried the boxes inside and unpacked the computer. Within a very few moments it was discovered that the monitor lead was the wrong one, so although it could be assembled, the computer wouldn't actually work. Immediately a call was placed to the helpline and a pleasant sounding voice answered the query with, 'No problem, I will put one in the post. It will be with you within 14 days' and promptly hung up.

Questions

1 As the purchaser, what do you think you should have expected from the computer supplier?

2 From the order being placed, how do you think this would have been processed by the supplier and who would have been involved in this process?

3 Where do you think the problems with supply lay and how might they have been avoided?

4 Do you think the purchaser would buy from this supplier again?

Further reading

Additional academic material to support the ideas and principles outlined in this chapter can be found in most 'marketing' texts and also in texts on strategy and management. Students wishing to read further are recommended to search under the 'key words' highlighted above but may also like to explore the following:

Barlow, N.M. (2001) *Batteries Included*. London: Random House Business.

Cook, S. (2002) *Customer Care Excellence: How To Create an Effective Customer Focus*. London: Kogan Page.

Williams, T. (1996) *Dealing with Customer Complaints*. Aldershot: Gower.

10 Customer-led communications

Rod Radford

LEARNING OUTCOMES

After reading this chapter you should be able to:

- **Use a variety of different models to explain how communication works**

- **Appreciate the importance of listening and customer feedback to effective communications**

- **Identify the role of communications in influencing both external and internal customers**

- **Determine how a range of organisations might employ communications to build and maintain relationships**

- **Better understand how communications messages are received by customers**

KEY WORDS

Brand communication

Communications campaign

Communications channels

Communications feedback

Communications mix

Communications objectives

Communications vehicles

Dialogue

Field of experience

Guerilla communications

Information and communication technologies (ICT)

Internal communications

Joined-up communications

Message

Micro-communications

Noise

Online and offline communications

P of promotion

Stakeholder publics

Total communications

INTRODUCTION

In Parts One and Two of the book we discussed how the organisation can move closer to customers. In the preceding chapter the importance of internal customers to external customer service was examined. Here we explore the dynamics of influencing both external and internal customer groups using managed communications based on customer-led information. Irrespective of whether we are talking about private or public sectors, B2C or B2B, or where crossing cultural divides, communicating effectively is central to building and maintaining quality customer relations. Communication is the 'face' of and indeed may be the very essence of our offer to and contact with our clients.

Initially, this chapter investigates the basic processes involved in customer-led communication. Based on a better understanding about how commercial communications work, we then explore how organisations actually influence and respond to their customers. We start from the organisation's perspective, then investigate how communications impact from the receiver's or customer's point of view. The chapter ends by examining how best to communicate with customers at the personal level. Good communication, as we will see, involves a combination of listening and understanding as well as skilful outbound messages. In Chapter 11, the long-term, even lifetime management of customer relationships emphasises the need for intensive and sustained communications with both external and internal customers.

10.1 CUSTOMER COMMUNICATION

We begin by focusing on the definitions, models and processes underlying informed customer communication. This is done as a prelude to establishing a framework for understanding communication and the two-way customer dialogue required with both external and internal customers.

Commercial communication

Communicating is something we all do and take for granted, yet if we want to manage and improve performance we need to understand communication more closely. It is about imparting and conveying information, involves two or more parties and requires transmission from one party to another. Most authors define communications as involving a transaction between parties and a transfer of meaning. As such, effective customer communication is central to marketing exchange and is at the 'sharp end' of doing business.

It is associated with the marketing mix **P of promotion** and the commercial communications tools of selling, advertising and a range of other activities in their support, such as public relations and merchandising. Some definitions of communication require intent but in the context of customer relationships it is clearly possible to communicate messages and values accidentally or by default.

Communication between organisations and their customers may also be held to operate at a number of levels but at its best involves listening and targeting. In quality terms, **internal communications** within the organisation as well as between the organisation and its external customers is important. It is a process capable of making or breaking customer loyalty.

Communicating with the customer, however, is more than just promotion. Each element of the marketing mix is capable of saying something, including our people, processes and the physical evidence of service we provide. Factors as diverse as word-of-mouth reputation, staff motivation and the company mission statement also communicate and influence customer relationships. In fact, at every point of customer contact, during each transaction, every 'episode' and within every part of a customer's experience there is an opportunity for **total communications** (see Figure 10.1).

The communications process

Organisations operate by communicating with their customers and we can model the process. The sender organisation encodes messages and then places them in various media **communications vehicles**, such as newspapers, magazines or television, and signals them to the receiving customer. If the **message** is meaningful, at the same time the receiver will decode, understand and hopefully respond. Effective transference rests on knowledge, feedback and skill, as well as a little luck sometimes. It depends on what is called a common **field of experience** between sender and receiver and on them understanding each other (see Figure 10.2).

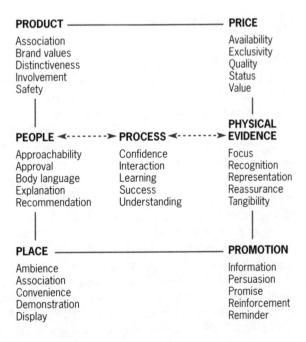

Figure 10.1 Extended mix communications

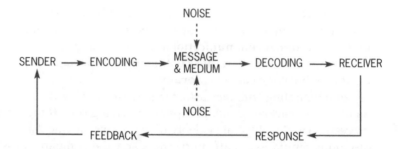

Figure 10.2   Communications model
Source: Adapted from Kotler (2000: 551)

The customer is not at all passive, however, and may interpret the signal in unintended ways. There may be unexpected reactions, interference or **noise** can block out or distort the signal or it may simply miss, for example where the customer is not tuned in during transmission. Noise, ranging from competitor action to customer distraction and plain physical interference may be completely outside our control. Without **communications feedback** an organisation may be none the wiser and repeat the signal pointlessly at great expense. Similarly, all publicity is not good publicity and the sender may be transmitting unintentional signals which are being picked up by customers and unintended receiver groups alike with negative effects. In this context, it's not just what we say and do, it's also how we do it. Where things go wrong a communications model is also a good fault-finding mechanism.

Spotlight 10.1

Creature comforts

In 1991 the Electricity Association launched its classic Heat Electric Campaign, a highly popular series of television advertisements. Ads featured a variety of cuddly plasticine animals, including a tortoise, a family of penguins and a 'laid back' Brazilian parrot, chatting to an interviewer about how much they liked electric central heating. They spoke into a large microphone and in homely 'fireside' accents explained the benefits of attractiveness, comfort, ease of use, reliability and how nice it is to return to a warm flat. The word 'electric' was scripted and clearly written on the microphone itself. People really loved the campaign.

In subsequent advertising research, recall was high. However, when asked, almost everybody thought the ads were for gas, the main rival to electricity as a domestic fuel. It appears the target audience's 'frame of reference' for traditional warmth included a flame which they associated with gas fires and not 'cold' radiators. The Electricity Association had been communicating on behalf of its rival at great expense. The campaign won top creative awards and continues to be liked, being voted the fourth most popular ad in Graham Norton's, *The 100 Greatest TV Ads* ITV show despite utterly failing to convey its core message.

In essence, organisations are attempting, by their actions and communications campaigning, to sequentially move the customer from a state of unawareness to a state of loyalty and repeat purchase. Magazine articles, simple advertising copy or a sales promotion may grab attention, remind and raise external customer awareness. Informative advertising communicating brand reputation, product comparison and demonstration can then engender liking and preference. Face-to-face sales persuasion, point-of-sales material and the recommendation of opinion leaders may secure subsequent conviction and purchase while continuing post-purchase involvement, support and, above all, positive experience can then reinforce customer value, cement loyalty and secure repeat purchase. This will need to be synchronised internally, involving parallel **dialogue** with service providers using presentations, training, in-house newspapers, etc. to inform and secure employee commitment. Messages are both communicated at a corporate, business unit level and through customer interaction with marketing and promotional mix variables (see Figure 10.3).

The role of communication

Customer communication completes the 'marketing cycle', linking customers with product and availability. At a societal level, in order to connect mass production and consumption there simply must be mass communications. At its best, commercial communication engages in real dialogue, transmitting value and meaning, while responding to feedback and remaining close to the external customer. Its role is to announce, inform, promise, persuade and influence customers to 'buy in' by communicating and delivering customer satisfaction. Putting thing right, saying sorry and supporting long-term relationships are increasingly also its goals. Recognising that employees deliver quality, internal communications encourages affiliation with organisational values as well as providing everyday working information. Communication to both external and internal customers is central to both marketing transactions and relationships. In the modern market place the core difference

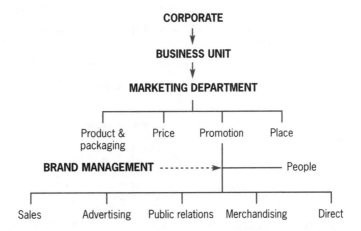

Figure 10.3 Levels of communication

and unique selling proposition of a product may be almost entirely created by the quality and credibility of **brand communication**. Brand value alone may be what customers are relating to and associating with when they repeat purchase. It is most emphatically not the role of marketing communication to misinform and where there is actually little or no substance to communicate there is little point in 'flogging a dead horse'.

Commercial communications should be based on clear intent. A **communications campaign** generally seeks to both 'push' product on to and 'pull' products off the shelf and 'position' the offer competitively in the mind of the consumer. Its component parts need to hang together as a cohesive whole and remain consistent with core brand values. Over a product life cycle communications may have very different roles to play. With new, introductory products, getting attention, trial and acceptance is the task, while when sales take off, brand identity will be promoted. Later, during market maturity, maintaining loyalty, defending market share and adding value become most important. In decline, the need to revitalise and reposition the product or direct customers towards alternatives, perhaps reducing communications to 'bare bones' dominates. Within a campaign individual messages may be charged with differentiating, reminding, informing or persuading (DRIP) or sequentially securing attention, arousing interest, building desire and promoting action (AIDA) and moving a customer from unawareness through purchase to brand loyalty (see Figure 10.4). It may be that there are considerable hurdles and countervailing forces to be overcome.

A systematic approach

If we hold that having a 'common field of experience' with customers is a strength, then we need a vehicle to deliver customer information. However formal or informal, our capacity to make 'output' decisions such as which **communications mix** to use

Figure 10.4 Commercial communications process

Source: Based on Wilson and Gilligan (2001: 469)

rests on obtaining and accurately processing good customer 'input' data. Of course, should we pay attention to all the information out there we would rapidly suffer 'information overload' and must actively filter much out. Communications managers make choices about what data to let in while paying attention to feedback loops indicating campaign results, but it is all too easy for a customer information gap to evolve. What is required is an information system that connects the various sources of customer information, ensuring that appropriate data reaches the decision makers who need it. B2B organisations with smaller numbers of customers and closer, more direct relationships may have the edge here. The maxim, however, remains the same, quality decisions rest on quality information and 'garbage in, garbage out'.

Not just 'joined-up' information processing but systematically **joined-up communications** need to be employed. Customer communications and campaigns need to be thought of as one thing and not a series of disjointed activities. To support an integrated focus, many organisations traditionally structured around their products are re-conforming themselves towards customers and channelling communications through designated 'customer champions', while taking a holistic view of total communications. The last thing a sales manager who has just secured an important new customer needs is to have weeks spent building up trust and rapport undone by an inaccurate, automatic 'red letter' demand for payment sent from the accounts office. An integrated communications campaign systematically builds upon itself to achieve a single objective (see Spotlight 10.2).

Spotlight 10.2

Campaign plan for opening of a new aerobics studio

NOV	*01	Book telephone directory entry
DEC		(*Christmas*)
JAN	*02	Advertise for and begin interviewing staff (*Ongoing*)
	*03	Press releases and interviews with exercise & lifestyle magazines
FEB	*04	Stand at health and fitness exhibition
	*05	Shop front complete and drop in visits possible
	*06	Website operational
MAR	*07	Local press advertising campaign commences (*Ongoing*)
	*08	Local BBC radio interview
	*09	Staff training and briefing begins (*Ongoing*)
	*10	Telephone sales campaign starts (*Ongoing*)
	*11	In-house newsletter and web bulletin board launched
	*12	Incentive vouchers issued
	*13	Pre-bookings accepted

Spotlight 10.2 *continued*

APR *14   Invitation/introductory sessions given during open week

    *15   Boards and signs out

    *16   Local cinema promotion

    *17   Interviews for local newspapers

    *18   Leaflet drops to selected local addresses

MAY *19   Fly sheets and sandwich board in the high street

    *20   Personality launch and grand opening

The importance of proactivity

It is important not just to respond and react to customer information but also to be proactive and create the type of competitive relationship desired. Few of us go to work dreaming of how to maximise negative feedback from customers, but it may even be necessary to initiate complaints. Where our customers regard our service negatively but don't tell us, there is little choice. We need to approach them and form a picture of what is going wrong. Judging customer satisfaction by action, even repeat purchase, may also not be wise. They may feel they have no option, that our competitors are just as bad, they cannot be bothered to change for now or are giving us one last chance. Inside the organisation things may be much the same for who dares tell the managing director that customer service is terrible. A modern manager needs to facilitate dialogue and feedback rather than assuming that 'no news is good news'. Feedback, even where negative, is more of an opportunity than a threat, and service recovery may well result in intensified customer satisfaction and loyalty. Listening is a critical part of effective communication.

We need to know what our customers like as well as dislike about our performance and it is equally within our power to find out. Likes can tell us more about the criteria consumers use when choosing us over our competitors and why they come back. They may then form the platform for future promotional messages and prove highly effective in retaining and attracting business or indeed staff. A restaurant manager, for instance, would impress a business user just by calling the day after a function to see if they were pleased, and could easily enquire what they liked the most and what they thought could be improved. Again, with positive feedback there is a need for proactivity and it is unwise to assume either external or internal customers will tell you. Praise is hard earned in British culture; when did your boss last say 'good job'?

Missed communication

Communicating with external customers does not always go smoothly and sometimes it seems if anything can go wrong it will, occasionally with unexpected results. Difficulties are experienced through the lack of clear objectives in the first place, insufficient resources, defective knowledge of the customer, weak messages or media, too much competing noise, entrenched customer attitudes and poor feedback information. Frequently there is a weak field of experience and don't assume the 'big guys' always get it right. Marlboro launched an advertising campaign in the Far East using the classic image of the lone cowboy gazing out across the prairie. While in the West this might communicate rugged, masculine individuality, in the East, with different cultural norms, it was interpreted along the line of lonely failure and outcast. Needless to say sales fell and now three cowboys feature.

Everything an organisation does, as well as the way its employees perform (e.g. smiling), communicates to its customers. This is particularly true when service is being provided and customers come into direct contact with the employees who perform it. To the customer these people are the organisation, yet almost inevitably they vary in their performance. Everybody needs to be motivated, 'singing from the same hymn sheet' and seeing themselves as an organisational representative. Here internal communication supports and nurtures external customer care. Opportunities for mismatch are legion where the rumour mill probably works very much faster than official **communications channels**. A Los Angeles advertising agency thought it would be fun and different to have a 'be rude to the customer day' and proceeded to humorously abuse everybody they spoke to. They had lost several of their clients by lunch time.

10.2 INFLUENCING EXTERNAL AND INTERNAL CUSTOMERS

Incorporating and building on the models and processes underlying informed customer communications, we now move forward to explore how organisations actually engage in influencing their external and internal customers.

Communicating with external customers

Once aware of external customer profiles (e.g. their age and lifestyle) and opportunities, organisations are in a position to target communications. Appreciative of customers' needs and wants and choice criteria, they are in a position to match benefits sought with products offered and communicate a promise to deliver. If we know that supermarket customers dislike being made to feel in the wrong when taking goods back, we might communicate that we are the company that doesn't make you feel bad, that it's safe to talk to us if you don't like something, and seek to differentiate ourselves from our competitors in that way. Kellogg's discovered that adult consumers associated their cornflakes with positive childhood memories and were able to add nostalgia for a bygone age to their products' attributes. Saga

Holidays, realising that marketing communication has traditionally been youth-oriented, launched their own highly successful magazine and created a 'mature' channel of communication with their customers who were aged 50 or more. Commercial communications campaigns, individual messages and indeed all organisational action signal a promise to external customers and attempt to trigger responses.

As we have seen in the previous section, an organisation attempts to influence and assist targeted customer groups to move up a ladder, beginning with total unawareness of a product and ending in repeat purchase. To this end communications may be sustained before, during and maintained after purchase as customers move through stages of awareness, interest, comprehension, liking, preference, conviction and purchase, and ultimately lead to brand loyalty. Within a communications campaign different communications tools will be sequenced to maximise effect, for example public relations information preceding personal selling and advertising for best results. It is important that the whole campaign concentrates on the organisation's core communications message (see Table 10.1).

Table 10.1 Properties of commercial communication tools

Advertising	'Mass selling' to gain attention, promise, remind and reinforce
Branding & packaging	Awarding difference, focus, personality and recognition
Direct marketing	Allowing access, interaction and rapid feedback
Merchandising	Incentivising and promoting sales at the point of sale
Selling	Face-to-face representation capable of demonstration, overcoming objections and personal persuasion
Public Relations	'Mass telling' and informing external and internal publics including
Exhibitions	To show, present and meet
Media exposure	To gain credibility and inform
Presentations	For direct explanation and feedback
Sponsorship	Allowing access and association
Company visits	Building relationships and goodwill
Hosted events	Creating impact and a platform for further communications

A typical communications mix and blend of methods of influence tend to distinguish different types of market. In B2B markets direct selling, exhibitions and trade public relations predominate. In fast moving consumer, 'self-service' markets the emphasis is on advertising, branding, packaging and merchandising, such as shelf positioning and incentives at the point of sale, while consumer durables such as cars also employ showroom selling. Public sector institutions may do little hard selling or advertising and concentrate on internal marketing communications and external customer information giving, while small organisations have no budget to initiate anything that is not 'in-house' and localised. As well as the high-profile techniques, a lot of persuasion is very low key and face-to-face. Whether seeking to influence their customers to buy, vote, volunteer or change working practices and/or their opinion, information and managed communication is increasingly the method.

Not everything is equally difficult to communicate, however. Sometimes campaigns take off because you are simply in the right place at the right time or the message's time has come. At other times spin-off media interest multiplies the impact of a single communication and occasionally a 'feeding frenzy' takes place. Some messages are easier to communicate than others (Spotlight 10.3).

Spotlight 10.3

Somethings are easier to communicate

In 1993 the Dyson Dual Cyclone DC01 bagless vacuum cleaner was launched on to the crowded UK market. Based on a revolutionary design, centrifugal force and in a range of bold colours, the machine retailed for over £200 and became the fastest-selling vacuum cleaner ever to have been made in the UK. At first an effective public relations campaign explained and profiled the product while demonstration and personal selling were available in department stores. This was followed by mass advertising and wider availability. Such rapid adoption of a relatively long-term commitment that is both new and expensive is not usual and may be largely explained in communication terms.

- A real advantage of being the world's first bagless vacuum cleaner with superior performance.
- Easy to compare with traditional cleaners and highly compatible with consumer knowledge and experience.
- An improvement rather than complete difference, still looking like a vacuum cleaner.
- Relatively simple to understand and easy to communicate, particularly visually.
- Proven track record, credibility, modernity and design ability of James Dyson.
- An unmatched ability to demonstrate suction properties through a perspex cylinder.

Source: Adapted from Rogers (2003)

Advances in **information and communication technologies (ICT)**, particularly to do with new database possibilities, the Internet and mobile telephones, is revolutionising business communications. Publishing and transmitting information, customer interaction, making transactions and linking up directly with others both internally and externally is increasingly possible, as well as cost-effective, worldwide. New technology makes direct, tailor-made messages, rapid responses and data-led listening to and tracking of customers easier. Developments in digital television and radio and broadband will further extend the possibilities for interaction and 'person-to-person' marketing communication. Another effect for the technically proficient has been to promote opportunist, quick, 'hit and run' **guerrilla communications** (often by smaller organisations) which exploit windows of opportunity or even seek to undermine the messages of competitors (e.g. by using a parallel website). Associated with unconventional, non-traditional communications which often go to the edge, they almost inevitably involve the Internet. Any modern communications plan is almost certain to contain online as well as offline components.

The customer's communication needs

However communications literate, consumers are engaged in making choices, problem solving and comparing between alternatives (see Figure 10.8 on page 263). They need enough information to form a judgement, are increasingly 'time poor' and face a bewildering array of competing information sources and 'information overload', yet rely on input information to construct a lifestyle. In addition, once a purchase has been made, they may seek the reassurance of further confirming communication. They demand to be listened to and treated with respect, and demand the ability to seek redress if not satisfied. They have the right to expect decency, legality, honesty and truthfulness (Advertising Standards Authority) and want communications they can understand. The clever use of copy, such as employing the term 'farmhouse' to describe factory-produced food and short-term 'spin' or 'hype', are increasingly seen as misleading. Communications managers need to be aware not only of the law and voluntary codes of conduct but also the need to communicate social responsibility. Consumers are also becoming resistant to unsolicited incoming messages and are hostile to the 'junk mail' and' spam' with which they are bombarded. Permission to inform and communicate with customers may need to be sought.

Evaluating performance

In order to maintain influence and adapt, organisations keenly evaluate and track the impact of their communications. Communications are important, high-profile and expensive in terms of both money and time, so considerable amounts of pre-testing and post-publication analysis can occur, for example tracking changes in customer attitudes or awareness and recall testing to ascertain if they remember where they saw or heard messages and understood what they were trying to say. Given the time lapses in response, the interactive nature of different communications methods and the impact of changing external variables, it is however notoriously difficult to evaluate the influence of individual tools, let alone whole campaigns. Coupon returns, enquiry rates, numbers of visitors to an exhibition and salesforce feedback may be measured along with changes in hard sales. When organisations test the market or trial their products they are largely evaluating the promotional mix and noting communication spend in order to 'gross it up', know what works and how much it costs to roll the campaign out nationally.

Communications may be appraised as both strategy and tactics, involving, for example, both a brand repositioning exercise and altered packaging. In the longer term it is likely that it will be evaluated for its contribution to strengthening the relationship between an organisation and its key clients. Each step along the way can also be monitored against shorter-term criteria, such as the time taken to achieve more rapid enquiry response rates or reduce customer waiting times. Some communications tools are implicitly tactical and more straightforward to measure, such as the sales promotional take up of special offers and competitions. The importance of setting SMART (specific, measurable, acceptable, realistic and timed) **communications objectives** to evaluate against cannot be overemphasised. Strategically, the idea may well be to move customer relationships from a focus on short-run sales to longer-term involvements and partnerships (see Figure 10.5).

Brand positioning

The distinctiveness of a product offering can be created by its name, symbols, style and packaging, and its attractiveness and associated brand values, which are largely created and sustained by marketing communications. Establishing brand reputation may award quality certification to both the product and its user. It communicates powerfully in itself and is associated with both customer preference and loyalty. Thus brand building is a major focus in commercial communications and an asset to both producer and customer. In 'commoditised' service markets with little tangibility or physical evidence almost virtual imagery may signify and communicate brand personality – a red telephone and jingle representing Direct Line Insurance – without which the organisation would be almost indistinguishable. Though Pepsi is generally perceived of as being younger than Coca–Cola, both continue to offer and communicate benefits to their respective customers, the former by sponsoring music artists who appeal to the youth market.

Competing brands are positioned in a market place and need maintenance from time to time. It may be necessary to reinforce drifting attributes such as masculinity in Bacardi rum or infuse additional properties. Periodically, in response to changing customer and competitive circumstances and in order to prolong their lives, brands will be repositioned from one domain to another (see Figure 10.6). Communications usually lead the way. For example, Guinness was successfully repositioned from

Figure 10.5 Communications ladder

Source: Based on Chartered Institute of Marketing (2001–02: 15), itself adapted from Luengo-Jones (2001)

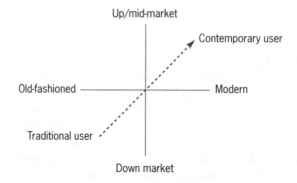

Figure 10.6 Brand repositioning map

something primarily associated with the traditional working-class, building trade and grannies drinking half pints for the iron content to a more up-market, fiercely independent post-Yuppie drink consumed by men, young and old. The chemical properties and the name Guinness remain the same, but its image, central distinctiveness and communicated values have all changed dramatically, helped immeasurably by ground-breaking advertising campaigns.

Well-blended, unconfusing communications maintain brand awareness and perception, sometimes over long time periods, for example we really do appear to perceive Andrex toilet tissue as being the softest. All elements of any sensible communications mix and plan will reinforce and contribute consistently to core brand values. Away from household consumer markets, B2B and not-for-profit organisations are also interested in maintaining and communicating their reputation and a good 'brand' name (e.g. Greenpeace) and are becoming more sophisticated. Large corporate bodies have long recognised the need to sustain a reputation for social responsibility via sponsorship and charitable giving, seeing it as important to employees and shareholders as well as external customers.

Dilemma 10.1

The world's largest brand 'makeover'

In 1997 Bob Ayling, Chief Executive of British Airways, announced a new corporate identity and changed aeroplane livery saying, 'We need a corporate identity that will enable us to become not just a UK carrier, but a global airline that is based in Britain'. In preparation for a new millennium, the old-fashioned Union Jack flag, adorning 308 aircraft tail fins worldwide, would have to go and be replaced by an assortment of more than 50 different individual designs. Ranging from Scottish tartan to the abstract imagery of a Californian artist, the new images were not only bold but originated from and recognised the regions of the world they served. 'Painting the Skies', as this aspect of the re-branding exercise

Dilemma 10.1 *continued*

became known, was designed to shed 'old Britishness' and convey the image of 'a global, caring company, more open, more cosmopolitan but proud to be based in Britain'. It also represented 'a new banner for our employees and business partners' and 'most importantly a signal to travellers all around the world that we want to be their favourite airline'. It all seemed to make sense and was projected to cost several million pounds over the next three years.

Instantly, there was a traditionalist backlash at home. Famously, at the televised unveiling of a model plane in the new livery, ex-UK Prime Minister Mrs Thatcher covered the tail fin up again disparagingly with her husband's handkerchief. Domestic public opinion and the media by and large failed to identify with or were perplexed at the range of different images and critical articles began to appear in the press. Some external stakeholders ultimately came to appreciate them but employees soon came to identify the new livery with the cost-cutting and negative industrial relations that emerged alongside restructuring. Finally, research indicated that the now controversial new designs were also becoming disliked by some overseas customers, who were also confused by the fact that BA's flagship Concord fleet continued to use the Union Jack. In 1999 British Airways decided to reverse their decision, undo a leading element of the world's largest brand makeover and adopt a new, 'Britpop' stylised British flag in the future for the tail fins of all their aircraft worldwide.

Nobody appeared to have fully understood, and in an effort to harmonise, modernise and communicate their brand globally a degree of domestic uncertainty and resentment had been created. At the same time customers were becoming disillusioned with the major carriers and interested in their newer, lower-priced rivals, such as Ryanair. It is notoriously difficult when repositioning a brand and communicating new values not to offend traditional customers, but by attempting to please many masters it is all too possible to please none.

Internal communications

Internal marketing communication was first proposed in the mid-1970s as a way to achieve consistent service quality. In services, the internal P of people, who ultimately control levels of customer access, interaction, participation and satisfaction is vital. Both training and communicating with the staff and adding customer value matter, particularly where staff are enabled and empowered to help customers at the point of contact and customer services are decentralised. Internal customers must be informed and appraised of what is going on, including being briefed about forthcoming external communications campaigns. At times, as an organisation adapts to customer and market conditions, changes to working structures and prac-tices will also be necessary. The quality of explanation, discussion and listening deeply affects levels of employee resistance, understanding, 'ownership of' and, ultimately, the likelihood of change succeeding. Customer-led organisations use multiple communications channels and are communications rich, their communica-tions objectives depending heavily on levels of internal awareness and experience.

Communications messages may well be adapted for different internal stakehold-ers, some of whom may be positive about the message, while others are indifferent towards or even negatively against what is being said and need more persuasion.

Majoring on public relations and personal persuasion, and typically employing the media of internal newsletters, staff magazines, bulletin boards and face-to-face briefings internal communications impart identity to workers and managers and signal organisational goals and values. They are also a useful conduit for feedback from those in customer contact and those responsible directly for delivery, along with the suggestions' box and more everyday management. The larger the organisa-tion the more important it is that internal service providers don't feel like 'mushrooms in the dark'. Recently, an insurance services provider informed its call centre staff they were being made redundant, leading to them walking out immedi-ately. Once again, how you communicate is almost as important as what you say.

The concept of internal customers and markets is also embedded in Total Quality Management, where downstream teams are seen as the customers of those before them on the production line and are empowered to refuse to accept sub-standard material. Communications links and instant feedback between teams drives quality and the pursuit of 'zero defects'. Such organisations facilitate communication and interaction, abandoning strict hierarchical structures and the 'need to know' cul-tures that are sometimes associated with large publicly accountable bodies which badly inhibit information flow.

Managing customer expectation

If quality is about meeting and influencing customer expectation and even delight-ing clients, then managing expectation matters. While not the only quality variable, our communications should not promise more than we can deliver, sometimes an all to tempting sales tactic. In addition, the more we deliver the more the customer

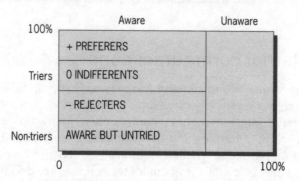

Figure 10.7 Map of internal stakeholder awareness

Source: Adapted from Kotler (1994: 604), itself derived from Ottensen (1977)

expects and, once given, is taken for granted. For example, long-running sales promotions become 'factored in', expected and are no longer an incentive. Customers, both external and internal, match their expectation with their experience and when this falls below a 'zone of tolerance' may easily become disillusioned, leading to low retention and poor motivation. Open, honest and transparent communications, along with effort, interest and the willingness to apologise, appear to retrieve disappointments somewhat but there are no easy answers.

Different customer groups may also have varying expectations and individuals have very different experiences, although in general customer expectation is increasing while tolerance for mismatch with experience is diminishing. Thus, not only ensuring that promises are kept and reliability is maintained, but communicating regularly is critical. Keeping in touch with customers, comprehending their expectations, apologising and explaining the limits of service possibilities can influence their expectations and may expand their 'zone of tolerance'. Most customers are reasonable, they know that when a low-cost flight is delayed a little they still have a good deal. What infuriates them is not being told the cause and how long the delay is likely to last. Skilled, working-class C2s, who are often self-employed or have their own experience of having to keep business promises, and who have hard earned money to spend, are least tolerant of unkept promises.

Internal expectations

Internally, a 'psychological contract' develops between managers and workers, denoting rights and obligations on both sides. Service providers also weigh their actions with their expectation of success and may even 'take their bats home' if they perceive that they are being misled. If internal customers feel there is little likelihood of being listened to, for instance, the suggestions' box will dry up and vital feedback will diminish. To avoid mismatch, dialogue is necessary. Quality internal marketing communications seek not only to provide information, assisting effective and efficient working, but also to engender 'ownership' and association with organisational values. Here as well unrealistically high or low expectations are influential on customer behaviour. As with external customers, zones of tolerance evolve. In this case they are influenced by, and are even created by, internal, everyday micro–communications within an organisation. Promises will be evaluated against experience and if there is no 'credit', trust or extra incentive, they will be discounted. Organisations that manage expectation, listen and communicate openly, honestly and transparently engender trust. Human resource and marketing management have overlapped.

10.3 HOW COMMUNICATIONS INFLUENCE CUSTOMERS

We have now explored several dimensions of communication as well as the ways organisations seek to influence their external and internal customers. In this final section we return to more closely understanding customers and examine how they receive, process and respond to the messages we send.

Stakeholder publics

Customers exist in a social context as part of and in relationship to the groups that make up their world. Groups may influence them positively (e.g. by their seeking the approval of friends and family), or negatively (e.g. a teenager rejecting and rebelling against family norms). Individuals both belong and aspire to belong to groups and disassociate themselves from groups they dislike or disapprove of. Whether at the level of the family, school, work, society, class or culture, association with, acceptance by and the approval of groups of people we care about and think important is highly influential on our behaviour. Opinion group leaders are particularly noticed and looked to. Conversely, social disapproval or linkage with a group from which a customer disassociates themselves may lead to their stopping or never buying a product. The very ownership of certain products may symbolise group membership and approval.

This is the context within which customers receive their information and it may be necessary to communicate to the groups that influence them and convince opinion group leaders and formers in order to make a purchase more socially desirable. At the B2B level it may require micro-communication to several members within a decision-making group in order to achieve a 'critical mass' of agreement and understanding. Certainly no double-glazing sales representative will attempt a 'pitch' unless both partners are present and I don't advise booking the family holiday without consultation even if you really like the look of the brochure. We should also remember that the customer may not be the person who uses and consumes our offering and that many products are obtained for, or given as gifts to, third parties by both businesses and individuals.

In relationship to the organisation, different **stakeholder publics** have a vested interest and may be expected to receive, decode and react to communications differently. Internal stakeholders (e.g. employees) exist within the organisation while connected stakeholders (e.g. shareholders, key suppliers and distributors) are outsiders with a direct interest. External stakeholder groups such as government, local community, media and pressure groups, and ultimately public opinion, may be influential. Public Relations has long since been attempting to communicate messages differently to its different internal and external 'publics'. Imagine the various receptions of the sudden announcement of the closure of a large local employer in a local newspaper followed by a refusal to comment by the company on that evening's local news. Emergency PR may be required, tailor-made and targeted towards different stakeholders.

Customer problem solving

Customers have physical and psychological needs and wants (learned needs), the latter predominating in a developed Western economy (e.g. need a drink but want an orange Fanta). Their motivation may differ (e.g. lack of sustenance, safety, social approval or self-esteem) but they are engaged in a problem-solving exercise, finding ways and making choices in order both to satisfy their immediate desire and to maximise and balance their lifestyle within their means. From their perspective, the marketing mix 4Ps of product, price, place and promotion equates to the 4Cs of customer value, cost, convenience and, not least, communication. Communication plays an important part in providing comparative information, promising benefits and offering solutions to their problems. They face standard or repeat and complex or new problems of varying difficulty and risk, and are said to be engaged in making either rational routine, limited difference, extensive and completely different or impulsive purchase decisions. The latter is associated with individual consumer purchases of 'supermarket goods' and not B2B purchases, where a more rational approach to problem solving prevails. Depending on which school of thought you subscribe to about customer decision making, communications may be seen to either actively inspire purchase or merely remind and incentivise customers to choose a product solution (from their 'buy set' of preferred and alternative brands) as they routinely and habitually make their household purchases (see Figure 10.8).

In simplistic terms, customers can be seen as engaged in a process of sequentially realising they have a need or want, being driven to search for solutions, acting (e.g. buying in) and, if successful, achieving, temporarily at least, satisfaction and drive reduction. The successful completion of this process is central to brand loyalty as repeat purchase is likely, is mirrored by communications objectives and is followed up by post-purchase contact to remind, reinforce and maintain positive feelings. Communications may trigger awareness in customers of a need or want and accelerate drive but may be seen as most potent in the search phase, when the problem solver most actively searches for and is most open to receive messages that otherwise may pass by unnoticed. It is also all too possible for there to be a mismatch between expectation and experience, leaving the customer disappointed, still with a problem and likely to switch brand. This is also a fertile time to communicate either to recover the situation or offer other, more reliable solutions.

The speed and style of customer decision making varies according to their familiarity with the product and process, their (largely learnt) personality and whether they are engaged in making autonomous or joint decisions. Each of these may colour communications. Whether customers are making a completely new, 'modified' or identical re-buy purchase will influence the amount of information required and may take longer, as does joint decision making where negotiation and accommodation with third parties is required. Extrovert personalities are said to prefer loud, social solutions and customers have very different approaches to risk, which

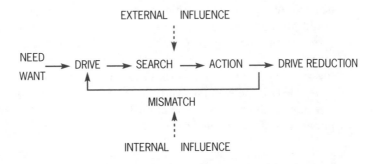

Figure 10.8 Consumer decision-making model

are reflected in the communications images to which they respond. Innovative, very early adopters enjoy being first, self-discovery and dislike direct selling. Advertising images of innovative opinion leaders may prove attractive and endorse the product to later, more risk-adverse customers, while laggardly individuals may only respond to communications from other traditionalists or never at all.

Self-orientation

From the customers' perspective the world starts from them. They have built up and stored a picture of their world based on hard-won experience which is of considerable use to them in interpreting and cataloguing new incoming stimuli. Having internalised, patterned and organised an accumulated 'world view', they are highly selective about what they will now pay attention to, recognise or change. In fact, customers are positively defensive of their psychological consistency, further seeking out, confirming and supporting messages, ignoring and avoiding conflicting messages and consciously rejecting and undermining the validity of challenging data (e.g. 'he would say that wouldn't he'). In many ways we see what we want to see and we hear what we want to hear, although there are some communications images that always seem to get attention: I cite the Wonder Bra poster campaign 'Hello Boys'. Some people are more open than others, but communications messages that are inconsistent and don't fit with the customers' 'world view' are likely to be ignored, rejected or forgotten (see Spotlight 10.4).

Spotlight 10.4

Classic rejection

In the 1990s the Central Office of Information (COI) launched a public service advertising campaign aimed at early hard drug users, indicating the ease and rapid impact of substance addiction. Repeating the headline, 'I can handle it', young men and women were depicted degenerating from recreational drug use, through dependence to total reliance and self-destruction. The general public wholeheartedly approved, supported the campaign and it was repeated to acclaim. Ads graphically demonstrated to them that users of hard drugs in fact could not handle it, and portrayed how stupid and weak they were. Tracking research with the target group, however, indicated that the campaign was largely ignored or rejected on a 'what do they know' basis. Being told you are an idiot (even if true) and stark confrontation of personal values (however valid) were never likely to be well received. Once associated with the 'establishment' view, rejection of the message was almost certain and the campaign had little or no impact where it was needed.

How customers perceive a situation, product or brand name is highly influential, even if incorrect. They may think our service is still poor, based on a single past experience, and, although now we are award-winning, 'wouldn't touch us with a barge pole'. We are only as good as an individual's last encounter, although oddly enough he/she may think more highly about our quality if we have put our prices up, there being a common perception that high price equates to better quality. Consumers also are not indifferent about what they experience, their attitudes being based on often deep-seated values and beliefs that prejudice their behaviour. Attitudes are enduring, self-supporting and hard to shift or overcome, and predispose an individual to most things, including communication. Not surprisingly, marketers spend a lot of time fostering and tracking positive customer attitudes and perceptions and making sure they are communicating consistently with a customer's attitude set. Where it is necessary to challenge and change customer attitudes, using 'fire to fight fire' and undermining 'cognitive consistency' are more likely to succeed than full-frontal confrontation. For example, the customer dislikes a product but likes a sports team which it starts sponsoring and to maintain consistency begins to feel more positively about the former.

Communications messages

Communications messages and experiences, even once committed to memory, may be forgotten. The message may never lodge firmly in the customer's memory, may fail to be recognised or retrieved for some reason or may have been dumped due to non–use over time. Overly complicated messages may exceed short-term memory processing capacity to absorb information. Memory is also selective, some images and feelings being repressed and rejected for use as too challenging. Communications messages frequently attempt to remind and refresh positive memories, offering clear cues and links to previous images to aid both storage and retrieval. Retrieval may be inhibited by new and old material overlaying each other (e.g. I can't remember a new telephone number because the old one gets in the way). Ideally, new messages need to be different enough from each other, older ones need to be stored separately and alongside rather than as replacements, and once again simple communications consistent with existing stored material are most easily remembered. It may also be possible to assist forgetting by never reminding or updating an aspect of communication. For example, Perrier found that communicating how they had got over a water quality crisis just served to remind customers, so they stopped and moved on and people began to forget.

Communication channels

Not only the message but also the communications channel used may transmit value to customers. Exposure varies significantly to a particular medium and different communications vehicles possess very different reader, listener or viewer profiles. In addition, individuals are not indifferent to, and associate with, their media of choice. It is said light-heartedly, for instance, that *The Telegraph* newspaper is read by the people who used to run the country, *The Guardian* by people who think they should be running the country and the *Financial Times* by people who actually are running the country. Some media are more believable than others and a mediums' status itself colours communication reception. The way people use communications channels also needs to be taken into account when communicating and should not be taken for granted. Both internal and external customers leave radios and, increasingly, television on all the time, like 'wallpaper', without paying attention and during the TV advertisements are just as likely to be making a cup of tea as watching. In general terms, editorial copy is believed more than advertising; customers just seem to prefer the straightforward money-off or added-value incentives they understand and remain suspicious of telephone contact at home regardless of the message. Different media are able to communicate in different ways (Table 10.2).

Table 10.2 Commercial media attributes

Cinema	Youthful profile: audience suspends reality and may associate product placements and brands with film stars
Outdoor & transport	Local, sometimes 'captive' audience: prone to erosion of quality and vehicle movement
Posters	Often 'drive past': able to secure attention, remind and reinforce although very subject to 'clutter' with limited ability to communicate detail
Press	Local, national and magazine: can have high 'last', reader association and secondary 'opportunity to see', awarding editorial credibility as well as advertising opportunities for detail and coupon response
Radio	Peak listening at commuting times: local impact, immediate, urgent, capable of awarding BBC authority but suffers from low attention levels
Television	Mass audio-visual medium: powerful home impact on receptive audience with ability to communicate mass brand values and build interest and desire cost-effectively

Brand focus

Brand communicates values to customers and is a symbolic shorthand and tag for information about the product. In communication terms, it awards recognition, credibility, distinctiveness and difference to a product as well as safety and quality assurance to the customer. Unless there is real 'brand confusion' or 'apathy', branding makes it quicker and more straightforward for customers to appraise a communication and more likely that they will respond. Association with a powerful, coherent brand personality should not be underestimated. It represents a 'coat hanger' for focusing expectation, values and qualities such as reliability and trust. Icon brand imagery in particular is a powerful mechanism for coherently marshalling and transmitting information. Brand reputation, while not static, is at the centre of customer interaction and association.

In contrast, straightforward word-of-mouth and personal face-to-face communications should never be discounted as effective communications media. Experience shows that a sale is up to three times more likely based on recommendation and appropriate new products may be strategically placed with opinion leaders and early adopters to create 'chatter' and exposure. Similarly, internal customers are an absolutely central communications vehicle to those outside the organisation. Even their body language communicates volumes and, while hard to define, we all know the difference between 'have a nice day', 'can't be asked' and 'don't bother me', and who we would rather approach.

Change and opportunity

Internet communications (the first interactive, mass communications technology since the telephone) and mobile phones (person-to-person rather than installation-to-installation) alone are revolutionising patterns of communication between organisations and both internal and external customers. It is hard to imagine a contemporary communications strategy which does not include **online communications** as well as **offline communications** elements. Media of communication have proliferated (e.g. through satellite, cable and digital technology), channels are fragmenting and communications mixes are becoming more complex, more global and more personalised. Electronic retrieval and database systems allow ever more sophisticated opportunities to record, connect and manipulate customer feedback data and are being used more fully. It is becoming increasingly possible to listen to, communicate with and target smaller customer groups (e.g. a single block of flats) and on the basis of improved database management, it is becoming possible to tailor-make messages. For example, in the near future entering a supermarket to be offered personalised sales promotions without 'swiping' your loyalty card will become commonplace. Potentially the location of anything can be determined quickly, we can contact customers anywhere, communicate 24 hour a day, communicate 'virtually' at a distance and connect our information systems with those of our suppliers and customers. The pace of change in communications and information processing technology is daunting yet it represents a clear opportunity to improve customer communications.

Neither are our customers static, being increasingly knowledgeable, demanding, cynical and less tolerant. At the same time, from a communications perspective, they are time poor, increasingly technologically proficient, have greater choice and are swamped with messages competing for their attention and business. Lifestyles are changing and along with the media, the market place is fragmenting and customer segments are getting smaller and more diverse. The new 'connoisseur consumer' (not necessarily young anymore) has more disposable income than ever before yet is beginning in well-established markets to conclude that one brand is much like any other. Average spans of attention are shortening, written media are decreasing in usage and multicultural diversity is impacting more strongly, while within organisations internal customers whom they rely on increasingly have higher aspirations, are less deferential and often feel they now 'live to work' rather than 'work to live'. It is increasingly necessary to communicate value and resolve the sometimes conflicting interests of external and internal customers, particularly in voluntary and not-for-profit organisations such as the charity Oxfam (Dilemma 10.2). Communicating intelligently has in fact become more important as a result of applying old models to finding new solutions.

Dilemma 10.2

The ethics of promotional spending

Oxfam is a high-profile charity with a mission to relieve poverty and distress in any part of the world by both direct development aid and, increasingly these days, education and campaigning. It is reliant on fundraising from small, large, corporate and governmental donors as well as the trading income from a chain of shops. It also relies on a small number of full-time staff and a much larger number of highly principled volunteers in order to operate. Associated tradition-ally with Third World emergency relief and provoking advertising imagery, Oxfam is a not-for-profit body accountable to both those who support it and those it seeks to assist. It is closely connected to world governments, other non-governmental agencies and public opinion. As may be imagined, spending any of its £187 million UK income on publicity and lobbying, let alone advertising, how-ever instrumental in getting things done, is likely to 'raise eyebrows' both inside and outside. In the year 2000–01 the cost of raising £63.6 million in non-govern-mental donations alone was £15 million, while education and campaigning consumed 6% of total expenditure.

A frequently asked question, requiring sensitive, transparent explanation, is why does Oxfam spend money on fundraising? Should everything not go directly to good causes? Oxfam spends money for the sole purpose of making money, regarding it as an investment which in the real world ensures the support and expansion of their mission. Furthermore, what is spent is not spent wastefully. Fundraiser campaign managers in fact work to tight budgets and have to prove that communications activities are effective before investing in them. They have to be very careful, maximising free or reduced cost promotional spend and agency support, use in-house public relations, volunteer participation and make creative use of the telephone and the Internet. 'When we first considered adver-tising on TV we tested the effectiveness of adverts in cheaper daytime slots on regional TV stations', explains the website (http://www.oxfam.org.uk). Justifying and persuading internal stakeholders, for whom 'big bucks' advertising and establishment links are deeply suspect, may not prove easy.

This kind of communications vulnerability to criticism and need to account for, and constantly justify, promotional spend is common to public and voluntary sector bodies. They are value-driven, believe in what they do and are reliant on internal customers who can 'take their bat home' if they want to. Ironically, they are also incredibly rich in communication possibilities.

SUMMARY

In conclusion, we are now in a position to form opinions about what constitutes best commercial communications practice. Effective communications are targeted, consistent with customer values, clearly in the customer's language and delivered in an appropriate medium at the right time. There is a lot to be said for simplicity. Good communications campaigns move the customer sequentially from initial unawareness to long-term loyalty, build relationships and meet, exceed and, where necessary, retrieve customer expectation. At their best they represent total communications, partnership and true, proactive dialogue with all key stakeholder publics. Resting on systematic listening, SMART objectives and evaluative feedback, their component parts are integrated, focused and consistent with core communications messages and brand values. They keep their promises, don't promise more than they can deliver and are rooted in a deep understanding and recognition of the importance of both external and internal customers. Although they may not win creative prizes, they significantly influence customers. Ultimately, the best communications and communications campaigns are well conceived, informed and managed, contributing hugely to transmitting and delivering customer satisfaction.

However you view it, winning future organisations will have to add value and be special and different by providing service and through communicating intensively with both their external and internal customers. Despite criticism of Customer Relationship Management (CRM), enhanced long-term relationships, integrated approaches and dialogue are the way. These are the subject of the following chapter. For almost all commercial and not-for-profit organisations there has never been a time when communications matter more.

Discussion questions

1   What constitutes effective commercial communication?
2   Why are integrated communications campaigns to be desired?
3   How can communications achieve brand focus?
4   What messages might an organisation's different internal and external stakeholder publics want to hear?

Case study 10.1 | *Metro*

Metro, the first urban national newspaper is a free, colour, 20-minute read targeted at 6.30am–9.30pm commuters travelling to and from work. The London edition was launched in March 1999 by Associated Newspapers and heralded what has become a publishing phenomenon. Subsequently rolled out to seven other major UK cities, *Metro* rapidly became one of the six largest circulation newspapers in this country and the worlds largest free sheet.

It was initially aimed at the younger and more affluent of the 400,000 regular London commuters that research indicated did not already buy a weekly newspaper. Distribution engaged their basic instinct to pick up something that was free, easily availabile, particularly at underground station entrances, and aroused their curiosity about what fellow travellers were conspicuously reading in otherwise dull circumstances. Carrying editorials and advertising that appealed directly to the target audience's busy, 'time poor' lifestyle, and in competition with the local radio, billboards and posters of a 'captive' environment, *Metro* soon became an essential part of London commuter life. Enough copies are now produced for 50% of the capital's 'rush hour' passengers.

The formula transferred rapidly to the estimated eight million adults living outside London who work but do not read a national daily newspaper (thus cleverly not cannibalising Associated Newspaper's existing customers). *Metro* is now available in the commuter transport systems of Birmingham, Edinburgh, Glasgow, Leeds, Manchester, Newcastle and Sheffield, as well as the capital, with a combined UK readership of around 830,000. Audience research indicates that its readers are predominantly ABC1, that is white-collar workers between the ages of 16 and 44, 60% male, and with an average age of 29. 'These are the people who work at the heart of the service economy; they are bright, intelligent, hard working and tell us what they want', says Doug Read, *Metro*'s Executive Director.

The profile of *Metro*'s readership and the fact they had never read or were lapsed readers of national daily newspapers made them highly attractive to advertisers. Space was sold to media buying agencies as a specific 'media moment', competing with radio and 'outdoor and transport' rather than as space in another traditional newspaper. Early on, advertising agency representatives were taken to London's Waterloo station. 'From an elevated balcony every morning you can witness an entire sea of blue created by commuters carrying hundreds of our blue front-page mastheads' explained Karen Wall, *Metro*'s Marketing Manager. Advertisers were convinced and within the first two years of its launch *Metro* took £40 million worth of display advertising revenue, becoming profitable after only 11 months of its initial launch. Long-term advertising deals were quickly secured for a wide range of market sectors, including retail, motoring, travel, finance and dot.com providers.

Metro's editorial continued to present a balanced, 20-minute mix of punchy national and international editorial wrapped around local information, including listings, tips and guides and engaging competitions, games and puzzles. Readers are encouraged to become part of local campaigns and petitions and to contribute their views. Interaction and association was further enhanced by the launch of http://metro.co.uk in November 2000, effectively taking the newspaper online. The website contains the *Metro Café* where readers can read highlights, updates, have their own say and not least access promotions on travel, retail and entertainment. 'We currently use this response mechanicism for data collection, which is used both for customer profiling to further our distribution channels and for a variety of commercial applications', relates Karen Wall. In addition *Metro* has established 'Urban Life', a panel of 3,000 readers whose views are monitored and tracked on a range of issues. Mike Anderson, the *Metro* supremo, who is also Managing Director of the *London Evening Standard*, believes that as well as helping Metro to stay close to its customers, 'the panel offers advertisers themselves the possibilities of unique feedback'.

As affluent urbanites tend to be wine drinkers, the *Metwines* brand was launched in 2000 as a joint venture with Virgin Wines. Given the opportunity to replicate success, it was not long before *Metro* was being introduced abroad. Commencing in 2001, the formula was successfully transferred to cities around continental Europe and North America and was aimed at their own long-suffering commuter publics. New cities in the UK have been earmarked as potential launch sites and it may only be a matter of time before every major city in the world has a *Metro* clone. While other press media experience falling circulations and incomes, and despite increasing competition, *Metro* continues to grow. 'Its readership cannot be reached in any other way, giving the company a degree of future proofing against any downturn in advertising revenue', states Jessica Hodgson of the *Media Guardian*. A new player has forged a place for itself and continues to prosper in the crowded press media market place.

Questions

1   Who are *Metro*'s main internal and external stakeholder publics?

2   What other products could be advertised successfully in *Metro*?

3   What does being free communicate to readers?

4   Why would *Metro* also want to be online?

Source: Adapted from the article, 'The fast track to success: *Metro*'s marketing strategy pulls new readers and advertisers', *Marketing Business*, April 2001: p 21; Jessica Hodgson, '*Metro* set for further expansion', *Media Guardian*, 24 April 2001; Roy Greenslade, 'So who actually reads *Metro*?', *Media Guardian*, 28 October 2002; and Jim Blyth (2003) *Essentials of Marketing Communications* (2nd edition). Harlow: Financial Times/Prentice Hall, pp. 67–8.

Further reading

Blythe, J. (2003) *Essentials of Marketing Communications* (2nd edition). Harlow: Financial Times/Prentice Hall.

BPP Study Text (2003) *Customer Communications*. London: BPP Professional Education.

BPP Study Text (2003) *Marketing Communications*. London: BPP Professional Education.

Chartered Institute of Marketing (2002) *Customer Communications*. Trowbridge: CIM Publishing.

Chartered Institute of Marketing (2002) *Integrated Marketing Communications*. Trowbridge: CIM Publishing.

Jobber, D. (2004) *Principles and Practice of Marketing* (4th edition). Maidenhead: McGraw-Hill, Chapters 12–16.

References

Chartered Institute of Marketing (2001–02) *Managing the Marketing/Customer Interface* (Study Text for December 2001 and June 2002 exams). London: BPP Publishing.

Kotler, P. (1994) *Marketing Management: Analysis Planning, Implementation and Control* (8th edition). Englewood Cliffs: Prentice Hall.

Kotler, P. (2000) *Marketing Management: Planning, Implementation and Control* (Millennium edition). Upper Saddle River: Prentice Hall.

Luengo-Jones, S. (2001) *All to One: The Winning Model for Marketing in the Post-Internet Economy*. New York: McGraw-Hill.

Ottenson, O. (1977) 'The response function', in M. Berg (ed.), *Current Theories in Scandinavian Mass Communications Research*. Grenaa, Denmark: GMT.

Rogers, E.M. (2003) *Diffusion of Innovations*. New York: Free Press.

Wilson, R. and Gilligan, C. (2001) *Strategic Marketing Management: Planning, Implementation and Control*. Oxford: Butterworth-Heinneman.

11

Developing and managing customer relationships

Simon Kelly

LEARNING OUTCOMES

After reading this chapter you should be able to:

- **Appreciate why customer relationships are important and how they deliver value**

- **Recognise the importance of value**

- **Understand the practice of building customer relationships – customer relationship management (CRM) and relationship marketing (RM)**

- **Understand the key principles of relationship marketing**

- **Appreciate the different types of customer relationship**

- **Understand the key properties of relationships**

- **Know how to build relationships into the planning process**

KEY WORDS

Customer relationship
management (CRM)
Lifetime value
Loyalty ladder
Mega marketing
One-to-one marketing

Perceived value
Permission marketing
Relationship marketing
Total cost of ownership
Value

INTRODUCTION

In recent years advances in technology have dramatically reduced product life cycles. This same technology has empowered customers with access to information that has shortened search times for new products and services and has improved their decision-making quality.

Today, if you want to take a weekend break in New York you can fire up an Internet search engine and within minutes you will be comparing offers from companies across the globe. Within half an hour you could be in a strong position to book the holiday based on a deep understanding of the comparative offers that are out there – with an instant view of price differentials. Some of us remember – only a few years ago – going from one high street travel agent to the next comparing offers – a fraught process that could take days. At the end of the Internet experience you are always left feeling that you have got the best value deal. This was rarely so in the old world as the best value deal had often gone by the time you'd compared offers!

In this environment, where price is completely transparent, organisations have to look for new ways to provide value to the customer and at the same time deliver long-term value for their shareholders, especially as this is set against a backdrop where customer expectations are rising (see Chapter 12). This chapter will examine how organisations seek to deliver long-term value through customer relationships – a true source of competitive advantage today.

The chapter will begin by looking at why customer relationships are important. Having definined value, we will examine the practice of building customer relationships through **relationship marketing (RM)** and **customer relationship management (CRM)**. After developing an understanding of the key principles of relationship marketing, we will explore the different types of customer relationship. This will allow us to look at the key properties of good relationships. Finally, we will examine how to build relationships into the planning process.

11.1 WHY ARE CUSTOMER RELATIONSHIPS IMPORTANT?

Over the past decade or so it became increasingly difficult to differentiate from competitors in serving general product needs. Now customers expect individual attention and companies have had to shift their focus to a customer orientation. Some believe the explosion in Internet usage during the 1990s put customers firmly back in control (Seybold, 2001). In the past, banks and insurance companies kept customers through inertia – even ones they didn't really want to keep – as moving accounts was difficult. Now customers can move their financial records and their relationships easily. In the past, manufacturers paid lip service to designing and configuring products for customers. Now they have the tools to make custom-manufacturing cost-effective and practical. Customers are flocking to companies like Dell, which allows customers to build a personal computer to their own specifications through its website. This shift in the business environment – and the resulting shift towards one-to-one marketing – is shown in Figure 11.1.

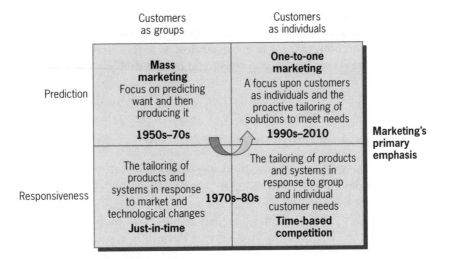

Figure 11.1 The shift from mass marketing to one-to-one marketing

Source: Gilligan and Wilson (2003)

The single-minded focus of this chapter will examine why companies seek to develop relationships with customers and how they deliver mutual value. In order to do this we need to be clear about what value is in the context of customer relationships.

11.2 WHAT IS VALUE?

One dictionary definition of **value** is: 'The desirability of something, often in terms of its usefulness or exchangeability'. Others are: 'An amount of money considered to be a fair exchange for something' or 'Something worth the money it cost'.

So, we can see that value – like beauty – is very much in the eye of the beholder. **Perceived value** is often seen to be the difference between the benefits gained and the costs associated with consuming a product or service:

Perceived value = benefits – costs

From the point of view of the consumer, costs can mean a lot more than just purchase price. A ticket for a Sheffield United match may cost £15 (a credit card booking over the telephone may incur a cost of £1). When you add to this the costs of a programme and half-time refreshments, the overall cost may be much more like £25. This is before anything is factored on for the cost of getting to and from the match, along with the opportunity cost you assign to the fact that you could have been doing something else. Costs can include:

- search costs – associated with finding the item you want to purchase;
- installation costs – to get the product working (e.g. a home computer);
- ancillary costs – for the items you need to help get the service you want (e.g. computer software);

- running costs (e.g. petrol for a car);
- maintenance costs – to keep the item in shape so that it continues to do the job you bought it for (e.g. car service) or to fix it if things go wrong;
- insurance costs – to protect you in case things go wrong.

All these costs added together would give you the **total cost of ownership** for a product or service. So a more accurate view of perceived value would be:

Perceived value = benefits – total cost of ownership

The benefits sought really depend on the needs customers are trying to address. Customers who are looking to buy a car just to get them from A to B are entirely different from those who are looking for a car that gives them status. Balancing the benefits gained against the costs allows customers to form a view about value for money: 'The restaurant meal was definitely worth £50 because the surroundings were excellent, the service was first-class and the food was well prepared.' If customers believe they got value for money the first time they made a purchase, they are likely to buy again.

From the point of view of the suppliers, they believe they are getting value from customers if the benefits they get from serving the customers are greater than the costs of serving them, which means they are making a profit from the customers. This is not straightforward as the acquisition costs for getting a customer in the first place are often very high. Companies frequently do not make a profit from a customer for quite some time.

How customer value is measured has certainly changed over time. Many organisations now use **lifetime value**, that is how much would the customers be worth if the company kept them for the rest of their lives? This puts an entirely different perspective on the supermarket customer who *only* spends £20 a week – they are actually worth in excess of £30,000 over a 30-year period.

So, creating mutual value is about satisfying customer needs so they keep coming back for more products and services, which produces greater profitability – or does it? We will now look at the case for developing long-term customer relationships.

11.3 THE CASE FOR CUSTOMER RELATIONSHIPS

Over the past few years the focus has shifted from customer acquisition to customer retention, as demonstrated in Figure 11.2. Developing customer relationships has become increasingly important for customer retention. Retention was felt to deliver results both by improved turnover and reduced costs. The longer customers stay with you, the more often they purchase and the greater the range of products they buy from you. The double whammy is that the more you get to know the customers the easier they become to handle. In addition, customers can apply their experience with the seller to raise the efficiency of providing the products, which all leads to reduced costs.

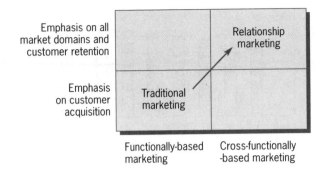

Figure 11.2 The transition to relationship marketing
Source: Adapted from Christopher *et al.* (2002)

Work by Reichheld and Sasser in the early 1990s proved the empirical case for customer retention. The financial services group MBNA found that a 5% reduction in customer defections led to a 60% increase in profits over the following five years (Reichheld, 1993). The result of a sector overlapping study (see Figure 11.3) showed that a 5% reduction in churn rate generated 25–85% higher profits.

A financial consultancy established that customer-related transaction costs decrease by around 60% between the first and second year of a customer relationship (Reichheld and Sasser, 1990). This happens because customers encounter fewer problems. More importantly, the financial consultant gains a better awareness of the customers' financial situation and investment preferences, which has a measurable impact on cost savings. An investigation into the life insurance sector further demonstrated that a growth in customer retention of 5% translates into cost reductions of 18% (Reichheld, 1993).

Finally, the total impact of customer retention on profits was analysed during the course of an active customer relationship. Figure 11.4 shows the results of this impact on profit as a result of the effects of word-of-mouth communication.

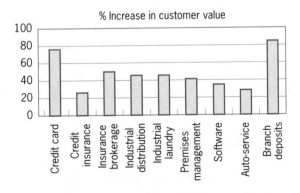

Figure 11.3 The consequences of a 5% reduction in customer losses in different fields
Source: Reichheld (1996). Reprinted by permission of Harvard Business School Publishing from 'The Loyalty Effect' by Frederick F. Reichheld. Boston MA 1996, pp. 36. Copyright © 1996 by Bain & Company, Inc. All rights reserved.

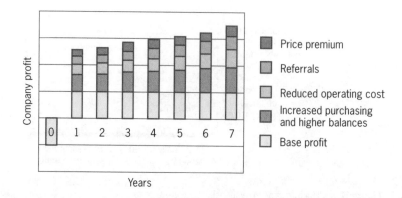

Figure 11.4   The development of value categories in the course of a customer relationship

Spotlight 11.1

Quantity or quality ? – O_2 versus T-Mobile

The landscape of the mobile telephone industry has changed dramatically in the last two or three years. Before this the dash for customers saw all the main network providers offering pre-pay packages. Performance was measured in the industry by the number of customers and total revenue. Now the focus is much more on quality and profitability, as highlighted in this performance comparison of T-Mobile and O_2 – the third and fourth largest network providers.

At the end of 2002, T-Mobile had 12.4 million customers, compared with O_2's 11.95 million. In the third quarter of 2002 T-Mobile added 659,000 new customers compared with 532,000 for O_2. In November 2002 T-Mobile overtook O_2 to become the UK's third largest network.

In the squeezed margins of the mobile industry it's quality not quantity that matters, which is why average revenue per user has become such an important measure. T-Mobile has reported average revenue per user (ARPU growth) from £204 in March 2002 to £226 in December 2002. This is still lower than O_2, Orange and Vodaphone. Over the same period O_2 grew ARPU from £231 to £243.

To increase ARPU, T-Mobile needs to increase the number of users on contract as opposed to pre-pay. Here it is way behind the competition with only 17.9% of its customers being on contract compared with 33% for O_2 (September 2002).

Finally, customer churn is important in the industry as a drop in churn rate of 1% increases profits by £5 million. Here T-Mobile is in front with an annualised churn rate of 21% compared with 28% for O_2. O_2 has put measures in place to reduce churn through its O_2 First Loyalty programme. The scheme uses customer data

Spotlight 11.1 *continued*

to send up to 4,000 copy variations in direct mail shots to offer advice on the most suitable tariffs. The scheme now has 1.8 million members. Among this group the churn rate is half that for other customers and customer satisfaction is 6% to 10% higher.

So, who has the best quality customer base – T-Mobile or O_2?

Source: Adapted from Curtis, J. (2003) 'T-Mobile vs. O2: the first year report,' *Marketing Magazine*, 19 April

As we can see from Spotlight 11.1, retaining customer relationships delivers long-term value to companies, increasing revenue, reducing costs and improving profits. The firm develops a much deeper understanding of its customers and, in return, the customers get value delivered back in the form of products and services that genuinely meet their needs.

The changing business environment, supported by the empirical case for customer relationships and retention, gave rise to the growth of the disciplines of customer relationship management and relationship marketing.

11.4 WHAT IS RELATIONSHIP MARKETING?

Traditional theory said that differential advantage was created, and sustained, by the intelligent use of the marketing mix. Originally, this was just 4Ps: product, price, promotion and place. With the rise in services this was no longer felt to be enough. Physical evidence, people and process management now form the three additional Ps in the extended marketing mix – or 7Ps.

This takes us right back to booking the weekend trip to New York. Competitive advantage in the traditional 4Ps can often be transient in the Internet world. With the rise of services, the intangible elements of the offer can often create competitive advantage. Anyone who has been entertained in a queue in a Disney theme park or used the fastpass facility to jump queues on their favourite rides will vouch for how important process management is.

In order to satisfy ever-demanding customers, organisations had to work with other companies to provide the range of services required. Competitive advantage was often gained by those who had the best partnership networks and customer relationships. This is the domain of relationship marketing.

Gummesson (1999) defined relationship marketing as 'marketing seen as relationships, networks and interactions'. *Relationships* require at least two parties who are in contact with each other. The basic relationship is that between a supplier and a customer, which he calls the simple dyad relationship. He sees a *network* as a set of relationships that can grow into a complex pattern which is required to develop and deliver service to the end customer. In order for this to work they have to engage in active contact with each other. This is *interaction*.

Gummesson took his inspiration from his time as a management consultant where he observed: 'Creating and maintaining a network of relationships – outside as well as inside the company – constituted the core marketing of the consulting firm.' (1999: 2). Gummesson criticised traditional marketing concepts, saying that they were based exclusively on getting the customer to transact with the organisation. Relationship marketing is about achieving customer loyalty.

The definition provided by Gummesson is very broad. Parvatiyar and Sheth (2000) provided a definition that usefully focuses on activities that add value to the customer and to the organisation, emphasising mutual value creation: 'Relationship Marketing is the ongoing process of engaging in cooperative and collaborative activities and programmes with immediate and end-user customers to create or enhance mutual economic value' (Bruhn 2003: 10).

In this chapter the focus will be on relationships with customers.

11.5 WHAT IS CUSTOMER RELATIONSHIP MANAGEMENT?

If relationship marketing is about engaging in collaborative activities with customers to create mutual advantage, it is important to know who your customers are and what their needs are. This is where customer relationship management (CRM) fits in. CRM is the technique or set of processes for collecting information from prospects and customers about their needs, and for providing information that

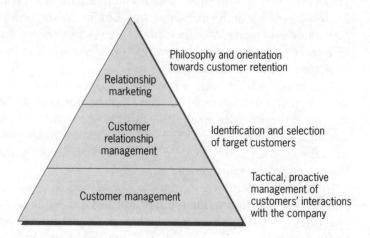

Figure 11.5 Relationship marketing and CRM – a hierarchy
Source: Christopher *et al.* (2002)

helps customers evaluate and purchase products that deliver the best possible value to them. It is a process for managing the company's resources to create the best possible experience and value for customers while generating the highest possible revenue and profit for the company.

A typical CRM system uses a centralised database to store data about marketing, sales and customer service. This gives employees a complete view of the company's relationship with each customer. The tactical management of customer interactions is known as customer management. Figure 11.5 shows how these three disciplines sit together. In simple terms, an organisation needs to begin with a philosophy that customer relationships and retention are important, that is relationship marketing. To do this it needs to know who its important customers are and what their needs are, that is customer relationship management.

11.6 PRINCIPLES OF RELATIONSHIP MARKETING

Loyalty snakes and ladders

If long-term customer relationships are to deliver increasing value to both parties, the aim is to keep profitable customers and move them up the 'loyalty ladder' (Christopher et al., 2002) (see Figure 11.6).

At the bottom rung of the ladder are your list of *targets*. You have performed your market segmentation and you now have a target market of customers you believe would benefit from your products and services. Having shaped your 7Ps to target this customer set, some will respond positively, indicating they want to talk more with you – these are your *prospects*. After engaging in dialogue with your prospects, some will decide to buy your services – these become your *buyers*. At this point the buyer will only have performed one transaction with the company. If he makes a repeat purchase, you would then begin to consider him as a *customer*. From this

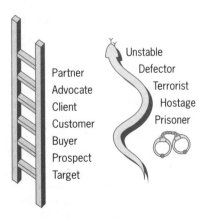

Figure 11.6 Loyalty snakes and ladders

point on the trip up the ladder is about the customer feeling that it is worth making the journey up to the top rung because he can see long-term value in the relationship. From the view point of the organisation, it will want to help the customer get to the top of the ladder if it sees the relationship as being profitable. So once the first purchase has been made, the customer will be prepared to buy more if his needs have been met or exceeded. Those who stay loyal and buy a greater and broader range of goods become *clients*. If the client is satisfied – or delighted – with the services he gets from the organisation, he will actively support the organisation until he becomes an *advocate*, who openly promotes the organisation. At this stage he may become a *partner*, where he starts to share resource and risk, potentially developing joint offers to take to market.

This is, of course, a fairly simplistic view of customer relationships as not everyone will want to carry on up the ladder. Relationships are more like a game of snakes and ladders – and we all know that if the objective is to get to square 100 the first snake is on about square 12! If at any point a customer becomes dissatisfied, he will become *unstable* and start to consider competitive offers. He may then decide to leave – he becomes a *defector*. Worse still, if his experience has been so bad he may even turn into a '*terrorist*' towards the company, not only causing extra costs, but also actively dissuading other potential and current customers. The dissatisfied customer of a monopoly provider or a public sector organisation may have nowhere else to turn and at that point becomes a '*hostage*' or a '*prisoner*'.

One-to-one marketing

The acquisition costs for new customers are high: it can cost an online e-tailer £450 to acquire a new customer and more than two years to recoup the costs (Bark, 2001). Keeping customers continually educated about new products and services is also time-consuming for both the organisation and the customer. This led Peppers and Rogers (1994) to put forward the view that the focus should be on keeping customers longer and getting maximum value from them over time. 'If AT&T spends hundreds of dollars to get a new long-distance customer, and that customer pays $20 a month for AT&T services, then they have to be figuring out how to generate revenue through their interaction with that customer, not spending all their energy getting yet another new customer' (Godin, 1999).

Peppers and Rogers (1994) suggest that organisations focus on four things when selling to customers:

1. Increase your 'share of wallet'. Figure out which needs you can satisfy, then use the knowledge you have, and the trust you have, to make the additional sale.
2. Increase the durability of customer relationships. Invest money in customer retention, because it's a small fraction of the cost of customer acquisition.
3. Increase your product offerings to customers. By being customer-focused instead of retail-focused or factory-focused, a manufacturer or merchant can widely increase its offerings, thus increasing share of wallet.

4. Create an interactive relationship that leads to meeting more customer needs. It's a cycle: by constantly asking the consumer to give more information the marketer can offer more products.

Peppers and Rogers have called this approach focusing on fewer customers and getting a greater understanding of their individual needs in order to create value 'one-to-one marketing'. One-to-one marketing is a philosophy of building relationships that lead to understanding the needs and priorities of each prospect and customer, and providing the products and services that meet those needs.

A CRM-enabled company implements one-to-one marketing by using a unified approach to marketing analysis, marketing communications, sales and service. This improved communication technique results in creating a one-to-one relationship of understanding each prospect's needs and showing that the company's products meet those needs, which encourages the prospect to select that vendor. In other words, a CRM approach to one-to-one marketing helps a company implement the learning and communications techniques that demonstrate the desire of the company – and the value to the customer – in forming a long-lasting relationship.

Permission marketing

Godin (1999) builds on the work of Peppers and Rogers. He developed the term 'permission marketing', which is about 'turning strangers into friends, then friends into customers'. He says that one-to-one marketing focuses on the relationship from the first sale onwards whereas permission marketing works from the first contact onwards.

Permission marketing is all about using customers' permission to market to them, from the point where they are a target onwards. For example, Levi's has built one of the largest brands of women's jeans in the USA. It has done so without having any jeans in the store. Instead, women have their measurements taken by a trained specialist, who sends them to a computerised factory. There a semi-custom pair of jeans is made to order. The shopper gets custom fit for a fraction of the cost. Levi's has a huge saving in inventory risks and advertising costs. Best of all, once a customer has given her measurements to Levi's, would she ever consider switching brands to save a few dollars?

One-to-one marketing uses the same techniques as permission marketing, that is using customer knowledge, frequency and relevance of contact to turn customers into super-customers. One-to-one marketing uses the permission that's been granted after someone becomes a customer and uses that permission to create even better customers. The more permission, the more mutual value is derived for the customer and the organisation.

The permission marketer works to change the focus from finding as many prospects as he can to converting the largest number of prospects into customers. Then he leverages the permission on an ongoing basis to create mutual value (see Figure 11.7).

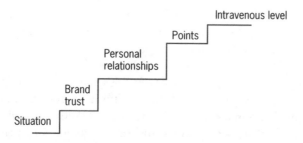

Figure 11.7 The five steps of permission marketing

There are five steps of permission marketing:

- *Intravenous level.* This is the level of trust you place in your doctor when you're in intensive care with a needle in your arm and medicine dripping into your veins. A company that has achieved intravenous permission is making the buying decisions on behalf of the customer.
- *Purchase on approval.* There is a second level on the intravenous step. Although not quite full intravenous, it's called purchase on approval. An example of this would be Britannia record club. Once you've signed up to be a member they choose which album to send you. They'll also advise you of what the choice is for next month. If you say no, they won't send it. If they've guessed your needs correctly, it comes automatically.
- *Points.* Points reward loyalty for repeat purchasing. Green Shield stamps, air miles or hotel honours cards are examples.
- *Personal relationships.* Surprisingly, Godin ranks personal relationships lower than points because they don't scale. This doesn't mean they aren't important, particularly in business-to-business (B2B) marketing. Many large sales are made in the IT industry through leveraging personal relationships. He recognises that it's the very best way to sell custom products or very expensive products. In these situations having a personal relationship can be the single best way to move someone up to intravenous levels. The point is you cannot develop an enormous business-to-consumer (B2C) organisation through personal relationships. In the B2C sector, you have to find an approach that can scale across thousands of customers. This is certainly being helped by the ability to provide personalisation on websites. This can give the feeling of a one-to-one approach to the customer and has scale.
- *Brand trust.* This is much lower down the permission ladder and is the trust that is placed when customers interact with a brand they are familiar with. Many fast moving consumer goods brands concentrate on brand building – supported by high advertising spend – to create a competitive advantage. You only have to look at the list of top global brands by valuation to see proof of this. This can count for nothing if a company loses touch with customer tastes and preferences. McDonald's earnings fell for seven out of the last eight quarters up to June 2003 as the trend towards healthy living hit their sales. Even the biggest brands have to keep in touch with the times and reposition themselves in line with the changing environment. The question is does McDonald's have sufficient permission from its customers to significantly change its offer through the power of its brand? (See Dilemma 11.1.)

Dilemma 11.1

Relationship through brand? – salads help boost McDonald's sales

After 14 consecutive months of decline McDonald's brought Jim Cantalupo out of retirement to become chief executive officer. In his previous 28-year career he had held all posts up to vice-chairman. During this time he had masterminded the global expansion of McDonald's, taking the international division from 2,350 restaurants to 15,000.

The challenges he faces are very different from the expansionary times. He needs to get McDonald's back on track. Many commentators believed that the decline was because McDonald's had not kept up with demands for healthier lifestyles.

Commenting shortly after his appointment, Mr Cantalupo said: 'Our competitors have done a good job of duplicating our standards but they can't duplicate our brand. McDonald's is like a Cadillac. It may need a wash and a polish, it may need tuning up but it's the Cadillac of the industry.'

Sales in May 2003 were up by 2.2%, the first rise for 14 months. The world's biggest fast food company said that the introduction of healthier items on its menu had played a significant part in the increase.

Critics claimed that McDonald's had jumped on the bandwagon by offering more salads and fruit, suggesting the company was responding to global concerns over obesity and poor diet. McDonald's insisted that it was just offering a broader choice to customers.

Shares in the company surged to a nine-month high as a result of the figures. Same-store sales in the USA, its largest market, were up 6.3%, the highest increase in four years.

'This outstanding performance was driven by customers' strong response to our nationally advertised Premium Salad line-up and extremely popular Happy Meal offerings [and] ... enhanced customer service', said Jim Cantalupo.

The company began offering sliced apples and grapes at its 1,200 UK outlets two months ago. Low-fat pasta salads, and mozzarella and sun-dried tomato flat-bread have also been introduced.

Does this mean that their brand has developed relationships strong enough to overcome their apparent initial failure to recognise the healthy food trend?

(Jim Cantalupo died suddenly in April 2004. He was owed a great debt by McDonald's after masterminding a turnaround in their fortunes with the introduction of a new healthier menu.)

Source: Adapted from Innes, J., 'Salads help boost McDonald's sales', *The Scotsman*, 7 January 2003.

- *Situational permission*. This is given at any point of interaction when a customer deals with an organisation. Godin sees this as being important because at the point of interaction there is the opportunity to add value to the sale – and for the customer. 'Do you want fries with that?' are the six most profitable situational permission marketing words in history. With 100,000 employees using this line to customers every day McDonald's has generated billions of pounds in extra sales using situational permission. The question is will 'Do you want a salad with that?' have the same effect. Early indications look good.

There is a lower level than this which is called SPAM. This is where there is no permission or relationship and the company practises 'interruptive marketing'. Godin includes television and radio adverts, direct mail to strangers and, above all, junk email in this category. This equates to the bottom rung of the communications ladder introduced by Rod Radford (in Chapter 10) (see Figure 10.5 on page 257). Now that millions of unsolicited emails can be sent out for less than £100, spam marketers can flood potential customers with millions of unwelcome interruptions. Add this to the proliferation of channels to customers and the number of interruptions runs into the thousands per week. No wonder customers are seeking relationships with companies that can solve their problems and create mutual value. The challenge for companies is to add value by making customer interactions anticipated, personal and relevant.

Now we have considered the case for relationship marketing, we can turn to different types of relationship.

11.7 TYPES OF CUSTOMER RELATIONSHIP

There are several different types of relationship where the attributes and dynamics of the relationships vary greatly. Here we examine a few important ones.

Business-to-business relationships

The unique feature of many business-to-business (B2B) relationships is that they typically involve many people from both the supplier and customer. Figure 11.8 shows a typical array of roles in B2B decision making. Taking IT and telecommunications as an example, it may be the marketing director who has *initiated* an enquiry into buying a new customer relationship management system to support customer retention. A key *influencer* in the decision-making process maybe the sales general manager, who wants to ensure that what is purchased is easy for his sales team to use and will drive up the number of quality leads coming from marketing campaigns. There are also likely to be key influencers inside the IT department, who may have a view on the best system for ease of integration into their current systems or who may just have a favourite supplier. If the CRM system is above a certain value it may be the managing director (MD) who will make the

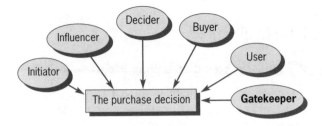

Figure 11.8 B2B decision making

final *decision* or, more frequently, it will be a committee of people headed by the MD. For high-value capital items the *buying* department will be involved and the finance director will take an active interest. High-value projects usually go to trial, at which point the view of the *users* will be taken very seriously. If it is too time-consuming to use and does not prove to deliver the stated benefits in trial, the project may go no further. Finally, there is always a *gatekeeper*, perhaps a person in the IT department who thinks that he has the right to decide who the supplier will see, when and why.

Clearly, to sell successfully into another organisation is complex as it can involve tens of people from the supplier and customer organisations. To win this one deal the supplier will have to understand where the power lies in the buying organisation and seek to influence all the key people. If there are already existing relationships, then the chances of winning will be much greater than the competing supplier who has no established contacts. To grow mutual value for both organisations, suppliers will take the customer up the loyalty ladder faster if they:

- work to develop a deep understanding of the customer, the industry and the business drivers;
- demonstrate that they understand how their own organisation can help the customer;
- can influence the organisation to develop new offers to create new opportunities for the customer;
- understand how technological developments in the industry can deliver value to the customer;
- can form partnerships with other suppliers to solve the customer problems;
- can open meaningful peer-to-peer relationships with the customer, leading to greater mutual understanding and resulting in delivery of higher mutual value (see Spotlight 11.2).

Electronic relationships

The electronic relationship is becoming more important as customers use the Internet extensively to learn, shop and buy. Increasingly, they are discovering the benefits of personalisation and customisation. Amazon.com recognises who you are after you've logged in and presents you with book choices based on stated prefer-

Spotlight 11.2

ICT Industry Executive Calling Programmes

A number of corporations in the ICT Industry, such as the Global IT services company IBM and the American telecommunications giant AT&T, run programmes where senior executives meet their counterparts in client organisations. These are sometimes referred to as Executive Calling Programmes.

Senior executives will be matched to senior clients either through previous relationships with individuals, aligned to their previous career experience, or by job function. If the executive vice-president of marketing for AT&T used to work with the chief finance officer of Global Bank Co., then they would be matched up on the calling programme. If the human resources vice-president for IBM used to work in the retail sector, he could well be assigned to an executive in the retail sector. Finally, peer-to-peer calling would take place, for example chief finance officer to chief finance officer.

The key objectives of such programmes are generally to form closer relationships, to share organisational learning and to help retain key accounts. The senior executives would meet on a periodic basis for mutually beneficial discussions. The most fruitful ones would be about sharing learning: How do you measure customer satisfaction? How do you retain customers? How do you share knowledge around your organisation? How do you use the Internet?

This puts the relationship above the basic account manager versus ICT buyer. It can lead to greater loyalty as this type of relationship is difficult to replicate. To run these programmes successfully organisations have found it useful to link it to executive performance.

ences or on your latest selections. They even email you when a new book in your preferred category is released. Timbuk2 designs, a US-based manufacturer of backpacks and messenger bags, is developing new direct relationships based on its ability to customise (see Spotlight 11.3).

Dell computers used the direct model to allow customers to customise their own personal computers to take them to the forefront of the home PC market. Nowadays customers are demanding e-relationships with companies as part of a multi-channel strategy. They want to choose when and how they buy – through the Internet, over the telephone or in a retail outlet. Companies ignore the importance of the e-relationship at their peril, not least for its capability to add long-term mutual value – the customer gets exactly what they want and the company gets to provide it at much lower cost. A bank account transaction was estimated to cost 15 pence over the Internet compared with £1.50 in a bank branch (Friedman and Furey, 1999) with probably less queuing and the task is performed at the customer's leisure. So e-channels

Spotlight 11.3

Timbuk2Designs

'Customers love the ability to custom-design their backpacks. But there's just no way to convince retailers to take custom orders in the stores. They can't handle one-off products. So we'll go direct to the customer and do it on the Internet. Customers can design their own backpacks, we'll ship them out the next day, and if retailers want to participate we'll set up a shop on their websites and put kiosks in their stores too!' (Brennan Mulligan, President, Timbuk2Designs)

Source: Patricia Seybold (2001) *The Customer Revolution*. London: Random House.

can create mutual value through better service at lower costs, allowing the organisation to learn more about the customer and deliver more value back over time.

In the B2B world moving routine repeat purchase tasks to the e-channel delivers the double whammy of lowering the costs to serve the customer and raising customer satisfaction. Companies like Cisco Systems have found that self-service customers are generally more satisfied (see Spotlight 11.4). In addition, time is freed up for the account teams, who no longer have to deal with the repeat orders and can now focus on building customer relationships. Spending more time in getting to understand the customer's business will allow suppliers to proactively suggest solutions to the customer business problems, delivering mutual value. This is much more fruitful than processing and chasing orders for small repeat purchase items.

Spotlight 11.4

E-channel at Cisco Systems

Cisco Systems is one of the world leaders in developing integrated information exchange systems based around the Internet. They are an $18 billion manufacturer of network routers and switches. As a leading provider of the electronic components, they provide the infrastructure underpinning the Internet. Naturally, the company has sought to exploit technology to improve the management of customer relationships. Features of their system include:

- an online customer enquiry and order placement system which handles over 80% of all orders received by the company

Spotlight 11.4 *continued*

- a website that allows customers to configure and price their router and switch product orders online

- an online customer care service which permits the customer to identify a solution from Cisco's data warehouse of technical information and then to download relevant data or computer software. The firm estimates that the facility has saved $250 million per annum in the cost of distributing software and a further $75 million savings in the staffing of their customer care operations.

Cisco tracks the percentage of customers who transact online and their satisfaction levels for two reasons: (1) the Internet yields a lower cost to serve customers; and (2) the self-service customers are more satisfied customers. In the third quarter of 2003, Cisco reported that gross margins had risen to 70.8% against turnover of $4.6 billion for the quarter. Cisco gets the triple whammy of better customer satisfaction, at less costs and more profit from their e-channel.

Sources: Adapted from David Jobber (2001) *Principles and Practice of Marketing* (3rd edition). New York: McGraw-Hill; and Patricia Seybold (2001) *The Customer Revolution*. London: Random House.

Mega marketing

Mega marketing is where relationships must be sought with governments, legislators and influential individuals in order to make marketing effective on an operational level. Clearly, for companies in regulated market places, such as electricity, gas and telecommunications, this has been extremely important over the last few years. The government privatised the state monopolies and allowed competition into these markets, in some cases for the first time. In order to ensure there was fair play in these new competitive markets the government set up 'watchdog' bodies to regulate the industries. This led to the creation of OFTEL, OFGAS and OFFER. In these markets mega marketing was a crucial activity, both for the incumbents and for those with aspirations to enter these new markets. For public sector organisations the policy direction of the government needs to be clearly understood before any marketing of local services can take place.

Classic dyad relationship

What is clear is that without effective management of the classic customer–supplier dyad relationship, investing time and energy in the other types of relationship is worthless. Reichheld and Sasser (1990) have provided the empirical evidence that long-term relationships are worth pursuing as they deliver mutual value for customers and suppliers. We have seen that developing customer relationships is the domain of relationship marketing, whose aim is to deliver mutual value by moving customers up the loyalty ladder (Christopher et al., 2002). This has led to a greater focus on customer retention and a belief that focusing on fewer customers and creating more value is the way to go, as outlined in their view of one-to-one marketing (Peppers and Rogers, 1994). Godin (1999) has prescribed that permission marketing is the way to develop customer relationships, turning strangers into friends and friends into customers. So, if the case for delivering mutual value through better customer relationships is in some way proven, what makes for a good relationship?

11.8 PROPERTIES OF EFFECTIVE RELATIONSHIPS

In B2B marketing a distinction has been made between three types of connection that together form a relationship between buyers and sellers (Hakansson and Snehota, 1995):

- Activity links, including activities of a technical, administrative or marketing kind.
- Resource ties, involving exchanging and sharing resources which are both tangible, such as machines, and intangible, such as knowledge.
- Actor bonds that are created by people who interact and exert influence on each other and form opinions about each other, for example like the peer-to-peer contacts mentioned earlier.

There are 13 properties that can be useful for planning to develop relationships and to aid decision making (Godin, 1999; Gummesson, 1999; Seybold, 2001):

- Collaboration
- Commitment, dependency and importance
- Trust, risk and uncertainity
- Power
- Longevity
- Frequency, regularity and intensity
- Closeness and remoteness
- Formality, informality and openness
- Routinisation
- Content
- Personal and social properties
- Anticipated, personal and relevant
- Customer centricity.

Collaboration

Collaboration could be linked to a single deal, for example, joining forces to win the supply of the CRM system. Alternatively, it could be continuous collaboration to achieve shared objectives. The CRM software company Siebel has grown through collaboration with the key IT service providers such as IBM and consultancies such as Accenture. In modern business, the term 'compete at breakfast, collaborate at lunch' is often used. Customers will now insist that companies bring the best partners to the table to solve their problems and this has driven the need for former competitors to collaborate. Clearly, a low degree of competition and a high degree of collaboration are the basis for a long-term harmonious relationship. These days collaboration is often a prerequisite for success and is demanded by customers.

Commitment, dependency and importance

If a relationship is important, then both parties are probably dependent on each other for mutual success and must commit themselves to making it work. If a company is operating a just-in-time (JIT) system, the production line will close down if the supplier does not commit to deliver on time. Dependency is therefore high. In the fast moving consumer goods market manufacturers are dependent on a small number of retailers (e.g. Tesco, Sainsbury's, Asda, Wal-Mart) for a large proportion of their sales. Conversely, retailers rely on a few key suppliers to deliver their product range (e.g. Procter and Gamble, Unilever). This level of dependency leads to high commitment from the senior management teams of these companies to work together to achieve joint objectives. If they don't, the end customers will be the ones who are dissatisfied because the stores don't stock what they want.

Trust, risk and uncertainty

The basis for many purchasing decisions is often risk reduction. People purchase certain brands because they associate them with a quality standard that is delivered consistently. It also makes decision making easy – when we see the familiar Coca-Cola bottle in a fridge that is packed with different drinks, and we are thirsty and in a hurry, then our choice is de-risked. This amount of certainty cannot be given in service industries where the output is less tangible. We only know how good an insurance policy is when we place a claim on it. Our lives are too cluttered to read the fine print so we trust the broker. This can be immediately lost if the customer experience doesn't live up to the trust placed. In B2B situations an additional factor is that any major purchasing decision usually has to be justified to your boss. For this reason, personal risk reduction is often a key purchasing criterion. In order to develop successful relationships in B2B marketing, companies have to actively seek to build trust. In the early days, this may involve removing some of the uncertainty in a customer's mind by offering to share risks.

Power

Rarely do two parties have the same amount of power in any relationship. It could be that one company is much bigger, has better access to customers, a larger market share, better technology or knows a particular market place more intimately. Exerting the position of power often and overtly is not good for sustaining long-term relationships. Here there is a strong link to dependency. Increasingly, large corporations rely on very small organisations to provide specialist services for them to deliver the product or service to the end customer. The big corporation needs to understand that the small company will deliver most effectively if there is a clear work plan with few emergencies and surprises because they don't have a huge amount of resource to call on. The small business will also be very dependent on the corporation for prompt payment of bills, and will not thank them for exerting their power to pay when they feel like it.

Longevity

We have seen that longevity can be a key to profitable relationships. Keep a customer for a long time and they become easier to serve, buy more of your products and are a lot more profitable than when the company first acquired them. This is why, year-on-year, students are offered ever more attractive incentives to join banks. The acquisitions costs are well justified as the bank could be acquiring a successful business studies graduate who goes on to become a chief executive of a FTSI 100 company. The banks are looking at the potential lifetime value of the student. Longevity should not be taken for granted as a recipe for success. In the B2B sector long-term relationships can become stale. The supplier can become blasé and fall into the trap of thinking there's a regular order regardless of effort or results delivered. At this point, relationships can be broken as they fail to deliver innovation and creativity.

Frequency, regularity and intensity

Some relationships are frequent and active, for example, people may use the same bus company to get to work every day. Others are less frequent, such as using the services of an undertaker, although loyalty to a certain provider can be strong. Other relationships can be intense for a period of time, for example, an undergraduate has an intense relationship with his university over a three to four-year period.

We have seen that in order to develop stronger relationships with customers organisations should look to have fewer customers with deeper relationships (Peppers and Rogers, 1994). Godin (1999) believes that gaining customers' permission to have a dialogue with them allows you to increase the frequency of contact, providing it is kept relevant. This is certainly the approach that BT has taken with its Insight executive service (see Spotlight 11.5) For those – like undertakers – who cannot make their relationship more frequent, the importance of delivering an excellent experience is the key to customer loyalty.

Spotlight 11.5

BT Insight executive – relevance through permission

In 1998 BT realised that for its major corporate customers things were changing. Most of its well-established relationships were with its customer telecom departments. With the advent of CRM technologies and business process improvement software, a large proportion of responsibility for ICT-related spend had moved to the functional directors, where BT did not have strong relationships. At this time a large percentage of its revenue streams were coming from traditional 'dial tone revenues' – a commoditising space. To be seen as a thought leader in the solutions provider space, BT created the Insight Interactive programme led by Tony Rice.

Tony and his team surveyed 30,000 people in their business customer base about their key business issues. They asked if they would like to have a dialogue with BT on these issues, how often and through what media.

The response rate to the survey was beyond expectations – at around 20%. It made Tony feel he'd struck a chord. Insight Interactive then became a service which provided thought-provoking information to clients' functional managers – linked to the business issues they were facing. Subjects included customer relationship management, e-business, supply chain management, etc. This was designed to help create a compelling reason to consider and reappraise BT, its core capabilities and the business value it offered.

So the customers gave BT permission to communicate interactively with them about issues that they felt were important to them through their channel of choice, proving the power of relevance through permission:

- More than 15,000 business people voluntarily signed up as Insight Interactive members, with another 10,000 accessing the site as guests.

- A survey of members demonstrated that active users' perception of BT had changed to that of a solutions company.

- A £50 million per annun pipeline of new business was created.

Closeness and remoteness

Closeness strengthens the feeling of security and can certainly help reduce the perceived risks in doing business with an organisation. The majority of relationships thrive on tacit understanding between parties and only a minority are regulated in contracts. This is why in the B2B sector account management has been a prominent feature in customer relationships – the account manager is there to develop a deep understanding of what drives the customer and to proactively offer solutions to the customers' issues. This, of course, facilitates the sale of the organisation's own products and services, thus delivering mutual value.

Good relationships are formed where an organisation deeply understands when closeness is important to a customer and when it is not. When was the last time you went into a bank branch to get money? There's really no need – you can use the ATM. Most people prefer to get an account balance from a machine rather than a person by using the ATM or Internet banking. We have already seen how Cisco and others have used the e-channel – although on the face of it a more remote form of contact – to provide customers with the ability to order online. Increasingly, customers look for a mix of channels, which vary in their personal closeness, to do business with organisations.

Formality, informality and openness

The more an organisation gets to know a customer, the less formal the relationship will become and, usually, the more open it will be. This is particularly the case in B2B situations. Problems will be resolved over the telephone, the finer points of a new contract can be ironed out over a game of golf, or in a football hospitality box. Often the most successful firms are the ones that make the informal part of a relationship work. Sometimes this can be brought about through the intelligent use of customer events, mixing formal and informal discussions. Using an attractive location, leading industry speakers, and offering a thought-provoking issue of the day to discuss will often attract senior business customers to spend time with their suppliers. In the evening, things become more informal over dinner when everyone tries to get to know each other better.

Clearly, the provision of certain products and services will be underpinned by legal contracts, but success is often effectively developing the informal relationships. This is not just the domain of the B2B sector. Anyone who has a local pub can experience the benefits of a drink on the house or just after the bell. Getting the email from Amazon saying 'Hi Simon – do you know the new Patricia Seybold book is out?' is putting informality into a formalised communication process.

Routinisation

In order to execute service delivery effectively all organisations need to have routine processes that the customer understands and feels the benefit from taking part in. Customers who use the bank ATM know that inserting their card and keying in the password will allow them to draw out money. A B2B relationship often involves raising a purchase requisition, followed by a purchase order, completion of work and an invoice. Making these processes effective is a prerequisite to developing effective relationships, as is understanding which processes the customers want to be routinised, such as online ordering.

Content

Business relationships used to be seen to be an economic exchange – money for goods. Increasingly it is becoming more about the exchange of knowledge and information. The fast moving consumer goods organisation shares market research into a particular product market with the retailer, who in turn provides sales results for product lines and customer feedback on certain products. The retail bank shares its views on where the industry is going with its information technology provider, who provides a future view on where technology is going. The further up the loyalty ladder you go, the more the relationship will be about knowledge and information sharing as it becomes a key to unlock new mutual value creation.

Personal and social properties

Going back to formality, informality and openness, imagine you are at the dinner table at the customer event, you start to strike up a conversation about football and the customer makes it quite apparent that he does not talk about anything other than business. Clearly, in future interactions you will stick to business conversations, as you have met someone who 'does not do informal'. Personal and social properties are age, sex, profession and personality type. These are very important considerations when trying to build relationships. In the B2B sector the supplier organisation will often mirror the customer organisation: if they are all MBA-level, middle-aged males, then the supplier may provide a similar type as an account manager. Depending on the service that is being provided, this can sometimes be a mistake. Organisations use creative agencies – advertising companies or event agencies – because they don't have these types of people in-house. If these suppliers 'go native', they put themselves in a good place to lose the business.

Anticipated, personal and relevant

In Chapter 10 we were reminded that we exist in an environment where we are all being bombarded with communications – email, mobile phone, telephone, TV adverts, billboards, newspapers, etc. As new methods of communication have come along, the old ones have not all gone away. So, the supplier has to cut through the noise the customer is experiencing. Relevance is becoming the order of the day.

I am interested in when the next Colin Gilligan book is being published so I give Amazon permission to tell me. When they do, it is relevant to me – I anticipated that they would tell me because I said they could, and it is personal to me. Compare this with the mass direct mail-type approach where people throw parties if they get a 2% return rate – the other 98% got a communication that was irrelevant and annoying. Besides, the more relevant your interactions are, the more time you must have spent understanding the customer's needs. Thus, the more value you are providing, the more value you will get back. It is a virtuous circle.

Customer centricity

How customer-centric a relationship is can be the key to creating customer value. This can be heavily determined by how suppliers view themselves, which will affect how they behave. Does the supplier think he sells hamburgers, or does he think he provides a family entertainment experience? Does she sell bank accounts or does she help customers manage their finances – or finance their ambitions? Does he sell telephones or does he provide his business clients with tools to help them manage their customer contacts more effectively? In short, if suppliers are only interested in punting their products – that is they are product-centric – they will soon run out of road. If the key to building customer relationships is deeper customer understanding – that is customer centricity – to help broaden the range of products you provide, you will not achieve it if you are spending all your time just selling today's products. As you move up the loyalty ladder the relationship becomes more about achieving mutual value. At this point transfer of information and knowledge may be more important than exchanging goods for money.

Now we have considered the properties of relationships we can move on to look at how companies can plan to develop effective relationships.

11.9 PLANNING EFFECTIVE RELATIONSHIPS

If organisations are serious about developing relationships that deliver mutual value, they have to ensure that relationships are built into their strategic planning process. This will allow them to plan to develop relationships with customers who will benefit from them – and deliver back increased profit to the organisation. Figure 11.9 sets out the key building blocks for effectively embedding relationships into an organisation's planning process and effectively executing them. In this section we will examine what's inside these building blocks.

Figure 11.9 Planning for effective relationships – the five building blocks

Block 1 – Audit

Before auditing relationships, an essential part of any marketing audit is to scan the external environment to see what is changing. Recent history is littered with companies whose performance collapsed because they did not keep a close enough eye on the world as it affected them:

- British Bikes – Triumph collapsed in the early 1970s because they didn't see the Japanese threat coming.
- IBM – Once seen as a shining corporate star in the 1970s, IBM recorded the biggest corporate loss in history in the 1980s because it failed to spot the move from mainframe to distributed computing to PCs. And yes, what a comeback!
- McDonald's – Heralded by many as a fantastic marketing organisation, McDonald's recorded seven periods of reduced revenues out of eight (up to June 2003) as it failed to respond to people's changing preferences towards a healthy lifestyle. Are there the first signs of an IBM-style comeback?

The list is potentially endless. The point is that customer relationships will only remain great if what is being offered remains in tune with their changing needs.

After performing an environmental scan to see what is changing out there, a company should closely examine the state of its current customer relationships. This will involve examining who are and who are not their customers. This will allow objectives for acquisition, retention and growth to be developed in the strategy block.

Block 2 – Strategy

If a company wants a relationship with a group of customers, then it needs to find customers with a common set of needs. This is what *segmentation* should deliver. This will allow companies to begin to target customers and to start to communicate with them in a way they recognise. Piercy (2000) recommends building relationships into the segmentation process by developing an understanding of who does and who does not value a relationship. This would lead companies to segment by:

- relationship seekers, who want a close and long-term relationship with suppliers;
- relationship exploiters, who will take every free service on offer but will still move their business elsewhere when they feel like it;
- loyal buyers, who will give long-term loyalty but who do not want a close relationship;
- arm's length transaction buyers, who avoid close relationships and move business based on price, technical specification or innovation.

After deciding which customers want meaningful relationships, companies can then segment the customers by where they are on the loyalty ladder, or in terms of permission marketing steps.

In the strategy block companies need to set customer acquisition, retention and growth goals, and develop a strategy for each.

Block 3 – Measurement

An organisation will not set out to deliver customer value if it does not measure it. Patricia Seybold (2001) put forward a set of measures based on a flight deck, focusing purely on customers monitoring navigation, performance, operational controls and the environment. The measures would focus on:

- number of active customers
- number of loyal customers
- customer satisfaction
- revenue per customer.

Contrast this with traditional measures of a purely financial focus and companies start to drive a different set of behaviours. Companies which Seybold cites as taking a customer-centric measurement approach are Egg and Charles Schwab.

If mutual value is delivered through retention and growth of the existing customer base, then actively measuring customer satisfaction is key. The results of the satisfaction surveys should drive business improvement and help shape development of the customer experience.

Block 4 – Systems

If a company wants its relationship development to succeed, it will need to have systems and processes in place to actively capture and record customer interactions. This will allow the company to build up a picture of customer needs, wants and preferences. The result will be better targeting and more relevant customer dialogues, leading to increased satisfaction and loyalty.

The drive to improve customer relationship management has led many organisations to invest in systems. Already these are falling into disrepute in some places as organisations have realised the key issue is cultural change. You can have the most fantastic CRM system in the world, but if people in the organisation who have regular customer contact don't keep it up to date, it will soon become useless. To overcome this it is essential that businesses start building this active record-keeping into the reward plans of customer-facing people. If they don't, there will always be a satisfaction delivery gap as companies fail to track changing customer needs. In addition, they will incur unnecessarily high market research costs. Market research is often a waste of money in B2B situations because intelligence should be coming back from the people having daily dialogues with customers.

Block 5 – Tactics

Finally, if relationships have effectively been built into audit, strategy development and systems and are being measured, the organisation puts itself into a strong position to shape its 7Ps to grow the relationships. Here are just a few ways this could be done.

Product – develop a strong brand personality

If a company is starting from scratch with a new brand, then once it has gone through the segmentation exercise it needs to develop a brand that is compelling to its target audience. Egg was born to address a younger more vibrant audience than the customer base of its parent company Prudential. Egg was chosen as the brand name because when it was researched the target audience saw it as 'fresh and new' – the perfect way to open a relationship with them.

Promotion – customer propositions

Get the customers to tell you what they want to talk to you about, when and how, and then you can cut through the noise with relevant communications by gaining permission.

Once you know what their key issues are, present your products and services back in a way that reflects this. BT discovered this through their Insight executive programme. Its business clients had issues about customer retention and business agility in the new economy. BT therefore presented its products and services to these customers as ways to improve customer relationship management and business agility. Egg went a stage further and gathered feedback from 30,000 customers, which helped to shape their overall value proposition and led them to develop better savings accounts, flexible mortgages and loans, and more convenient service (Seybold, 2001).

Offering customers what they say they want is a novel way to move them up the loyalty ladder.

Place – develop a channel mix that customers want to use

Increasingly customers are making choices based on the channel mix that companies offer them. If they want to buy a trip to New York over the Internet, they will. And if a company cannot service this need they will not get the business. Many customers use the Internet to research offers and then go to a shop to make the purchase. An Internet-only organisation would not win business from this type of customer.

If customers want to order routine re-buys over the Internet, then give them the ability to do it – like Cisco has. The good news is that this is triple whammy territory: the organisation saves cost as repeat purchases are moved to the Internet, customers get what they want, and the account managers have more strategic discussions with the customers.

At the same time service has to be seamless across all channels. If a company does not know that the customer placed an order over the Internet when he phones into the call centre to check progress, it could well lose the customer. If an account manager goes to see a customer and does not realise he had a problem with his last big Internet order, she will soon find out.

To move a customer up the loyalty ladder a seamless experience is essential. Once a company has set up its multi-channel strategy it has put itself into a position to develop interactive relationships. In B2B situations, the face-to-face account managers are left to develop closer relationships with customers rather than wasting time chasing orders. At this point the account managers need to open up peer-to-peer contact with their key clients, thus making the relationship relevant and interactive.

If customers say they want to be regularly emailed about product developments, then fine. If they want to exchange views on a website chat room, then a company should set one up. To get to the top rung of the ladder and stay there relationships have to be interactive because growing mutual value is about being passionate about understanding the customer and giving them more and more of your products and services.

SUMMARY

In a world where customers have much more choice and many more channels through which to deal with suppliers, customer relationships have become extremely important. Nowadays the emphasis is on customer retention, seeking to grow relationships and grow mutual value. The empirical case for customer retention was first put forward by Riechheld and Sasser (1990), and since that time organisations have embarked on customer relationship marketing and relationship marketing.

We have seen that there are many facets to relationship marketing, which is why many organisations are still grappling with it. What is clear is that it is crucial in the Internet economy – and in the face of the 'new' customer, which is the subject of Chapter 12.

Discussion questions

1 Why are customer relationships important?
2 What is perceived value?
3 What is relationship marketing?
4 What is customer relationship management (CRM)?
5 For a company of your choice describe what they could do to move customers up the loyalty ladder.
6 Describe a situation when you have defected as a customer. What caused you to defect? What could the organisation have done to keep your custom?
7 What is one-to-one marketing?
8 Describe the five steps of permission marketing.
9 What are the properties of effective relationships?
10 Describe an organisation that you feel you have an effective relationship with. Why is it effective? How do you benefit from this relationship?

Case study 11.1 | Text R for relationships?

Next time you pick up your mobile phone, try to imagine how futuristic it would look to someone from ten years ago. Back then, mobile phones were far less sophisticated devices – expensive and owned by few. Brick-like, they had tiny monochrome screens and ungainly protruding aerials, and they were only used for one thing: talking to other people. Today's latest models, in contrast, are elegantly shaped pocket computers. Your current handset may well have a large colour screen and a built-in camera; as well as being a telephone, it can send and receive text messages, and may also serve as an alarm clock, calendar, games console, music player or FM radio.

Research and consulting agency Gartner estimates that global mobile phone sales will reach 580 million units this year – making it a £50 billion global industry. Demand for new handsets is being fuelled by the boom in cheaper camera phones combined with a surge in upgrades in the USA, Europe and Korea. In the US last year 110 million handsets were sold of which 90 million were replacements.

Changing technology and consumer preferences are leading to a shift in the balance of power among mobile phone manufacturers. In its prime Nokia controlled about 60% of the global market. While Nokia remains market leader research group Strategy Analytics estimates that market share has slumped to 29.2%. Motorola is in second spot with about 16% with Samsung third with 13%.

Nokia built its success partly on the fashionable design of its handsets. This trait once helped it overtake Motorola as market leader. While others were concentrating on manufacturing excellence Nokia stole the march on the market by designing phones customers wanted. Its products appealed because of the development of a simple to use standard for all of its handset keypads. The aesthetics and simplicity of the handsets helped to maintain brand loyalty.

Nokia's supremacy in these two fields is under threat. Rivals are starting to design their own handsets with simplicity in mind and Nokia's mantle of fashionable trendsetter is beginning to slip. Motorola has brought out 25 new models to appeal to every type of market. The designs include clamshell handsets, MP3 music-playing capabilities and, most importantly, cameras. Samsung is hitting the market hard with a wide range of compact, silver clamshell mobile handsets.

Nokia's own pride has compounded the problems it faces. Just over a year ago the company dismissed the idea of making clamshell phones. This seems to have been a big mistake as clamshells are considered to be one of the main reasons for Motorola's success. Nokia loves to differentiate itself from rivals and following the lead set by Motorola will be a galling admission of defeat.

The rise of competitor handset manufacturers, such as Samsung and Sony Ericsson, has been helped by the demand for camera phones above all else. According to Strategy Analytics, only 6% of Nokia phones sold last year had a camera, compared with 30% of Sony Ericsson phones.

Competition is set to hot up for two main reasons. First, the barriers to entry have fallen. Hardware and software have, to some extent, been commoditised, and there is far more scope for outsourcing of design and manufacturing than there used to be.

This has allowed original design manufacturers (ODMs), consumer-electronics firms and even start-ups to enter the handset business. The old vertical industry model has been undermined. And it is the rise of the ODMs in particular that is doing the most to disrupt the industry's established order – Nokia, Motorola and Samsung.

Secondly, the drive to create one device for consumers for music, gaming, video, computing, voice and data brings into play some powerful new competitors – no less than Sony, Microsoft and possibly even Apple.

Questions

1   Begin by conducting a short survey among your colleagues: what mobile phone do they own? When did they last change? What are the main functions they use?

2   How did Nokia initially achieve 60% market share?

3   Why did Nokia lose market share so quickly?

4   How could relationship marketing have helped Nokia retain market share?

5   What can Nokia do to retain and grow market share now? What part can relationship marketing play in helping Nokia regain market share?

Further reading

Bruhn, M. (2003) *Management of Customer Relationships*. Harlow: Pearson Education.
Buttle, F. (1996) *Relationship Marketing – Theory and Practice*. London: Paul Chapman Publishing.
Cartwright, R. (2000) *Mastering Customer Relations*. Macmillan.
Seybold, P. (2001) *The Customer Revolution*. Random House.

References

Bark, B. (2001) 'One-to-one marketing', available at www.1to1.com.
Bruhn, M. (2003) *Management of Customer Relationships*. Harlow: Financial Times/Prentice Hall.
Christopher, M., Payne, A. and Ballatyne, D. (2002) *Relationship Marketing*. Oxford: Butterworth-Heinemann.
Friedman, L.G. and Furey, T. (1999) *The Channel Advantage*. Oxford: Butterworth-Heinemann.
Gilligan, C.T. and Wilson, R.M.S. (2003) *Strategic Marketing Planning*. Oxford: Butterworth-Heinemann.
Godin, S. (1999) *Permission Marketing*. London: Simon & Schuster.
Gummesson, E. (1999) *Total Relationship Marketing*. Oxford: Butterworth-Heinemann.
Hakansson, H. and Snehota, I. (1995) *Developing Relationships in Business Networks*. London: Routledge.

Parvatiyar, A. and Sheth, S.N. (2000) 'The domain and conceptual foundations of relationship marketing', in J.N. Sheth and A. Parvatiyar (eds), *Handbook of Relationship Marketing*. Thousand Oaks, CA: Sage.

Peppers, D. and Rogers, M. (1994) *The One to One Future Currency*. New York: Doubleday.

Piercy, N. (2000) *Market-led Strategic Change: A Guide to Transforming the Process of Going to Market*, Oxford: Butterworth-Heinemann.

Reichheld, F.F. (1993) 'Loyalty-based management', *Harvard Business Review*, March-April: 64-73.

Reichheld, F.F. (1996) *The Loyaly Effect*. Boston: Harvard Business School Publishing.

Reichheld, F.F. and Sasser, W. (1990) 'Zero defections: quality comes to services', *Harvard Business Review*, August–September: 105–11.

Seybold, P. (2001) *The Customer Revolution*. London: Random House.

12

The emergence of the new consumer: coming to terms with the future

Colin Gilligan

LEARNING OUTCOMES

After reading this chapter you should be able to:

■ **Appreciate how the changes within the marketing environment that we have discussed in earlier chapters of the book have created a 'new marketing reality'**

■ **Recognise how an important part of this new marketing reality is the emergence of a very different type of consumer**

■ **Understand in detail the characteristics of this 'new consumer'**

■ **Understand the implications of the new consumer for the marketing planning process**

KEY WORDS

Brand promiscuity
Cash-poor/time-rich
Cash-rich/time-poor
Extra value proposition
Generation X

Kidults
New consumer
New marketing reality
Relationship marketing myopia
Super-powered consumer

INTRODUCTION

The effectiveness of any marketing programme is determined to a very large extent by the marketing planners' understanding of the customer and, in particular, by their understanding of how and why customers behave as they do. The deeper this understanding, the more likely it is that marketers will be able to predict how customers are likely to respond to different types of marketing activity. In the vast majority of markets, however, buyers often not only differ enormously in terms of how and why they buy and how and why they respond to marketing stimuli, such as the different elements of the marketing mix, but they are also currently changing in a series of significant and far-reaching ways, something that is making the job of marketing planners far more difficult and complex. In many consumer markets, for example, buyers typically differ not just in terms of their age, income, educational levels and geographical location, but also, and more fundamentally, in terms of their personality, lifestyle, perceptions, lifestage, needs and expectations.

Nevertheless, and despite these complexities, the need for the marketing planner to understand the detail of the buying process and exactly why people do – or do not – buy should be self-evident, since the costs and competitive implications of failing to do so are likely to be significant. As just one example of this, there is a considerable amount of research evidence that suggests that something in the region of 80% of all new products launched fail, a failure rate that is due very largely to a misunderstanding on the part of marketing planners of customers and their expectations. Because of this, a great deal of attention has been paid in recent years to detailed analyses of customers in order to provide us with a level of customer understanding that enables marketing planners to predict far more readily and accurately exactly *how* customers will behave in any given situation and how they will respond to different types of marketing strategy.

Within this chapter we examine a number of the more important changes that have taken and are taking place within the marketing environment and how, together, they have created a **new marketing reality**. We then discuss the implications of this new marketing reality for the marketing planning process. In doing so, we argue that because of the nature and significance of these changes, the ways in which marketing planners need to understand customers has also changed. In practice, though, it appears that many marketing planners still view customers in much the same way that they did ten years ago. Against this background, we then turn to the characteristics of what we have labelled the 'new consumer' and how marketing planners might possibly respond to this

12.1 THE CHANGING MARKETING ENVIRONMENT (OR THE EMERGENCE OF A NEW MARKETING REALITY)

If there is a single issue or theme that now links all types and sizes of organisation, it is that of the much faster pace of environmental change and the much greater degree of environmental uncertainty than was typically the case even a few years ago. This change and uncertainty have been manifested in a wide variety of ways and have led to a series of environmental pressures and challenges with which managers have had to come to terms. Taken together, these changes, some of which appear in Table 12.1, have led to what we refer to here as the 'new marketing reality'. This new reality is significant for a number of reasons, but most obviously because of the ways in which it is forcing many marketing managers to rethink how they operate.

Although the ten points identified in Table 12.1 are not intended either as a complete or definitive list of the sorts of environmental challenge that marketing managers now face, they illustrate some of the ways in which marketing environments are changing and how the pressures upon managers are increasing. Of these changes, the one with which we are most concerned here is that of the very different cultural and social pressures that have led to what we refer to as the 'new consumer'. However, before we examine the new consumer, the reader should not automatically assume that rapid environmental change always leads to problems or threats for an organisation. Instead, many changes lead to windows of opportunity. The real challenge for managers can therefore be seen to be that of developing a sensitive environmental monitoring system that is capable not only of identifying as quickly as possible the nature and significance of any threats – and *opportunities* – but that then provides marketing planners with the information needed to respond to these cleverly.

Table 12.1   The changing marketing environment and the emergence of a new marketing reality

---

Among some of the most significant and far-reaching environmental changes of the past few years have been the following:

1. A much greater degree of economic volatility and uncertainty.

2. The opening up of a series of new and often very different geographic markets (think about the emergence of China and the Central and Eastern European markets).

3. High and seemingly ever higher levels of political change and uncertainty in many parts of the world.

4. The far greater pace of technological change.

5. New forms of distribution and access to markets, including through the Internet.

6. New and often more unpredictable competitors and forms of competition.

7. The increasingly global nature of many markets.

8. The erosion of many of the traditional bases of competitive advantage.

9. A significant downward pressure upon prices.

10. Very different social and cultural pressures that have led to a different type of consumer (this is the new consumer referred to in the title of the chapter).

Although the impact of any one of these factors may, by itself, be relatively small, their combined effect is significant and has created a new marketing reality which demands that marketing planners be infinitely more aware of the changes taking place within the market and infinitely cleverer in how they respond. In essence, therefore, the new marketing reality has highlighted the way in which many of the traditional market paradigms are no longer really appropriate and now need to be rethought.

12.2 THE RISE OF THE NEW CONSUMER

The new consumer is a phenomenon that emerged throughout the 1990s very largely as the result of a series of major social, political, economic, technological and cultural changes within society. Insofar as it is possible to identify how the new consumer differs from the old, it is that they are typically:

- far more demanding
- far more discriminating
- much less brand loyal
- much more willing to complain than customers in the past.

A more detailed picture of the new consumer appears in Table 12.2.

The significance of the new consumer can perhaps best be understood by focusing upon just two of these factors, that of the changed and changing roles of men and women and, at least in some parts of the market, the greater emphasis upon

Table 12.2   The emergence of the new consumer

The marketing environment of the past 10–15 years has been characterised by a series of fundamental and far-reaching economic, social and political changes. One consequence of this has been the emergence of what we can refer to as the 'new consumer'. Although, as Gilligan and Wilson (2003) suggest. 'this new consumer is not necessarily new in any absolute sense, they differ in a wide variety of ways from traditional consumers in that their expectations, values and patterns of behaviour are all very different from those of the past. The consequences of this are manifested in several ways but most obviously by the way in which the marketing planner's levels of understanding of customers' motivations must be far greater and the marketing effort tailored more firmly and clearly to the patterns of specific need.' This new consumer is characterised by:

- new and very different sets of value systems;
- a greater emphasis upon value for money and higher levels of price awareness;
- less technophobia;
- a greater willingness to accept more and exciting new products;
- a tendency to experiment with new products, ideas and delivery systems;
- lower levels of brand and supplier loyalty;
- higher levels of brand promiscuity;
- a far more questioning and sceptical attitude towards government, big business, politicians, the church and brands;
- higher levels of environmental awareness and a greater 'greenness';
- major changes in family structures and relationships, with changed and changing roles of men and women;
- the emergence of a far more media, advertising, brand and technologically literate generation of consumers.

value for money. In the case of the car market, for example, slightly more than 40% of new cars that were bought privately in 2003 were bought by women; this compares with less than 6% in 1970. The implications of this for the car manufacturers have been enormous and have had to be reflected not just in terms of the design of cars, but also in the type of market research that is conducted, the nature of the advertising used to promote the cars, the media vehicles that are used, and the approaches to selling. At the same time, the search for greater value has led customers to be willing to use less traditional ways of buying cars, including through car supermarkets, through the Internet, and through companies that specialise in importing cars from those parts of the world where prices are lower than in the UK. The implications of this for car manufacturers, with their traditional dealer networks, have been significant and have forced them to refocus substantial parts of their marketing strategies, but most obviously their approaches to pricing, distribution, dealer support and after-sales service.

The new consumer and the youth market

The differences that exist between the new consumer and the old are even more apparent, and more extreme, in the case of young(er) consumers (for our purposes here, we see these to be aged between four and 19), in that this segment, when compared with other customer groups, is also typically:

- far more media literate;
- infinitely more advertising literate;
- much more brand literate, brand sophisticated and brand discriminating;
- far more technologically literate.

To a large extent, these higher levels of media, advertising, brand and technological literacy can be seen to be the direct result of having been exposed to a far greater number and a much larger variety of media than any previous generation. Included within this are 24-hour television, satellite broadcasting, and a huge upsurge in the numbers of newspapers and far more finely targeted magazines. The advertising literacy then follows directly from this in that the sheer number of advertisements to which they have been exposed is higher than ever before. Brand literacy emerges from brands having been an integral part of lifestyles for as long as this generation has been alive, something that was not always the case with older consumers. Equally, the technological literacy follows from their exposure to technologies such as information technology from a very early age. The combined effect of this is the emergence of a very different type of buyer who has very different and often much more unpredictable patterns of buying.

In many ways, the emergence of this new type of consumer, be it in the teen market or those aged 20–55, represents one of the biggest challenges for marketers, since their expectations of organisations and the nature of the relationships that they demand are very different from anything that existed previously. Recognising this, if marketers fail to come to terms with it, the implications for organisational performance and marketing planning are significant (see section 12.4 for further discussion).

Dilemma 12.1

The success of the new Mini

First launched in 1959, the original Mini proved to be one of the motoring icons of the 20th century. Almost 40 years later, in 1998, production of the car finally came to a halt. Two years later, the announcement by BMW, by then the owners of the Mini brand, that they were investing £200 million in the development and launch of the new Mini was therefore received with enormous enthusiasm.

The launch proved to be a huge success, with customers falling very broadly into one of two target groups. The first consisted of people aged 25-35 who bought the Mini as their primary car in preference to a similarly priced Toyota, Volkswagen or Renault. The second group consisted of people in their 40s who bought it as their second or third car and who were looking for what the company described as 'youthful motoring fun'. The factor though that seemed to be common to both groups was that buyers were often bored by the increasingly similar looking competitive products that dominated the market and were looking for something that was slightly different and possibly quirky. The car's image was reinforced by an advertising campaign that was based around a series of 'Mini adventures' such as finding lost cities and saving the world from a Martian invasion, and an Internet campaign that made it appear as if the site's home pages were being attacked by Martians and disgruntled Zombies.

By the middle of 2004, the company could look back at what had proved to be one of the most successful launches of a car ever. The dilemma they faced, however, was that as sales increased yet further, they were being drawn into a very different type of market segment with buyers who were arguably rather more traditional in their approaches and expectations

In what ways would you change the marketing strategy to reflect the differences between the initial target groups (the innovators and the early adopters) and the new targets within the mass market?

12.3 THE CHANGING SOCIAL, CULTURAL AND DEMOGRAPHIC ENVIRONMENTS

Many of the factors that have led to the emergence of the new consumer can be seen to be the almost inevitable result of the often radical changes that have taken place within the social, cultural and demographic environments of the past 20–30 years and it is to these areas that we now turn our attention.

Western societies have been and are currently still undergoing a series of significant and far-reaching changes (for a more detailed treatment of this area, see Gilligan and Wilson (2003: Chapter 6). Included within these are:

1. *An upsurge in the number of single-person households*, with the size and importance of this SSWD group (single, separated, widowed, divorced) having grown enormously over the past 20 years. This upsurge has been driven by a series of changes across society that include:
   - people getting married at a later stage than in the past
   - a rapid rise in the divorce rate (about one-third of all marriages in the UK now ends in divorce)
   - the increasingly high failure rate of second marriages
   - an upsurge in the numbers of one-parent families (see Spotlight 12.1)
   - a much greater degree of social and geographic mobility
   - higher income levels, especially among women, that give people the freedom to live alone if they wish to do so.

2. *A significant growth in the number of people sharing a home*, with this becoming increasingly like the first stage of marriage. At the same time, the number of households with two or more people of the same sex sharing has also increased.

3. A rapid increase in *group households* with three or more people of the same or opposite sex living together and sharing expenses.

4. A greater tendency for *young adults not to leave home* but, because of the rapidly increasing costs of property, to stay at home for longer, a phenomenon that is seen as its most extreme in Italy where many children do not leave the family home until their early 30s. There is also the phenomenon of young adults leaving home for short periods but still seeing the parental home as 'their' home and returning to it frequently. Labelled the 'boomerang generation', the factors

Spotlight 12.1

The growth of the single-parent family

Between 1986 and 2001, the number of single-parent families in Britain doubled to the point at which they represented more than a quarter of families with children. These figures, published by the Office for National Statistics, also suggested that there were 1.75 million one-parent families and that almost 2.9 million (or 26%) of children aged under 19 live in a one-parent family. The report highlighted the way in which virtually every kind of one-parent family had risen in relative numbers, but that the sharpest rise was the number of single lone mothers – women who had never married. The 26% of families that lone parent units accounted for compared with just 14% 15 years earlier. At the same time, we have also seen an upsurge in the number of couples who decide not to have children, with one in four now falling into this category.

The implications for marketing of changes such as these have already proved significant in a variety of ways and have been reflected in an increase in demand for more starter homes, smaller appliances, food that can be purchased in smaller quantities, and a greater emphasis upon convenience products generally.

that have contributed to this are partly cost, but also a reluctance to accept the full responsibilities of adulthood. The significance of this is shown by the way in which a study in 2002 by the Social Market Foundation, an independent think tank, revealed that one in four people in the 20–30 age group are now returning to live with their parents

5. *A far greater degree of social mobility* that has developed across the Western world as the result of consumer cultures changing, income levels increasing and very different lifestyle expectations emerging. Taken together, this has led to the creation of a far larger and far more powerful middle class, which exhibits fewer specifically national characteristics and a greater number of common expectations and patterns of buying.

6. The *ever greater urbanisation of society* as a higher proportion of the population, but especially the young, move into the centres of population.

7. A substantial increase in the *numbers of young people going into higher education*. In the 1960s, about one in 17 of the population went to university. By the mid-1990s the figure was about one in three. Current government targets suggest a figure of one in two. The implications of this are significant in a variety of ways, but most obviously in terms of the ways in which education not only broadens perpectives, but also career expectations and lifelong earnings potential increase.

8. The collapse of the idea of a *job for life*.

Rethinking and redefining ideas about demographics

The implications of the eight points referred to above have been significant and have led to a rethinking of how marketing planners view consumers and age and social profiles. Rather than being tied to the traditional and largely simplistic perceptions and preconceived notions of how people behave initially as teenagers and then through their 20s, 30s and so on, there is now a far clearer understanding of the complex ways in which attitudes and behaviour, as well as a series of other factors, interact with age to create new types of consumer group. These include:

1. *The youthful elderly*. Although it has long been recognised that changing demographics in many countries are leading to increasingly elderly populations, surprisingly little attention has been given to the characteristics of these people and, until very recently, to their buying habits, expectations and potential. However, the notion of the youthful elderly is based on the way in which, as the children of the 1960s move into middle age/late middle age (this is the 'baby boomer generation'), they are increasingly retaining their youthful lifestyles and attitudes. (For a fascinating and detailed discussion of this, see Richardson, 2001.) Benefiting from higher levels of health and fitness, and having more money than previous generations, the youthful elderly or the baby boomer generation not only expect but are also able to live life to the full. Given this, age largely becomes an attitude of mind and has led to the notion of psychological age (in other words, how old do I feel I am? rather than how old am I in chronological terms?).

Although many planners, other than those in the specialist companies such as Saga, have previously largely ignored this market, its real size, value and potential are shown by the way in which, in the UK, more than one-third of the population is currently over 50. (The situation in Japan is even more extreme as the country heads towards a demographic profile of almost 50% of the population being aged 60 or more.) Over the next 40 years, the number of people in the UK aged between 60 and 74 will grow by 43%. Its value is also illustrated by the way in which numerous products such as Reebok and Adidas are owned by as many 25–44 year-olds as 15–24 year-olds.

2. *Ageing children (the under 14s).* At the same time that we are seeing the elderly becoming much more youthful in their attitudes and buying habits, a whole series of changes have also been affecting the children's market, with the numbers in these segments dropping significantly. Using 2000 as our starting point, the numbers of those who are in the 5–9 years age segment, for example, will have declined by 6% by 2005. The 10–14s will remain static and the 15–19s will increase by 5%. By 2010, the 5–9s will have declined by 11%, the 10–14s will have declined by 5% and the 15–19s will increase by 6%. However, the numbers alone paint only a small part of the overall picture. The much greater availability of technology and media means that this group of ageing children is being exposed to the adult world much earlier. It is now aware of advertising and its role by the age of three. One result of this is that they are more demanding of brands and their environment, with this being due in part to more spoiling by time-pressured parents and the far greater availability of luxuries. They are also more sophisticated, are far more unforgiving with regard to brands, typically have low boredom thresholds and have an expectation of constant and/or instantly available entertainment.

3. *Ageing children (the teens).* Although the teenage market has traditionally been seen to be among the fastest changing segments of consumer markets, there is now considerable evidence to suggest that this segment is changing even faster than in the past. In part, this is because of the ways in which teenagers today have been exposed to a greater number of stimuli, something that, as we suggested earlier, has led to the emergence of a generation that is now far more advertising, media, technologically and brand literate than any of those that have gone before.

The general picture that emerges from these sorts of changes is that, increasingly, there are now far fewer set lifestages and much less behaviour that is age-appropriate in the traditional sense. Children, for example, are exposed to an infinitely greater number of stimuli (half of all four-year-olds have a television in their bedroom) and are far more brand conscious, while adults are staying younger for far longer. The age at which many people have children is getting later as they concentrate on having 'fun' (this is the rise of 'middle youth' – people in their 30s and 40s who still haven't 'settled down', something that has been manifested in the rise of adventure holidays targeted at this group.) These changes have also led to the emergence of what is sometimes referred to as **kidults**, a phrase that is used to refer both to children who grow up – or have had to grow up – far more quickly than in the past, and adults who refuse to fully accept their age and who buy products that might normally be seen to be aimed at teenagers. In addition to the example cited above of companies such as Adidas and Reebok, which have a high penetration of the kidult market, companies such as Sony with its Playstation, Microsoft with the X-Box and Nike have all recognised the value of this market sector.

Developing the broader picture

At the same time as the social and cultural changes have been taking place, the world has also been experiencing a variety of other significant shifts in demographic structures, all of which need to be understood by marketing planners and reflected in the marketing planning process. Included within these are:

1. *The explosion of the world's population*, with a substantial amount of this growth being concentrated in those nations in the Third World which, because of their low standards of living and economic development, can least afford it.
2. *A slowdown in birth rates* in virtually all of the developed nations. With many families today opting for just one child, the implications for a wide variety of companies have been significant. Johnson & Johnson, for example, responded to the declining birth rate by very successfully repositioning its baby oil, baby powder and baby shampoo in such a way that the products also appealed to young female adults. Similarly, cosmetics companies have placed a far greater emphasis on products for the over-50s.
3. *Major changes in family structure* that have emerged as the result of the sorts of factors to which we made reference earlier, including fewer and later marriages and very different roles for men, women and children.
4. *Higher levels of education* and an increasing number of families in what has traditionally been seen as the middle class.
5. *Major geographical shifts in population*.
6. *A growth in telecommuting*.
7. *A rapidly ageing population* as advances in medical care allow people to live longer. One result of this trend, which has in turn been exacerbated by the slowdown in the birth rate, has been an increase in the number of empty nesters who have substantial sums of discretionary income and high expectations (see Spotlight 12.2).
8. *A growth in emigration*, as far greater numbers of people move from the undeveloped and underdeveloped parts of the world to the more affluent West.
9. The rise of *the '99 lives' phenomenon*. The idea of the '99 lives' was first identified by Faith Popcorn, the American trend forecaster, and involves recognising that a consumer can play a very large number and wide variety of roles (e.g. mother, wife, manager, outdoor enthusiast) and that typecasting under a single broad heading and then trying to appeal to the 99 lives consumer in a simplistic way is almost certainly doomed to failure.

Spotlight 12.2

The changing consumer – the growing power of the grey market

For many years, the over-50s market was seen to consist of largely passive consumers who were of little real interest to marketeers. The reality, however, as a series of studies published at the end of the 1990s revealed, is often very different (see, for example, Golik (ed), *Mature Thinking* (2003)).

Prominent among the drivers of the growing importance of this market is the way in which the baby boomer generation is now moving into its 50s and that, in terms of size, the market is growing. In the UK, for example, there are now more people aged over 60 than those under age 16. In Japan the profile is even more stark, with forecasts suggesting that more than 50% of the population will be over 60 by 2010. The essentially active nature of the market is revealed by a variety of statistics, including that 30% of expenditure on household goods comes from households where the head is over 50.

Undoubtedly, one of the biggest mistakes that marketers have made in the past is to view the over-50s as a single consumer group. Given that the market now accounts for 44% of the population (in 20 years, one in two adults will be over 50), it is in reality a remarkably heterogeneous group. Recognition of this has led the specialist 50-plus advertising agency Millennium Direct to segment the market in terms of 'thrivers' (50–59), 'seniors' (60–69) and 'elders' (70 plus). By contrast with the typically time-poor 30-somethings who have mortgages to pay and young children to look after, the over-50 market is frequently time-rich and, in many cases, has a high disposable income. It tends also to be a market in which levels of brand loyalty are high. If anything, the significance of the over-50s market is likely to increase dramatically over the next few years, not just because of its greater size and higher total net worth (older people hold 80% of all wealth and 75% of all stock portfolios), but also because the values of the baby boomer generation are very different from those who went before.

Social and cultural change: an overview

Taken together, the net effect of the changes referred to above has been significant, and is continuing to prove so, with the marketing strategies of nearly all companies being affected in one way or another. At their most fundamental, these changes have led to a shift from a small number of mass markets to an infinitely larger number of micro-markets, differentiated by age, sex, lifestyle, education, and so on. Each of these groups differs in terms of its preferences and characteristics and, as a result, requires different, more flexible and far more precise approaches to marketing which no longer take for granted the long-established assumptions and conventions of marketing practice.

A summary of some of the major changes that are taking place, broadened slightly to take account of all four elements of the European political/legal, economic, social/cultural and technological (PEST) environments, appears in Table 12.3.

Table 12.3 European consumers: the changing PEST environment

Political & legal trends	Economic trends
• The decline of the nation state and the centralisation of power as a result of the growth of the European Union • The integration of Central/Eastern Europe into Western Europe • More cross-border legislation • Fundamental shifts in the political/economic power balance • The privatisation of welfare provisions	• An increase in real income growth • Higher energy costs • The globalisation of economies (not only industries, but also services) • The end of jobs for life • The decline of cross-border economic barriers • The (further) development of the three nations society and the emergence of ever greater gulfs between the rich and the poor • The decline of mass brands • Changes in the savings/debt ratio • The rise of the virtual organisation

Social trends	Technological trends
• The fragmentation of formerly homogeneous market segments and groups and the emergence of a pluralism of lifestyles • Greater individualism and the emergence of an event-based society that reflects a search for excitement, experience and adventures • Greater social and economic mobility • A generally faster pace of life with dramatically changed and changing roles of men, women and children • The rise of the 'kidult' • The search for new identities, new ways of life and new values • The rise of the middle class • Greater scepticism towards politicians, big business, institutions and brands • A greater emphasis upon 'green' issues and environmentalism • Higher levels of cross-border migration • A rapidly ageing population and the social and economic rise of the 'grey' market • The end of jobs for life • Higher levels of education	• The faster pace of technological change and the growth of the digital decade • The growth of artificial intelligence and virtual reality • The commoditisation of information • The convergence of technologies • More intrusive and 'clever' technologies • A digital decade, with information management centred around access to knowledge and information

Social change and the three nations society

Recognising the nature and significance of the sorts of changes within society that we have discussed so far, the Henley Centre in the mid-1990s highlighted the ways in which there is an interaction of time and money and how this has led to the emergence of a sizeable **cash-rich/time-poor** segment in society. The profile of this segment which they referred to as 'the first nation', differs in a number of significant ways from that of what they labelled the second and third nations; the characteristics of the three segments are illustrated in Table 12.4. The 20% of the people in the first nation segment are characterised by being willing to spend money to save time, something that distinguishes them from the other 80% of society. By virtue of their income levels, this segment of society also has open to it a greater spectrum of product choices, and has responded by being more willing than other segments to pass on to others some aspects of the management of their lives.

The significance of the cash-rich/time-poor segment: the growth of the service support sector

It should be apparent from Table 12.4 that the first nation identified by the Henley Centre is of enormous potential significance to marketers. Because more and more people are working longer hours, the service sector has grown enormously to fill the time gap. The idea of getting someone to do something for you is no longer seen to be a sign of laziness, but is instead a sign of people valuing their life and being far clearer about their priorities. Other factors that have led to the growth of the service sector to serve this market include the following:

- 72% of women of working age are now employed and while statistics show that women still do the majority of housework, young women are less inclined to do it than their mothers. The number of single-person households is also increasing and so these people have no one else to do it for them.
- The desire for convenience and the intention to exploit fully the limited time that people do have. They are therefore willing to pay for time, quality and simplicity.
- The 24-hour society that has been driven by:
  - the Internet being 'open' 24 hours a day, something that helps to confirm this notion of the 24-hour society;
  - home delivery and the easy availability of products when and where you want them;
  - an increase in stress-related diseases.

Table 12.4 The three nations society

The first nation	The second nation	The third nation
• 20% of the population	• 50% of the population	• 30% of the population
• 40% of consumer spending	• 50% of consumer spending	• 10% of consumer spending
• Cash-rich	• Cash-constrained	• Cash-poor
• Time-poor	• Time-constrained	• Time-rich

The significance of the cash-poor/time rich segment: the search for greater value

At the other end of the spectrum to the first nation society is the **cash-poor/time-rich** third nation group, a group that has very different spending patterns and whose significance is shown by the way in which:

- although 40% of households are affluent, one in three is poor and getting poorer;
- high levels of price consciousness continue to thrive, with retailers such as Wal-Mart, Aldi and Netto all set to capitalise on this;
- even the wealthier, older households will feel squeezed as they live longer and more of their discretionary income goes on health, education (that of their grandchildren) and private insurance;
- consumers are becoming ever more demanding of quality and see price/value solutions more than price by itself to be important.

12.4 THE RISE OF THE NEW CONSUMER AND THE IMPLICATIONS FOR MARKETING PLANNING

Throughout this chapter we have suggested that the 1990s saw the emergence of a very different type of consumer. Among those to have discussed this in detail are Lewis and Bridger (2000) who in their book *The Soul of the New Consumer* suggest that 'consumers have evolved from being conformist and deferential children, reared on the propaganda of the post-Second World War and who were prepared to trust mass advertising, into free-thinking, individualistic adults who are sceptical of figures of authority such as politicians, big business and mega brands' (see Figure 12.1).

Old Consumers, they suggest, were 'typically constrained by cash, choice and the availability of goods, New Consumers are generally short of time, attention and trust' (this is the cash-rich/time-poor first nation generation that we referred to in Table 12.4). Mass society, they argue, has shattered and been reduced to a mosaic of minorities:

> In a hypercompetitive world of fragmented markets and independently-minded, well-informed individuals, companies that fail to understand and attend to the needs of New Consumers are doomed to extinction. Currently, the average life of a major company only rarely exceeds 40 years. In the coming decade, any business that is less than highly successful will find that lifespan reduced by a factor of at least 10. (Lewis and Bridger, 2000)

Although it might be argued that the picture that Lewis and Bridger paint is a little dramatic, the changes that are taking place are undoubtedly significant and have major implications for marketing planners. In discussing this, Gilligan and Wilson (2003) argue that there are four key areas to which planners need to pay attention:

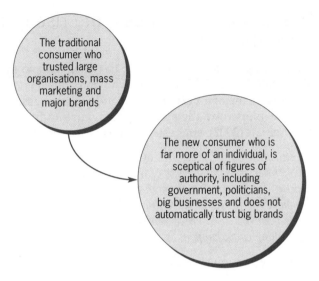

Figure 12.1 The shift from the old to the new consumer

1. How best to (re)connect with the new consumer. The roll call of those who have failed to do this includes some of the biggest brands in the world, some of which have found it difficult to recognise the new consumers' often very different patterns of behaviour, much higher expectations and lower levels of brand loyalty.

2. How best to direct and subsequently manage their messages to increasingly critical audiences who have access to technology and who, through tools such as the Internet, are able very quickly to publicise often highly critical reviews of new products, services or films that can be far more influential than the formal advertising campaigns.

3. Recognise the real potential of innovative forms of communications, such as viral marketing, to deliver their message to new consumers. Among those who have done this well are some of the niche teenage fashion brands whose target market is largely the urban street warrior who in the early days is attracted to a brand not on the basis of mass advertising, but of word of mouth. As soon as there is any danger of the brand moving anywhere near the mainstream, the urban street warrior – and his friends – move on to another brand.

4. How best to individualise and tailor services to the consumers' needs to a far greater extent than has typically been the case in the past. This sort of response, which can be labelled 'complicated simplicity', means the end of a mass audience-oriented approach and the far greater acceptance of an audience-of-one approach (refer back to Chapter 11's discussion of one-to-one marketing and the growth of permission marketing). This shift is likely to be driven, in part at least, by the consumer empowerment movement which, among other things, demands a far greater degree of price transparency. The implications of this are potentially significant, since organisations face the pressure of having to cut costs and maintain profitability, while having little opportunity to raise prices.

The new assertiveness: the rise of the complaining consumer

It should be apparent from what has been said so far that the new consumer is a very different type of consumer, who demands a very different approach to marketing. This theme of a very different and far more assertive type of consumer has also been developed by the advertising agency Publicis, which, in its report *The New Assertiveness* (2002), suggests that this new type of consumer:

> *Infuriated by the pressures of twenty-first-century living and a feeling of having little control over many aspects of their lives, consumers are attempting to regain control and vent their frustration through their buying habits. ... Seventy per cent of those surveyed believe the future is more uncertain than it was in their parents' day – an anxiety that has been increased since September 11. Many now feel vulnerable to the possibility that anything could happen, at any time.*

The study goes on to argue that:

> *This insecurity and frustration is breeding a new generation of consumer. Increasingly, we are buying products or services to cheer ourselves up – 31 per cent of adults surveyed said their consumption was motivated by this, a figure that rose to 50 per cent among 15 to 24 year-old respondents. (2001/2)*

The report also highlighted the way in which consumers' expectations of product quality and levels of service are outstripping satisfaction, with 96% of respondents having made a complaint about a product or service during the previous 12 months.

The new consumer moves on: the genie of the super-powered consumer

Arguably one of the most significant and far-reaching characteristics of new consumers is, as we suggest above, their willingness to complain. This has, in turn, led to the emergence of what might loosely be termed the **super-powered consumer**. Super-powered consumers are typically media literate, have access to their own mass-media channel of communication (the web), have a number of tools for a fast response to problems (the mobile phone), and often have a public relations strategy and an ability to hurt companies. They are also often well informed and frequently politicised in their behaviour patterns. Examples of super-powered consumers in action include the anti-global brand demonstrations in Seattle in 1999; French farmers attacking the 'imperialism' of McDonald's; European and North American customers asking questions of Nike about their manufacturing policies in Southeast Asia; and the green lobby forcing the British government to change its policy on genetically modified foods.

In a number of ways, however, the emergence of the super-powered consumer represents something of a paradox. Marketers have worked hard to create this type of consumer by giving them greater access, more information and more influence over how business is done, and how brands communicate. Having been encouraged to ask questions, consumers have become far more discriminating and cynical, with the result that marketing planners are now under far greater pressure and need to respond with communication that is more open.

The new consumer and youth culture: the rise and fall of Generation X and the emergence of Generation Y

Published in 1991, Robert Coupland's *Generation X* defined a slice of *zeitgeist* that was characterised by young people who in many cases had dropped out of society and rejected the idea of work. They, it was claimed, were the future. However, just four years later, **Generation X** vanished to be replaced by a very different type of youth culture. In an attempt to come to terms with this, the advertising agency BMP DDB Needham conducted a major study of Britain's youth in 1995/96. Labelled ROAR (Right of Admission Reserved), the research focused upon consumption habits, jobs, incomes, loves and hates, and hopes and dreams.

The ROAR research, in common with a great many other youth studies, focused upon trying to find the style leaders. Based on the 'trickle down' theory, each social group, the theory suggests, will have *Purists*, the handful of people who create the fashion; *Style Leaders*, who pick up on it first; *Early Adopters*, who crave recognition by the Style Leaders; *Happy Compromisers*, who know they're not Style Leaders but know what's hip and what they want from it; and the *Unsophisticated*, who dress up – perhaps strangely – but probably get things six months too late. This approach to structuring youth is used by many brands targeted at the young. The product is placed with Purists or Style Leaders in the hope it will 'trickle down' to the Early Adopters and finally to the remainder of the target market.

Although the sorts of groupings that emerged from the ROAR study have an initial attraction, the dangers of categorising markets in this way should not be underestimated. Despite our earlier comment about many young consumers being relatively conservative in their choice of brands, there is also a strong element of heady individualism among young consumers. This individualisation, together with an accelerating culture, leads to a sizeable part of the youth market being inherently and intensely brand promiscuous. The idea of **brand promiscuity** reflects the way in which many new consumers show far lower levels of loyalty to brands than in the past and constantly switch between one brand and another, despite any incentives offered through the marketing mix.

Following the decline of Generation X, Generation Y began to emerge. However, unlike the earlier Generation X, who had grown up during an era of downsizing and restructuring, members of Generation Y have been shaped by the experience of entering the workforce during one of the longest and strongest economic booms in history. It was also this generation that was brought up in the decade of the child, when the psychology of self-esteem drove a great deal of thinking about how children should be raised. In discussing this generation, Tomkins (2002: 43) suggests that:

> On entering the job market, the twentysomethings were in big demand not just because of the booming economy but because, as the first generation to have grown up with computer technology, they were seen as leaders of the biggest business upheaval since the industrial revolution. Small wonder these cosseted, sought-after youngsters were optimistic and self-confident – or that their elders may have seen them as arrogant.

However, with the end of the dot.com boom, it was this segment that was hit the hardest. In the USA, for example, unemployment among those aged 16–24 is now much higher than among those aged 25 and over – a reversal of what happened in the last recession, when companies downsized by cutting older, more experienced workers.

In the longer term, though, Generation Y represents a powerful market, since not only will demographics weigh heavily in their favour as populations age and the demand for younger workers outstrips supply, but it is also this market that we are referring to when we discuss the higher levels of media, advertising, brand and technological literacy.

The almost desperate struggle to understand youth markets in detail is driven by a combination of factors. In part, it is the sheer size, value and volatility of the market. However, perhaps more importantly, this is a market which has many, many years of buying ahead of it. Because many consumers are invariably relatively conservative, they tend to stay with the brands of their youth for some time.

12.5 THE NEW CONSUMER AND THE GROWTH OF RELATIONSHIP MARKETING

Against the background of everything that we have said about new consumers and their typically much higher and very different sets of expectations, there is the question of how marketing planners need to respond. Among the most obvious or necessary responses is the need to develop and build much closer and more cost-effective relationships with the consumers. Gilligan and Wilson (2003) suggest that there are numerous ways in which relationships can be managed proactively, including by redefining and extending the marketing mix. As markets have become more competitive, the extent to which marketing planners can differentiate purely on the basis of the traditional 4Ps of the product, price, promotion and place has become increasingly more difficult and more questionable. To overcome this, the focus in many markets has moved to the 'softer' elements of markets and the additional 3Ps of people, processes and proactive customer service. In emphasising the softer elements of marketing, marketing planners are giving explicit recognition to the way in which the product or service is typically delivered through people and that it is the organisation's staff who have the ability to make or break the relationship. This, in turn, is influenced either positively or negatively by organisational processes and the effectiveness of process management (process management is concerned with the ways in which the customer is handled from the point of very first contact with the organisation through to the last). The third of the soft Ps is that of proactive customer service and the ways in which levels of customer satisfaction can be leveraged by proactive rather than reactive service standards and initiatives (refer back to Chapter 9's discussion of the service delivery gap).

Relationship marketing myopia

But although relationship marketing and relationship management have an obvious attraction, they also have their critics. Nigel Piercy (2002), for example, has identified what he terms **relationship marketing myopia**, or the naive belief that every customer wants to have a relationship with its suppliers. He goes on to suggest that 'customers differ in many important ways in the types of relationship they want to have with different suppliers, and that to ignore this reality is an expensive indulgence', (2002: 72). This, in turn, has led him to categorise customers in terms of those who are:

- *Relationship seekers* – customers who want a close and long-term relationship with suppliers.
- *Relationship exploiters* – customers who will take every free service and offer but will still move their business elsewhere when they feel like it.
- *Loyal buyers* – customers who will give long-term loyalty, but who do not want a close relationship.
- *Arm's-length, transaction buyers* – customers who avoid close relationships and move business based on price, technical specification or innovation.

In categorising customers in this way, Piercy gives recognition to the need for relationship strategies to be based upon the principles of market segmentation and customers' relationship-seeking characteristics:

> *Relationship investment with profitable relationship seekers is good. Relationship investments with exploiters and transactional customers are a waste. The trick is going to be developing different marketing strategies to match different customer relationship needs.* (Piercy, 2002:73)

Piercy's comments are interesting for a variety of reasons and raise the question of whether there is a direct link between customer satisfaction and customer loyalty. Although a link might appear obvious, there is in fact little hard evidence to suggest anything other than the existence of what is at best an indirect relationship. Instead, it is probably the case that it is customer *dissatisfaction* that leads to customer disloyalty, although even here the link may be surprisingly tenuous. While this may seem to be a strange comment to make, the reality in many markets is that there is often a surprisingly high degree of inertia within the customer base. Given this, customers or consumers may be in a position where they simply cannot be bothered to change their source of supply until levels of dissatisfaction reach a very high level.

The problems of customer and brand promiscuity: the need for the extra value proposition

One of the principal themes that we have tried to pursue throughout this chapter is that many of the traditional assumptions that have been made about customers and that have driven thinking on marketing strategy are quite simply no longer appropriate. In the case of customer loyalty, for example, rather than being able to take customer loyalty for granted, the reality for many marketing planners today is that, as customers have become more demanding, more discriminating, less loyal and more willing to complain, levels of customer and brand promiscuity have increased dramatically. In a number of ways, this can be seen to be the logical end-point of the sorts of ideas discussed by Alvin Toffler in his book *Future Shock* (1970), when he predicted that we would be living in a world of accelerating discontinuities where 'the points of a compass no longer navigated us in the direction of the future'.

Among Toffler's predictions was that, as the pace of change accelerates, so the nature of relationships becomes much more temporary. For marketers, the most obvious manifestation of this is the fracturing of the relationship between the organisation and its markets and the decline of brand loyalty. In part, this can be seen to be the result of the way in which customers are now faced with so many stimuli in the form of advertising, promotions, point-of-sale offers, poster sites, and sponsorship, that there is the danger of a considerable amount of marketing activity simply becoming white noise, that is noise that cancels out other noise so that nothing can be heard. Given this, there is a need to rethink the nature of the relationship between the consumer and the brand. One of the ways in which this can be done is by focusing upon added value and the **extra value proposition** (EVP), customer-driven strategies and permission marketing. In the absence of this, there is the very real danger of competitive oblivion, particularly as web-based strategies reduce market entry barriers and costs.

Looking to the future

There is in many organisations the temptation to focus upon the short term. There are several explanations for this, the most obvious of which stems from the (greater) feeling of security that managers derive from concentrating upon the comfort zone of the areas and developments that are essentially predictable. A more fundamental explanation, however, emerged from a survey in the *Asian Wall Street Journal*. The study, which covered large firms and multinational corporations, illustrated the extent to which many senior managers are forced to demonstrate higher and more immediate short-term results than in the past. The implications for strategic marketing planning are significant, since strategic planners have little incentive to think and act for the long term if they know that they will be evaluated largely on the basis of short-term gains and results. The sorts of trade-off that emerge from this have, in turn, been heightened as the pace of change within the environment and the need to manage ambiguity, complexity and paradox have increased. Nevertheless, strategic marketing planners must, of necessity, have some view of the longer term and of the ways in which markets are likely to move. Doyle (2002) identifies ten major trends within the environment:

1. The move towards what he terms the fashionisation of markets, in which an ever greater number of products and markets are subject to rapid obsolescence and unpredictable and fickle demand.
2. The fragmentation of previously homogeneous markets and the emerge of micro-markets.

3. Ever higher expectations.
4. The greater pace of technological change.
5. Higher levels of competition.
6. The globalisation of markets and business.
7. Expectations of higher service.
8. The commoditisation of markets.
9. The erosion of previously strong and dominant brands.
10. A series of new and/or greater governmental, political, economic and social constraints.

Although the list is by no means exhaustive (it fails, for example, to come to terms with the detail of a series of the major social and attitudinal changes that we have discussed within this chapter) and, in a number of ways, focuses upon the broadly obvious in that much of what he suggests is simply a continuation of what exists currently, it does provide an initial framework for thinking about the future.

A somewhat different approach has been taken by Fifield (1998) who has focused upon tomorrow's customers. He suggests that these customers will not simply be a replication of the customer of the past, but will instead be characterised by a series of traits that include being:

- inner-driven and less susceptible to fashion and fads;
- multi-individualistic and multifaceted;
- interconnected with a far stronger awareness of different facets of their lives;
- pleasure seeking;
- deconstructed in that they will view work, family and society very differently from that in the past;
- unforgiving in that they will not only expect more, but they will demand more and retaliate if and when this is not provided.

SUMMARY

Within this chapter we have focused on the ways in which the marketing environment is changing and how one of the most significant of these changes has proven to be the emergence of the new consumer. This new consumer, as we have discussed, differs in a whole series of ways from consumers in the past, something that has significant implications for the marketing planning process. Faced with this, marketing planners can take one of two approaches. Either they can fight to come to terms with these differences and then rethink – possibly in a radically different way – how the organisation approaches the market, or they can pay lip service to these changes and continue with the same approaches as in the past. The consequences of this second approach are likely to be reflected in an increasingly obvious mismatch between market demands and organisational behaviour and, given this, it is unlikely to be a realistic strategic option.

Discussion questions

1. We refer in section 12.3 (page 31) to the ideas of the youthful elderly, ageing children (the under 14s), ageing children (the teens) and kidults. What examples can you identify of organisations that have deliberately targeted each of these groups? How have they done this?

2. The three nations society (see Table 12.4) highlights a series of differences that supposedly exist between different parts of society. To what extent do you agree with this concept and where do you see evidence of organisations adopting different strategies to appeal to each of the three groups?

3. Relationship marketing has been an area upon which many marketing planners have focused in recent years. Identify three examples of organisations where relationship strategies have been pursued either successfully or unsuccessfully. What lessons might be learned from these?

Case study 12.1 | **The new consumer and the rise of the Internet – new rules for the new world**

The background

The characteristics of the new consumer and, in particular, their much higher levels of technological awareness and technological literacy have provided enormous opportunities – and enormous threats – for large numbers of organisations. In the case of the retail sector, many of the traditional players have been hit hard by new entrants to their markets and have struggled to come to terms with the consumers' new shopping habits and the development by new entrants of what we can loosely refer to as new rules for the new world. Internet shopping has grown exponentially over the past few years and in December 2003 accounted for 7% of total UK retail sales. Amongst the winners in the battle for consumer spending power have been the Internet banks such as Smile! and Egg which have blended 24-hour access with far higher levels of service than the traditional banks; the low-cost airlines such as easyJet and Ryanair, both of which have made the travel agent redundant by operating only through the Internet; and Amazon.com which has reinvented the rules for book selling by rejecting the traditional high street book selling business model.

The growth of Amazon.com

Launched in 1995, Amazon.com's founder and CEO, Jeff Bezos, astutely recognised the potential offered by the technology of e-commerce and the willingness of a time-constrained and far more experimental consumer to use the new technology as a means of maximising their choices, reducing the prices that they had to pay for the products they were buying, and increasing levels of convenience by buying at the time of the day that *they* wanted rather than the times that the traditional retailer dictated and found more convenient.

In many ways, Bezos's strategy was deceptively straightforward and based on a combination of:

- the astute application of a new and rapidly growing technology to a product area that had high and demonstrably sustained – and sustainable – levels of demand;
- an obsessive customer focus designed to ensure that the company constantly got closer to the customer;
- the use of technology to develop consumer profiles and consumer insights that became ever more detailed each time a customer dealt with the company;
- the adding of value at every stage of the process;
- an emphasis upon constant change and development;
- ongoing innovation that was reflected in the company's move from books into music, consumer electronics, toys and games, clothes, kitchen and household goods, and so on;
- clear core value propositions (convenience, the size of the stock, selection, service and price);
- an emphasis upon customer management and retention; and
- a managerial perspective that gave explicit recognition to the way in which the new consumer is not simply a North American or Western European phenomenon, but is in fact truly global.

Amazon and the issue of value

From the outset, at the heart of the company's strategy there has been a deep-seated recognition that the new consumer searches for value and new experiences. Given this, the core proposition centres around low cost, easy consumer access, the quick and easy selection of books, and the development of a value delivery network.

The notion of a value delivery network highlights the way in which players within the chain, and not just Amazon itself, are used to add value to the customer experience. This is done most obviously by customers providing reader reviews, authors who provide comments, and the personalisation of the offer (customers would indicate the types of books – either in terms of subjects or authors – they liked to read. Having signed up for this, they then receive regular e-mails with reviews of the books that Amazon's editors feel will appeal to the customer).

The implications for the competition

Faced with a 'clicks' based business model, many of the traditional 'bricks' players found Amazon, particularly in the early days, to be a notoriously difficult competitor with which to come to terms. Some responded by ignoring Amazon, seemingly on the basis that they felt that Internet shopping would never really take off. Others responded simply by trying to copy the Amazon model but then, as late entrants, found this to be costly and that they had no obvious competitive advantage.

Given this, the constraints that the players in the second wave of entry to the market have faced in competing with Amazon can be seen to revolve around:

- the costs;
- the difficulties of achieving meaningful position within the market;
- the question of how best to attract customers who currently buy from Amazon and who are generally satisfied with the service they provide;
- the difficulties of moving quickly and cost effectively through the internet learning curve;
- the need to build a supporting infrastructure.

However, at the same time, it needs to be recognised that Amazon too may be faced with problems as the market moves into the next stage of its development. Among the most obvious of its potential problems include:

- others entering the market and the market then becoming too crowded;
- strategic drift on the part of Amazon and the gradual and general erosion of its competitive advantages;
- the question of how exactly to position itself in what might be seen to be the second stage of the market's development;
- how the organisation might keep differentiating itself in a meaningful way;
- the financial costs of developing and coming to terms with new forms of competition;
- the failure to deliver the ever higher levels of service that the new consumer typically demands;
- niche players who 'cherry pick' by focusing upon the high-margin parts of the market;
- prices – and margins – throughout the market decreasing;
- the general costs of competition increasing; and
- perhaps most importantly from our standpoint within this chapter, the dangers of customer promiscuity, with customers showing little real loyalty to the company.

Questions

1. Assume that the technology available in 1995 had been available five years earlier. How successful do you think Amazon would have been if it had attempted to launch its offer at that stage?

2. Given the nature of the new consumer, how would you suggest that Amazon operates to ensure that customers do not defect to the emerging competition?

3. What other examples can you identify of companies recognising the needs and expectations of the new consumer and responding cleverly to these developing demands?

Further reading

Hamel, G. (2001) *Leading the Revolution*. Boston, MA: Harvard Business School Press.
Klein, N. (2000) *No Logo: Taking Aim at the Brand Bullies*. London: Flamingo.
Lindstrom, M. and Seybold, P.B. (2003) *BRANDchild: Remarkable Insights into the Minds of Today's Global Kids and their Relationships with Brands*. London: Kogan Page.
Ridderstrale, J. and Nordstrom, K. (2000) *Funky Business: Talent Makes Capital Dance*. Harlow: Financial Times Prentice Hall.

References

Coupland, R. (1991) *Generation X: Tales for an Accelerated Culture*. New York: Little Brown & Co.
Doyle, P. (2002) *Marketing Management and Strategy* (3rd edition). Harlow: Prentice Hall.
Fifield, P. (1998) *Marketing Strategy* (2nd edition). Oxford: Butterworth-Heinemann.
Gilligan, C.T. and Wilson, R.M.S. (2003) *Strategic Marketing Planning*. Oxford: Butterworth-Heinemann.
Golik, B. (ed.) (2003) *Mature Thinking*. Shipley: Millenium plc.
Lewis, D. and Bridger, D. (2000) *The Soul of the New Consumer: Authenticity, What We Buy and Why in the New Economy*. London: Nicholas Brealey.
Piercy, N.F. (2002) *Market-led Strategic Change: A Guide to Transforming the Process of Going to Market*. Oxford: Butterworth-Heinemann.
Publicis (2002) *The New Assertiveness*. London: Publicis.
Richardson, S. (2001) *The Young West: How We Are All Growing Older More Slowly*. San Diego, CA: University of California Press.
Toffler, A. (1970) *Future Shock*. New York: Bantam Books.
Tomkins, P. (2002), *Sunday Times*, 10 February.

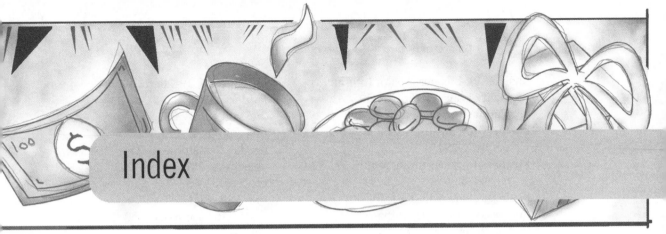

Index

ACORN system 153–4
acquisition costs 276, 282, 293
activities (lifestyle 148–9
adjustment function 129
advertisements 31, 54–5, 248–9, 256, 264, 266, 309
Advertising Standards Authority 54–5, 256
advocate 281, 282
affective component (attitudes) 127
affective learning 120
after-sales service 197
age factor 17, 145–6, 312–15, 322
AIDA 250
airlines 7
ancillary costs 275
arm's-length, transaction buyers 323
assessment of quality 206–7
ATEX Directive 44
ATOL 192
atomisation 139
attitudes 60, 126–31
audit (of relationships) 297, 298
augmented product 173, 174–5, 197
Automobile Association 52

baby boomer generation 315
Back to the Floor (BBC) 6
badge, quality as 189, 192–3
bargaining power 69
barter 9–10
behaviour
    ethical *see* ethics
    see also customer behaviour

behavioural intentions 127–8
behavioural segmentation 145, 150–3
beliefs 32–3, 127–8
benefit segmentation 150
benefits 155, 157, 275–6
birth rate 314
Body Shop 60–1
boomerang generation 311–12
Boots 69
Boston Consulting Group 30
brand beliefs 32–3
brand cannibalisation 141
brand communication 250, 266
brand equity 178
brand focus 266–7
brand image 130, 131
brand literacy 309
brand loyalty 115, 263, 308, 315, 319, 321, 324
brand name 6, 125
brand personality 177, 257, 266, 300
brand positioning 257–9
brand promiscuity 308, 321, 323–4
brand stretching 178
brand switching 263, 283
brand trust 284–5
branding 175–80
    corporate identity 258–9
British Airways 258–9
British Association of Removers 55
British Telecom (BT) 58, 294
business-to-business sector
    communications 251, 254, 258
    customers 25, 27, 38–43, 158

business-to-business sector (*continued*)
  quality issues 189, 192, 205–7
  relationships 284, 286–8, 292–6, 299
business-to-consumer sector 27, 28, 38, 167, 284
business-to-government sector 27, 39, 43–4
business chain 216–17, 220
business markets 151, 155–8
buyer 38, 69, 158, 281, 287
  see also consumer; customer
buying decisions 112–16
buying roles 38–9

Cadbury 144
call centres 64, 84, 197, 225–6, 300
CAP Code 55
capital equipment 169
caravan park 15
cash-poor/time-rich segment 318
cash-rich/time-poor segment 317
centralised purchasing 155, 157
Chambers of Commerce 88
channel mix 300–1
charities 18, 208, 268
ChildAid 90
children 90, 313
choice (purchase decision) 34
Cisco Systems 289–90
class 59, 147
classical conditioning 122, 123, 124–5
client 26–7, 281, 282
closeness (relationships) 294–5
closure 125
cognitive component (attitudes) 127
cognitive customer 37
cognitive dissonance 34
cognitive theory/school 122, 124–5
collaboration 292
commitment 292
communications 231
  change in 267–8
  channels 253, 265–6
  customer-led 245–72
  external/internal 253–61
  feedback 247, 251–2, 260, 261
  influence of 19–20, 261–8
  ladder 257, 286
  messages 247, 265
  mix 250–1, 258
  needs (of customers) 256
  objectives 251–2, 257, 263, 269
  process 247–9
  role 249–50
  systematic approach 250–2
  vehicles 247
Companies House 156
company structure 218–20
competition 10–11, 13, 327–8
competitive advantage 279, 284
  information and 81–3, 93, 100–1
  market segmentation and 143, 144
competitive environment 5–6, 100
competitive forces 68–9
competitive market 13
competitor analysis 70, 100–1
competitors 50, 68–70
complaints 91, 203, 204, 239–40, 320
complex decision making 115
components 168
concentrated marketing 139
conformance to requirements 189, 190–1
connative component (of attitudes) 127
connectionist school 122–4
'connoisseur consumer' 267
consistency (quality) 16
consumables 169
consumer
  definitions 25–6, 216
  new (emergence) 305–29
  privacy 55, 66
  protection 61–2, 175
  roles (99 lives) 314
  spending (UK) 28–30
  see also customer; customer behaviour
consumer-oriented organisation 25
consumerism 61–2
continuous innovation 182–3
core product 172, 173–5, 201
Corgi 192
corporate capability 230, 233

corporate identity 258–9
cosmetics for men (case study) 104–5
costs 275–6, 282, 293
counterfeiting 204–5
country-of-origin effect 194, 195
critical events segmentation 145, 153
cues 121
culture/cultural issues 59, 310–18
customer 4, 101
   adoption of new products 183–4
   buying decisions 112–16
   communications *see* communications
   definitions 25–7, 218
   expectations *see* expectations
   influences on 19–20, 50, 261–8
   loyalty *see* loyalty
   in micro-environment 66–7
   perception 188–211, 222, 230–1, 237
   problem solving 36–7, 120, 125,
      262–4
   purchase decisions 31–6
   retention 276–9, 282, 291, 299, 300
   segmentation *see* market
      segmentation
   types of 27–8
   see also consumer; external customer;
      internal customer
customer-centric relationship 296–7
customer-focused approach 4, 45, 165,
      166–7, 282
customer-led communication 245–72
customer-led organisation 167
customer-oriented organisation 81–3, 91
Customer, Quality and Innovation
      (CQI) 225
customer–supplier relationship 19–20,
      22–3, 158
   case study 241–3
   dyad relationship 280, 290–1
   interactions 220–6
   rules of engagement 231
   see also customer relationship
      management; relationship
      marketing
customer acquisition 276–7, 282, 293
customer behaviour 81, 109–36

'customer champions' 251
customer dissatisfaction 4, 5, 239, 323
customer information 66, 76–103
   see also information
customer losses/defections 277
customer management 280, 281
customer needs 163–87, 256
customer promiscuity 323–4
customer relationship management
      19–20, 269, 273
   case for 276–9
   definitions 279–81
   effective relationships 291–301
   importance of relationships 274–5
   principles of 281–6
   types of relationships 286–91
   value defined 275–6
customer relationships, external 237–40
customer satisfaction 4–8, 114, 199,
      221, 238, 252, 299
   information and 81, 95
   loyalty and 35, 323
customer segments 15
customer service 65, 221, 228–9, 239–40
customer situations 17–19
customer value 102–3, 296, 299
   total 4, 5, 26
customisation 288–9

Data Protection Acts 55, 66
Day Chocolate Company (case study)
      60, 72–4
decentralised purchasing 155, 157
decider 38, 287
decision makers 101
decision making 292
   model 263
   process 31, 36–7, 43, 45, 111–16,
      286
   unit 28, 38, 114
defector (customer) 281, 282
demographic environment 310–18
demographic segmentation 143, 148
demographics 60, 148, 312–14, 322
dependency 292, 293
dialogue 249, 252, 261, 293–4

differentiation 174–5, 178, 250
dissatisfiers 14–15
distribution 64
    case studies 73–4, 135
    chain 216, 217, 219, 237
    channels 181, 204
distributors 68
dog kennels 11
domestic markets 155, 156
drive 117–18
drive-time maps 154
drug use campaign 264
Dyson Dual Cyclone 166, 255

e-commerce *see* Internet
e-procurement 44
early adopters 264, 267, 321
Early Followers 30
early majority 183, 184
economic/rational customer 37
economic factors (PEST analysis) 50,
        56–9, 316
economic growth 57
education levels 314
effective relationships 291–301
Egg 39
ego-defensive function 129
elderly population 17, 312–13
electric guitars (case study) 132–6
Electricity Association 248
electronic relationships 287–90
emigration 314
emotion 37, 118
employees 81, 221, 229
    co-operation 230–2
    ensuring standards 233–7
    relationships 236–7
    roles 220, 234–6
environmental awareness 61, 208–9,
        308
environmental scanning 50, 52–3
environmental uncertainty 306–7
EPOS system 156
ethics 32–3, 144, 268
    marketing environment 60–1, 72–4
    quality and 207–9

ethnicity 18, 59
Euro-consumers 155
European Union 43–4, 55–6, 66, 88, 104
evaluation
    information collection process 101–3
    performance 256–7
    personal (quality) 189, 194
    post-purchase 34–6
    purchase decision 32–4, 113, 116
exchange rates 58
exchanges 4, 9–13, 22–3
expectations 4, 6, 10–11, 114
    managing 260–1
    matching 222–3
    quality and 201–5
expected product 172–3, 175
experience, quality as 189, 194
experts 201–2
extensive problem-solving 36–7
external customers 215–17
    communicating with 253–9
    definitions 218–19
    interaction 220–6
    managing relationships 237–40
    service culture 226–37
external information 80, 83, 90
external stakeholders 262
extra value proposition (EVP) 323–4
extremity (attitudes) 128

factor analysis 149
Fair Trade (case study) 72–4
family 28–30, 147–8, 311, 314
fast-moving consumer goods 176, 178,
        181, 203, 284, 292, 295–6
feedback 247, 251–2, 260, 261, 300
feelings, attitude and 127–8
felt needs 118
field of experience 247
Flybait 41
First-of-the-Masses 30
focus group 97
football (on television) 25–6
for-profit business 4, 18
Ford 165
formal quality assessment 206

formality 295, 296
Fox Safety Lamps 44
French culture 19, 20
frequency of contact 293–4
functional priorities 234–5
functional value 33
future trends/approaches 305–29

gatekeeper 38, 287
GE Capital 42
Generation X 321–2
Generation Y 321–2
geodemographic segmentation 145,
    153–5
geographic segmentation 143, 147,
    155–6
geographical shifts (population) 314
gestalts 125
government 88, 195, 290
  as customer 27, 39, 43–4
grey market 315
grey marketing 204, 205
guerilla communications 256

Happy Compromisers 321
health sector 54, 194–6, 200, 202
high involvement 114–16, 118, 177
home entertainment 119
hostage (customer) 281, 282
Hutchison 3G 151
hybrid segmentation 145, 153–5

importance (in relationships) 292
income 57, 146–7
individual customer 28–30, 37
industrial customers 167–9
industrial markets 151, 155–8
industry structure 70
industry type 155, 156
inertia 115
inflation 57
influencer 38, 286, 287
informality 295, 296
information
  collection 93–103
  on customer 66, 76–103

external 80, 83, 90
internal 80, 81, 83, 90
needs (of organisation) 77–85
primary 86, 87, 90, 96–7
qualitative 91, 92, 96, 97–8
quantitative 91, 92, 96, 97
reliability 84–5, 200
secondary 86–7, 88–9, 90, 95–6
sharing 295–6
sources 86–92
information and communication
  technologies (ICTs) 255–6, 267, 288
'information overload' 251, 256
information search 32, 113, 116
initiator 38, 286, 287
innovation 180–4, 189, 193–4
innovators 183, 184
inseparability (services) 171
installation costs 275
instrumental conditioning 122–4, 126
insurance costs 276
intangible benefits 15, 26, 201
intangible element (services) 169–70
integrated communications 251–2
intensity (relationships) 293–4
inter-employee relationships 236–7
interaction 279–80, 283
interest rates 59
interests (lifestyle) 148–9
internal communications 247, 259–61
internal customer 9, 18, 19, 27, 39,
    45–6, 224–6, 259–61
internal expectations 261
internal information 80, 81, 83, 90
internal stakeholders 260, 262
internal suppliers 218–20, 224, 231
international markets 58, 155, 156
Internet 65, 143, 225, 256, 274, 300–1
  electronic relationships 287–90
  new consumer and (case study) 326–8
  shopping 30, 32, 62, 68, 150, 200,
    326–8
  source of secondary data 88, 89
interruptive marketing 286
intravenous level (permission
  marketing) 284

Investors in People 192
involvement (high/low) 114–16, 118,
        176
ISO 9000 series 192, 236

joined-up communications 251
junk mail 256, 286
just-in-time system 158, 275, 292

key customer values 102–3
kidults 313–14
knowledge 77, 80–1, 129, 295–6

laggards 183, 184, 264
late majority 183, 184
league tables 189, 192–3
learned behaviour 120
learning 120–6
legislation 54, 55
level (quality) 16
Lever Brothers 112
Levi Strauss (case study) 160–1
lifestyle 143, 145, 147–9, 150, 267
lifetime value 276, 293
Likert scales   149
limited problem-solving 36
location 155, 156
longevity 293
Love Bug Virus 63
low involvement 114–16, 118, 176–7
loyalty
    brand 115, 263, 308, 315, 319, 321,
        324
    customer 35, 101, 177, 257, 280,
        282, 284, 323–4
loyalty ladder 281–2, 287, 291, 296,
        297–8, 300–1
loyalty segmentation 152–3
luxury goods 201, 211

McDonald's 284–5
macro-environment 53–66, 81
mailing list companies 156
maintenance costs 276
major innovation 182
management 202, 203–4

management information system 232
managing director (MD) 286–7
manufacturers 40
manufacturers' brands 179, 180
market aggregation 139
market analysis 99–100
market challenger/leader 79
market developments (case study) 72–3
market opportunities/threats 80–1, 307
market research 295–6, 299, 309
market segmentation 137, 281, 298,
        313
    advantages/disadvantages 140–2
    behavioural segmentation 145, 150–3
    case study 160–1
    criteria used to identify 145–55
    definition 139–40
    hybrid segmentation 145, 153–5
    industrial markets 155–8
    principles/process of 138–9
    profile segmentation 145–8
    psychographic segmentation 145,
        148–9
    viable (requirements) 142–4
market share 79–80, 81, 91, 105
market structure 58
market value/volume 80
marketing 7, 13, 110, 230, 249
    mass 139, 275, 319
    one-to-one 275, 282–3, 284, 291, 319
    permission 283–6, 291, 294, 298, 319
    relationship, new consumer and
        322–5
    viral 65, 319
marketing environment
    analysing 53–70
    case study 72–4
    changing 306–7
    definitions 50–1
    environmental scanning 50, 52–3
marketing mix 53, 81, 279, 306, 322
    communications and 246–7, 250, 263
marketing planning 306, 318–22
markets 13
mass marketing 139, 275, 319
mass production 164, 165, 249

measurement (relationships) 297, 299
media 266, 267, 309
mega marketing 290
memory 265, 319
message 247, 265
Metro (case study) 270–1
micro-communication 262
micro-environment 53–4, 66–70
micro-markets 324
Mini (re-launch) 310
minimum order size 157
missed communication 253
Mister Minit 170
mobile phones 63, 278–9, 302–3
moderator 97
modified re-buy 43, 263
money exchanges 10
Morgan Cars (case study) 186–7
MOSAIC system 153
motivation 116, 117–19, 121
multiple supplier policy 155, 158
mystery shopping 97, 242

National Health Service 27, 196, 200,
    202
needs 117–19, 138, 262, 263
    see also customer needs
negative reinforcement 122, 124, 126
Network Rail 202–3
networks 279–80
new consumer
    changing environments 306–7, 310–18
    emergence/rise of 308–10, 318–22
    Internet and (case study) 326–8
    relationship marketing (growth)
        322–5
new entrants (to industry) 69
new marketing reality 305, 306–7
new product development 64, 110,
    180–4
new task 43
'99 lives' consumer 314
noise (in communications) 248, 250, 324
Nokia (case study) 302–3
not-for-profit organisations 4, 18, 27,
    39, 45, 90, 159, 258, 268

O₂ 278–9
objective measurement (of quality)
    206–7
observation 97
offline communications 267
one-to-one marketing 275, 282–3, 284,
    291, 319
online communications 267
open tender 43–4
openness 295, 296
operant conditioning 123
opinion leaders 249, 262, 264, 267
opinions (lifestyle) 148–9
opportunity 80–1, 267–8, 307
opportunity cost 275
order size (heavy/light) 155, 157
organisation
    characteristics 155, 156
    control 202, 204–5
    customer satisfaction and 5–8
    employee contribution 229–32
    information needs 77–85
    as process (functions) 226–7
    understanding customer behaviour
        109–36
organisational customer 27, 39–46
organisational problems 155, 157
own brands 179–80, 193, 201
Oxfam 208, 268

parallel importing 204
partner 281, 282
passive customer 37
Pavlov's experiment 123
people 247, 259, 279
perceived value 16–17, 275–6
perception, quality as 189, 194
performance evaluation 256–7
perfume industry 78–9
perishability (services) 172
permission marketing 283–6, 291, 294,
    298, 319
persistence (of attitudes) 129
personal evaluation 189, 194
personal interviews 97
personal relationships 284, 296

personality 177, 179, 263–4
PEST analysis 50, 54–66, 316
PetFood Inc. 84–5
physical behaviour 120
physical evidence 247, 279
Pinpoint system 153
Pioneers 30
place 247, 263, 279, 300–1, 322
points (permission marketing) 284
political and legal factors (PEST
    analysis) 50, 54–6, 316
positive reinforcement 126
post-purchase evaluation 34–6, 112
post-purchase processes 113, 114, 116
potential product 173, 175
power (in relationships) 293
pre-conception/pre-conceived ideas 222
premium pricing 201
prepotency 118
price 247, 263, 279, 319, 322
pricing (Tokai case study) 135
primary information 86, 87, 90, 96–7
prisoner (customer) 281, 282
proactivity 232, 252, 322
problem recognition 31, 93–4, 113, 116
problem solver 38
problem solving 36–7, 120, 125, 262–4
process management 279, 322
product-focused approach 164–5
product life cycle 250
product range 72, 134, 156, 292
product specification (quality) 189
production (Tokai case study) 134–5
productivity measurement 236
products 4, 32, 70, 247, 263, 279, 322
    augmented 173, 174–5, 197
    brand personality 177, 257, 266, 300
    differentiation 174–5, 178, 250
    for industrial customers 167–9
    knowledge 155, 157
    levels 172–5
    new (development) 64, 110, 180–4
    services and (differences) 169–72
profile segmentation 145–8
promotion 65, 73, 135–6, 279, 300, 322
    communications 246–7, 263, 268
prospect 281

psychographic analysis 149
psychographic segmentation 145, 148–9
psychological contract 261
public relations 260, 262
purchase 113, 152, 155, 157, 284
    decisions 31–7, 114–15, 116
Purists 321

qualitative information 91, 92, 96–8
quality 4, 13–15
    customer perceptions of 188–211
    perceived value 16–17, 189, 194
Quality Assurance Agency 22, 192–3
quality control 228, 231, 236
quality standards 189, 192–3, 230–1,
    233–7
quantitative information 91, 92, 96, 97
questionnaires 97

Ratner 8
raw materials 168, 217, 227, 228
recruitment 233
regional differences 59
regularity (relationships) 293–4
regulatory bodies 54, 195–6
reinforcement 121–2, 123, 124, 125–6
relationship building 19–20
relationship exploiters/seekers 323
relationship management see customer
    relationship management
relationship marketing 274, 276–8
    definitions 279–80, 281
    myopia 323
    new consumer and 322–5
    principles of 281–6
relevance 87, 294, 296
reliability (information) 84–5, 87, 200
religion 59
remoteness (in relationships) 294–5
repurchasing 155, 157
resistance (of attitudes) 128–9
resources 57
respondents 96, 98
response 121
Retail Motor Industry Federation 55
rewards 236, 284

Right of Admission Reserved (ROAR) 321
risk 114, 118, 292
rivalry (between competitors) 69
routine purchasing decisions 36
routinisation 295
Rover Group 56
running costs 276

Saga Holidays 17
salient attributes 32
sampling 98
satisfiers 14–15
saturated market 140, 142
scientific testing 206–7
search costs 275
secondary information 86–90, 95–6
segmentation *see* market segmentation
selection (purchasing) 32–4, 113, 116
selective tender 43–4
self-actualisation 153
self-orientation 264–5
self-regulating groups 54–5
self-service customers 289–90
semi-finished products 168
service clients 41–3
service culture 226–37
service delivery 64, 223–4, 322
service encounter/expectations 222
service specification 189, 191–2
service support sector 317
services 4, 26, 32, 70, 167–72
    quality 197–205
sex variable 145, 146
SIC codes 156
single-parent family 311
single supplier policy 155, 158
situation segmentation 152
situational permission 284, 286
skin care (case study) 104–5
Skinner's experiment 123, 124
Škoda 131
small and medium enterprises (SMEs)
    159
SMART objectives 257, 269
social change 315–17
social class 59, 147

social environments 310–18
social factors (PEST analysis) 50, 59–62,
    316
social mobility 311, 312
social responsibility 60–1, 144, 258
Sony Walkman 141
'spam' 256, 286
Stadium Ltd (case study) 47–8
stakeholder publics 262
stakeholders 45, 207–8, 260, 262
standard, quality as 189, 192–3, 233–7
Standard Industrial Classification 156
Stationery Express 99
stereotypes 130, 148–9
store choice 113, 116
straight re-buy 43
strategic actions 84
Strategic Business Unit (SBU) 229
strategic planning 297, 324
strategy (relationships) 297, 298
Style Leaders 321
subjective assessment (of quality) 206
substitute products/services 69
super-powered consumer 320
superior product 189, 191–2
Superprofiles system (CDMS) 153
suppliers 4, 12, 67–9
    internal 218–20, 224, 231
    multiple/single (policy) 155, 158
    see also customer–supplier relationship
supply chain 40–1, 204–5, 216, 217,
    237
supply chain management 158
symbolic learning 120
systems (relationships) 297, 299
Sytner BMW 174

T-Mobile 278–9
tactical actions 84
tactics (relationships) 297, 299–301
tangibility (services) 169–70
tangible benefits 15, 26
Target Group Index 154
target market 73, 121, 281
taxation 58
teamwork 237

technological factors (PEST analysis) 50, 62–6, 316
technology 155, 156, 236, 255–7, 267, 288
telecommunications 63
telecommuting 314
telephone banking 225–6
tendering process 43–4
terrorist (customer) 281, 282
Tesco 69
Third World 314
Thorntons 152
threats, opportunities and 80–1, 307
three nations society 317–18
Timbuk2Designs 289
time-based competition 275
Tokai (case study) 133–6
topic guide 97
total communications 247
total cost of ownership 276
total customer experience 197–205
total customer value 4, 5, 26
Total Quality Management (TQM) 225, 236, 260
trade associations 55, 88
Trades Description Act 200
trading blocs 58
training 207, 233–4
trickle down theory 321
trust 189, 194–6, 284–5, 292
24-hour helpline 228–9, 242

UK consumer spending 28–30
uncertainty 292, 306–7
unemployment 57
university choice (case study) 22–3
Unsophisticated (consumers) 321
unstable customer 281, 282
urban street warrior 319

urbanisation 312
usage patterns 150–2, 155, 157
user 38, 287
utilitarian motives 118
utility value 33

valence (of attitudes) 128
validity (information) 84–5
value 318, 327
    definition (in CRM) 274, 275–6
    extra value proposition 323–4
    perceived 16–17, 275–6
    quality and 13–15
    see also customer value
value-expressive function 129
value added 217, 219, 227
    branding and 178–9
    extra value proposition 323–4
    quality and 189, 193–4
value chain 216, 217, 227
value for money 189, 191, 193, 211, 276
variability (services) 171
variety seeking 115
viral marketing 65, 319

wants 117–18, 262, 263
wastage/waste 228–9
white noise 324
world view 264

Yorkshire Tea 208
youth market 309–10, 321–2
youthful elderly 312–13

zero defects 260
zone of tolerance 198, 261